Psychoanalysis in the Age Totalitarianism

C000213551

'This volume is unique in exploring what its editors call "the two-way traffic between ideas of psychoanalysis and totalitarianism". We recognize that, whatever its focus on introspection, psychoanalysis is a social and political enterprise. It thrived in postwar Germany because it had a subject, the immediate Nazi past, and a heroic leader, Alexander Mitscherlich, who both interpreted the Nazi movement and lived out his opposition to it. We also learn how psychoanalysis can succumb to its own dogmas and confusions. We emerge with many questions about totalitarianism ("totalism" better serves us psychologically) but with a deepened sense of psychoanalysis in the world.'– **Professor Robert Jay Lifton**, author of *Witness to an Extreme Century: A Memoir* and *The Nazi Doctors*.

'Among this book's contributions, two stand out forcefully. It widens and deepens the meaning of both psychoanalysis and totalitarianism, in the context of a history of the Western world from the 1920s to the 1960s. It also evidences the movements of minds at work around these topics, exploring connections between different realms of phantasy and actuality, such as children's mental health in relation to democratic, authoritarian and totalitarian political attitudes; imagination, belief and transference in relation to freedom; psychoanalysis in relation to intelligence work and political torture; and economic and political oppression, including colonialism, in relation to the loss of subjectivity and unconscious dependency. The result provides fascinating reading and opens up new thoughts in transdisciplinary fields of knowledge.' – **Professor Luisa Passerini**, European University Institute, Florence, author of *Fascism in Popular Memory*.

'This important and wide-ranging book explores psychoanalysis, its endeavour to enhance psychic freedom, and the totalitarian forces that aim to make free thought impossible. These essays show us psychoanalysis in radical conflict with dictatorship, discuss the consequences of totalitarian regimes for the psychoanalytic movement, highlight the power of racism and suggest how much political thought and sociology may have to gain from psychoanalytic conceptualisations.' – **Dr Franco De Masi**, training analyst, Italian Psychoanalytical Society and former President, Centro Milanese di Psicanalasi, author of *Making Death Thinkable* and *The Enigma of the Suicide Bomber*.

Psychoanalysis in the Age of Totalitarianism provides rich new insights into the history of political thought and clinical knowledge. In these chapters, internationally renowned historians and cultural theorists discuss landmark debates about the uses and abuses of 'the talking cure' and map the diverse psychologies and therapeutic practices that have featured in and against tyrannical, modern regimes.

These essays show both how the Freudian movement responded to and was transformed by the rise of fascism and communism, the Second World War, and the Cold War, and how powerful new ideas about aggression, destructiveness, control, obedience and psychological freedom were taken up in the investigation of politics. They identify important intersections between clinical debate, political analysis, and theories of minds and groups, and trace influential ideas about totalitarianism that took root in modern culture after 1918, and still resonate in the twenty-first century. At the same time, they suggest how the emergent discourses of 'totalitarian' society were permeated by visions of the unconscious.

Topics include: the psychoanalytic theorizations of anti-Semitism; the psychological origins and impact of Nazism; the post-war struggle to rebuild liberal democracy; state-funded experiments in mind control in Cold War America; coercive 're-education' programmes in Eastern Europe, and the role of psychoanalysis in the politics of decolonization. A concluding trio of chapters argues, in various ways, for the continuing relevance of psychoanalysis, and of these mid-century debates over the psychology of power, submission and freedom in modern mass society.

Psychoanalysis in the Age of Totalitarianism will prove compelling for both specialists and readers with a general interest in modern psychology, politics, culture and society, and in psychoanalysis. The material is relevant for academics and post-graduate students in the human, social and political sciences, the clinical professions, the historical profession and the humanities more widely.

Matt ffytche is Director of the Centre for Psychoanalytic Studies at the University of Essex, and Editor of *Psychoanalysis and History*. He is an Academic Associate of the British Psychoanalytical Society and has written widely on Freud and American neo-conservatism, psychoanalysis and mid-twentieth-century social science, and the relation between psychoanalysis and literature.

Daniel Pick is a psychoanalyst and historian. He is Professor of History at Birkbeck, University of London, and a Fellow of the British Psychoanalytical Society and of the Royal Historical Society. An editor of *History Workshop Journal*, he is also a member of the editorial board of the New Library of Psychoanalysis, as well as the advisory boards of *Psychoanalysis and History* and Cambridge Studies in Nineteenth-Century Literature and Culture.

The New Library of Psychoanalysis
'Beyond The Couch' Series
General Editor: Alessandra Lemma

The New Library of Psychoanalysis was launched in 1987 in association with the Institute of Psychoanalysis, London. It aims to promote a widespread appreciation of psychoanalysis by supporting interdisciplinary dialogues with those working in the social sciences, the arts, medicine, psychology, psychotherapy, philosophy and with the general book reading public.

The *Beyond the Couch* part of the series creates a forum dedicated to demonstrating this wider application of psychoanalytic ideas. These books, written primarily by psychoanalysts, specifically address the important contribution of psychoanalysis to contemporary intellectual, social and scientific debate.

Current members of the Advisory Board include Giovanna Di Ceglie, Liz Allison, Anne Patterson, Josh Cohen and Daniel Pick.

For a full list of all the titles in the New Library of Psychoanalysis main series and also the New Library of Psychoanalysis Teaching Series, please visit the Routledge website.

TITLES IN THE 'BEYOND THE COUCH' SERIES:

Under the Skin: A Psychoanalytic Study of Body Modification
Alessandra Lemma

Engaging with Climate Change: Psychoanalytic and Interdisciplinary
Perspectives *Edited by Sally Weintrobe*

Research on the Couch: Single Case Studies, Subjectivity, and
Psychoanalytic Knowledge *R.D. Hinshelwood*

Psychoanalysis in the Technoculture Era *Edited by Alessandra Lemma
and Luigi Caparrotta*

Moving Images: Psychoanalytic Reflections on Film *Andrea Sabbadini*

Reflections on the Aesthetic Experience: Psychoanalysis and the
Uncanny *Gregorio Kohon*

Psychoanalysis in the Age of Totalitarianism *Edited by Matt ffytche
and Daniel Pick*

Psychoanalysis in the Age of Totalitarianism

Edited by Matt ffytche and
Daniel Pick

Routledge
Taylor & Francis Group

LONDON AND NEW YORK

First published 2016
by Routledge
2 Park Square, Milton Park, Abingdon, Oxon OX14 4RN

and by Routledge
711 Third Avenue, New York, NY 10017

Routledge is an imprint of the Taylor & Francis Group, an informa business

© 2016 selection and editorial matter, Matt ffytche and Daniel Pick; individual chapters, the contributors

The right of the editors to be identified as the authors of the editorial material, and of the authors for their individual chapters, has been asserted in accordance with sections 77 and 78 of the Copyright, Designs and Patents Act 1988.

All rights reserved. No part of this book may be reprinted or reproduced or utilized in any form or by any electronic, mechanical, or other means, now known or hereafter invented, including photocopying and recording, or in any information storage or retrieval system, without permission in writing from the publishers.

Trademark notice: Product or corporate names may be trademarks or registered trademarks, and are used only for identification and explanation without intent to infringe.

British Library Cataloguing in Publication Data
A catalogue record for this book is available from the British Library

Library of Congress Cataloging in Publication Data
Names: ffytche, Matt, editor. | Pick, Daniel, editor.
Title: Psychoanalysis in the age of totalitarianism / edited by Matt ffytche and Daniel Pick.
Description: New York : Routledge, 2016. | Includes bibliographical references and index.
Identifiers: LCCN 2015046123| ISBN 9781138793880 (hardback) | ISBN 9781138793897 (pbk.) | ISBN 9781315760773 (e-book)
Subjects: LCSH: Psychoanalysis—Political aspects. | Totalitarianism. | Subconsciousness—Political aspects.
Classification: LCC BF175.4.S65 P796 2016 | DDC 150.19/5—dc23
LC record available at https://lccn.loc.gov/2015046123

ISBN: 978-1-138-79388-0 (hbk)
ISBN: 978-1-138-79389-7 (pbk)
ISBN: 978-1-315-76077-3 (ebk)

Typeset in Times New Roman
by Swales & Willis Ltd, Exeter, Devon, UK

In memory of John Forrester (1949–2015)

Contents

Notes on contributors   xii
Foreword   xvi
CATALINA BRONSTEIN

PART I
Frameworks   1

1   **Introduction**   3
    DANIEL PICK AND MATT FFYTCHE

2   **Totalitarianism: a sketch**   20
    JOEL ISAAC

PART II
Reckonings with fascism   27

3   **Studies in prejudice: theorizing anti-Semitism in the
    wake of the Nazi Holocaust**   29
    STEPHEN FROSH

4   **Inner emigration: on the run with
    Hannah Arendt and Anna Freud**   42
    LYNDSEY STONEBRIDGE

5   **The superego as social critique: Frankfurt School
    psychoanalysis and the fall of the bourgeois order**   55
    MATT FFYTCHE

PART III
Precarious democracies   71

6 Psychoanalytic criminology, childhood and
   the democratic self   73
   MICHAL SHAPIRA

7 'The aggression problems of our time': psychoanalysis
   as moral politics in post-Nazi Germany   87
   DAGMAR HERZOG

8 Totalitarianism and cultural relativism: the dilemma
   of the neo-Freudians   102
   PETER MANDLER

9 D.W. Winnicott and the social democratic vision   114
   SALLY ALEXANDER

PART IV
Writing the history of psychoanalysis   131

10 Totalitarianism and the talking cure: a conversation   133
   JOHN FORRESTER AND ELI ZARETSKY

PART V
Mind control, communism and the Cold War   145

11 Psychoanalysis and American intelligence
   since 1940: unexpected liaisons   147
   KNUTH MÜLLER

12 Therapeutic violence: psychoanalysis and the
   're-education' of political prisoners in Cold War
   Yugoslavia and Eastern Europe   163
   ANA ANTIC

PART VI
Colonial subjects   179

13 Spectres of dependency: psychoanalysis
   in the age of decolonization   181
   ERIK LINSTRUM

14 The vicissitudes of anger: psychoanalysis
    in the time of apartheid   193
    ROSS TRUSCOTT AND DEREK HOOK

PART VII
Why psychoanalysis?   205

15 Total belief: delirium in the West   207
    JACQUELINE ROSE

16 The totalitarian unconscious   221
    MICHAEL RUSTIN

17 Post-psychoanalysis and post-totalitarianism   239
    RUTH LEYS

    Bibliography   252
    Index   279

Contributors

Sally Alexander is Emeritus Professor of Modern History, Goldsmiths, University of London, a founder editor of *History Workshop Journal*, and her most recent book is *History and Psyche: Culture, Psychoanalysis, and the Past*, edited with Barbara Taylor (2012). Her interest in psychoanalysis and social democracy continues through a research project, 'Quest for Democracy and Welfare', based at the European University in Florence.

Ana Antic is a post-doctoral fellow at Birkbeck, University of London, on the project 'Reluctant Internationalists: A History of Public Health and International Organisations, Movements and Experts in Twentieth-Century Europe'. Her research focuses on the history of modern Europe and the Balkans, history of war and violence, and history of psychiatry. Her first monograph, *Therapeutic Fascism: Experiencing the Violence of the Nazi New Order in Yugoslavia*, is forthcoming with Oxford University Press.

Catalina Bronstein, MD, is Visiting Professor in the Psychoanalysis Unit at University College London. She is a training analyst at the British Psychoanalytical Society. She trained as a psychiatrist in Argentina and later as a child psychotherapist at the Tavistock Clinic and as an analyst at the British Psychoanalytical Society. She is the former London Editor of the *International Journal of Psychoanalysis* and currently sits on its board. She has written numerous papers, chapters in books and monographs on a wide variety of subjects. She edited *Kleinian Theory: A Contemporary Perspective* (2001) and co-edited *The New Klein-Lacan Dialogues* (2015). She works in private practice and at the Brent Adolescent Centre, London. She is currently the President-elect of the British Psychoanalytical Society.

Matt ffytche is Director of the Centre for Psychoanalytic Studies at the University of Essex, and editor of the journal *Psychoanalysis and History*. He is author of *The Foundation of the Unconscious: Schelling, Freud and the Birth of the Modern Psyche* (2012) and various articles on psychoanalysis and mid-twentieth-century social science and intellectual culture, and on W.R. Bion. He is an Academic Associate of the British Psychoanalytical Society.

John Forrester, who died in 2015, just before this book went to press, was an internationally renowned Freud scholar and historian of psychoanalysis. He was Professor of History and Philosophy of the Sciences at the University of Cambridge. His publications include *Language and the Origins of Psychoanalysis* (1980), *The Seductions of Psychoanalysis: Freud, Lacan and Derrida* (1990), (with Lisa Appignanesi) *Freud's Women* (1992), *Dispatches from the Freud Wars: Psychoanalysis and its Passions* (1997) and *Truth Games: Lies, Money and Psychoanalysis* (1997). A major new work, completed with Laura Cameron, *Freud in Cambridge*, a study of the reception of psychoanalysis in Britain in the early twentieth century, will shortly be published.

Stephen Frosh is Pro-Vice-Master and Professor in the Department of Psychosocial Studies at Birkbeck, University of London. He has a background in academic and clinical psychology and was Consultant Clinical Psychologist at the Tavistock Clinic, London, throughout the 1990s. His publications include *Psychoanalysis Outside the Clinic* (2010), *Hate and the Jewish Science: Anti-Semitism, Nazism and Psychoanalysis* (2005), *For and Against Psychoanalysis* (2006), and most recently *Hauntings: Psychoanalysis and Ghostly Transmissions* (2013) and *A Brief Introduction to Psychoanalytic Theory* (2012).

Dagmar Herzog is Distinguished Professor of History and Daniel Rose Faculty Scholar at the Graduate Center, City University of New York. She has published extensively on the history of religion, the history of the Holocaust and its aftermath, and the histories of gender and sexuality. Among her books are *Sex after Fascism: Memory and Morality in Twentieth-Century Germany* (2005) and *Sexuality in Europe: A Twentieth-Century History* (2011). She is currently working on a transatlantic history of psychoanalysis in the post-war era, with particular attention to the themes of desire, trauma, and aggression.

Derek Hook is an associate professor in the Department of Psychology at Duquesne University, and an extraordinary professor of Psychology at the University of Pretoria. He was a founding editor of the journal *Subjectivity*, and is the author of *Foucault, Psychology and the Analytics of Power* (2007), *A Critical Psychology of the Postcolonial* (2012), *(Post)Apartheid Conditions* (2014) and the forthcoming *Lacan and 'the Psychological'*. He is currently editing, with Calum Neill and Stijn Vanheule, a three-volume commentary series on Lacan's *Écrits*. He underwent psychoanalytic training at the Centre for Freudian Analysis and Research in London.

Joel Isaac is Senior Lecturer in the History of Modern Political Thought at the University of Cambridge. He is the author of *Working Knowledge: Making the Human Sciences from Parsons to Kuhn* (2012). His current research examines the ways in which neoclassical economics has shaped political thought in the twentieth century.

Ruth Leys is a historian of the human sciences with a special interest in the history of the neurosciences, psychoanalysis, and psychiatry. Recent publications include *Trauma: A Genealogy* (2000); *From Guilt to Shame: Auschwitz and After* (2007); and 'The Turn to Affect: A Critique', *Critical Inquiry*, Spring 2011. She is currently finishing a book provisionally entitled *The Ascent of Affect: A Critical History From the 1960s to the Millennium.*

Erik Linstrum is Assistant Professor of History at the University of Virginia. He is the author of *Ruling Minds: Psychology in the British Empire* (2016). He is now working on a history of knowledge about colonial violence in post-war Britain.

Peter Mandler is Professor of Modern Cultural History at the University of Cambridge and Bailey Lecturer in History at Gonville and Caius College, and has served, 2012–16, as President of the Royal Historical Society. His most recent book is *Return from the Natives: How Margaret Mead Won the Second World War and Lost the Cold War* (2013). He is currently working on the transition to mass education in Britain since 1945, and on the language of social science in everyday life in Britain and the US *c.* 1930 to *c.* 1970.

Knuth Müller is a clinical psychologist, social worker, and psychoanalyst, with a private practice in Berlin. He is a member of the International Association for Relational Psychoanalysis and Psychotherapy (IARPP), a visiting lecturer at Steinbeis University and the author of *Auftrag der Firma: Geschichte und Folgen einer unerwarteten Liaison zwischen Psychoanalyse und militärisch-nachrichtendienstlichen Netzwerken der USA seit 1940* (2015).

Daniel Pick is a psychoanalyst and historian. He is Professor of History at Birkbeck, University of London and a Fellow of the British Psychoanalytical Society. He currently holds a senior investigator award from the Wellcome Trust for a project entitled 'Hidden Persuaders? Brainwashing, Culture, Clinical Knowledge and the Cold War Human Sciences'. His publications include *Faces of Degeneration: A European Disorder, c. 1848–1918* (1989), *War Machine: The Rationalisation of Slaughter in the Modern Age* (1993), (as co-editor with Lyndal Roper) *Dreams and History: The Interpretation of Dreams from Ancient Greece to Modern Psychoanalysis* (1994), *Svengali's Web: The Alien Enchanter in Modern Culture* (2000), *Rome or Death: The Obsessions of General Garibaldi* (2005), *The Pursuit of the Nazi Mind: Hitler, Hess, and the Analysts* (2012), and *Psychoanalysis: A Very Short Introduction* (2016).

Jacqueline Rose is Professor of Humanities at Birkbeck Institute for the Humanities. She is a co-founder of Independent Jewish Voices in the UK and a Fellow of the British Academy. Her books include *Feminine Sexuality: Jacques Lacan and the École Freudienne*, which she co-edited with Juliet Mitchell and translated, *Sexuality in the Field of Vision* (1986), *The Haunting* *of Sylvia Plath* (1991), *States of Fantasy* (1996), *On Not Being Able to Sleep: Psychoanalysis and the Modern World* (2003), *The Question of Zion* (2005), *The Last Resistance* (2007), *Proust Among the Nations: From Dreyfus to the Middle East* (2011), and the novel *Albertine* (2001). *Women in Dark Times* was published in 2014.

Michael Rustin is a professor of sociology at the University of East London, a visiting professor at the Tavistock Clinic and at the University of Essex, and an associate of the British Psychoanalytical Society. He has recently co-edited, with David Armstrong, *Social Defences against Anxiety: Explorations in a Paradigm* (2014); *After Neoliberalism: The Kilburn Manifesto*, with Stuart Hall and Doreen Massey (2015); and co-authored *The Inner World of Doctor Who*, with Iain MacRury (2013). In 2016, *Reading Melanie Klein*, written with Margaret Rustin, will be published by Routledge in the New Library of Psychoanalysis Teaching Series.

Michal Shapira is Senior Lecturer of History and Gender Studies at Tel Aviv University. She previously taught at Columbia University, Barnard College as an ACLS New Faculty Fellow and at Amherst College as a Visiting Assistant Professor. Her research deals with the domestic, socio-cultural, cross-national, and imperial legacies of the Second World War in Britain and beyond, and focuses on total war, gender, and the development of expert culture. She is the author of *The War Inside: Psychoanalysis, Total War and the Making of the Democratic Self in Post-war Britain* (2013).

Lyndsey Stonebridge is Professor of Modern Literature and History at the University of East Anglia. She has published widely on psychoanalysis, modern literature and, most recently, the cultural history of rights and justice. Her publications include: *The Destructive Element: British Psychoanalysis and Modernism* (1998), *Reading Melanie Klein* (co-edited with John Phillips, 1998), *The Writing of Anxiety* (2007), and *The Judicial Imagination: Writing after Nuremberg* (2011). She is currently completing a new study of statelessness in the twentieth century, *Placeless People: Rights, Writing and Refugees.*

Ross Truscott has held fellowships in Interdisciplinary Feminist Studies at Duke University, at the Interdisciplinary Center for the Study of Global Change at the University of Minnesota and, while writing this chapter, at the Centre for Humanities Research, University of the Western Cape. He has published on a range of topics, including post-apartheid melancholia, obsessional whiteness, race, gender and sexuality, postcolonial and psychoanalytic theory, empathy and political transition.

Eli Zaretsky is Professor of History at the New School for Social Research, New York. His works include *Capitalism, the Family and Personal Life* (1976), *Secrets of the Soul: A Social and Cultural History of Psychoanalysis* (2004), *Why America Needs a Left* (2012) and *Political Freud: A History* (2015).

Foreword

Catalina Bronstein

Totalitarian regimes aim not only at attaining full control of the state, but also at 'the total penetration of the human subject' (Joel Isaac, writing below, p. 22). This book greatly helps in understanding the different mechanisms involved in the creation of internal and external conditions that promote a culture of fear, as well as attacking values which are intrinsic to humanity: the respect for life, human rights and freedom of thought, including the capacity for critical thought and the right to possess one's own identity. Psychoanalysis, with its particular emphasis on free association and freedom of thought, can provide a significant contribution to the understanding of both the emergence of totalitarian regimes and the effect they have on the individual and the group.

In her illuminating chapter Lyndsey Stonebridge asks: 'How can one endure reality so defined by the threat of total obliteration?' (p. 43). She responds that, for many, survival comes through mental flight; for others, the price paid is permanent exile. She also remarks that both Hannah Arendt and Anna Freud shared the conviction that reality must be confronted and that 'it was only by engaging with reality . . . that it was possible to remain in the world' (p. 43). How far a sense of reality can be retained and discriminated from delusional thinking in times of totalitarianism itself merits consideration. Perhaps this opens up the question as to how far an individual can successfully engage with reality when subjected to a profound state of uncertainty, fear and confusion created by a mixture of information, misinformation and disinformation.

My question here is prompted in part by a personal experience I went through with friends, colleagues and relatives who disappeared during Argentina's 'dirty war'. The fate of the 30,000 'disappeared' illustrates not just the extreme aggression and murderous activity of the then-prevailing military government towards its people, but also the sadistic quality involved in the manipulation of information and lies that the families of the 'disappeared' had to endure as they were left suspended in a state of unknowing, uncertainty, and hope for the return of loved ones (Corsi, 2015). An estimated 500 children, born to mothers who were in detention and later 'disappeared', were robbed of their true identities as they were given to families, many of them military families, who registered the babies as being legally theirs. It was only many years later, after the exhaustive work of the 'Mothers and Grandmothers of the Disappeared', that some of the kidnapped children – now adults – could be reunited with their original extended families.

In Argentina the state terrorism that imposed what was called the 'National Reorganization Process', which took place between 1976 and 1983, left deep scars which will take many years to heal. As in other Latin American countries, this was not the first military coup that toppled democratically elected governments. For example, there was another military coup in Argentina in 1966. In Chile in 1973 President Allende was overthrown by the armed forces and national police. Within a year of the coup Allende's appointed army chief, Pinochet, assumed power. These military coups counted upon support from the United States, which saw the potential for communism in Latin American countries as extremely dangerous, a threat to political stability and to their economic policies. The activity of guerrilla groups was seen as a justification for the abolition of democracy and the persecution of anybody who appeared to challenge the so-called 'principles of law and order', even though the same government that claimed to be the representative of 'the law' acted in profoundly unlawful ways. The terrorist actions of the guerrilla groups led to a counter-propaganda system which, by fuelling the fear that, in the words of the country's then de facto president, 'Argentine society was on the brink of disintegration' (Videla, 1980, my translation), convinced many Argentinians it was necessary to support the authoritarian government. Factory workers, students, journalists, psychoanalysts, psychologists and other professionals, nuns and priests – anybody who was opposed to the government – were seen as potentially 'subversive'. The promise to bring 'law and order', to exercise 'authority' to protect Christian values, or 'family values', had great appeal for a large number of people. As Michael Rustin describes in his contribution to the present volume, totalitarian regimes enact the split between good and evil that was described by Melanie Klein as characteristic of the paranoid-schizoid position.

Arendt makes a distinction between 'suspect' and 'objective enemy'. She writes that in totalitarian regimes the 'objective enemy' is defined by the policy of the government and not by an individual's desire to overthrow it. 'He is never an individual whose dangerous thoughts must be provoked or whose past justifies suspicion, but a "carrier of tendencies" like the carrier of a disease' (Arendt, 1973 [1958]: 423–4). In this respect, the military government in Argentina used the fight against left-wing guerrilla movements as a justification for viewing anybody who had democratic ideas, or who dared question the government's actions, as a dangerous 'carrier of a tendency' and an 'objective enemy'. It was certainly not essential to be part of a forbidden organization to be considered an enemy and to be at risk of being eliminated.

Assessment of reality and the capacity to differentiate what comes from us from what comes from the other is heavily influenced by our projections. This assessment sustains our actions, our rational behaviour which, as the psychoanalyst Roger Money-Kyrle described, could be:

defined . . . in relation to instincts, as the pursuit of the most effective means,
so far as an undisturbed assessment of the situation enables us to see them,
of the basic instinctual life-aim. This aim, at its source in the unconscious, is
to win a battle, against that part of the destructive impulse not harnessed in
its support.

(Money-Kyrle, 1961:100–1)

He continues, 'irrational behaviour has a suicidal quality about it; for it is at least
the passive, and sometimes the active, ally of the suicidal impulse in us'.

In totalitarian times the capacity to judge what is real, and to differentiate
what comes from the external world from what is the result of one's projections,
can prove extremely difficult. Equally, it can be very hard to establish the differentiation between what is rational behaviour from what is an irrational (and
suicidal) process of thinking, or course of action. When the state uses violent
unlawful measures that thwart individual liberties; when the police are not at the
service of protecting civilians but instead serve the military government; when
the simple fact of being opposed to a government and speaking against it endan-
gers the subject; when telephone conversations are intercepted, and to appear in
an 'enemy's' address book is sufficient to make anybody into an 'enemy'; when
any books that are remotely connected to 'banned' social and political ideas have
to be disposed of – then the only way to survive emotionally is by exercising
a certain amount of denial. Hollander suggests that a culture's thoroughgoing
violence can force individuals into paranoid-schizoid defences, such as splitting,
projective identification, denial and idealization, leading to a diminished capacity to distinguish between internal and external sources of persecutory anxiety
(Hollander, 1998: 205). The denial of reality can act as a defence against feelings
of confusion, helplessness and doubt when confronted with potential annihilation, though it actually places the subject in greater danger and at risk of taking
irrational and suicidal decisions. The horror of knowing about the reality of gas
chambers in Nazi Germany, or that the 'disappeared' in Argentina were actually
tortured, killed and disposed of by the military by throwing them from planes
into the River Plate, might well be otherwise impossible to withstand. The fact
that during totalitarian regimes large sections of the population are in denial
and continue to lead a 'normal' life can increase the sense of isolation, fear and
paralysis in those citizens who are more aware of the dangers stemming from
these regimes.

When denial is no longer effective, a state of confusion and self-imposed
paralysis can take over. During the mid to late 1970s I undertook my psychiatric
and psychotherapeutic training in a small psychiatric Unit in Buenos Aires. In
the space of three years our group supervisor, an analyst, was jailed, one of the
psychologists 'disappeared' and one of my close colleagues and friends left the
country soon after finding his apartment had been searched by the secret services
or the army. Our department was not unique in this regard. Several colleagues
from other specialities also 'disappeared'. I was on duty one day when I saw a

patient, a young woman in her late twenties (whom I will call Ms C). She was beset by anxiety, looked drained and persecuted. As soon as she sat down she pleaded with me to admit her to hospital. She looked around the room as if there were somebody behind her. She spoke fast in a low voice, and in a panicky way described how she had got home from work the previous day to find her husband was not there. She was told that the army had taken him away. He 'disappeared'. She then tried to reach some close friends, but to her horror, they had all disappeared as well. 'They are after me now!' She was clearly disturbed and at times I could not quite make sense of what she said. I also started to feel confused. I initially believed her account, then doubted it and wondered whether she was hallucinating: was she hearing voices? Why was she turning round, examining the room with her eyes, looking behind her back? Was she looking for real military personnel or was she hallucinating? She explained that somebody might have placed microphones in the room – something not unusual in the political climate at the time. For some reason, however, she convinced herself that I was a safe person.

Her insistence that she needed to be admitted to a hospital ward, and that the army, the secret services and the police were after her, made me also feel quite anxious for her and, unavoidably, for myself. If she was not in fact ill, but was simply wanting to be admitted to the psychiatric ward as a way of escaping the secret services and armed forces, this might actually put her at even greater risk, as many hospitals were under military control. Some hospitals (such as the Posadas Hospital) operated clandestine detention centres. But if she was going through a psychotic breakdown then I should admit her. Her awareness that I was wondering about the reality of her account, but even more, that I did not share her belief that the hospital would provide a safe haven from the army, police and secret services, visibly increased her anxiety. I decided to consult with my head of department who, after spending another hour with Ms C, did not seem to be able to reach a diagnosis either. With hindsight I think that this young woman was suffering from a psychotic breakdown as a reaction to a highly traumatic situation that could not be contained and which brought on a state of ego disorganization. In this case, delusion and reality came together. Terror can be disorganizing. While she seemed clear as to the identity of the enemy from whom she needed protection, I felt confused. Was the enemy within or without? I think it was both. We decided to keep her in our service for some hours, gave her some medication to reduce her anxiety and helped her see that neither the hospital nor we ourselves could protect her from the risk of being taken away, and to face the fact that she might need to look elsewhere for a safe refuge. I gave her an appointment for the next day but I never saw her again. I was left uncertain about whether this was because she was hiding, and simply did not trust us any more, or whether she had become another 'disappeared' person.

Psychoanalysis – and psychoanalytical institutions – are easily influenced by the political power of totalitarian regimes. Even though, as John Forrester and Eli Zaretsky mention (present volume, p. 139), psychoanalysis can survive and even thrive under certain circumstances in totalitarian regimes, such as it did in Argentina in the 1970s and early 1980s, this does not mean that psychoanalysis was not profoundly affected. Moreover, while the regime was apparently tolerant of psychoanalysis, at the same time many psychoanalysts were jailed, persecuted, or 'disappeared', and many had to leave the country. In effect, the relationship that totalitarian regimes establish with psychoanalytical institutions may differ greatly from the way individual practitioners belonging to those institutions are treated by the state. Under such circumstances, the relationship between psychoanalysts and their own institutions may become strained.

Marie Langer provides an interesting example of this process when she describes how difficult it was for her, in Vienna, to 'live with psychoanalysis and the Communist Party'. She was in psychoanalytic training when, in February 1934, the Gestapo captured the analyst Edith Jacobssohn (later Jacobson) after following one of her patients. Langer writes:

> In order to protect psychoanalysis and its patients, the staff met with Herr Professor, as everyone referred to Freud, and decided that no analyst could be active in a clandestine party, still less treat persons who were. The Socialist Party, the Communist Party, even the National Socialists, in other words the overwhelming majority of political organizations, were banned.
>
> (Langer, 1989: 78)

Her analyst (Sterba) informed her of this fact and told her that they would have to abide by the decision. This measure, which was apparently proposed by Federn, brought Langer into direct conflict with Bibring, who was the director of the Institute of Psychoanalysis, as Langer herself was arrested for trying, along with other doctors, to create a pacifist organization. She was helped through this crisis by Kurt Eissler and by Sterba, and was not expelled. But it well illustrates the strain and political confusion which can beset psychoanalytical organizations attempting to operate under totalitarian regimes, and the diverging positions that organizations and individual analysts may take, whether they are located in the affected countries or outside them, as Knuth Müller's chapter below also illustrates. In Argentina in 1971 a number of analysts of the APA (*Asociacion Psicoanalitica Argentina*) questioned the role of psychoanalysis and the psycho-analytical institution in relation to society, and insisted upon the need to think not just in terms of the life and death instincts, which belong to the essence of being human, but also to provide a structural analysis of aggression, to acknowl-edge that both analysts and analysands live within the same social structure (Dubcovsky *et al.*, 1971).

This book greatly contributes to the understanding of these complexities, explor-ing the different elements that are to be encountered at the crossroads of psycho-analytical, cultural and political thought, and helps us to remain mindful of the devastating effects that totalitarianism and its culture of violence and fear have on human beings.

Part 1

Frameworks

Chapter 1

Introduction

Daniel Pick and Matt ffytche

This book seeks to alter the way psychoanalysis is positioned in the political landscape of the twentieth century by locating it in 'totalitarian' times.[1] It argues that the rise of fascism, the trauma of the Second World War, and the transformation of that struggle in the Cold War, shifted the centre of gravity within the profession as well as the social understanding of its role. Collectively these decades from the 1920s through to the 1960s – a period of large-scale growth, development and repositioning of the psychological sciences as a whole – were permeated by anxieties over the threat of totalitarian societies and the nature of totalitarian 'mind', as well as deliberation over the psychological basis for freedom in society. We investigate how particular visions of the mind, therapy and politics interacted during the age of Total War and Cold War, and ask how the history of psychoanalysis might be rewritten in that light.

Freud and the movement he founded have often been associated with liberal and cosmopolitan values. Psychoanalysis, invented by a self-proclaimed 'Godless Jew' who inhabited Vienna in the declining decades of the Habsburg Empire, was in obvious ways bound up with Enlightenment ideals (even as it demonstrated the very limits of reason). It was and largely remains sympathetic to individualism, pluralism and the presumption of a right to privacy and confidentiality in the clinical domain. Freud himself tended to view religion or political idealism with irony and treated rituals of faith as versions of obsessional neuroses. Moreover, regimes that have succeeded in collapsing much of the distinction between the private and public sphere have usually shown little tolerance for psychoanalysis, or for sustaining the modicum of security and freedom the practitioner requires in order to work, or the patient needs to 'free associate' whilst trusting in the clinician's discretion.

Yet whatever the ideals and ideal context for psychoanalysis, its practice did not remain confined to liberal forms of polity. Psychoanalytical theories about self and group in our period ramified far beyond the conceptions of the early movement, even as they informed an increasingly large range of social and intellectual activities. At times ideas and techniques drawn (loosely or otherwise) from Freud's repertoire were deployed for quite other purposes from those he had envisaged, for example as a tool of political or commercial persuasion, in methods of inducing personal 'recantation', or in endeavours to ensure the 're-education' of colonized people. In exploring the history of psychoanalysis in 'totalitarian' times, we thus approach contentious debates from the past, consider how 'the talking cure' has been applied in or used to challenge particular modes of political thought, and map practices and ideas that, for better or for worse, came to be associated with psychoanalysis during the middle decades of the last century.

The Cold War arguably provided Freud's movement with its greatest opportunities for public attention and certainly added to its political relevance. It was during the Cold War that psychoanalysis gained its firmest purchase on public life, at least in America. Whether or not this wider legitimation was a direct consequence of the turbulent context, or simply coincided with it, the development of psychoanalysis as a more global, professional and politically active force was undoubtedly deeply entangled with the experience of widespread conflict and political instability. The 'Age of Totalitarianism' called forth particular versions of psychoanalysis that aimed to meet the demands of violent times.

Totalitarianism

Between the 1920s and 1950s the concept of 'totalitarianism' emerged and took root. But it did not always mean the same thing. Soon after the First World War influential supporters of the Italian Fascist Party, for instance, wrote in praise of totalitarian systems of government, and Mussolini quickly adopted the word. It served, rhetorically, to point up the contrast between an old Italy marked by individualism, regional differences, factionalism, and selfish materialism, and the new regime's idealized 'total' community, which bound individual and collective interest together in a common aim, while providing a bulwark against liberalism and Bolshevism.

By contrast with Freud's notion of unavoidable psychic division, fascism envisioned minds in harmony with each other, and with the state. The fascist utopia, no less than the communist version, proposed to reshape bodies and minds, to create citizens fit for regenerated and unified societies. Many liberal and conservative commentators in America and Britain saw some merit in, or in some cases even enthusiastically welcomed, European fascist political experiments on the grounds that they restored order. By the 1930s, however, with the Duce's ruthlessness, violence, and imperial ambitions ever harder to ignore, previous agnostics abroad were, often enough, expressing unbridled dismay, even as many Italians continued to reveal powerful feelings of devotion to and desire for their leader (Alpers, 2003; Duggan, 2012). During that decade, Freud would address Mussolini – ironically or not – as a 'cultural hero', while gifting him a copy of *Why War?*, Freud and Einstein's extended correspondence, which had been sponsored in 1932 by that ever-more fragile and notional entity, the League of Nations (Gay, 1998: 448, n).

Dramatic though the Italian case appeared, Germany's was to prove overwhelmingly more important and fearsome in the transformation of Europe and the wider world. Nazi ideologues had also seized upon this notion of totality, and with a vengeance. Through the 1920s, 30s and early 40s, Nazism became ever more radical in its ambitions to create a unified state and *Volk*, in which the supposed purification of 'race' would be achieved through the elimination of population groups designated as 'degenerate', above all the Jews. The new 'imagined communities' in Italy and in Germany had been reinforced by collective displays of euphoria during the interwar decades. At the same time both Mussolini and Hitler pursued the violent intimidation, and where necessary elimination, of those who stood in their way. The battle-hardened mind and the war-ready nation were extolled by numerous enthusiasts (not for the first time in history) as essential antidotes to decadence. Different forms of fascism around the world have relied upon different levels of intimidation and terror in practice, but violence and the mobilization of fear have always been essential hallmarks, as has the ecstatic performance of allegiance. Demonstrations of popular affiliation with the Nazi cause at the Nuremberg rallies and elsewhere were carefully choreographed; but that is not to deny the extent of the admiration and fervour that huge numbers of people felt on seeing or hearing the Führer.

The phenomenon of the Show Trials in Moscow in the late 1930s brought home another element of what came to be viewed as 'totalitarian' practices, and subsequently generated considerable debate about the possibility of political 'brainwashing'. Communism, at some key historical moments, made much of such staged public confessions. In *Darkness at Noon* (1940) Arthur Koestler famously depicted an old but suspect 'comrade', confined to a bleak cell, eventually embracing the required confessional narrative before his inevitable execution. A terrifying cult of the leader, many commentators showed, required a corresponding abjection of political subjects – 'captive minds', ultimately with nowhere to go. Meanwhile, amidst the violence and the excoriation of degenerate or renegade types, both fascist and socialist realist art portrayed model men and women as purified, unified, and remade, happily obedient, under the command of a benevolent supreme authority.

Whilst nobody who took any close interest in such matters could deny the many differences between social and political life under Stalinism and Nazism, or between Stalinism and Maoism, various notable theorists looked for the shared, monolithic qualities of the new 'total state' (in all its forms). Thus critical commentators drew parallels between the kinds of obedience sought from populations under fascism and communism, or between the ruthless purges conducted by both Hitler and Stalin, as essential features held in common. By the 1950s, 'totalitarian' had become a widely used word in political discourse, signifying, as the *Oxford English Dictionary* puts it, 'of or pertaining to a system of government which tolerates only one political party, to which all other institutions are subordinated, and which usually demands the complete subservience of the individual to the state'.

War in the mind

One element this definition neglects is the role of psychology. A crucial concern in post-war narratives on totalitarianism developed by Hannah Arendt,

Jacob Talmon and many others, was the capacity of totalitarian states successfully to invade the *minds* of their subjects. No shortage of commentators also wrote of the risk that totalitarian enemies would successfully export their ideas abroad; the Cold War was cast precisely as a global battle of ideas and beliefs. Hence, it was often argued, the urgent need for liberal democracies to shore up the psychological strength of their populations against these dangerous lures. Roosevelt (United States president from 1933 to 1945) and his successors, Truman and Eisenhower, needed little convincing that psychological expertise was a powerful part of the political toolkit, as relevant in shaping analysis of foreign affairs and decoding enemy propaganda as in securing support for controversial policy measures at home. Through radio and other media, the twentieth-century leader could speak directly to the citizen, in the intimacy of the home. Electors were often portrayed as susceptible to hidden and orchestrated forms of influence, or as unconsciously captivated by causes, rather than rationally choosing between options. The argument had been powerfully set out before the war, for example in *The End of Economic Man: A Study of the New Totalitarianism* (1939), a work by Peter Drucker, émigré to America, prolific writer and specialist in management theory. Mussolini or Churchill, Hitler or Roosevelt might well have agreed at least on the fact that electorates are swayed by powerful emotional forces, and therefore require strong leadership figures. To recognize such an unconscious domain of psychic factors in collective action and belief was, admittedly, far from a novel insight in political thought in the 1930s. The psychology of 'the masses' had already emerged in the late nineteenth century as a supposedly scientific field of study in its own right. But the combination of mass democracy and those ever-more pervasive technologies of cinema, radio and, later, television changed the terms of the discussion. Moreover, the human sciences were themselves coming into service in industry and commerce, or in the 'messaging' strategies of diverse political parties, with the aim of influencing the prior opinion of consumers and voters. In short, the notion of politics as a field in which individuals might consciously weigh up and exert choices according to their personal inclination was often seen as hopelessly outmoded.

Freud's nephew, Edward Bernays, a pioneering public relations consultant in America, had already attempted, during the interwar period, to make use of psychoanalytic ideas in his commercial work and advice to government. Alarmed by the rise of the far right in Europe and by Goebbels' skilful use of radio and other means of propaganda in Germany, his writings, such as *Speak up for Democracy* (1940) and *Democratic Leadership in Total War* (1943), called for action to sustain vulnerable minds and consolidate allegiance to American values in a time of global uncertainty. The very techniques of mass persuasion and unconscious domination that characterized those modern highly illiberal European states, he suggested, might need to be deployed in the 'Land of the Free', even at the price of corroding that freedom to some degree. No shortage of political theorists in the 1930s, such as Harold Lasswell, also argued forcefully that the phenomenon of 'Hitlerism' required a sophisticated combination of political *and* psychological response if there was to be any hope of defeating it (Pick, 2012: 95–6, 123). By the war years a substantial body of opinion in Washington, especially in the field of intelligence, accepted that psychoanalysis and anthropology (among other disciplines) were necessary forms of expertise in a world struggle between liberty and fascistic or communistic forms of tyranny. Not long after its creation in 1947, the CIA developed experimental projects in universities and sometimes hospitals to harness medicine, and the research evidence gathered within human and natural sciences, in order to foster still further the endeavours of its predecessor, the Office of Strategic Services, which had already pioneered political profiling, new interrogation and officer selection techniques, 'black' propaganda and 'dirty tricks' operations.

Though not all post-war philosophical inquiries into freedom of mind, or psychological experiments on authority and obedience, made explicit links to the Cold War conflict and the preceding struggle against fascism and Nazism, such contexts were pervasively present. Psychologists and psychiatrists even invented new words to describe states of mind, or perhaps the annihilation of mind, congruent with totalitarian regimes. 'Menticide' for example, a 1950s coinage, directly expressed Cold War visions of the total state's capacity to murder the mind; meanwhile the word 'totalism', favoured by Erik Erikson and Robert Jay Lifton, captured instead a sense of completely boxed-in mental life. 'Totalism' described a situation where a subject is held in thrall by an absolute system, operating within a 'sacred language', and allowed no leeway for doubt or dissent (Lifton, 1961).

'Totalitarianism' was likewise to prove an extraordinarily fertile idea in culture and political thought. It was cast by a large range of critics on both the Left and the Right as the quintessential modern form of tyranny, and as both cause and effect of a warped form of thinking in individuals and groups. Along with German or Soviet villains, sinister Asian, or specifically Chinese, brainwashers, capable of interfering with the unconscious minds of their foes, became commonplace stereotypes of the post-war years. Advocates of CIA-experimental projects on mind control could point to the stories, true or fanciful, of vulnerable PoWs having their emotions worked over, and their opinions turned, during the Korean War. Experiments in behavioural modification, mind-bending drugs and sensory deprivation that, unlike more obvious forms of torture, left few marks upon the body, continued, building on wartime precedents. (Whether skilful operators could truly mesmerize their subjects to act out of character, and to what extent 'brainwashing' was a myth, fascinated political and psychological commentators alike.)

Such practical attempts to harness or protect the minds of post-war citizens ran in parallel to (and sometimes directly fuelled) an array of literary and cinematic conceits concerning psychological warfare, or politics as a form of mental interference or derangement. *The Manchurian Candidate* (a novel in 1959, and a film in 1962), portrayed the shrill atmosphere of McCarthyite America, even as it depicted (more or less facetiously) communist apparatchiks skilled in the new techniques of 'brainwashing'. The Chinese and the Russians are seen working together in this tale, skilfully harnessing the 'psy' sciences not merely to 're-educate' enemy soldiers but to turn them into automata. In *Dr Strangelove or: How I Learned to Stop Worrying and Love the Bomb* (1964), the direction of the lens was turned from Moscow to Washington. Kubrick's film featured, amongst other memorable characters, a paranoid US military officer prepared to unleash nuclear Armageddon whilst convinced not only that communists were tampering with the fluoridization of water (a common fear of the period), but also that an international conspiracy was underway 'to sap and impurify all of our precious bodily fluids'. In the same year, the historian Richard Hofstadter's essay entitled 'The Paranoid Style in American Politics' (which first appeared in *Harper's Magazine*, and has been much quoted since) suggested that this pathological strain of thought in US political life had long pre-dated the Cold War (Hofstadter, 1964).

'Totalitarianism', as all of this might well suggest, though potent as a cultural metaphor, is a highly problematic concept in contemporary and historical analysis. It is difficult, or perhaps impossible, to extricate it from the intense and often fantastical projections that were made during the Cold War, when rhetorical accounts proliferated about the psychology of entire enemy populations. Totalitarianism may handily conjure up a sense of Nazi Germany, the emergence of Stalin's dictatorial leadership in Soviet communism, and the triumph of Mao in China. But the label is itself very obviously also a *product* of particular forms of political rhetoric and Cold War cultural fear. The reader will find some of our contributors regard the term 'totalitarian' as hopelessly contaminated by that history, some seek to retrieve it and put it to new uses, while for others again it is simply a source of confusion, given the very notable differences between the various most prominent cases, most obviously of all Nazi Germany and Stalin's Soviet Union (cf. Kershaw, 2004). Here we seek to examine rather than just assume the term (the scare quotes, although not insistently flagged every time the word is mentioned, are used advisedly). So the reader will encounter discussion of its history, semantic range and diverse applications (see particularly the contributions by Joel Isaac and Michael Rustin, as well as the discussion between John Forrester and Eli Zaretsky, chaired by Daniel Pick).

Psychoanalysis

Of all the psychologies current in this Cold War context, psychoanalysis was particularly concerned with explaining liberal anxieties about the resilience and perils of democracy, the paranoid and schizoid mechanisms in 'group think', and the attractions of subservience that fostered the growth of 'authoritarian personalities'. In its earliest incarnations, Freud's work had been associated with the *individual* patient's experience of the talking cure, and with inquiry into the repressed sexual motives underlying human behaviour. However, psychoanalysis was also concerned with the way everyday life might be riddled with concealed sadistic and masochistic impulses, with powerful unconscious identifications, as well as melancholic or manic 'solutions' to anxiety and conflict that demagogues could easily exploit. By the 1920s, just as fascism arose, psychoanalysis had moved more firmly into the domain of *group* psychology, placing aggression, the death drive and the superego centre stage. Moreover, Freud was not only interested in the mass fervour and nationalist identifications that the Great War had inspired, but also in the way particular social organizations such as the Church and the Army bound individuals together.

Psychoanalytical concepts appeared well suited to the interpretation of the developing extremist mass movements, their bellicose rhetoric and toxic well of racial ideologies. Freud was not alone in pointing out the prevalence of such passions as envy, hatred and resentment in politics, but he offered a particularly influential account of how cruelty and destructiveness seeped into political ideologies and shaped the psychic life of individuals and societies. A range of followers took up such thinking, combining it with ideas from cultural anthropology, to arrive at various investigations of 'national character' (Mandler, 2013). However, psychoanalysts also suggested that more aggressive, perhaps more 'totalitarian', passions were present to a degree in all of us. Murderous feelings, a narcissistic sense of entitlement, wishes to enslave the other or merge with the leader, or even a profound unconscious desire to break human links and bonds apart, might be seething beneath urbane social appearances. They might emerge in lacerating forms of guilt complex, or be projected onto neighbours who could then, as Melanie Klein would put it, be annihilated as the 'bad objects' in which all the violence of intolerable feelings had been relocated.

Between the 1940s and 60s, clinical experiments in groups (for instance by Wilfred Bion, S.H. Foulkes) fed into such discussions of authoritarian and totalitarian mental states. In the same period, 'totalitarianism' was trickling into analytic vocabulary itself. Psychoanalytic writing in the 1930s might still occasionally employ the word to mean 'complete', as a contributor to *The Psychoanalytic Review* indicated when he wrote of 'the totalitarian point of view', meaning 'the whole person rather than some fragment' (Anon., 1937). However, the word's sinister political meanings were more commonly assumed. In a 1940 commentary in *American Imago*, Paul Federn argued that '[s]elf-knowledge, and self-government are contrary to most of the totalitarian and imperialistic tenets of today' (Federn, 1940: 65). Federn contrasted domains where dogmas are hammered into the heads of the masses through the leader's 'thunderous call', or more clandestinely through the use of 'suggestion and hypnotism', with a system based on 'progress through scientific information, and democratic striving for better principles of social order [that] correspond to psychoanalysis' (Federn, 1940: 66). Another significant example was Ernst Kris and Hans Speier's extensive project to analyse 'totalitarian communication', which led, amongst other things, to *German Radio Propaganda: Report on Home Broadcasts during the War* (1944).

References to totalitarianism were also evident in the writings and lectures of British analysts. In 1944 Ernest Jones, invited to lecture at a joint session of the American Psychoanalytic and Psychiatric Associations on the centenary of the latter, spoke on 'Psychology and War Conditions', reporting on the 'leaderless group test' devised by Bion. According to Jones, this exercise illustrated 'the contrast between the British outlook and the German or, more broadly, between the demo-cratic outlook and the totalitarian one'. The test corresponding to it in the German Army was designed to assess the candidate's responses when under command or in command – 'apparently no other situation is envisaged as thinkable than a definitely superior or definitely subordinate one'. This, Jones argued, was perhaps characteristic of the military point of view, 'which is as averse to the very idea of a group without a leader as it is to guerilla warfare or to mob rule' (Jones, 1945: 10).

Another notable commentator on such matters was the psychoanalyst Roger Money-Kyrle, who had participated in the denazification process in post-war Germany. His 'Social Conflict and the Challenge to Psychology', read before the Medical Section of the British Psychological Society in 1947, begins with the psy-chologist's dilemma: 'For more than three decades psychologists have been saying that the problems of the world are not purely economic, but also partly psycho-logical. They have been saying, in effect, that it is ill' (Money-Kyrle, 1978: 198). His talk explored the 'totalitarian fallacy' that 'the welfare of the abstract state is best served by sacrificing the welfare of all its concrete citizens', but pitched this in Kleinian terms as 'lack of conformity between the inner and the outer object' (Money-Kyrle, 1978: 198). He further suggested in 1957 that the consistent denial of 'the individual's unconscious sense of responsibility for predatory aggression led in the end, not to the emancipation of individuals from their sense of guilt, but to the mass projection of conscience, in its most ferocious form, into totalitarian states which sought to control even the thoughts of individuals' (Money-Kyrle, 1978: 305).

Psychoanalysis built up a strong case as the pre-eminent discipline for under-standing psychic possession by the other, identifying the vicissitudes of individual and mass allegiance to liberty, and pinpointing distortions in the inner life of author-ity. Especially salient was the notion that the political subject could be uncon-sciously enslaved from within, not simply mastered from outside. Freud, Klein, and Jacques Lacan (whose thesis about the capture of the ego in the 'mirror stage' was first developed in the 1930s), all explored the capacity for illusion, misconception, even total psychical enslavement, while Wilhelm Reich's *The Mass Psychology of Fascism* (1933) and Fromm's *Escape from Freedom* (1941) linked this directly to the terrifying totalitarian potential. A key task of modern political thought, these authors suggested, was to understand the unconscious predilection for submission. The analysis of subjects held captive by others, existing at the mercy of familial or political father figures, was soon extended by writers on both sides of the Atlantic to show how individuals in mass society were hollowed out from within, controlled by 'public opinion', or seduced by ersatz sirens, advertisers, or cults.

Much of the psychoanalytic attention to extreme forms of politics focused upon fascism rather than upon communism (Stalinist or otherwise). No doubt this was in part because many of the German psychoanalysts, during the 1920s and 30s at least, were sympathetic to social democracy and Marxism (for example Karen Horney, Otto Fenichel, as well as Fromm and Reich). But it also reflects the massive and direct impact of fascism and Nazism upon the lives of so many of Freud's followers. Many psychoanalysts had suffered directly under Hitler's dictatorship, the prime bases of the early movement having been in Austria, Germany and Hungary. Psychoanalytic theory, just as Freud had anticipated, was rejected as a 'Jewish science' – Freud's books were burned in the German capital in 1933, and the old Berlin Society (some of whose members had been active in the 1920s developing free psychoanalytic clinics, as an experiment in social care) was remodelled as the notorious Göring Institute. It was no surprise, therefore, that the analytic societies of North America, whose membership lists were swelled by so many displaced colleagues from Europe, committed themselves to grappling with the psychological roots of anti-Semitism, fascism, ultra-nationalism and militarism, in Germany and elsewhere. The fact that many of the essays in this book return to the presumed psychopathology of the far right therefore corresponds to emphases apparent in the original psychoanalytic literature itself.

Nevertheless, some psychoanalysts sought equally to identify the desire for ultra-egalitarian societies as an expression of infantile wishes, building on Freud's sceptical remarks about Bolshevism. They argued that those who yearned for complete equality in the state might be playing out dreams of a family without differences or hierarchies. For the Scottish analyst W. R. D. Fairbairn, communism was an improbable dream of delivery from Oedipus (1935: 233–46). Once the word and the wider concept of 'totalitarianism' gained traction in the 1940s, the two forms of psychic and political problems associated with the 'pathologies' of extreme left and right could be seen to be almost one and the same. Just as political theorists were constructing their narratives of the 'totalitarian state', numerous clinicians were reporting on the totalized mind, for example at the International Congress on Mental Health in London in 1948 (*Proceedings*, 1948). Frankfurt School sociologists, in exile in America, also famously merged aspects of their account of fascism with critiques of US mass culture, seeing totalitarian society as a product of technological modernity *per se*.

What counts as 'analysis'?

This book focuses upon *interactions* between psychoanalysis and other perspectives on totalitarianism. This raises historiographical and methodological issues, including a question as to exactly what counts as 'psychoanalytic'. The boundaries of the discipline, which had been hard to define from its origins, continued to be blurred in the 1940s and 1950s as psychoanalysis was imported into new fields by trained practitioners as well as by non-clinicians who had become convinced of the usefulness of its insights and concepts. Furthermore, numerous psychiatrists (with or without formal psychoanalytic training themselves) borrowed ideas or techniques piecemeal and incorporated them into quite different clinical as well as ideological agendas, while some Cold War behavioural scientists were combining psychoanalysis with social science, psychology and biology.

Such ambiguous 'osmosis' between specialisms, and debates over the meaning and limits of psychoanalysis, were apparent much earlier, but arguably became still more pronounced after 1945 when Hollywood, popular magazines, cartoons, novels, and newspapers opined ever more frequently on the talking cure. Moreover, whilst it is true that very many psychiatrists trained as analysts, above all in the United States, the work of such clinicians often stretched the definition of analysis to the limit (or beyond). Thus in discussing psychoanalytic influence the historian faces a dilemma: is it best to include whatever was said or done in its name, or, at the other extreme, attempt to stay close to those versions of the theory and practice provided by Freud and his inner circle? Disputes about who were Freud's most effective *and* faithful heirs were of course important features of the landscape: differences existed between Klein, Anna Freud and Winnicott, and divergences between Lacan and other influential analysts in France were also soon apparent, as were contrasting emphases amongst the neo-Freudians, ego psychologists and their rivals in the United States. The second and third generation of psychoanalysts often believed themselves to be following faithfully in Freud's own footsteps while pursuing remarkably disparate paths. And of course many of those who claimed the mantle of psychoanalysis in political or cultural commentaries owed allegiance to none of these clinical traditions and had no training in the field at all.

Historians rightly challenge too doctrinaire a version of what constitutes 'real psychoanalysis' during this period of radical development in its theory and practice around the globe, since so many of the significant elements of its complex dissemination initially appeared as 'fringe' only to become more widely accepted later, or *vice versa*. However, the question of boundaries is particularly fraught when it comes to understanding how the talking cure merged with other psychological and psychiatric techniques. At times, as is shown in several chapters below, psychoanalysis not only provided interpretive tools for understanding the phenomena associated with totalitarianism, but was also drawn into the orbit of penal and authoritarian confessional practices, or experiments in coercive persuasion on both sides of the 'Iron Curtain'.

The contents

Acknowledging, then, the need for caution in the way the terms 'totalitarianism' and 'psychoanalysis' are applied, we argue that the period roughly from 1933 to 1963 (from the installation of Hitler as German Chancellor to the death of Kennedy, not long after the Eichmann trial and the Cuban Missile crisis) decisively shifted the agendas of the 'psy' professions and consolidated the role of an increasingly diversified psychoanalysis within new and influential kinds of psychopolitical debates. No previous volume, as far as we are aware, has yet attempted to consider the field in quite this way, focusing on the two-way traffic between ideas of psychoanalysis and totalitarianism. Much historiographical attention, until recently, was directed towards the invention and early history of psychoanalysis. Important studies have also been produced of conflicts within the profession and the movement during the 1930s and 1940s, and various illuminating national histories have been written. Particular features of the interaction between colonialism, post-colonialism, critical theory and psychoanalysis, as well as the impact of specific branches of analytic thought, such as 'object relations', on developments in post-war welfare and democracy in western states, have been mapped in significant recent publications (e.g. Anderson *et al.*, 2012; Hook, 2012; Shapira, 2013; Linstrum, 2016). Even so, more inquiry is needed into how and why, after 1945, psychotherapy, psychology, psychiatry and psychoanalysis reached into new geographical and disciplinary spaces or gained influence in social and foreign policy debates.

Parts of this story of how psychoanalysis influenced, and was influenced by, a Cold War climate can be pieced together by drawing upon studies such as those above, along with other landmark accounts produced in the last twenty years. Anyone pursuing these questions owes a strong debt to research already conducted, for example, on the Soviet Union by Alexander Etkind (1997) and Martin Miller (1998). More recently, an excellent volume of essays edited by Joy Damousi and Mariano Plotkin (2012) explores the fate of the psychoanalytic movement under conditions of restricted political freedom in Europe and the Americas. Eli Zaretsky's panoramic history, *Secrets of the Soul* (2004), is also an essential backdrop, whilst Martin Jay's *The Dialectical Imagination* (1973), Geoffrey Cocks' *Psychotherapy in the Third Reich* (1985) and Tom Harrison's *Bion, Rickman, Foulkes and the Northfield Experiments* (2000) provide crucial studies of particular developments that complement and inform the present discussions. The current volume attempts to deepen insight into how psychoanalysis was affected by, even as it shaped, the discussion of totalitarianism. It invites comparison of psychoanalytic and other modes of thought on the politics of mind, the political conditions in which psychoanalysis may exist, or flourish, and unearths and analyses occasions when 'the talking cure' contributed to the interpretation of global or national politics. We are interested in affinities and differences between psychoanalytical approaches, and in setting these alongside contemporaneous interventions in political philosophy. In this regard, several of the essays here (notably by Lyndsey Stonebridge, Jacqueline Rose and Michael Rustin) re-examine Arendt's rejection of Freudian thought in her contributions to discourse on totalitarianism, holding up against this her own parallel emphases on the psychological illusions and distortions driving political reality.

We have divided the analysis into seven parts. 'Frameworks' pairs this Introduction with Isaac's sketch of the history of the term 'totalitarianism'. The second section, 'Reckonings with fascism', contrasts the views of exiles on the horrors of Nazi Germany – émigré psychoanalysts in the US and Anna Freud in Britain; the sociology of the Frankfurt School; and Arendt's writings on humanity in dark times. Stephen Frosh focuses on the psychoanalytic theorization of anti-Semitism, and the attempt to safeguard democratic society from the violent deformations of racial and ethnic prejudice, while Matt ffytche's 'The superego as social critique' explores how Frankfurt School sociologists engaged with Freudian thinking whilst their critique of totalitarianism underwent various permutations, from an assault on patriarchy in Weimar Germany to a defence of the family in 1950s

America. Lyndsey Stonebridge compares Arendt's and Anna Freud's attempts to understand how children and adults retreat internally from violent external events, and the ethical possibilities or dangers such psychological manoeuvres can present.

Where the second section largely concerns the catastrophic effects of Nazism, Part III, 'Precarious democracies', concentrates upon how psychoanalysis was mobilized to reconstruct a healthy society, defined against totalitarian sickness or presumed abnormality. These chapters explore different faces of the Cold War political situation, and a common dilemma: how to break free of the wartime logic of 'us and them', and arrive at a more complex understanding of the relation between health, democracy and violence. Peter Mandler traces the influence of the neo-Freudians on American anthropology, and shows how those using psychoanalysis were torn between the need to work as propagandists for the United States, and a less partisan attempt to appreciate and study cultural difference. Michal Shapira recounts the history of the Institute for the Scientific Treatment of Delinquency in London, and efforts by psychoanalysts there to reorient the criminological approach towards antisocial behaviour along more therapeutic lines. Sally Alexander's chapter on 'D.W. Winnicott and the social democratic vision' contextualizes and illuminates Winnicott's radical attempts to acknowledge the threat of hostile forces within, while Dagmar Herzog examines the trajectory of West German debates in the 1960s and 1970s sparked off by Konrad Lorenz's theories of innate aggression. German psychoanalysts were riven by competing desires to ally their theories with biology, while not dehistoricising the violence of recent political experience or disabling the possibility of social transformation through psychotherapeutic awareness. Part IV, which takes the form of a conversation between Forrester, Pick and Zaretsky, provides something of an interlude and free-ranging overview of the historiographical opportunities and problems presented by putting psychoanalysis and totalitarianism together in the first place.

Chapters in Part V, 'Mind control, communism and the Cold War', draw on little-known archival material and suggest how certain clinicians, East and West, sought to break down and then rebuild the personality at the behest of state agencies. Each of these chapters suggests the degree to which talking therapies and clinical knowledge could be mobilized in the pursuit of coercive political goals. Knuth Müller's 'Psychoanalysis and American intelligence since 1940' describes analysts' work in propaganda and connected aspects of the war effort, before turning to experiments into psychic regression funded by the CIA and other agencies in Cold War America. Ana Antic examines the implication of certain 'psychotherapeutic' ideas and techniques in brutal forms of political re-education pursued in the Goli Otok camp in Tito's Yugoslavia. Following on from this – and recollecting the discomforting connections Arendt drew between the development of fascism and Nazism, and the broader history of European imperialism – Part VI concerns experiences and theories of 'colonial subjects'. Erik Linstrum writes about the process of decolonization, which was associated by psychoanalysts in various global contexts with a process of weaning; nationalist movements correspondingly being viewed through the lens of political immaturity.

Ross Truscott and Derek Hook illustrate how psychoanalysis was mobilized in political debates in South Africa, and how the 'health' and 'pathology' of deep-seated emotions such as rage were taken up in the struggle against the apartheid state. Finally, 'Why psychoanalysis?' contains three richly suggestive responses to our themes by Jacqueline Rose, Michael Rustin and Ruth Leys, each of whom also presents a distinct case for the importance, potential subtlety and value of psychoanalytic thought in political debate, past and present.

Psychoanalysis, we see here, is anything but dead, despite the popularity of claims that it's a relic of the past, all of whose premises are long out of date. New biological (or biologistic) models of the emotions have gained an important purchase on contemporary culture and thought. The endeavour to draw psychoanalysis and the neurosciences into a new unified paradigm has been influential, even if many neuroscientists, psychiatrists and 'affect theorists' declare Freud's entire *oeuvre* to be defunct. What often goes missing in current discourse on the emotions, and especially on the nature of traumatic experience, is sustained inquiry into meanings. We are creatures, after all, according to psychoanalysis, shaped, and often enough governed, by unwitting beliefs, motives and phantasies. As Leys suggests, we make and endlessly reconfigure meanings, even as we suffer actual wounds. We endure external (sometimes accidental, or sometimes intentionally catastrophic) impacts, but we also have to make 'sense' of our lives and patch things together, loading onto new 'traumas' something of ourselves and of our psychic pasts. From the idea of the drives in Freud, to the emphasis upon the unconscious work of phantasy in Klein, to the exploration of how we may seek to decipher what it is that others want from us in Lacan, psychoanalysis always suggests we are animals with a difference. (For a contemporary discussion of trauma from a psychoanalytic point of view, see for example, Garland, 1998; Lemma and Levy, 2004; cf. Micale and Lerner, 2001, for the vexed history of the concept of 'trauma'.)

Totalitarianism in the clinical encounter

At the London conference from which the present book first emerged, several notable contributions were made by speakers, and from the floor, that cannot be included here. We are aware that another set of essays would be required to examine uses of political metaphors in the consulting room, and to consider more broadly the competing therapeutic aims expressed by clinicians who have claimed an allegiance to Freud during the twentieth century. A further highly relevant field of investigation (as movingly illustrated in Catalina Bronstein's personal reflections in her foreword to this book) is the writings by practitioners about their own psychic struggles and the difficulty (or impossibility) of analytic work in states where the police have arbitrary powers of arrest or may kill with impunity, and where the walls of each private house or office might really 'have ears'. Less attention has been paid, perhaps, to the nature of the pressures that are placed upon analysts in coercive situations, than to the normative values that are sometimes imposed upon patients (or used to discriminate against would-be candidates for training) by analysts themselves.

For instance, much critical discussion has been focused, in recent years, upon the prejudices of some analytic practitioners, or has identified how entire institutions sought to generalize about, as well as to pathologize, homosexuality. Attempts to pressurize and 'convert' patients, it can well be argued, flies in the face of the very radicalism and openness of Freud's own approach, in which all forms of identity or 'orientation' are potentially open to analytic inquiry. Besides Freud's transgressive understanding of the 'polymorphous' potential of desire, however, one must also reckon with his own sometimes conservative acceptance of social mores, reflecting rather than challenging the patriarchal and heteronormative assumptions of his time. We cannot pursue this question further, but would not dissent in this regard from Eli Zaretsky's *Secrets of the Soul*, which has characterized the profession as 'Janus-faced' in its relationship to the exploration of gender and sexual politics. The same can be argued, even more so, in its relation to colonial structures. Especially relevant here, if one were to chart the history of critiques of analysis as a normative discipline, are Michel Foucault's writings on psychoanalysis as a reinvention of Catholic confessional practices, according to which, even at its freest, this speech was never free, but corralled by techniques designed to solicit and construct subjectivity in a particular fashion.

In the field of analysis itself, much has been written on the gross as well as the subtle and ambiguous ways that patients or analysts, or both, may generate an atmosphere that decries free thought and attacks difference, treats doubt as weakness, or conversely invites the endless proliferation of doubt in order to attack all forms of conviction, so satisfying various unconscious purposes (Feldman, 2009). Interestingly, even as Money-Kyrle, Fromm and Adorno regarded psychoanalytic ideas as precious tools for analysing the mechanisms of thought control in totalitarian societies, the term 'brainwashing' had also percolated into the language of clinicians *and* patients, rebounding upon the therapeutic treatment itself. Sometimes the term appears as a charge against the Freudian approach, or against the 'psy' sciences at large (for instance in the writings of a number of prominent 'anti-psychiatrists', such as R.D. Laing), and is linked directly to ideas about social control and 'totalistic' modes of thought. Sometimes 'brainwash', in clinical contexts, as in common parlance, slides free of its original Cold War moorings and seems interchangeable with other words such as 'hypnotize' or even just 'manipulate'. The author of a psychoanalytic paper in 1965, for example, described a patient, Mr B, who '[f]or the first time . . . showed real anger. He accused me of being unfeeling, dogmatic, mechanistic. He said I only wanted to brainwash him into mediocrity and take all his money in the process' (Kasper, 1965: 479).

A paper by the British psychoanalyst Nicholas Temple at our London conference was especially thought-provoking, showing how useful political metaphors can prove in considering transference and countertransference dynamics, and in reflecting upon possible 'enactments' in a session.[2] Temple presented the experience of a 'totalitarian' state of mind 'that can dominate a patient's internal world'. This, he suggested, is a form of 'mental organization that draws its power from the death instinct and contains strong defences against guilt and vulnerability'. A patient who is subject to such a 'dictatorship of the superego' can appear to be 'living in an internal totalitarian state' in which 'freedom of thought is suppressed and attachment to and dependency on good objects are attacked'. In the case Temple described, attempts on the part of the analyst to introduce ideas that might question the confined mental system were automatically attacked. Moreover, the analyst found himself at least temporarily inhabiting a world with his patient in which 'this tyrannical state of mind is ruthlessly defended, despite the arid and deadened state which it actually creates for the patient and the analyst'.

Temple found his efforts to engage the patient in the analytic process strongly opposed, and he surmised that this was at least in part because of the challenge offered to the defensive system by the analysis itself. Here Temple builds on earlier landmark papers including, within the Kleinian tradition, those of Herbert Rosenfeld (himself an émigré from Nazi Germany) and John Steiner. Such work conceptualized pathological 'organizations' within the psyche in terms of particular, often entrenched, clusters of psychic defences that (however restricting and deadly) sometimes serve to fend off still greater calamities in mental life (Rosenfeld, 1971; Steiner, 1993). Temple noted how a clinician entering into the heavily internally-policed world of certain patients comes under 'pressure to collude since there is a real threat that the collapse of the defences will result in a catastrophic experience of guilt'. The analyst may in fact collude without even realizing it, 'in order to avoid being attacked and treated like a dissident who should be punished and silenced because of opposition to the internal regime'. He described how a particular patient, Ms B, experienced him as a 'bullying, cruel, dictatorial figure who was forcing dogmatic views onto her'.

Temple's work was brought to a premature end when Ms B abruptly terminated the analysis. 'In other patients, it has been possible for the analysis to survive and gradually to lead to a change which allows for a stronger resistance against the totalitarian system.' He ended with a reference to Freud's observation in *Civilization and Its Discontents* (1930) that a capacity for guilt is necessary for a civilized society, a burden it must inevitably bear because of the fact of human destructiveness. By contrast, for Temple, 'the totalitarian state bases itself on its capacity to project guilt into the enemies and victims of the system and to commit crimes to keep this control, so that it continually enacts human destructiveness and uses its crimes to avoid guilt, effectively functioning in the paranoid schizoid position'.[3]

Present crises

Today, the word 'totalitarian' may be less frequently invoked than during the Cold War proper. Nevertheless it still persists, along with other terms indicative of ominous forms of state power, mass fervour or the cult-like devotion that have so often accompanied it. If 'totalitarian' has receded from political discourse, concern about neo-fascism, or visions of an 'Orwellian world' in which cyberspace creates new possibilities for the total 'surveillance state' have certainly not.

The newspapers comment daily on dehumanized 'terrorist acts'; phenomena which are matched by state policies to kill those deemed 'terrorists', and all in their proximity, with impunity, often from a vast distance by an operative seated at a computer monitor, in an ever-expanding use of 'drone warfare' (Chamayou, 2015). Meanwhile, public concern about the militarization of policing, the dwindling of public spaces, the scope for the exercise of personal freedom or collective protest, the domination of consumer culture, and invisible controls and forms of data management exerted through the 'online community', is widespread, and reprises in new forms (and in the face of new technologies) many of the alarming commentaries of earlier Cold War times. If a previous generation feared the unleashing of full nuclear war between the superpowers, we live in an age of equal uncertainty and no less apocalyptic possibility, overshadowed by a climate change catastrophe that is already unfolding, with inevitable vast population movements and new struggles for material resources. Even the 'traditional' forms of Cold War manoeuvring and mind games have returned with force. North Korea, amongst other recent nuclear powers, continues to generate alarm (not only in neighbouring countries) and 'Kremlinology' is back in fashion in Britain and America, as the actions and further intentions of Putin and his circle (legitimate national self-protection, paranoia or imperialistic ambition?) divide the media commentariat.

A sustained consideration of the relationship between what we have termed 'the Age of Totalitarianism' and these most immediate and contemporary psychological and political issues lies beyond the remit of this book. Suffice it to say that the material explored here is not only of value in reconstructing a crucial and turbulent episode in the global development and applications of psychoanalysis, but also sheds light on the present, as Rustin, Leys and Rose also argue in the concluding essays to the book. There are clearly many continuing anxieties to be faced and protests to be made about the coercive and secretive uses of political power, the management of individuals in contemporary mass societies, and the causes of public acquiescence and denial in face of the assault upon hard-won post-war legislation to protect human rights. As Arendt remarked, what always requires vigilant attention is how insidious strands of totalitarian thought can be silently accommodated within contemporary political and social reality, even without a manifest tyrant in power:

> Political, social, and economic events everywhere are in a silent conspiracy with totalitarian instruments devised for making men superfluous . . . Totalitarian solutions may well survive the fall of totalitarian regimes in the form of strong temptations which will come up wherever it seems impossible to alleviate political, social, or economic misery in a manner worthy of man.
>
> (Arendt, 1973 [1958]: 459)

Arendt concludes her book with the warning that the totalitarian potential is 'an ever-present danger', and likely to stay with us from now on (Arendt, 1973 [1958]: 478).

Though 'totalitarianism' is heavily freighted by its Cold War history, we may not be best served by regarding it merely as a moribund artifact. True, it extended its grip over the popular imagination after the Second World War, and as such was often a facet of Western propaganda for the 'open society' and the 'open mind', featuring heavily in political philosophical critique of the 'road to serfdom'. But the problems and terrors that 'totalitarianism' captured in a single, vexed, but highly suggestive word are likely to continue to reverberate, for good reason, in the politics, cultures and psychologies of the future.

Notes

1 Our particular thanks to Andrea Brady, John Forrester, Gordana Batinica, Marcia Holmes, Alessandra Lemma, Peter Mandler, Isobel Pick and Lyndsey Stonebridge for useful comments on an earlier draft of this introduction, or responses to other material in the book; to Shaul Bar-Haim and Danae Karydaki, for their assistance in arranging the London conference; to Ian Magor for suggesting the cover image; to Nicole Mennell and Sophie Richmond for helpful editorial advice, and to David Armstrong, Robert Jay Lifton and Michael Roper for illuminating discussions of this topic as the book took shape. We are also grateful to the Wellcome Trust in London for facilitating two exploratory workshops and funding an international conference on psychoanalysis and totalitarianism in London in 2012, where many of these chapters were first developed, and to Michal Shapira for organising a valuable follow-up conference on post-war psychoanalysis and history, at the Heyman Center, Columbia University in 2014.
2 We are grateful to Nicholas Temple for permission to quote from his unpublished paper here.
3 Further examples especially relevant here, by Eric Brenman, Otto Kernberg, Robin Anderson and others, are discussed in Pick (2012, Chapter 11). For the uses of psychoanalysis in exploring racial and other forms of hate and prejudice in psychic life and politics, see also Clarke, 2003; Frosh, 2005; Figlio, 2006; Davids, 2011.

Chapter 2

Totalitarianism

A sketch

Joel Isaac

This book examines psychoanalysis in the age of totalitarianism. A number of questions can be asked about this intriguing formula. Just what are the connections between psychoanalysis and totalitarianism? How strong is the relationship between these two terms? Does 'the age of totalitarianism' bear only an external connection to psychoanalysis – say, as an organizing framework for writing its history? Or is there something inherent in our way of thinking about the theory and practice of totalitarian rule that calls for psychoanalytic and psychological categories? Perhaps certain forms of psychoanalysis are uniquely well equipped to understand the appeal of totalitarian politics, or the contents of the 'Nazi mind'. It may be useful, as a way of getting a provisional grasp on these problems, to highlight some key features of the history of the idea of totalitarianism. That is my purpose in this brief introductory chapter.

We may begin with the question of novelty. One does not have to read far into the scholarly literature to encounter the claim that totalitarianism is a concept, and a form of politics, unique to the twentieth century. One of the founders of totalitarian studies in the post-war United States, the political scientist Carl J. Friedrich, made the core of his theory of totalitarianism the claim that 'totalitarian society is historically unique and *sui generis*' (1954: 47). Claims about the uniqueness of totalitarianism have typically been defended as follows. When we survey the ideologies and clashes of values that define twentieth-century politics, what we see, for the most part, are ideas that trace their lineage to the nineteenth century, if not even further back. As Tony Judt observed of the passage of history running from 1919 to 1989, the core political categories of this period, '[n]eoclassical economics, liberalism, Marxism (and its Communist stepchild), "revolution," the bourgeoisie and the proletariat, imperialism and "industrialism" . . . were all nineteenth-century artifacts' (2008: 3). In contrast, however, the concept of *totalitarianism* and its kin ('total war', 'total state' and 'total mobilization') had no obvious precedent in the political thought and practice of the preceding centuries. The totalitarian idea is the twentieth century's special contribution to the history of political thought.[1]

I think this claim about novelty is basically correct, but it is necessary to enter some caveats. Historians, if only as a matter of professional honour, tend to be suspicious of *sui generis* types of argument. Appropriately enough, then, historical studies of 'total' war and 'total' mobilization have been pushed back as far as the late eighteenth century (see e.g. Bell, 2007). Moreover, who could doubt that political violence, political messianism and utopian fantasy – those outriders of totalitarian regimes – also played their part in the events of 1789, or 1848, or 1914? And even if fascism and National Socialism seem in some sense without obvious avatars before the 1920s, Soviet communism can still be viewed as an offspring of the Enlightenment, as in fact recent studies of the Cold War have insisted (see Westad, 2005: 4–5). In addition, if these considerations encourage scepticism about the notion that totalitarianism is unique to twentieth-century political thinking, further pause for thought is given by the remarks of the major intellectual critics of totalitarianism, especially Isaiah Berlin, Karl Popper and Friedrich Hayek. For it was their view that the typical features of totalitarian regimes – the deification of the state as the source of political legitimacy and social identity, the disdain for individual rights, private space and civil liberties – traced long historical arcs of development: back to certain strands of Enlightenment rationalism (Berlin, 1969), or to the scientific and political revolutions of the seventeenth century (Hayek, 2001 [1944]) or indeed to the tribal, kinship-based societies of prehistory (these being Popper's (1945) archetypes of the 'closed society'). From these broader perspectives, there seems little new in twentieth-century totalitarian politics save the putting into terrible practice of principles and thoughtways long nurtured in the modern West.

We ought to keep these extended genealogies in mind when thinking about the uniqueness or otherwise of the 'age of totalitarianism'. Nevertheless, the claim of genuine historical novelty still has purchase. It doesn't seem entirely wrong to let etymology play a role in deciding the case, and when we do it is evident that both the vocabulary and concept of totalitarianism emerged within less than a decade following the Italian journalist and politician Giovanni Amendola's coining of the term 'totalitarian' in 1923. Amendola began using the term thereafter to describe the extremity of Italian fascism and its striking contrast with the liberal principles of representative government, majoritarianism and the rule of law. In various combinations, the word began to circulate thereafter in fascist circles in Italy and Germany as a badge of honour. In more careful, if no less partisan, terms Carl Schmitt and Ernst Jünger in Germany began to speak of the 'total state' and 'total mobilization' as counterpoints to the attenuated liberal state and its bourgeois values (Gleason, 1995: 13–30).

We have the historian Abbott Gleason to thank for these insights into the genesis and development of the idea of totalitarianism; what I wish to underscore in his findings is that it is clear that the language and practice of totalitarian politics came to European and American political discourse historically rather late in the game, during the 1920s and 1930s. Ideas of the 'total state' were felt self-consciously to be new departures in these years. Moreover, the logic of total mobilization, of the absorption of society by the state, produced forms of government and political economy that do in fact appear to be *sui generis*. This, at any rate, is the message of recent studies of Nazi economics and Nazi imperialism by Adam Tooze (2006) and Mark Mazower (2008). We deny ourselves important perspectives on fascist rule if we subscribe to the view that there can be nothing new under the sun, and that totalitarianism is as ancient as organized human community itself.

It is also worth pointing out that even the liberal critics of totalitarianism believed that, whatever its long historical development, there was something so novel in totalitarianism as to elude conventional categories of political thought. Part of Hayek's point in writing *The Road to Serfdom* (2001 [1944]) was to insist that totalitarianism was easy to miss: it took a special awareness of the typical traits and aetiology of totalitarian rule to grasp that welfare state capitalism was, as Hayek saw it, a first step on the road to totalitarian rule. To take another example, the American diplomat George F. Kennan, speaking at the 1953 conference that helped to launch totalitarian studies in the United States, wasn't just being modest when he said that nothing in his considerable education had prepared him to make sense of totalitarianism. Said Kennan (1954: 18):

> When . . . I look into my own mind today to see what might be there in the way of general appreciations about the nature of totalitarianism, I find a great disorder of undigested impressions and a number of actual blanks where I know that knowledge and deduction ought to be and aren't.

In sum, there was something in totalitarianism that defied conventional historical or social-scientific thinking, and which required a bottom-up reconstruction of conceptual categories.

So there is something unusual and unique about the 'age of totalitarianism' as an epoch in modern thought and political practice. There remains the challenge, however, of explaining in what the uniqueness of totalitarianism, as an idea and as an epoch, consists. This problem has both empirical and methodological components: we need to know *what* to study and *how* to study it. Psychoanalysis enters the picture here. Historians have noted that, in our search for defining characteristics of totalitarianism, we cannot appeal straightforwardly to criteria such as political violence, utopianism, total mobilization and so on. These cannot – at first blush anyway – distinguish totalitarianism from earlier political or militant organizations. But when we look to the origins of the *idea* of totalitarianism, we see that it was linked to something like the total penetration of the human subject by the state or party. A strong link exists between fascist rule and the making and unmaking of subjectivity or personality.

In fact, the claim was that fascism was designed, not merely to command total obedience from the subjects of its rule but to make people into something more than objects of political control. Fascist selves were conceived as vehicles for the 'totalitarian spirit'. Amendola, looking back in 1923 at a year of political crisis since the March on Rome, observed that:

This spirit will not allow any new day to dawn that has not rendered the fascist salute, just as it does not allow the present era to know a conscience that has not bowed the knee and confessed: 'I believe'. This remarkable 'war of religion', which has been raging for over a year in Italy . . . denies you the right to possess a conscience – of your own, not one imposed by others.

(quoted in Gleason, 1995: 14)

Leading fascist ideologues like Giovanni Gentile were likewise eager to insist that totalitarian rule would reach into every area of human life, thereby obliterating distinctions between state, nation, party and the individual. Totalitarianism was a doctrine of political order that reached into the psychological constitution and the mental lives of its subjects. It went hand in hand with the denial of a realm of social value open to conscience and individual discretion. To be sure, some of this territory is already investigated under the heading of 'political religion' (see e.g. Burleigh, 2006); some of Amendola's remarks about the confessional dimensions of totalitarian rule fit very well with this distinctive approach to the study of totalitarianism. Nevertheless, the mechanisms of social control and psychological warfare inherent in fascist rule are well suited – and were by scholars of the 1950s thought to be well suited – to the methods of psychoanalysis in its different forms.

To sum up what I have argued thus far: the idea of totalitarianism does indeed seem to be *sui generis* in the history of modern politics, and psychoanalysis would seem to have some special claim on our attempts to account for the history and theory of totalitarian politics. In closing, I want to make a final point about the use of the category of totalitarianism in writing the history of psychoanalysis. The ways in which I have invoked the category thus far rest on a large assumption: namely, that there is a common doctrine or set of standards to be extracted from the study of regimes like those of fascist Italy, Nazi Germany, Soviet Russia and Communist China. But it must be pointed out that the equation of these regimes, and the notion that they bear comparative assessment in ways that, say, the study of Hitler's Germany and Franklin Roosevelt's United States do not, is an achievement that emerged rather late in the history of the concept of totalitarianism. If the 'age of totalitarianism' runs, roughly speaking, from Mussolini's power-grab in 1922 to 1989, then the very idea of totalitarianism as an 'ism' belongs to the identification of the regimes of Soviet Russia and Nazi Germany, which became a legitimate and widespread move only as the Cold War heated up during the late 1940s and early 1950s. It is of course true that these kinds of comparisons were not alien even to Mussolini, Schmitt and Jünger, and gained more traction after the Nazi–Soviet Pact of 1939. Nevertheless, the notion of fascism and communism as species of the same political genus took hold in large part thanks to the work of scholars in Soviet studies in North America. It has been observed of this shift in focus of the theory of totalitarian rule at mid-century that it was the obverse and ideological foil, if you will, of accounts of the essential 'pluralism' of the

American political system that emerged during the same period and were often published by the same scholars (see Cieply, 2006; Solovey and Cravens, 2012). Given an account of totalitarianism, one could reverse-engineer a model of a liberal society and vice versa. *There* we have the single-party state, the ruthless suppression or control of voluntary organizations, the command economy and thought reform, while *here* we have open institutions, interest-group politics, the free market, confessional pluralism and the cultivation of creativity and open-mindedness.

The theory of totalitarianism is itself, in part, an artifact of a certain kind of post-war liberalism. If we insist on this point, however, it is important to stress that liberalism was in the picture from the beginning, and that perhaps in describing the history of psychoanalysis in the age of totalitarianism we are describing the connections between psychoanalysis and the emergence of a certain kind of qualitative or existential liberalism, rather than merely procedural or legalistic liberal politics. The ideals of personhood, conscience, privacy, psychic health and social relations that have woven their way through the reception and transformation of psychoanalytic theory in the United States may therefore also be considered components of a reordered and reinvigorated mid-twentieth-century liberalism (see Cohen-Cole, 2014; Thomson, 2006).

It was not always thus. The earliest invocations of the totalitarian spirit and the total state by Gentile and Schmitt, for example, involved centrally the contrast with decadent or ineffectual liberal institutions – representative government, constitutionalism, the rule of law, civil society and so on. During the 1920s and 1930s, liberal ideas, even in the United States, were undergoing a catastrophic collapse in legitimacy. Insofar as these rested on a largely procedural and legalistic understanding of liberal government, it was clear that those kinds of claims about the essence of liberal values were hard to maintain when crisis governments and emergency legislation held sway even in the so-called Anglo-Saxon countries. Before Carl Friedrich became the leading theorist of totalitarian dictatorship, he and his students devoted themselves to working up a defence of *constitutional* dictatorship that could accommodate Roosevelt's extensive use of war powers for domestic political purposes and the spread of American military governments across the globe.[2] Meanwhile, in the late 1930s and early 1940s, theorists of totalitarianism associated with the Frankfurt School were apt to argue that totalitarian states grew out of the liberal-capitalist order and its crisis, and so could not be considered the antithesis of liberalism.[3]

That liberal theory could draw strength from the contrast with totalitarian regimes was by no means a given; that it eventually *did* needs some historical investigation. Part of the explanation, I suspect, may centre on the shift in liberal thought away from legal and institutional languages and towards accounts of the self and its social context that drew succour from psychoanalysis and the social sciences.[4] The complex intertwined histories of liberalism, the theory of totalitarianism, and psychoanalysis may usefully be kept at the forefront of our minds as we consider the chapters in this volume.

Notes

1 For a general account of totalitarianism in the history of political thought, see Isaac (2003).
2 Carl J. Friedrich, 'The Development of Executive Power in Germany', *American Political Science Review* 27 (1933): 185–203; Ibid., *Constitutional Government and Politics: Nature and Development* (New York: Harper & Brothers, 1937); Frederick Watkins, 'The Problem of Constitutional Dictatorship', *Public Policy* (1940): 324–79.
3 See e.g. Max Horkheimer, 'The Authoritarian State' (1940), in *The Essential Frankfurt School Reader*, ed. Andrew Arato and Eike Gebhardt (New York: Continuum, 1982), 95–117.
4 On the rise of psychology in liberal thought after the Second World War see Cohen-Cole, *Open Mind* and Ellen Herman, *The Romance of American Psychology: Political Culture in the Age of Experts* (Berkeley: University of California Press, 1995).

Part II

Reckonings with fascism

Studies in prejudice

Theorizing anti-Semitism in the wake of the Nazi Holocaust

Stephen Frosh

Asking questions about hatred: the mission of *Studies in Prejudice*

In the period immediately after the Second World War, the question of how the murder of millions of people mainly on racial grounds could have come about in the centre of Europe fuelled interest in both the sociology and the psychology of authoritarianism, fascism and prejudice.[1] The topic of anti-Semitism was one focal point for this, understandably because of the specific fate of the Jews under Nazism but also because anti-Semitism could be seen as a prototype of, or perhaps a core element in, all racial hatred. Comprehending what had happened and how to prevent it recurring was a crucial moral and political endeavour, and it also may have seemed to many people that without a conscious effort the lessons of the immediately preceding period might be lost before they had even been learnt. This was certainly the view of the editors of the American Jewish Committee-backed series *Studies in Prejudice*, produced by adherents of the Institute of Social Research, the 'Frankfurt School'. In their Foreword to the series, Max Horkheimer and Samuel Flowerman famously asserted (1950: v), 'Today the world scarcely remembers the mechanized persecution and extermination of millions of human beings only a short span of years away in what was once regarded as the citadel of Western civilization.' The claim that forgetfulness was already happening, that the memory of what had not yet come to be called the Holocaust was being lost, is explicit here and was to become an orthodox point of view amongst many historians in subsequent years. The argument ran that immediately after the war this forgetfulness was motivated by an emotional inability to face the facts of what had happened, a need to focus on personal and social reconstruction, fears provoked by the Cold War and possibly by a triumphalist discourse necessary for the foundation of the State of Israel. In governmental circles, the perceived dangers of communism had overtaken the actual experience of Nazi barbarism, in a shift that had all the hallmarks of the psychoanalytic process of denial writ large. This version of things has now been put severely in doubt, not just by ideologues such as Norman Finkelstein (2000) who have traced the explosion of more recent interest in the Holocaust to the efforts of American Jews and Zionists to create a favourable climate for themselves. More careful scholarship has also revealed a substantial amount of writing and activity around 'remembering' the Holocaust that started immediately at the war's end (and even before it in some cases) and never really ceased, even if it did not come together until towards the end of the 1950s. In his Introduction to the edited collection *After the Holocaust: Challenging the Myth of Silence* (Cesarani and Sundquist, 2012), for instance, David Cesarani comments (2):

> The purpose of this essay collection is to present evidence that in the wake of the Second World War the Jewish survivors of Nazi persecution and mass murder were not 'silent' and that, over the ensuing fifteen years, the world was gifted a plenitude of information about the horrors that had so recently occurred in Europe.

The evidence the collection presents is indeed compelling on this, but it also offers some explanations as to why people who it might be assumed wrote in good faith about the 'silence' could have thought it had existed. One reason was language: much personal testimony written in the early years was in Yiddish or Polish and was not translated; in addition, it was very difficult to sustain networks of international collaboration and memorializing once the post-war East–West divisions were fully in place. This all means that the situation was much more complex than Horkheimer and Flowerman's statement about 'scarcely remembering' suggests: there was plenty of activity, even if keeping track of it and institutionalizing it was hard.

Of course, Horkheimer and Flowerman were not naïve. On the one hand, the warning about forgetting was an important factor in setting the work of the authors of *Studies in Prejudice* and that of the American Jewish Committee in a strongly moral and therapeutic framework – their role was to remind the world of the horror that it had just witnessed and was in the process of denying. But Horkheimer and Flowerman were also aware that the forgetting was nowhere near absolute: they continued by suggesting that the trend they identified towards denial had not fully silenced the troubling questions posed by Nazism; and that these have something to do with the fragility of the structure of civilization within which supposedly advanced cultures live.

> Yet the conscience of many men was aroused. How could it be, they asked each other, that in a culture of law, order and reason, there should have remained the irrational remnants of ancient racial and religious hatreds? How could they explain the willingness of great masses of people to tolerate the mass extermination of their fellow citizens? What tissues in the life of our modern society remain cancerous, and despite our assumed enlightenment show the incongruous atavism of ancient peoples? And what within the individual organism responds to certain stimuli in our culture with attitudes and acts of destructive aggression?
>
> (Horkheimer and Flowerman, 1950: v)

This sets up the work very clearly as an attempt to understand *irrationality* and mass psychology. What is articulated here is a polarization of the 'culture of law, order and reason', which one might assume to be the enlightenment project, against 'irrational' forces that are left over as 'remnants of ancient racial and religious hatreds' and which are visible in the willingness of people to tolerate violent destructiveness. 'Irrationality' here is a kind of vestigial but still active process; the account is reminiscent of Freud's (1927: 48) seemingly despairing response to the continued hold of religion over people who should know better: 'surely infantilism is destined to be surmounted'.

The way Horkheimer and Flowerman articulate this similarly draws on the idea of a developmentally 'primitive' state that puzzlingly sustains itself and breaks into the mature organism to do damage. The dominant images are colonial and bodily, running together the idea that there is a primitive stain in civilization ('atavism') with the equally familiar one of an apparently healthy body politic that is subjected to a spreading illness. The shock of Nazism was that it could appear as an 'irrational remnant' in a 'culture of law, order and reason' – as if psychoanalysis had not already told the world that such 'culture' is built on shaky foundations, that irrationality is not just something it contests, but is its permanent underside. The 'incongruous atavism of ancient peoples' breaks through, damaging 'our assumed enlightenment' and in this formulation echoing Freud's own colonial imagery of the 'primitive' and the 'savage' (Freud, 1913). Switching from this language of primitivity and 'ancientness', Horkheimer and Flowerman also attribute the going-astray of western civilization to the attack on it by a bodily pathology: 'What tissues in the life of our modern society remain cancerous?' they ask. The key point, softened by their use of 'assumed' in 'assumed enlightenment', is that there is something left over or extraneous that is damaging contemporary culture, and it is this we need to understand – rather than that it is the culture itself that is wrong. That is to say, they do not prefigure the later suggestion, for example from Zygmunt Bauman (1989), that the Holocaust was not an aberration, but an *expression*, of modernity; rather, they maintain the simplification that there is a fundamental opposition between civilization and barbarism, between the cultured and the primitive, between the healthy organism and that which invades it to make it ill. This is a view not consistently held by Freud himself, despite his push to oppose the civilized European by the other as 'primitive'. Indeed, that the seeds of destruction might be *intrinsic* to 'a culture of law, order and reason' is suggested by his own account of how culture originates in acts of violence (the murder of the father in *Totem and Taboo* and in *Moses and Monotheism* – Freud, 1913, 1939) as well as by the broader psychoanalytic proposal that each human subject, however 'cultured' she or he may be, is inhabited and preoccupied by irrational, unconscious urges that may even take the form of a drive towards death.

Still, Horkheimer and Flowerman ask excellent questions. 'How could they [i.e. 'many men'] explain the willingness of great masses of people to tolerate the mass extermination of their fellow citizens? . . . And what within the individual organism responds to certain stimuli in our culture with attitudes and acts of destructive aggression?' These questions remain timely: how can it be that such things can (be allowed to) take place? In the full glare and gaze of the populace, with everyone's knowledge, in full daylight – because this is what happened and happens, even if there were shadows too, in which much of the detail was hidden – something bursts through that excites some people into destructive action and terrorizes others into silence, and brutalizes everyone until they hardly see it for what it is. And asking such questions was no trivial matter in the immediate post-war period, even if the claim is heavily overstated that there was little discussion of the Holocaust. As details of the concentration camps seeped into public aware-ness; as people started to rebuild their lives and particularly as the Jews who had escaped began to trace what had happened to those who had been left behind, the force of these questions was sometimes too much for people to take in and silence was at least sometimes the preferred response (e.g. Roseman, 2001). In articulating the issues at all, the authors of *Studies in Prejudice* were very much on the side of those brave enough to risk seeing what was there.

In search of useful answers, Horkheimer and Flowerman draw heavily on psy-choanalysis and social psychology. They are in fact alert to the possibility that they will be criticized for their psychological focus, and attend quickly to it; after all, the Frankfurt School was one of the most influential and sophisticated groups of sociologists and social theorists of the twentieth century. Nevertheless, they choose to stay with psychology in regarding the essential intervention that will follow from their studies as one of *education* and through that protection of the individual against the possibility of being led astray again; and for them, such educational interventions are individually and psychologically based. 'Once we understand, for example, how the war experience may in some cases have strength-ened personality traits predisposed to group hatred,' they write (Horkheimer and Flowerman, 1950: v), 'the educational remedies may follow logically. Similarly, to expose the psychological tricks in the arsenal of the agitator may help to immu-nize his prospective victims against them.' The model here is pedagogic and therapeutic; the point is to understand 'irrationality' and 'atavism', and indeed susceptibility to 'agitators' advancing extremely prejudiced views. And for them, this is a personal affair: 'education in a strict sense is by its nature personal and psychological', which means that one has to understand just what the personal and psychological element in 'prejudice' might be in order to find ways to 'eradicate' it. This psychological focus both allows for a nuanced and powerful utilization of psychoanalytic theory, and raises questions about what *Studies in Prejudice* might offer for a fully social analysis of what nowadays we might more easily recognize as racist hate. The rest of this chapter takes up these points in relation to the core racialized component of *Studies in Prejudice*, the issue of anti-Semitism, asking about the limits of the approach taken by the Frankfurt School theorists of the time, and also about how it feeds into some later developments, with particular reference to some of the ideas of Slavoj Žižek.

Cultural nomadism

Given the emphasis on psychology, the persuasive power of authoritarianism and the 'irrationality' of prejudice and hate, it is not surprising that psychoanalysis was one of the conceptual systems drawn on in *Studies in Prejudice*. Its influence can be seen very profoundly in its best-known volume, Adorno, Frenkel-Brunswik, Levinson and Sanford's (1950) *The Authoritarian Personality*. For Adorno and

Horkheimer, the lead figures in the Institute for Social Research, the stakes were high. Wiggershaus (1995 [1986]: 275) describes how, by 1940, Adorno was seeing the Jews as 'the proletariat of the world-historical process of enlightenment, deprived of every vestige of power', so that analysis of the Jewish situation and of anti-Semitism would cut to the heart of the issues of domination and oppression. Adorno developed a vision of the Jews as representing 'nature' (in the form of an attachment to 'nomadism') against the depredations of 'civilized', alienated class society. This provokes envy amongst non-Jews, with the Jew representing a happier, less constrained humanity, in which the forces of rationality and alienated labour are kept at bay.

It has to be said that this seems an unlikely portrait of Jews, who throughout the twentieth century were more characteristically viewed as urban. Indeed, distance from 'nature' was often used in the rhetoric directed against them, in particular through the trope of 'rootless cosmopolitanism' and divorce from the 'land' or 'soil'. On the other hand, Adorno's reference to nomadism is resonant of some of Carl Jung's notorious commentaries in the pre-war era, in which the Jew is seen as parasitical on the more substantial and genuinely creative Aryan consciousness.

> The Jew, who is something of a cultural nomad, has never yet created a cultural form of his own and as far as we can see never will, since all his instincts and talents require a more or less civilized nation to act as host for their development.
>
> (Jung, 1970 [1934]: 165)

What is apparent here is that the representation of the Jew as nomadic, which is understood by Adorno as a source of anti-Semitic envy, is turned by Jung into an accusation of parasitism. This combines the idea of rootlessness with a more general feeling that has recently become central to some psychoanalytic thinking on racism: that the core racist fantasy is of having something stolen. The others enjoy themselves too much; this is envied – there is so much freedom in it – and the question arises, why do *they* have so much pleasure, and *we* so little? The answer has to be, because our deserved enjoyment for which we have worked and suffered so hard, has been taken away from us by underhand means. The Jew has stolen the money, the black has stolen sexuality: this is what drives much racist fantasy. For Slavoj Žižek, prime exponent of this view of the racist imaginary, such a fantasy is premised on the repression of a different awareness, that what has been 'lost' or stolen in this way was never part of the subject at all:

> What we conceal by imputing to the Other the theft of enjoyment is the traumatic fact that *we never possessed what was allegedly stolen from us*: the lack ('castration') is originary, enjoyment constitutes itself as stolen.
>
> (Žižek, 1993: 203)

Be that as it may, there is a direct line of thought from the presentation of anti-Semitism as constituted around the idea of the Jew as parasite to the broader theorizing of racism as a psychic structure organized around fantasies of the theft of enjoyment. The *currency* of Adorno's thinking in current work (Žižek engages with him thoroughly in several places, for example in a discussion of psycho-analysis and political liberation in Žižek, 1994) is very marked in this way, as it is in many others.

The image of the cultural nomad successfully captures a sense of the Jew as standing outside the social order – the Jew as other – that is powerfully engrained in much anti-Semitic thinking. Building on this in their *Dialectic of Enlightenment* (1989 [1944]), Adorno and Horkheimer make a link between Jews and women, understanding the hatred towards them both as deriving from their status as outsid-ers to the coercive power of domination. The point here is not so much the more conventional psychoanalytic claim that weakness is despised because it reminds the oppressor of her or his own vulnerability, although this notion is present in *The Authoritarian Personality*. It is rather that women and Jews are excluded from the realm of culture, yet they continue to exist; this makes them less alienated (because less acculturated, hence more 'natural') and so produces envy in the 'strong', who are the victims of their own alienation. Where Jews differ from other minorities, according to Adorno and Horkheimer, is in the unusual combination of this asso-ciation with nature and 'weakness', and the striving of the Jew for something non-material or spiritual – an argument very much akin to Freud's (1939) idea that the key characteristic of Judaism is the belief in an abstract God and that this provokes antagonism from the more regressed, *less* intellectually cultured (Christian) other. The impact of this, somewhat as in Freud's theorizing, is supposedly to elicit envy in those who are subject to what Wiggershaus (1995 [1986]: 341) calls the 'failed civilization'. It is worth noting that the idea that the oppressed group bears the responsibility for preserving 'nature' is resonant of some later psychoanalytic accounts of the relationship between slavery and anti-black racism (e.g. Kovel, 1995), in which the repressed sexuality of the white is understood to be projected onto the supposedly animalistic body of the black. If it still seems slightly odd to extol Jews for their closeness to nature, it is nevertheless stimulating to consider that anti-Semitism may in this way connect more strongly with the general fantasy structure of racism: the derogated other who is made subject to racism stands in for what is imagined as having been lost or stolen, that thing that would bring the satisfaction which the 'failed civilization' denies.

Purity and projection

There are a number of shared themes that emerge from work in the *Studies in Prejudice* tradition. One is the location of responsibility for anti-Semitism firmly with the anti-Semite: Adorno *et al.* (1950: 301) state 'anti-Semitism is not so much dependent on the nature of the object as upon the subject's own psychological wants and needs'. The search for purity, both pure goodness within and pure evil without, as a key element in the anti-Semite's consciousness is an example of such 'psychological wants and needs', and links this work with later psychoanalytic traditions of thinking on racism, which suggest that it is one of many refusals to deal with doubt and ambivalence (Rustin, 1991). Denial of the multifariousness of social and psychic phenomena forms the basis of what Adorno *et al.* refer to as 'psychological totalitarianism', the impulse to keep everything completely in its place, under the sway of one powerful, paranoid organizing principle. The cost of this is great because the anti-Semite lives in terror of the persecutory universe she or he has created, but the benefit is that at least this universe makes sense, and nominates one single, identifiable source of danger – the Jew. For *The Authoritarian Personality*, it is the violence of this psychic process that characterizes the fascist and anti-Semitic state of mind, closing down anything soft and welcoming, replacing it with a repudiating harshness that damages the subject as well as the hated other, and that reflects (again to use the anachronistic mode of expression) a kind of enjoyment that masks an inner emptiness.

> It is as if the anti-Semite could not sleep quietly until he has transformed the whole world into the very same paranoid system by which he is beset: the Nazis went far beyond their official anti-Semitic programme . . . The extreme anti-Semite silences the remnant of his own conscience by the extremeness of his attitude. He seems to terrorize himself while he terrorizes others.
>
> (Adorno *et al.*, 1950: 324–5)

This compellingly captures both the extremity of the anti-Semitic state of mind and its perversity, a point followed up in other work including Klaus Theweleit's (1987 [1977]) exploration of what he references as the 'monumentalism' of fascism, the way it acts to preserve psychological and social boundaries in the most rigid way, setting them up as a bulwark against fluidity. 'Terrorizing' anti-Semitism is seen by Adorno *et al.* as a kind of addiction demanding increasingly intense satisfaction if it is to leave the subject satisfied, yet with every 'fix' there is something more that is needed, and something more that is lost. Any 'difference' becomes a threat and has to be wiped out, but the more tightly the boundaries around what is acceptable and 'same' are drawn, the more likely it is that difference of one form or another will be encountered. So it is that the capacity of the self to tolerate anything 'outside' is continuously reduced, and the intensity of hatred of all that is other is exponentially increased. This account offers a relatively simple yet quite durable model for understanding anti-Semitism in a psychosocial framework: the Jew is a figure chosen initially for its cultural congruence as a hate object, but is then excessively invested in as a carrier of all this otherness; conspiracy is to be found everywhere. This produces a spiralling of paranoia and hatred, as the Jew serves both to contain and to exaggerate the projected impulses of the anti-Semite. Psychosis is in the air, kept at bay only by endlessly increasing rigidity and escalating anti-Semitic hate. The Jew is a safety valve for destructive impulses, but this use of the Jew has a profound personal and social cost.

This material indicates the weight placed on psychological interpretation of anti-Semitic phenomena, a characteristic shared by many studies of Nazism in the preceding years, as Daniel Pick (2012) has recently shown. That is, like Nazism, anti-Semitism is viewed as a kind of madness that might be responsive to the vocabulary of psychology (prejudice) and psychoanalysis (repression and projection); this also holds the psychopolitical hope that comprehending it in these terms might offer a route towards the 'treatment' or therapy of society. 'The educational remedies may follow logically', state Horkheimer and Flowerman (1950: vii), buying into the Freudian and enlightenment idea that knowledge transforms the uncontrollably irrational into the amenably rational. Given the circumstances, one might wonder whether this is an instance of failing to learn from immediately preceding history, in which the rationalistic model implying the inevitability of enlightened progression to mental and political balance so conspicuously failed. On the other hand, it is perhaps ironic to think that there might be a link to ego psychology, the dominant form of psychoanalysis in the USA after the war, which was so despised by some of the Frankfurter theorists, notably Marcuse (1972 [1955]). The usual criticism is that ego psychology, which emphasizes the role of the ego in mediating between unconscious impulses and the requirements of 'external reality', turns too readily into a conformist psychology stressing adaptation to social norms. However, considering what the psychoanalysts who developed it (who were mostly forced emigrants from Nazi Europe, many of them Jewish) had been through, perhaps one should not be too single-minded about pillorying ego psychology's attempt to reinstate rationality as a moral force. The wish to restore some semblance of rationality as an ideal could seem like a genuinely therapeutic and civilized response to the explosion of irrationality so recently endured.

The Frankfurt School theorists were very alert to the potential limitations of their psychological reading of anti-Semitism and balanced it by linking it closely to social and economic analysis. For example, according to Bronner and Kellner (1989: 7), Horkheimer's (1989 [1939]) essay 'The Jews and Europe' 'basically interprets anti-Semitism in terms of its usefulness for monopoly capitalism'. Even in this article and with this caveat, however, Horkheimer manages to convey the energy and intensity of Nazi anti-Semitism as 'intimidat[ing] the populace by showing that the system will stop at nothing', but also serving psychic needs.

> People can secretly appreciate the cruelty by which they are so outraged. In continents from whose produce all of humanity could live, every beggar fears that the Jewish émigré might deprive him of his living. Reserve armies of the unemployed and the petty bourgeoisie love Hitler all over the world for his anti-Semitism, and the core of the ruling class agrees with that love. By increasing cruelty to the level of absurdity, its horror is mollified . . . Pity is really the last sin.
>
> (Horkheimer, 1989 [1932]: 92)

At this time, Horkheimer was generally scathing about the uses of psychological theories applied to social phenomena, but his analysis here is already pointing to the emotional hold that terroristic forms of anti-Semitism might have, even over those who ostensibly oppose them. It also shows the ambiguities that this psychic arrangement produced: 'pity is the last sin', not only pity for the other, but also the pity mobilized by recognition of the actual emotional needs of the hate-filled self.

If the fault lies not with the Jews, then why are the Jews so consistently chosen as the recipients of this particular form of racialized violence? The simple answer is that in the history of western civilization – specifically its Christian history but, as the Nazis had shown, underpinned by a good dose of paganism – the figure of the Jew constitutes a ready-made container for the destructive urges of the anti-Semite. That is, the psychological formulation provided by psychoanalysis is made *psychosocial* through the thesis of a socially and historically legitimized mode of expression of these psychological forces. For Adorno *et al.*, Jews are suitable 'substitute objects' because of the work that has been done on them historically in the culture, producing a fantasy that is compelling, rigid, and exhaustive. This produces the Jew as a perfect '"object" of unconscious destructiveness', fitting all the necessary requirements to fulfil that role:

> It must be tangible enough; and yet not *too* tangible, lest it be exploded by its own realism. It must have a sufficient historical backing and appear as an indisputable element of tradition. It must be defined in rigid and well-known stereotypes. Finally, the object must possess features, or at least be capable of being perceived and interpreted in terms of features, which harmonize with the destructive tendencies of the prejudiced subject.
>
> (Adorno *et al.*, 1950: 300)

According to Adorno *et al.*, the Jew is the ideal, prepared-for hated other for the disturbed individual, who latches onto this escape route in order to preserve psychic integrity when faced with internal destructiveness and an oppressive social order. In addition, the system of domination works to confuse the prejudiced person, creating a sense of being alienated from society, of not understanding how it works or what are the sources of its actual impact. Politically unsophisticated, the anti-Semite seeks respite from a mystifying reality in the reassuring story of the single enemy, a rigid narrative of existence strong enough, and widely-shared enough, to seem to make sense, and one supported by a social order that ensures opposition is directed against an externalized other rather than against itself. The Jew's 'alienness' serves as shorthand for the alien nature of society itself, but the materiality of Jews makes them accessible as an object of hate in the way that society in general is not.

> Charging the Jews with all existing evils seems to penetrate the darkness of reality like a searchlight and to allow for quick and all-comprising orientation. The less anti-Jewish imagery is related to actual experience and the more it is kept 'pure', as it were, from contamination with reality, the less it seems to be exposed to disturbance by the dialectics of experience, which it keeps away through its own rigidity.
>
> (Adorno *et al.*, 1950: 310)

It is interesting to note that this theme of the irrelevance of Jews to anti-Semitism – the way anti-Semitism perpetuates itself even, or perhaps especially, in the absence of Jews – is one that continues to thrive in the literature, and has been taken up for example by Žižek. He tracks the ways in which the very unreality of the denigrated other sustains it in the face of violence, making an escalating phenomenon of hatred: 'This paradox, which has already emerged apropos the Jews in Nazi Germany . . . the more they were ruthlessly exterminated, the more horrifying were the dimensions acquired by those who remained' (Žižek, 1994: 78). Being unreal, being fantastic, the hated other cannot actually be eradicated; in a sense, the perfect enemy is the one who does not exist.

In one of Otto Fenichel's last pieces (Fenichel, 1946), written for Ernst Simmel's *Anti-Semitism: A Social Disease*, the situation is still starker and more psychoanalytically specific. He takes up the position also found in *The Authoritarian Personality* that anti-Semitism arises in periods of socially induced misery: the anti-Semite, immersed in confusion and led astray by ideological forces, 'sees in the Jew everything which brings him misery – not only his social oppressor but also his own unconscious instincts, which have gained a bloody, dirty, dreadful character from their socially induced repression' (29). Jews are the ideal object for projection of these unconscious urges 'because of the actual peculiarities of Jewish life, the strangeness of their mental culture, their bodily (black) and religious (God of the oppressed peoples) peculiarities, and their old customs' (Ibid.), which remind the anti-Semite of 'old primeval powers' that non-Jews have given up (18). Jews seem uncanny because of these peculiarities, adding to the sense of threat and disgust they provoke. However, the most significant element leading to the intensity of anti-Semitic hate is the way the Jew is the recipient of the anti-Semite's own destructive feelings and also of the fantasized retaliation against them, induced by the individual's own superego. That is, both the repressed impulses and the punitive internal response to these urges are projected outwards, onto the Jew. Linked to this is a more profound identification between the Jew as foreign and uncanny, and the site of foreignness within: 'It can be expressed in one sentence' writes Fenichel (1946: 20): 'one's own unconscious is also foreign. Foreignness is the quality which the Jews and one's own instincts have in common.' The Jew as foreigner and preserver of archaic customs can be the object of projection of what is feared and hated within oneself, the 'foreign' unconscious; they thus carry the sense of destruction and desire, of 'what is murderous, dirty and debauched' (19), and racist hate is magnified by the anti-Semite's terror of these inner urges. Again this theme can be found exemplified in some of Žižek's writings, but here turned not into a fundamental psychic structure, but one that is socially overdetermined, the structure of capitalism.

> Is capitalism's hatred of the Jew not the hatred of its own innermost, essential feature? For this reason, it is not sufficient to point out how the racist's Other presents a threat to our own identity. We should rather invert this proposition: the fascinating image of the Other gives a body to our own innermost split, to what is 'in us more than ourselves' and thus prevents us achieving full identity with ourselves.
>
> (Žižek, 1993: 206)

Against the implication that it is the inner state of the subject that is primary in seeking out an external cause, Žižek (1997: 76) also gives us a more elaborated version of anti-Semitism in which it is produced by the structure of capitalism itself: 'social antagonism comes first, and the "Jew" merely gives body to this obstacle'. Culture's investment in this figure of the 'Jew' produces it as an element in the unconscious, and with it arises the widespreadness of anti-Semitism itself.

Ernst Simmel (1946), writing in the volume of essays that he edited out of a symposium on anti-Semitism organized by the San Francisco Psychoanalytic Society in 1944, draws a familiar parallel here, using the discourses both of Marxism and of anti-Semitism-as-illness and making the connection between modernity ('civilization') and the canker that destroys it.

> Applying our method of psychoanalytic-dialectic thinking, we must infer not that anti-Semitism annihilates the achievements of civilization, but that the process of civilization itself *produces* anti-Semitism as a pathological symptom-formation, which in turn tends to destroy the soil from which it has grown. Anti-Semitism is a malignant growth on the body of civilization.
>
> (34)

For Simmel, thinking back on the Nazi phenomenon, anti-Semitism is both a cancer and a mass psychosis, a 'social disease', despite the individuals concerned not being psychotic; or rather, it is the existence of this mass psychosis that *protects* anti-Semites from becoming psychotic themselves. Although it is the case that there may be various neurotic processes at work within individual anti-Semites, the individual anti-Semite is 'normal'. However, when this person joins a group the crowd dynamic takes over, distinguished particularly by 'unrestricted aggressive destructiveness under the spell of a delusion' (39) – exactly the characteristic of psychosis. This is also the epitome of the splitting process: 'he can split in two the re-externalized parental power: into the leader whom he loves and into the Jew whom he hates' (50). All this further clarifies the comfortable way in which the anti-Semite can live with irrational beliefs:

> The anti-Semite believes in his false accusations against the Jews not in spite of, but *because* of their irrationality. For the ideational content of these accusations is a product of the primary process in his own unconscious and is conveyed to his conscious mind through the mediation of the mass-leader's suggestions.
>
> (Simmel, 1946: 51–2)

The lie at the heart of racism, as Rustin (1991) describes it, comes out in full force here as a mode of psychic truth – not in the sense of an ethical truth, which it clearly is not, but rather as a symptomatic statement and a mode of containment-by-excess. The anti-Semite is attracted to 'irrational' beliefs precisely because they express the turmoil of a mind at war with itself and with the world, yet one that is structurally and socially weak, and needs the prop of its containing madness to keep itself sane. And at the root of this turmoil, according to Simmel, is 'the process of civilization itself', taking us back to the original theme that has at times been hard to preserve: that anti-Semitism is not something grafted onto modernity as an external force that disturbs what would otherwise be 'a culture of law, order and reason'; rather, as in Bauman's (1989) articulation, it is expressive of the irrationality that lies within modernity itself, and is generated by it.

Conclusion

It can be seen that despite the sophistication of the social theory on which these post-war writers drew, there is quite a simple psychosocial argument about anti-Semitism being posited. Society is anti-Semitic in its construction of the Jew as a hate object; and this construction allows individual anti-Semites to project their unconscious disturbances into that hate object. This simplicity is part of the reason both why the argument remains accessible and influential, and why it is also important to see how it is developed and deepened in later work. One question is, is it possible to go further than this essentially static presentation of the individual– social divide when considering anti-Semitism and other forms of social hatred? For example, might one build more fully on Simmel's argument that the contradictions in society are not simply accompaniments of, or accidental parallels to, the contradictions of the unconscious, but that they actively *produce* them, through all the micro- and macrosocial processes (parental interactions and anxieties; socialization practices; familial beliefs; gendered and 'racialized' institutional practices, etc.) out of which each person is made? Part of the point of the links made here with some later psychoanalytically-imbued sociological writing is to suggest that the ideas developed by the *Studies in Prejudice* authors prefigure a possibly more nuanced understanding of how the dynamics of racism and anti-Semitism are intrinsic to modernity and of the mechanisms through which this works to make them both 'personal' (in Horkheimer and Flowerman's sense) and fundamentally social, produced by 'the process of civilization'. For example, Slavoj Žižek, who has appeared frequently in this chapter, often turns to the exposure of anti-Semitism as a key topic, and even goes so far as to see anti-Semitism as paradigmatic for an understanding of racism itself. In this regard he writes that today, '"normal", non-exceptional, non-anti-Semitic racism is no longer possible' (Žižek, 1994: 74). His suggestion is not only that some basic psychic mechanisms are at work, but also that the fantasy structure of anti-Semitism is central to that of racism in general. For Žižek this turns on the idea of enjoyment and its theft, on how deprivation is clung to by the anti-Semite and on how the Jew is constructed, we might say, as the one who 'gets away with it', who can always turn the law to advantage. It should be noted that Žižek is often criticized for the way in which he approaches this material, for his own apparent 'enjoyment' of the anti-Semitic discourses that he describes (Frosh, 2011). Nevertheless, the detailed examination of the fantasy structure of anti-Semitism and racism that he uses can be seen to lean on the work of the critical theorists of the Frankfurt School, but also to radicalize it through its articulation of the *social* imaginary as the source of, and arena for, psychoanalytic exploration.

In all this, the figure of the Jew is a particularly powerful instance of the figure of the 'other' in general. Through its historically-derived cultural pervasiveness it is perpetuated as a representation of that which is needed yet despised, that which holds in place the otherwise potentially intolerable destructiveness of a social system founded on inequality and alienation. Such systems *create* their own psychic structures and psychological disturbances; thus, given the organization of Western society, anti-Semitism is as much an element in the unconscious of every subject as is any other psychosocial state – love, loneliness or loss, for example. The Jew is a constitutive feature of Western consciousness, primed by centuries of Christian anti-Semitism; and it is therefore one element out of which subjectivity is made. However, there are plenty of others, as postcolonial theory and feminism respectively have shown around racism and sexism, so anti-Semitism is by no means unique. One additional question that this gives rise to is over the extent to which the very specific and urgent focus on anti-Semitism that dominated in *Studies in Prejudice* limits or facilitates the application of its thinking to other modes of racist activity. Is it the case that European anti-Semitism's roots in the history of Christianity mean that what is theorized about the cultural function of the Jew as other is too specific to have lessons for, say, American anti-black racism? Or, as psychoanalysts have tended to assume, are we dealing with universal psychic mechanisms called into play under certain social conditions (extreme economic insecurity, for example) that then seek out whatever category of denigrated othering might be made available by the particular history of that culture? Whilst to the psychoanalytically attuned ear this seems a plausible assumption, the work still remains to be done, as some of the debates around the appropriateness of using psychoanalytic meta-categories in postcolonial theory have shown (Khanna, 2003) and as criticisms of psychoanalysis' own colonial and at times racist assumptions have also made clear (Brickman, 2003).

The post-Second World War effort to trace the psychodynamics of 'prejudice' was understandably focused on the recent experience of fascism and Nazism and concern over the danger of their resurgence; but it was also highly productive. These texts embody a principled attempt to construct a sophisticated psychosocial theory in the sense of one that understands the structure of personal life as inextricably bound up with social forces. However, the pull back to psychologism in this work inhibits the full development of such an account, effectively polarising the theory so that the social becomes either the true cause of anti-Semitism, or the 'container' for individual pathology. This makes sense within the prevalent discourse of Nazi 'madness', but perhaps is not so persuasive when one considers the durability of anti-Semitism and racism across time and space.

Note

1 Some material in this chapter was used in Stephen Frosh (2005), *Hate and the Jewish Science*. London: Palgrave.

Chapter 4

Inner emigration

On the run with Hannah Arendt and Anna Freud

Lyndsey Stonebridge

> They must remember that they are constantly on the run, and that the world's reality is actually expressed by their escape.
>
> Hannah Arendt, 'On Humanity in Dark Times:
> Thoughts about Lessing'

> I would [. . .] like to tell you what leaving Vienna has meant to me and how strange it is to carry a past within oneself which can no longer be built upon. With this experience, I have come to a new understanding of the process involved in repression and infantile amnesia.
>
> Anna Freud, letter to August Aichorn, 1946

'They must remember that they are constantly on the run': the migrants Hannah Arendt described in the lecture with which she accepted the Lessing Prize in 1959, were not, like her, actual refugees from totalitarianism, but fugitives of the mind only, 'inner emigrants' under the Reich who had retreated from totalitarianism in their heads (Arendt, 1983). The theme of Arendt's speech, 'thinking in dark times', would have held few initial surprises for her Hamburg audience, who might have anticipated her focus on Lessing's famous *Selbstdenken*, thinking for oneself.[1] Nonetheless, any self-identified inner immigrant in the audience might also have been arrested by Arendt's criticism of their contemplative detachment from the realities of totalitarianism. Don't think all your lofty freethinking somehow allowed you to rise out of the world's darkness, she also told them; inner immigration is as much a symptom of political times as it is a retreat from them: 'the world's reality is actually expressed by their escape'.

Biographer, political thinker and psychoanalyst, the late Elisabeth Young-Bruehl was one of the first to recognize the centrality of the themes of migration, exile and statelessness to Arendt's writing on totalitarianism in her still unsurpassed 1982 biography (Young-Bruehl, 1982). She was also the first to make the comparison with psychoanalyst Anna Freud's parallel experience of enforced migration, the subject of her second, equally definitive, biography (Young-Bruehl, 1988). The chapter 'Stateless Persons', in the middle of the Arendt biography, is echoed directly by 'Another Life' in the Anna Freud book. Like those of so many key thinkers of the last century, these are lives bisected by the before and after of exile.

Arendt would have been uncomfortable with the comparison implied by the two biographies, not least because she tended to assume that psychoanalysis encouraged the very self-absorbed and apolitical inner emigration she found so deeply suspect. Yet, as Young-Bruehl's careful attention to the models of mind developed by both her subjects suggests, there is more to this particular comparison than a shared migrant history. Tireless theorist of the ego's defences, Anna Freud was better placed than most to address the question implicit in Arendt's Lessing address: what happens when the mind retreats from a reality it finds intolerable? Or, as Arendt might have put it, how does the mind migrate from totalitarianism?

For Anna Freud, inner emigration is already the psyche's default position: for the ego, both the inside world and the outside world are always at some level difficult to tolerate. In dark times, she wrote in 'About Losing and Being Lost' (the remarkable essay about mourning and exile begun in 1946, but not published until 1967), the ego becomes even more damagingly defensive; the temptation is to 'turn away from life altogether, and to follow the lost object into death', she writes (1998 [1967]: 104). In her Lessing lecture, Arendt had similarly warned that, in his personal contemplation, the inner emigrant risked disappearing into the same 'holes of oblivion' that engulfed totalitarianism's real victims.

How can one endure a reality so defined by the threat of total obliteration? For many, mental flight was the best option in the worst of possible circumstances; for others, of course, permanent exile was the price paid for survival itself. But if Arendt and Anna Freud shared one thing it was the conviction that reality, however intolerable – mad even (as Jacqueline Rose demonstrates in her chapter in this volume) – must be confronted. It was only by engaging with reality, both women would come to argue, that it was possible to remain in the world, and to love it enough to want to make it worth living in again. Read together, Hannah Arendt and Anna Freud, the one concerned with political, the other with psychic, reality, ask not only what it means to escape totalitarianism, but also to defy it.

Hannah Arendt

When Arendt chided the inner emigrants in her Hamburg audience for forgetting about the reality of totalitarianism for the refugee, she knew full well that she was scratching at a recent local wound. In 1945 the term 'inner emigration' had been at the heart of an undignified argument among German intellectuals and writers (see Brockmann, 2003). Who was most culpable, went the debate – those who left willingly or those who stayed and emigrated in their heads? It perhaps says something about the failure to grasp the reality of Nazi totalitarianism that this debate could happen at all. This was Thomas Mann's point when he publicly declared that he would not be returning to Germany. In an earlier address to the Library of Congress in 1943 Mann had eloquently lamented the 'abnormal and pathological' condition of discovering one's own country to be the 'deepest most hostile foreign territory' ('Believe me: for many there Germany has become just as foreign as it is for us; an "inner emigration" with numbers in the millions there is just waiting for the end, just as we are waiting' [quoted in Brockmann, 2003: 14]). Two years on, the magnitude of the Nazi genocide meant that inner emigration risked sounding like little more than a piece of badly timed retrospective self-justification.

Arendt was of a similar mind. Always suspicious of popular psychological explanations that let history and its agents off the moral and political hook, she gave short shrift to the idea that inner resistance to Nazi totalitarianism (a resistance which was undoubtedly felt) was a persuasive moral, let alone legal or political, defence. 'In recent years, the slogan of the "inner emigration" has become a sort of joke', she complained in her Eichmann reports (Arendt, 1994 [1963]: 127). Thus Otto Bradfish, former member of the *Einsatzgruppen*, responsible for the killing of at least 15,000 people, could tell a German court that he had always been 'inwardly opposed' to what he was doing all along. He may well have been, Arendt remarked, but the point was that, even if millions had fled totalitarianism in their heads, this particular mass exodus remained a surprisingly and, as it turned out, fatally well-kept secret.

It was the facile moral politics of the 'inner emigration' debate that repelled her. For Arendt, the issue was not only about finding out which parts of the mind or population were culpable, but discovering a way of relating the activity of thinking to the reality of totalitarianism. This was the question at the heart of her Lessing lecture, where she gave a far more complicated and vexed account of the plight of the inner emigrant under totalitarianism than in the Eichmann commentary.

Where the trial reports were a very public coda to the history she had described in *The Origins of Totalitarianism* (1973 [1958]), the 1959 lecture was a public staging of the question at the heart of *The Human Condition* (1958) published one year earlier: how to create a politically meaningful humanity in the wake of totalitarianism? Lessing's vision of a fraternity of freethinking friends was the model of humanity against which Arendt tested both the recent past and her audience. The question provoked by Lessing after totalitarianism, in Arendt's words, was this:

> The question is how much reality must be retained even in a world become inhuman if humanity is not to be reduced to any empty phrase or phantom. Or to put it another way, to what extent do we remain obligated to the world even when we have been expelled from it or have withdrawn from it?
>
> (Arendt, 1983: 22)

Measure for measure: the amount of reality that can be kept back is proportionate to the future of humanity as a meaningful category. But the reality Arendt wants to hang onto here is not just the true state of everything that lies beyond the all-too-evident lies of totalitarian rule. It is the reality of being in the world together, of being obligated. This is the reality that all of totalitarianism's exiles – those who have been expelled and those who have withdrawn in their heads – must struggle to retain.

Putting the victims together with the bystanders like this looks audacious, even by Arendt's piety-busting standards. But Arendt is far from drawing easy equivalences here. It is precisely the reality of the pariah's existence that she is urging the inner emigrant to keep in mind, often in the dialogic irony of her prose itself. Only 'the warmth and fraternity of closely packed human beings' compensated 'for the weird irreality that human relationships assume' under totalitarianism, she noted, for example, of the unique fraternity found among the expelled (1983: 16). Few in her Hamburg audience could have missed the brute historical referent crammed in among those 'closely packed human beings'. The freedom of thought so prized by Lessing always had its geopolitical correlates – this is Arendt's belated message to Germany's inner emigrants. While the pariahs huddled together in the historical twilight, the inner emigrants withdrew into themselves: two different refuges, same reality. In contrast to the pariah's fraternity (a humanity seized from the reality of genocide at an atrociously high price), however, the lonely dilemma of the inner emigrant is suggested in her near-oxymoronic nomenclature. On the one hand she feels like an emigrant, an alien inside the state; in reality she is an alien inside her head only.

Arendt described inner emigration as an 'ambiguous phenomenon', as well she might: she counted several good friends among Germany's inner emigrants (notably Karl Jaspers), and could have wished that others might have emigrated further inside (notably Martin Heidegger); later she would say that it was not the behaviour of the Nazis that caused her the most astonishment, but that of her friends (Arendt, 2003 [1964]). What bothered her was not the phenomenon of inner emigration itself: far from it, Arendt was committed to the virtues of a Stoic retreat from public life and the cultivation of an 'inner polis'. As Rei Terada (2004: 855) has wittily summarized, for Arendt, 'self-involvement looks better and better as society goes out of its mind'. But only under certain conditions, for what really matters, what never ceases to preoccupy Arendt, is the *way* in which one migrates from the world; and it is at this point – both despite and because of her protests to the contrary – that her writing moves onto a terrain familiar to psychoanalysis.

More often than not inner emigration can end up being little more than escapism, a self-absorbed flight into the false refuge of the inner world. In the face of a 'seemingly unendurable reality' the temptation is to 'ignore that world in favour of an imaginary world "as it ought to be" or as it once upon a time had been' (Arendt, 1983: 19). But on the other hand, for Arendt, the work of enduring that reality, of testing and even eventually defying it, can begin only in the migrant mind – the mind that knows there is something to be escaped from. Between the madness of being at home in totalitarianism and the delusions of denying its existence, Arendt offered her audience a third option, in which to retreat from the world is actually to develop a sense of its reality, and so endure it. Paradoxically, turning away from the world could be a form of engagement with it, or possibly even a method of resistance:

Flight from the world in dark times of impotence can always be justified as long as reality is not ignored, but is constantly acknowledged as the thing that must be escaped. When people choose this alternative, private life too can retain a by no means insignificant reality, even though it remains impotent. Only it is essential for them to realize that the realness of this reality consists not in its deeply personal note, any more than it springs from privacy as such, but inheres in the world from which they have escaped. They must remember that they are constantly on the run, and that the world's reality is actually expressed by their escape. Thus, too, the true force of escapism springs from persecution, and the personal strength of the fugitives increases as the persecution and danger increase.

(Arendt, 1983: 22)

This is a remarkable passage, even by the standards of a lecture so freighted with the imagery of fight, flight and resistance. Arendt puts the inner emigrant on the run. The 'realness of reality' is revealed *because* of the effort to escape it; in the same move, 'escapism' begins to move into the territory of its opposites, engagement and defiance. Fleeing the world, it turns out, can also be a way of testing its reality and, perhaps, even retaining some of it for humanity.

'What is home, but a feeling of homesickness/for the flight's lost moment of fluttering terror?' asked Robert Lowell (1963) in the poem 'Pigeons', his 'imitation' of Rilke's *Die Tauben*, which he dedicated to Arendt. Fluttering between registers and contexts, between inner and outer emigrants, Arendt's lecture was an attempt to compel the reality of that terror into public view. This was not, she knew, a gesture without risks: it is the nature of reality under totalitarianism to get lost. One of the reasons why efforts to come to terms with Nazi totalitarianism had been so facile, she argued, was that many had emigrated so far into fantasy that little of the reality of the experience was grasped in the first place. To this extent, the organized guilt around which post-war Germany was invited to imagine itself, like the organized crime that preceded it, was not a coming to terms with historical reality but a reaction formation, a fantasy that covered up the fact that so many in the Reich had not, in fact, experienced its reality at all.

How then can reality be retained? How stay in the world you must, at the same time, run from? Fiction is the possibly surprising answer Arendt offers towards the end of her lecture. By fiction she does not mean lying; the totalitarian or political lie is its own species of language event, as she will insist later in her response to the Pentagon papers, 'Lying in Politics' (Arendt, 1972; see also Arendt, 2003). Fictions are narrations that, by repeating reality from a distance, permit it to be endured; fictions put the inhuman in discourse, allow the unspoken to be spoken. The example Arendt brought to Hamburg was William Faulkner's haunting evocation of the First World War, *A Fable*, published in 1954. That book, she argued, claimed some measure of reality back for humanity some thirty years after the event. Generically speaking, fables have a distinguished pedigree for telling political and historical truths that are hard to bear. Faulkner's, in this respect, is a typically late-modernist type of fable: a work of mourning for the sublime terror of trench war. Arendt was not saying, as Nietzsche famously did, that reality itself has become a fable (*'wie die "wahre Welt" endlich zur Fable wurde'* (Nietzsche, 1992); if anything, she wanted the novel to demonstrate the opposite: that the 'inner truth' of a historical event could be retained in spite of the 'weird irreality' of the times. The thought that under totalitarianism truth itself might dissipate into fiction was nonetheless present in her example – perhaps too present for Arendt's own comfort.

An anxiety about protecting a sense of reality from a potential world of fictions might also account for Arendt's preference for Faulkner's depiction of the First World War over the narratives of the Nazi genocide that were beginning to appear in the late 1950s (she cited the recent success of *The Diary of Anne Frank* as a counter-example of a kind of remembering that reduced moral horror to sentiment).[2] As much as the historical and aesthetic distance of Faulkner's novel provided her with an example of a reality returned, it also kept the reality at the core of her own lecture at a distance. Arendt herself describes *A Fable* as a 'less painful' example to deal with. Less painful for whom, some in her audience may have wondered? Terada again: 'As a lover of reality testing, the hardest fact for Arendt to bear is the fact that there are things that even she can't bear' (2004: 850).

Arendt's skittishness about sentiment is well known and is of a piece with her characterizations of psychoanalysis as a form of self-indulgence. But it is not just feelings that are the problem here. On the one hand, Arendt wanted to say that humanity can be re-imagined only by the recurrent narrations that are available to be heard: 'We humanize what is going on in the world and in ourselves only by speaking of it, and in the course of speaking it we learn to be human' (1983: 25). On the other hand, she wanted to maintain an absolute distinction between enduring reality and denying it, and between those narrations that return reality to humanity (Faulkner's, Lessing's, Arendt's own lecture) and those that condemn it to fantasy (at best the story the rapt reader of *Anne Frank* tells herself, at worst Otto Bradfish's and Adolf Eichmann's shameless self-expiations). The question of how one might arrive at one rather than the other remained unanswered.

That question emerged again in her 1964 essay 'Personal Responsibility under Dictatorship' (Arendt, 2003 [1964]). What distinguishes the defiant inner emigrant from the fantasist in this essay is the former's ability to test reality against her own experience. This ability is the prime (and frequently the only) defence against two of totalitarianism's defining features: the unprecedented way it smashes customary standards and general rules, and the extent to which it reaches into absolutely all spheres of human life. The person who keeps her moral wits about her, inwardly at least, is the one capable of measuring the unprecedented against her own experience. This testing is what Arendt calls thinking. In this context, the refugee who can take only her experience with her when all else has been lost (and whose presence I have also been tracking throughout the first part of this chapter) is the model of a resisting and resistant subjectivity. 'We had to learn everything from scratch, in the raw, as it were – that is, without the help of categories and general rules under which to subsume our experiences' (Arendt, 2003 [1964]: 25).

What perplexed Arendt, the refugee who learned how to think from scratch, was how difficult, if not impossible, active contemplation seems to have been for those who stayed at home. The horror of totalitarianism resided not only in its crimes, but also in the moral collapse resulting from the reluctance of so many simply to think:

> We see here how unwilling the human mind is to face realities which in one way or another contradict totally its framework of reference. Unfortunately, it seems to be much easier to condition human behaviour and to make people conduct themselves in the most unexpected and outrageous manner, than it is to persuade anybody to learn from experience, as the saying goes; that is, to start thinking and judging instead of applying categories and formulas which are deeply ingrained in our mind, but whose basis of experience has long been forgotten and whose plausibility resides in their intellectual consistency rather than in their adequacy to actual events.
>
> (Arendt, 2003 [1964]: 37)

What is it that makes people so unwilling to contemplate reality? Why is it so difficult to learn from experience? In her classic 1936 study of the ego's defences, Anna Freud had already rehearsed a psychoanalytic version of Arendt's problem: 'We do not yet know precisely what takes place in the adult ego when it chooses delusional gratification and renounces the function of reality testing' (1967: 82). In other words, we do not know what it takes to think in defiance of one's own delusions: the intrapsychic problem Anna Freud identified in 1936 had become, for Hannah Arendt by 1964, the central perplexity of moral and political life under totalitarianism.

Arendt remained so perplexed, we might claim in the context of the project of this book, because she could not imagine a role for the unconscious in resisting totalitarianism. The alien inside the inner emigrant is an alien only to the world, not to the thinker herself. It follows that feeling guilty about something that you are not directly responsible for (like not feeling guilty because you didn't really agree with what you were doing at the time), in Arendt's terms, is simply a gross 'moral confusion'. The thought that unconscious guilt might have something to do with totalitarianism's all-intrusiveness was not one that she seems to have found helpful. That one might be able to lie to oneself in good faith, as Jacques Derrida has argued, was anathema to Arendt's commitment to the truth and the law.[3] Even when the state is completely derelict, as it was in Nazi Germany, for Arendt a deep 'feeling for lawfulness' must remain as a spur for resisting the corruption of law (2003 [1964]: 40–1). The idea that this same deep 'feeling for lawfulness' (the superego of psychoanalysis, let us say) might sometimes also be the driver for compliance with state violence conceded too much power to the unconscious for this 'lover of reality testing' to contemplate.

Anna Freud

When you have had to flee a reality that nobody else wanted to see, insisting that its realness ('the realness of reality' in Arendt's emphasis) be recognized is not so strange; it is, perhaps, the only form of defiance left. It is no coincidence that in exile Anna Freud shared Arendt's commitment to reality testing. Jacques Lacan (1988) once described her account of the ego as the 'depiction of a moralist' (we can assume the equivocation between the ego's morality and Anna Freud's is deliberate). As with Arendt, in Anna Freud the moral imperative to engage with reality was born of the effort to escape and defy totalitarianism. In her biography, Young-Bruehl reminds us that under Anna Freud's leadership in the mid 1930s, the Vienna Society became a 'refugee placement agency'; the same might be said of the ego whose defensive manoeuvrings she mapped with such diligence in the same period (Young-Bruehl, 1988: 200). A 'placement agency' for the unconscious in a hostile and bewildering world – viewed in the context of her enforced migration, Anna Freud's efforts to educate the ego in the service of reality perhaps emerge less as the taming of the unconscious for ego analysis, for which she is frequently criticized, than as an attempt to win back the unconscious for the project of democracy.

This is Suzanne Stewart-Steinberg's important argument in her recent study of the figure she calls 'Anna-Antigone'. For Stewart-Steinberg, the problem Anna Freud encountered in her effort to preserve psychoanalysis for politics was 'that rational, consenting, and choosing subjects cannot be ruled by the unconscious', because democracy demands that we get the 'unconscious under some form of control. The looming threat, otherwise, is a return to a totalitarian logic' (Stewart-Steinberg, 2011: 5).[4] In other words, Anna Freud arrived at the same dilemma as Arendt, but from the opposite direction: where Arendt guarded against the unconscious by keeping it out of her account of totalitarianism, Anna Freud began with the lies that we tell ourselves all the better to understand why reality testing is so difficult – and so painful. In Hamburg Arendt insisted that the inner emigrants in her audience keep the reality of the victims of totalitarianism in mind; Anna Freud offers an excavation of that mind which drills down into the very places that Arendt assumed were off limits, even to totalitarian politics: the unconscious, fantasy and the nursery.

The psychoanalytic theory of reality testing begins in that apparently most private of places, at the breast. When the infant can no longer hallucinate satisfaction in its absence, Sigmund Freud wrote famously in 'Formulations on the Two Principles of Mental Functioning' (1911), the mind has to represent the reality of the world as it actually is, even as it is disagreeable. The reality principle thus emerges first through a denial born of disappointment, followed by the capacity to imagine a world we do not like: 'not what was pleasant was any longer imagined, but what was real, even though it should be unpleasant', Freud wrote in perhaps one of the least quoted passages from his work (1984 [1911]: 37).[5] While it is difficult to imagine Arendt taking her writing anywhere near a breast, she would have approved of the thought that this early thinking is also a kind of action in the world. Indeed, for both Freud and Arendt (as for her mentor Karl Jaspers), as Terada notes, 'realism arrives when the self can register facts and feelings that it does not accept' (2004: 846). When Anna Freud is accused of a too normative concern with getting the ego to adapt to reality, what is often missed is that, exactly like her father (and Arendt), her account begins not with assuming that reality can be known, still less accommodated, but with the capacity to imagine accurately a reality which is unpleasant – and which one wants to change.[6]

Where refugees are the model reality testers in Arendt's account, it is children who experiment with its limits in Anna Freud's. Faced with an intolerable reality the adult can at least (in non-totalitarian contexts) pick herself up and go; locked into a situation of total dependency, by contrast, the child has no ticket out; some kind of inner emigration seems to be her only refuge. But this flight turns out to be no escape: fantasy, phobia, symptoms, the dreams, daydreams, stories and games through which Anna Freud charts the ego's resistances are very far from being safe havens from the world; on the contrary, they are how we engage with what we find difficult to tolerate – how we learn to learn from experience, to adapt Arendt's terms. Recall the passage from Arendt's lecture: 'Flight from the world in dark times of impotence can always be justified as long as reality is not ignored, but is constantly acknowledged as the thing that must be escaped' (1983: 22). For Anna Freud, the story of the ego's defences, its flights and denials, also contains within it an acknowledgement of the very reality that is so difficult to bear: as Stewart-Steinberg puts it, 'defenses can never be silent' (2011: 178).

It is because the defences can never be silent that we know that there is a war going on in the ego. Anna Freud's bold descriptions of this war bring two new emphases to her father's account of reality testing. First, a clearer sense that the path to realism always involves the fictive, the fantastical: Little Hans, for example, Sigmund Freud's only case of child analysis, developed his animal phobias in order to deny the reality of his father's incontestable power. In Anna Freud's re-reading of the case, this was not simply a pathological escape from the world (an imaginary world of 'once upon a time it had been' in Arendt's terms, a delusion in Sigmund Freud's), but a normal part of development. 'Hans *denied reality by means of his fantasy*; he transformed it to suit his own purposes and to fulfil his own wishes; then, and not till then, could he accept it' (1967: 73, italics in original). Accepting reality means making it available to inventive narration (turning your father into a horse, or calling in the plumber to make you as anatomically powerful as him, to cite two of Hans' more creative narrative fantasies). Of course, what for the child might provide a path for the unconscious into reality, in the adult would still be a delusion; but for Anna Freud, as for Arendt, the stress is on how every defensive flight from the world also has a story to tell about the mind's struggle with that reality. Or, as her father described it in *Moses and Monotheism*, every delusion contains a kernel of historical truth – Young-Bruehl (1988: 204) reminds us that Freud's text (surely his own most exuberantly creative refugee narrative?) was indebted to his daughter's work on the silent war revealed by the defence mechanisms.

Even more so than for her father, however, and in a second new emphasis that puts her in direct conversation with Arendt, for Anna Freud the war within the ego is always a profoundly moral conflict. It is so precisely because of the difficulty both for the child and, indeed, for psychoanalysis, of distinguishing between the anxieties we feel about our own desires and those caused by the world: the 'anxiety of conscience', for Anna Freud, is so intense because we defend ourselves against the world in the same way we flee from our own desires. As Stewart-Steinberg (2011: 198) points out in a compelling comparison with John Rawls, Anna Freud thus thinks about justice as much as any political or moral philosopher but does so in 'affective and fictional terms'. She is as intrigued as Arendt as to why some people are able to test their experience against reality, while others remain deluded inside their inner shells (at one point Hans, like some of the inner emigrants Arendt no doubt had in her sights, decided simply to stop going outside altogether). Anna Freud's casting of that problem, however, lays bare the extent to which this is less a 'moral confusion' than a moral conflict. Far from being the escapist retreat Arendt feared, this psychoanalytic account of the mind begins with a sense of reality that is conflicted precisely because that reality is shared with others.

This is perhaps the point where Lacan's barb about Anna Freud's moralist mind can be flipped for a more historical, and possibly more political, reading of her theories of the defences (theories developed, it is perhaps worth saying again, from inside the heart of totalitarianism). In a later exchange with Joseph Sandler, Anna Freud qualified her moralism in these terms:

> *Sandler:*   I am rather puzzled, Miss Freud, when you speak of what people should *really* do.
> *Anna Freud:* When I say things like 'what they should really do' I always speak from the point of view, not of the outside observer, but of the internal conflict.
>
> (Freud, Sandler *et al.*, 1985: 210)

The syntax here belies the simplicity of the statement: speaking from the point of view of the internal conflict (which has its own view of the outside observer) is the grammar of the psychoanalytic transference. When Arendt despaired that people 'really should' have thought and judged the reality of things better in her essay on personal responsibility, she presumed a political subject who could reason with her own desires – her later defence of thinking would begin with the ability to dialogue with oneself (Arendt, 2003 [1971]). Writing out of the same hole of oblivion, Anna Freud reminds us that social and moral life begins with a mind overcrowded (and frequently overwhelmed) by inner voices; and a subject always unconsciously at odds with herself.

All of this would not, of course, have prevented Arendt from arguing strenuously against any suggestion that what happens, or does not happen, in the nursery of the mind could in any way give a proper moral, historical or political account of totalitarian compliance. For Arendt, the easy determinism to which popular versions of psychoanalysis are prone at best normalizes and at worst denies what is most uncomfortable about our political choices under totalitarianism. The nursery is emphatically not the same as the world of politics, she argues testily in the 1964 essay on 'Personal Responsibility' (Arendt, 2003 [1964]). If anything, kindergarten bears more resemblance to the slave camp (the striking comparison is Arendt's): both the child and the inmate are helpless; total dependence assures total compliance. By contrast, Arendt insists, in the political world it is the leader who becomes helpless if he defies his supporters (2003 [1964]: 47). This insistence on the persistence of the political contract under totalitarian dictatorship looks particularly stubborn, perverse even, in the context of an argument that is perplexed by the capacity for political self-delusion. But maybe we should not be too quick to see this simply as another example of Arendt's dogged commitment to the truth of politics. There is a logic that emerges from her repudiation of the blind obedience to the leader thesis that puts her closer to Anna Freud's thinking than she might have appreciated: if you defend your compliance by comparing yourself to a child, then you are in some sense acknowledging the moral and political reality from which you wish to escape; the truth of the matter is that you prefer to submit, that you have, indeed, registered reality and reacted to it – by imagining that it is not there.

'True morality' is the term Anna Freud uses to describe the moment when we unravel our disavowals and begin to really take on reality (1967: 119). Unlike Arendt, however, she also offers an account of what it is it that makes the political contract so difficult to maintain, which is not the same thing as saying it doesn't exist. To say that politics begins in the nursery, after all, need not imply that it should stay there. She once commented that she recognized herself in her father's *Group Psychology and the Analysis of the Ego* ('everything was in there, my old daydreams and all I wanted'; quoted in Young-Bruehl, 1988: 217). What that text taught her was just how hard the desire to submit to the leader's authority made the reality testing so central to her theory ('social anxiety' again). The reason why racism and xenophobia are not 'reversible by experience', she remarked in her 1948 essay 'Notes on Aggression', which we can now read almost as a direct reply to Arendt's perplexity about the inability of people to learn by experience, is that they are 'not rooted in a real assessment' but designed to keep hold of the fantasy that it is others you hate, not your loved ones (1998 [1949]: 46). At the root of identification with the aggressor is the inability to reality test (it perhaps took the daughter of psychoanalysis to make the connection between filial desire and political reality).

This is also the root of the very escapism Arendt feared and trivialized: a flight into the personal life of fantasy that then explodes (and a hatred as intimate as this can only explode) into the world not just as compliance, but as the psychopathology of the politics of terror. Better, under these circumstances, to turn the father into a horse, Anna Freud might have said of psychic life; better for political life to turn the dictator into a man with no mandate, Arendt might have added.

Conclusion

True morality, we might say after Hannah Arendt and Anna Freud, begins when denial is transformed into defiance. If this is a defiance based on 'knowing precisely' what that reality is and 'enduring it', in Arendt's terms, it is also one best reached by a kind of tactical retreat: an inner emigration that allows you to imagine the world not as you would like it to be, but in all its grim outrageousness. In conclusion, it is worth emphasizing again that the accounts of that inward turn presented in this chapter were produced by two women who experienced the reality of being a refugee first hand. This is not to claim any privilege to wretched historical experience on behalf of either Arendt or Anna Freud. It is rather, with them, to try to understand better the lived reality of total domination.

In the end, the stakes of her focus on the moral ego for Anna Freud were as political as Arendt's refusal to let Germany's inner emigrants off the hook in her Hamburg lecture. In another poignant exchange with Joseph Sandler, you can hear a very similar impatience with the persistence of denial in the world to Arendt's:

> *Anna Freud:* You know, in our everyday dealings with other human beings, we find their denial of reality extremely disturbing. We find that it's terribly difficult to convince somebody of something they have denied, or to get them to alter their behaviour if they are using denial . . . This means that what he does is non-adaptive, or rather it is felt by others to be non-adaptive.
>
> *Sandler:* But intrapsychically it is, of course, a very successful adaptation at times.
>
> *Anna Freud:* Very, but only if that person is the only person in the world.
>
> (Freud, Sandler *et al.*, 1985: 150–1)

Only if that person is the only person in the world: this is a very Arendtian response, in both tone and substance. Totalitarianism, Arendt argued famously, often makes you feel as if you are the only person in the world (hence the lonely fate of the inner emigrant) (1973 [1958]: 474–77.). The imperative expressed in her writing to confront reality derives not, as is sometimes assumed, from a lofty belief in the superior efficacy of thought and judgement; for Arendt, as for Anna Freud, we are obligated to reality precisely because we share it with others – because we are not the only person in the world. One final quote from Arendt's Lessing lecture to set alongside Anna Freud's refusal to normalize denial in moral terms; Arendt ends by parsing Lessing's famous homage to the power of human fraternity, *Nathan the Wise*, for her own dark times:

> [I]n the case of a friendship between a German and a Jew under the conditions of the Third Reich, it would scarcely have been a sign of humanness for the friends to have said: Are we not both human beings? It would have been a mere evasion of reality and of the world common to both at that time:

they would not have been resisting the world as it was. A law that prohibited the intercourse of Jews and Germans could be evaded but it could not be defied by people who denied the reality of the distinction. In keeping with a humanness that had not lost the solid ground of reality, a humanness in the midst of the reality of persecution, they would have had to say to each other: A German and a Jew, and friends.

(Arendt, 1983: 23)

On the run from totalitarianism, both Hannah Arendt and Anna Freud knew the full price of 'humanness in the midst of the reality of persecution'.

Notes

1 Philosopher and dramatist, Gotthold Ephraim Lessing (1729–81), was a key figure in the European Enlightenment. Distinguished by its irony, his writing is a dramatization of free thinking in pursuit of human reason as, for example, famously in *Nathan the Wise* (1779), assumed to be based on his own friendship with the philosopher of the Jewish Enlightenment (*Haskalah*), Moses Mendelssohn. In the 1930s, Arendt had criticized Nathan/Mendelssohn for a naïve assimilationism, blind to the realities of European Jewish history. Her return to Lessing in 1959 is a poignant revision of this earlier view. For a recent account of Lessing's importance to post-war debates see Ned Curthoys, 'A Diasporic Reading of *Nathan the Wise*' (2010).
2 Arendt also neglects to mention that *A Fable* is a messianic tale about the power of passive resistance. One man's refusal to fight inspires an entire battalion to lay down its arms. In other words, the story rehearses the silent reproach implicit throughout Arendt's lecture: why didn't you resist?
3 Derrida (2002: 51) describes the way Arendt pointedly 'neglects the symptomal or unconscious dimension of totalitarianism', even as her writing gestures toward an understanding of a political reality in which the absolute truth can no longer be the ground of resistance.
4 My reading of Anna Freud is indebted to Suzanne Stewart-Steinberg's *Impious Fidelity: Anna Freud, Psychoanalysis, Politics* (2011), and to Stewart-Steinberg's comments on an earlier version of this chapter.
5 Translation modified. The Strachey translation reads: 'what was presented in the mind was no longer what was agreeable but what was real, even if it happened to be disagreeable'.
6 Jacqueline Rose was the first to demonstrate that Anna Freud's account of the ego was far more complex and troubled by history and politics than previously assumed. See Rose, 'War in the Nursery' (1993).

Chapter 5

The superego as social critique
Frankfurt School psychoanalysis and the fall of the bourgeois order

Matt ffytche

The superego in political contexts

The 'superego', coined by Freud in his 1923 paper on 'The Ego and the Id' (Freud, 1923), became one of the most widely deployed and debated psychoanalytic terms of the next few decades. Within the psychoanalytic movement itself it was a stress-point in the controversial discussions between Kleinians and Freudians in Britain in the 1940s – particularly in arguments over the dating of infantile conscience (King and Steiner, 1991). It also formed a significant new bridge with the social sciences. The superego became a key concept, for instance, in the work of Theodor Adorno and Norbert Elias, while in 1952 Talcott Parsons hailed it as 'one of the most important points at which it is possible to establish direct relations between psychoanalysis and sociology' (Parsons, 1970 [1952]: 17). But what equally pushed the concept far beyond its original clinical frame, and into the limelight of social debate, were the unfolding political events, social anxieties and conflicts during the 1930s and 1940s. The turbulent social context, in effect, drew this term – which promised to isolate the internal structure of authority – into the foreground, as both psychologists and social scientists struggled to make sense of the formation and collapse of modern states, and to discover what drove the individual's relation to authority in an era of mass social change.

The period during and immediately after the Second World War saw a significant expansion of psychoanalytic presence in education, health, criminology and social theory (see chapters by Shapira, Mandler and Alexander in this volume). For many working in these areas, the superego was the point through which psychoanalytic observations in the clinical field could be usefully extended into the theorization of broader social phenomena such as the operation of groups, conscience and self-regulation, the internalization of social rules and moral laws, and the psychology of political leadership. Such trends also strengthened the presence of psychoanalytic ideas in anthropology, where a much-contested relationship had earlier been established via Freud's work on the Oedipus complex and the prehistorical narratives of *Totem and Taboo* (Freud, 1913). Emerging a decade later, the superego had strong genetic links back to this text, particularly its hypothetical account of the murder of a 'primal' father, which Freud speculated had given rise to an original communal guilt complex around which primitive forms of social organization and religion coalesced.

Importantly, Freud supposed the murdered father would have been reinstated or psychologically internalized as an ideal. With the emergence of the superego concept ten years later, these ideas were rearticulated – this time in terms of a child's internalization of a set of parental prohibitions (themselves expressive of archaic cultural taboos) as a way of resolving the Oedipus complex. The result was to set up a permanent agency within the mind, forming the foundation for experiences of guilt, self-criticism, conscience and moral law:

> The child's parents, and especially his father, were perceived as the obstacle to a realization of his Oedipus wishes; so his infantile ego fortified itself for the carrying out of the repression by erecting this same obstacle within itself. It borrowed strength to do this, so to speak, from the father, and this loan was an extraordinarily momentous act. The superego retains the character of the father, while the more powerful the Oedipus complex was and the more rapidly it succumbed to repression (under the influence of authority, religious teaching, schooling and reading), the stricter will be the domination of the superego over the ego later on – in the form of conscience or perhaps of an unconscious sense of guilt.
>
> (Freud, 1923: 34–5; see also Freud, 1924a; Freud 1933: 57–80)

Closely connected with these ideas was the 'ego ideal' – the idealized image of oneself (what one would like to be) modelled on equally idealized others – which had played a crucial role in Freud's *Group Psychology and the Analysis of the Ego* two years before. This further reinforced the relevance of the superego in discussions of authoritarian or totalitarian society, as Freud had demonstrated the function of the ego ideal in relation to models of leadership in the army and the church, while also examining the nature of crowds and masses.[1] The superego, then, came with a particular sociological spin which appeared to many as having anticipated the pathologies of authority in wartime, or in totalitarian states. For Adorno, Freud's portrait of the 'primal father of the horde' might as well be a portrait of Hitler, while the superego, 'anticipates almost with *clairvoyance* the post-psychological de-individualized social atoms which form the fascist collectivities' (Adorno, 1991 [1951]: 136). Likewise, when Edward Glover updated his analysis of the superego as an agency of the mind indelibly tinged by sadism (the 'primitive unconscious conscience') for the re-edition of *War, Sadism and Pacifism* in 1946, he suggested that the destructive procedures of modern warfare 'are much closer to (what we now know to be) infantile unconscious phantasies of destruction than to the ordinary fighting habits of the individual adult' (Glover, 1946: 185). That is to say, analysts who had been concerned with 'inner' sadism in the 1920s, such as Karl Abraham and Melanie Klein (who pioneered the concept of a particularly archaic and destructive superego operating in early infancy) had correctly discerned underlying psychotic trends in all minds, whose presence then emerged more indubitably in the Second World War. In Glover's interpretation, the sanction for aggressive impulses, granted to soldiers in the conflict, reinforced the sadism of their 'unconscious mentor or superego' which psychoanalysis had discovered to be lodged in infantile parts of the mind. The implication was, firstly, that 'moral conscience' was precariously based on an unstable and aggressive foundation; but also that such latent sadism was now 'licensed by the War Office' (Glover, 1946: 42) – it was intrinsic to the Allies as much as to the fascists.[2]

At the same time as psychoanalysts were promoting the relevance of the concept for the analysis of militarization, sadism or dictatorship, political contexts of the 1930s and 1940s were feeding back into the clinical vocabularies used to define the operations of the superego. Karen Horney described this part of the mind as 'a secret police department' (Horney, 2000 [1939]: 211), while the psychoanalyst and social psychologist J.C. Flugel, picking up on the Nazi jargon for the compulsory co-ordination of individuals with the agenda of the regime, argued in1945 that war raises the ego to the level of the superego and 'a sort of spontaneous *Gleichschaltung* occurs' in the nation (Flugel, 1962: 372–3). In fact, the concept has proved particularly prone to absorbing political vocabularies since its inception. In Freud's *New Introductory Lectures* the superego introduces a garrison into regions of the psyche inclined to rebellion (Freud, 1933: 110); for Erik Erikson in the 1960s it was a colonial governor-general who deals with insurrection by using native troops (Erikson, 1974: 86); more recently, Jessica Benjamin has written of the 'fundamentalist tendencies that make the destructive superego supreme' in political groupings, and from this arrived at the phrase 'internal fundamentalists' (Benjamin, 2002: 476).

This chapter will explore such political and social applications of the superego through a focus on the work of the Frankfurt School and its Institute of Social Research, active (like the superego itself) from 1923 in Germany, relocated to America in 1934, and then reconstituted in Cold War Germany in 1951 (Wiggershaus, 1994; Jay, 1973; Müller-Doohm, 2005; Wheatland, 2009), and including amongst its members or affiliates, Erich Fromm, Max Horkheimer, Theodor Adorno and Herbert Marcuse. Aside from their highly productive critical engagements with fascist and 'totalitarian' forms of subjectivity (which they applied equally to Nazism, mass culture in the US, and the history of Western reason), their engagement with psychoanalysis is particularly instructive for the way it spans the whole of the period from the early 1930s through to the 1970s. Striking, too, is the complexity and sheer variety of their attempts to mobilize Freudian ideas within a shifting analysis of authoritarian political cultures. Moreover, the superego itself forms an especially recurrent motif in their work. In the large group volume of *Studien über Autorität und Familie* ('Studies in Authority and the Family') published in 1936 – the culmination of the project to understand the formation of political character in Germany developed by Max Horkheimer, the Institute's Director from the early 1930s – Erich Fromm's 'Social-Psychological' section begins with an account of 'Authority and the Superego'

(Fromm, Horkheimer, *et al.*, 1936). In the early 1940s, the concept was deployed in Horkheimer and Adorno's various analyses of fascism and anti-Semitism – most famously in the series of empirical studies on *The Authoritarian Personality* (Adorno, Frenkel-Brunswik, *et al.*, 1950) which are relentlessly insistent on the unconscious impact of the father on the child. Horkheimer pointed out that, typically, an interviewee, when asked whom he regarded as the greatest personalities in history, answered 'my parents' – thus revealing an 'absolute submission to familial authority in early infancy' on the part of subjects deemed susceptible to fascist propaganda (Horkheimer, 1949: 368).

The same period produced some of the Frankfurt School's more celebrated polemical works, such as the jointly authored *Dialectic of Enlightenment*, Horkheimer's *Eclipse of Reason* and Adorno's *Minima Moralia* – all of which have sections dealing specifically with the superego. But the concept also winds up in Adorno's critical work on television (Adorno, 1998 [1953]), while his 'Notes on Kafka' take bearings from the theory of the primal father (Adorno, 1967). In the mid 1950s, by which time the frame of their analysis had shifted more obviously towards a critique of standardization and conformity in American culture as itself 'totalitarian', the superego reappears at the core of Marcuse's arguments in *Eros and Civilization* (Marcuse, 1972 [1955]). Here it enforces the demands 'of a *past* reality', retarding mental development so that the individual, and society, is instinctually reactionary (Marcuse, 1972 [1955]: 41). Even in the 1960s, when Adorno was re-established in Frankfurt and engrossed in Kantian epistemology, the superego remained a component of his work on conscience and the transcendental subject, some pages being devoted to it in his late masterpiece *Negative Dialectics* (Adorno, 1990 [1966]).

Authority, totalitarianism and the superego

As a way into this material, which is diverse and complex and spread between different authors responding to various political situations over at least three decades, I want to begin with a comparison of two distinct historical moments – one from the mid 1930s, and one from the mid 1940s. These will give an immediate sense of the diverging, even contradictory, ways in which the concept was mobilized in order to interpret totalitarianism. They will also show how, from early on, Frankfurt School accounts of the superego were radically altered by the authors' own historical experiences – the nightmare developments of the Third Reich, but also their cultural and intellectual disaffection in American exile.

The first example is the earlier Marxist project on 'Authority' (not to be confused with the later *Studies in the Authoritarian Personality*). In 1932 Horkheimer had urged the need to supplement historical and sociopolitical analysis with psychology as part of the Institute's investigation into the brakes on social change and, more particularly, why the German working class, which had appeared to reach a revolutionary moment of development in the 1920s, was now acting against its own best interests and submitting to increasing political control. The Frankfurt theorists at this time (official members of the Institute included Horkheimer, Erich Fromm, Friedrich Pollock, Leo Lowenthal and Herbert Marcuse, but not yet Adorno) centred their analysis of authority on the family – to quote Lowenthal, from a text written in 1934 for the studies, but not published until 1987: 'Having ceased to produce directly, the bourgeois family now acquires the important role of establishing one of the most crucial conditions of production, namely, reinforcing the authority necessary for the maintenance and reproduction of bourgeois society' (Lowenthal, 1987: 287). There was a natural convergence here with classical psychoanalysis which, from its own psychological direction, equally identified the family as the key site through which relations to authority were settled, particularly through the child's experience of the Oedipal drama whose outcome was the superego. The overlap between sociological and psychoanalytic accounts was further facilitated because both appeared to hinge on the role of the father – though Freud also referred to the superego as an internalization of *parental* prohibition, he typically construed this patriarchally, as did much of the associated literature at the time.[3]

Horkheimer's position can be sketched only briefly here. Essentially, his lengthy contribution to the group study, later translated as 'Authority and the Family' (Horkheimer, 2002 [1936]) developed a critique of patriarchy which drew on Erich Fromm's notion of the 'patricentric complex' (Fromm, 1991 [1934]). In Fromm's view, the patriarchal family produced psychical attitudes which maintained the stability of class society – including dependence on and identification with fatherly authority, pleasure at dominating weaker people, and a strict superego with a stress on duty, which led to feelings of guilt and the acceptance of suffering as punishment. All these attitudes were established and internalized as irrational givens (Horkheimer and Fromm draw on depth psychology to corroborate this). Essentially, patriarchal authoritarianism predisposed individuals towards a fascist structure of authority (the timing of the study, which aimed to facilitate a political intervention, made the analysis a matter of urgency). Society had stalled within an outmoded organizational structure which engineered authority rather than rational self-consciousness: 'authority is the ground for a blind and slavish submission which originates subjectively in psychic inertia and inability to make one's own decisions' (Horkheimer, 2002 [1936]: 71).

However, Horkheimer saw light at the end of the tunnel because the very form of the family (bourgeois or working class) had for a long time been under threat from the impact of large-scale manufacturing and unemployment, and had to be artificially sustained by the State to survive in its present form.[4] Although fathers might still retain a tyrannical image, they were now relatively politically impotent and their power within the family could crumble overnight allowing new social forces and structures to emerge.[5] Horkheimer suggests in passing (and rather unconvincingly, given his persistent patricentric focus), that 'there can arise a new community of spouses and children', and it will not, in bourgeois fashion, form a closed community over against other families of the same type (Horkheimer, 2002 [1936]: 124).

If one moves ahead ten or fifteen years to works such as Horkheimer's *Eclipse of Reason* (2004 [1947]) or Adorno's 'Freudian Theory and the Pattern of Fascist Propaganda' (1991 [1951]), one finds that, although aspects of the analysis remain constant, there have been some crucial shifts. 'Each human being experiences the domineering aspect of civilization from his birth', wrote Horkheimer in the early post-war climate. 'To the child, the father's power seems overwhelming, supernatural . . . The child suffers in submitting to this force.' It is forced 'to adopt a superego embodying all the so-called principles that his father and other father-like figures hold up to him' (Horkheimer, 2004 [1947]: 75). This much is consistent with the earlier studies. However, he now argued that 'the displeasure attached to submission persists, and [the child] develops a deep hostility to his father, which is eventually translated into a resentment against civilization itself' (75). The same structure that previously gave rise to psychic inertia, now encourages resistance and critique. According to Horkheimer, 'The resistant individual remains loyal to his superego, and in a sense to his father image' (77).

That is not all. 'As industrialist society passes into a stage in which the child is directly confronted with collective forces, the part played in his psychological household by discourse, and consequently by thought, decreases. Thus conscience, or the superego, disintegrates' (75). This, from the perspective of the mid 1930s, might have been the utopian moment – a shift not only in the structure of patriarchy, but in the whole moral and psychological organization supporting the endless reproduction of the bourgeois world. But in 1947 – by which point Horkheimer and Adorno (who joined the Institute formally in 1938) had experienced both the total disintegration of that pre-war German world, and the dislocation of exile in America – the bourgeois family had become a crucial bastion against the forces of conformity, against mass culture. For instance, in 1944 Adorno was moved to issue this warning:

> With the family there passes away, while the system lasts, not only the most effective agency of the bourgeoisie, but also the resistance which, though repressing the individual, also strengthened, perhaps even produced him. The end of the family paralyses the forces of opposition.
>
> (Adorno, 1978: 23)

Equally for Horkheimer, writing in 1941, 'the relation between father and son has been reversed' since Freud (Horkheimer, 1941: 381) – the father 'may still possess a superego, but the child has long unmasked it' (377). This shift in the way authority was internalized socially correlated with other trends which aimed at hardening people by 'breaking down their individuality' – a process 'consciously and planfully undertaken in the various camps of fascism', but which also 'takes place tacitly and mechanically' throughout mass culture, and 'at such an early age that when children come to consciousness everything is settled' (381). Part of the analysis here rested on their fear that the family was being undermined by a monopoly culture in which the state assimilates the individual directly – either through terror (as in Nazism), or through the use of consumer gratification (as in America). Against this, the family enclave and the despotism of the father, including the resentment he inspires in his children, provides a seedbed for critical faculties which can later be transferred into the social domain.

There are a number of ironies that can be brought out here. The obvious one is that, whereas in the 1930s the dismantling of the patriarchal family was the solution, now it is the disaster. Not only had Horkheimer been forced to shift his reading of the historical trend in the light of the actual history of Europe and America in the intervening years – 'Today the individual ego has been absorbed by the pseudo-ego of totalitarian planning' (Horkheimer, 1941: 377) – but he had come to *reverse* his political reading of the function of patriarchy. The dismembering of patriarchal authority appeared retrospectively as the wrong goal. At the end of the 1940s, in an edited collection of essays on *The Family: Its Function and Destiny* (part of an interdisciplinary Science and Culture series published by Harper whose other titles included *Beyond Victory* and *Our Emergent Civilization*) Horkheimer urged dramatically that

> the moral and religious ideas . . . derived from the structure of the patriarchal family still constitute the core of our culture. Respect for law and order in the state appears to be inseparably tied to the respect of children for their elders. Emotions, attitudes, and beliefs rooted in the family account for the coherence of our system of culture. They form an element of social cement. It appears to be imperative that society keep them alive, for it is a question of the life and death of civilization in its present form.
>
> (Horkheimer, 1949: 361)

Some pages further on he noted in addition: 'The same economic changes which destroy the family bring about the danger of totalitarianism. The family in crisis produces the attitudes which predispose men for blind submission' (365). A remarkable turnaround from the 'blind and slavish submission' which the same family produces in 1936 (Horkheimer, 2002 [1936]: 71).

A different kind of irony, emerging in the same period, relates to the high-profile collaborative studies on *The Authoritarian Personality*, produced as part of a five-volume series of 'Studies in Prejudice' funded by the American Jewish Committee, in this instance as a joint initiative with the Berkeley Public Opinion Study directed by social psychologist R. Nevitt Sanford. The superego is one of the key concepts through which the empirical data on potential authoritarian, fascist or anti-Semitic character traits in the American population is interpreted. Adorno was especially involved in this study, being official co-director of the research alongside Sanford, and contributing a lengthy qualitative section containing thematic analyses of the material, as well as a chapter which established 'Types and Syndromes'.[6] Almost every syndrome Adorno identifies in his portion of the study is presented as resulting from some permutation of the superego. For instance, for the 'Conventional' type, who succumbs to fascism merely through following the crowd, 'The superego was never firmly established and the individual is largely under the sway of its external representatives' (Adorno *et al.*, 1950: 753), while for the 'Tough Guy' or 'Psychopath', 'the superego seems to have been completely crippled through the outcome of the Oedipus conflict' (763). Alternatively, amongst low-scorers on the authoritarian scale, the 'Rigid' type is characterized by 'strong superego tendencies and compulsive features', though paternal authority is 'frequently replaced by the image of some collectivity, possibly moulded after the archaic image of what Freud calls the brother horde' (771), and so on.

But around the same period Adorno was also keeping his own more philosophical notes on the obsolescence of psychology and the liquidation of the individual. Thus already in 1941, in 'Notes Towards a New Anthropology', he explored the possibility that egoism, the Oedipus complex, and the psychology of the unconscious itself had reached a point of historical dissolution (Müller-Doohm, 2005: 552).[7] In 'Freudian Theory and the Pattern of Fascist Propaganda' written in 1951, the year after *The Authoritarian Personality* was published, Adorno stated unequivocally that: 'the psychological processes, though they still persist in each individual, have ceased to appear as the determining forces of the social process' (Adorno, 1991 [1951]: 136); thus 'fascism as such is *not* a psychological issue' (135). But in this case, what of the categories used throughout the contemporaneous empirical study, based on childhood psychological development?

There are a number of ways one can read this disparity. One is that Adorno was simply ambivalent – both about the nature of empirical research and about the categories drawn from Freudian theory. Another view is that the empirical studies represented one of the few routes the Frankfurt School exiles had towards funding and gaining orthodox recognition. (On a similar front, they were keen to ally themselves with the psychoanalytic establishment and to dissociate themselves publicly from the work of the dissident Fromm (Wheatland, 2009: 223–4).) But perhaps a more convincing answer (given Adorno's continuing interest in the superego into the 1960s) is that the term was mobilized in the service of different agendas in different works – and was prized, as was Freud's contribution in general, for the variety of ways in which it could be situated: now as something categorical; now as the manifestation of a historical process; now as a piece of provocation, an attack on conventional psychology. Although *The Authoritarian Personality* has remained a landmark study (albeit more for the nature and scale of the attempt than the reliability of its conclusions) its importance as a piece of 'Frankfurt School' literature has more recently been eclipsed by the bolder, more philosophical and polemical pieces which Adorno and Horkheimer wrote during the same period. These works dealt primarily with the experience of historical change – typically, they aim to pinpoint catastrophic shifts (social, cultural and cognitive) under totalitarianism. The value of the 'superego' in this more critical writing often lay in the authors' ability to demonstrate that individuals in contemporary society were in danger of losing their inner lives. Thus what was being mobilized here was not data analysis, but shock value: if you don't act now, you could wake up to find your superego, your psychology, gone.[8]

Mourning the fathers

Such observations about the redundancy of psychological thinking can naturally lead to assumptions that, the earlier contributions of Fromm aside, psychoanalysis featured only marginally and ambivalently on the horizon of the critical models generated by the Frankfurt School. In the 1930s, despite drawing on psychoanalysis, they were also critical of its example because Freud's theories echoed, even universalized, the irrational power structures in the family which needed to be dismantled (though precisely for this reason they were useful, polemically, for articulating those structures). By the 1950s, this ambivalence was expressed in the idea that the world to which Freud's psychology pertained was obsolete. 'Private life asserts itself . . . hectically, vampire-like, because it really no longer exists', challenged Adorno in *Minima Moralia* (1978: 33); for Horkheimer psychoanalysis was the owl of Minerva which 'took its flight when the shades of dark were already gathering over the whole sphere of private life' (1941: 376). The new focus of attention was mass culture, the world of Marcuse's 'one-dimensional man'. Certainly, it's not hard to find statements which present psychoanalysis as now part of the problem: for instance, Adorno also described it as a technique by which 'one particular racket among others binds suffering and helpless people irrevocably to itself, in order to command and exploit them' (Adorno, 1978: 64). The 'racket' label is significant here because it formed the basis for the Institute's 'racket' theory of Nazism, proposed as a group project in the early 1940s. Adorno's 'Reflections on Class Theory' gives a brief sketch of the idea: 'The image of obvious usurpation produced today by the peaceable leaders of capital and labour shows history as a history of group struggles, gangs, and rackets' (Wiggershaus, 1994: 319).[9]

But the situation was ultimately more complex than this, and in this second half of the chapter I want to pursue a set of more nuanced readings of how the literature produced by the Frankfurt School, and the psychoanalytic models of internal life, became increasingly implicated in each other, as critical theorists fled Nazi Germany into American exile. These readings turn not so much on the 'official' positions taken up towards psychoanalysis, or technical pronouncements on the superego, but on more implicit or understated observations emerging in their historical reflections, as thinkers such as Horkheimer and Adorno struggled to come to terms with the meanings of 'before' and 'after' Nazism, reassembling their critical models on the move in response to constantly changing circumstances.

At this point, too, I want to suggest a more nuanced understanding of the superego itself, as it emerged gradually in Freud's formulations during and after the First World War. Although the concept undoubtedly became serviceable to analysts and social psychologists in the 1930s who were searching for technical terms through which to explore the question of social conscience, or how authority is internalized, the superego as Freud viewed it (and also Klein) was never just about authority, guilt and the rule of law. It was always also preoccupied with the problem of how children deal with the loss of parental attachments, once their more original, intimate and passionate relationship has to be given up as the Oedipus complex is surmounted. This aspect to the superego comes out more clearly when one tracks the formation of the idea back beyond 'The Ego and the Id' and 'Group Psychology' (where the emphasis falls more often on issues of retention: how future character is formed from the precipitates of internalized object relations) to 'Mourning and Melancholia' (1917), where Freud's more general preoccupation is with loss and rage against loss – behaviour which he describes as a 'mental constellation of revolt' (Freud, 1917: 248). Or back beyond this to *Totem and Taboo* with its ambivalent love and destruction of the father. In 1923, Freud will re-emphasize this primal murder of the father as the historical point at which the superego first emerges as a psychical condition of humanity.

It is worth considering further the way in which Frankfurt School critique comes to function in relation to mourning. Whence did their antagonism to modern society derive? What drove their critical arguments? Early on, this antagonism stemmed most obviously from their desire to adopt a standpoint beyond the bourgeois world – to write for a society to be, entailing various levels of commitment to a Western Marxist project.[10] But post 1940 they more routinely wrote from a different sense of crisis – which was the historical loss or deformation of certain forms of individuality and autonomy associated with the bourgeois world itself. In *Minima Moralia* Adorno observed that Goethe, aware already in the late eighteenth century of the damage to human relationships in emerging industrial society, had proposed a self-imposed relinquishment of passion and unalloyed happiness; but, 'What has happened since makes Goethean renunciation look like fulfilment' (Adorno, 1978: 36) – later in the same text the libidinal achievement demanded of the healthy individual now makes 'the old renunciation of identification with the father' seem like child's play (58).

There are a few different points raised here. One is that 'things just got worse', and this more than anything altered Horkheimer and Adorno's perspective on bourgeois liberalism. Though they nowhere argued for turning back the historical clock, typically they maintained a foothold on the recent past (rather than an anticipated socialist future) as a point from which to measure the enormity of the crisis of the present. So the connection to what is already lost and antiquated becomes fundamental to their notion of critique. The influence of Walter Benjamin's *Arcades Project* was key in this regard. This vast and uncompleted work was devoted to unearthing the 'repressed' recent past of the late nineteenth century as a way of exploding triumphalist narratives of modernity. Such narratives, so Benjamin argued, had a tendency to naturalize or objectify the bourgeois vision of progress, in a variety of dazzling technological and consumer spectacles, while at the same time burying the evidence of their contingent origins, as well as the utopian socialist thinking which had originally fuelled them. Adorno was well placed to absorb Benjamin's lesson – one of the few people in this position for some decades – as his first job on joining the Institute in 1938 was to be the link with Benjamin, stuck in Paris, attempting to pursue this research to completion under ever more precarious circumstances. If the early-1930s Frankfurt perspective was that, psychologically, society lagged behind its economic and political potential (and the Institute drew on Marx, Freud, Weber and Nietzsche to make this case), the view from New York in the 1940s took in far more what was left behind – critique as a form of recollection.

There's another point, which is that having given up earlier hopes for positive social change, the task now became the more diminished (though no less urgent) one of simply keeping the idea of freedom or 'autonomy' alive. Hence Horkheimer's declaration in a letter to Salka Viertel in 1940, restated by Adorno in his *Minima Moralia*, that 'In view of everything that is engulfing Europe and perhaps the whole world, our present work is of course essentially destined to be passed on through the night that is approaching: a kind of message in a bottle' (Müller-Doohm, 2005: 262). The aim then was to preserve in their intellectual work something of the culture within which freedom and individuality could at least still be imagined. From this perspective, too, the crisis was about more than the camps, and the horrors of Nazism – these were concrete and extreme instances of a wider tectonic shift in the nature of modern subjectivity which affected every area of culture, thought and feeling. For this reason, the critique, and their pessimism, was maintained throughout the post-war period. There was no cause for victory celebrations within this larger frame.

Returning to Freud, the perhaps counter-intuitive, but thoroughly Adornian implication, then, is that if psychoanalysis has become redundant, that would transfigure it all the more into a significant critical tool: it belonged to the pre-fascist world in which individuals had not yet been 'reduced to a mere sequence of instantaneous experiences which leave no trace' (Adorno and Horkheimer, 1989 [1944]: 216). This touches very clearly on the cleavage within their perception of psychoanalysis – on the one hand, as now wedded to professional psychiatric culture in the US, with an instrumental brief devoted to dissolving resistances in personal life or facilitating adaptation; but on the other hand, looking back to Freud, as emblematic of a nineteenth-century world of psychological depth, complexity and obscurity, with which individuals used to be surrounded, but which was now being eroded by a culture of functionality and immediacy.

Horkheimer complained in 1949 that 'the image of the mother in the minds of children [in contemporary American society] sheds its mystical aura' (Horkheimer, 1949: 366).[11] She ceases to be a 'mitigating intermediary between him and cold reality and becomes just another mouthpiece of the latter'. In *Minima Moralia* Adorno mourned the fact that 'Every sheath interposed between men in their transactions is felt as a disturbance to the functioning of the apparatus' (1978: 41); there is 'no longer room for human impulses' (42). The Freudian unconscious, and its complex accounts of interiority – including the superego – was *par excellence* an intermediary, interposed between people and their transactions; or it was a gateway to concealed psychological dimensions in which experience leaves deep and complex traces. When Horkheimer defined the 'resistant individual' as one who remains 'loyal to his superego' (Horkheimer, 2004 [1947]: 77), he was also making a point about remaining loyal to the more 'unaccountable' psychoanalytic narrative of interiority, as a form of resistance to, for instance, the standardization of the culture of psychological enquiry. Likewise, Horkheimer, in a discussion of young 'rebels without a cause', the demons of 1950s America, warned that: 'These children behave like little savages because they have no psychological shelter' (Horkheimer, 1949: 373). He meant both that these children lacked a strong father and secure home and family, but also that they lacked the shelter of inner psychological space – as if the psychological paradigm itself (which would act as a buffer between them and the more mindless activities of the group) had been lost.

It is instructive that Frankfurt School theorists were so incessantly drawn towards the superego as the concept that most spoke to their accounts of the historical development of subjectivity, because of the psychological 'history' implicated within the concept itself: that is, the superego has to do with the recollection and internal preservation of something now transformed beyond recognition (the child's ambivalent love towards its parents). Something within the concept mirrors the Institute's own modelling of historical internalization and recollection – a process in which, by the 1950s, Horkheimer and Adorno were now primarily engaged. Alongside the critiques of authoritarianism, there emerged this longer-range mourning of a recently lost bourgeois culture which sets in in their work from the 1940s onwards, and makes intellectual culture itself a place of preservation in times of crisis. In *Minima Moralia*, Adorno surmised that, 'Since the demise of the old bourgeois class', certain ideas have 'led an after-life in the minds of intellectuals, who are at once the last enemies of the bourgeois and the last bourgeois' (Adorno, 1978: 27). That ambivalence about bourgeois culture chimes (in a psychoanalytic context) with their ambivalence about the father – a recurrent emblem of that culture in their work. It appears that their theoretical analysis, when combined with their historical experience in the later 1930s and 1940s, led them to a position in which they were at one and the same time enemies of the world of the classical superego, and engaged in a process of mourning, internalizing and preserving that world – not only the theoretical paradigm conjured by the concept; but the experiential world within and for which the concept had been articulated. Hence the superego continued to function in their work as something both historically eradicated, and as something in need of restatement and recollection as a necessary portion of social consciousness.

A couple of additional points can be made here about Adorno and Horkheimer's views on the father. One is that the emerging conservative element in the Frankfurt School critique of society put them into the same camp as other conservative liberals in America in the 1940s and 1950s when it came to the family, but also when it came to Freud. For instance, they had affinities with the New York Jewish intellectuals connected to the magazine *Commentary* (launched in 1945 and, like the Studies on Authority project, funded by the American Jewish committee) which included Irving Kristol and Norman Podhoretz, who later on become ideologues of neoconservatism. *Commentary* and the relocated Institute for Social Research in fact had their offices across the hallway in the same New York building, and there was some traffic to and fro – including the sociologist Nathan Glazer, who worked as a consultant for Horkheimer in 1944 but then joined the *Commentary* editorial team (Glazer also reviewed *The Authoritarian Personality* for the journal in 1950).[12] Both Kristol (associate editor of *Commentary*) and Podhoretz (later editor) were acolytes of American literary critic and cultural theorist, Lionel Trilling, absorbing his reading of Freud as a point of anchorage for contemporary liberal society, which they mobilized in many different polemical pieces on culture and politics in the succeeding decades (ffytche, 2013).[13]

However, I want to round off these observations on the way the superego acted as a compass for some Institute theorists, as they navigated their experiences of fascism, totalitarianism and mass culture, with a few reflections of a more psychoanalytic cast. These have to do with the fact that, because of the historical time-frame, when Adorno and Horkheimer intellectually reconstructed and remembered the pre-fascist world – as they so often did in the late 1940s – they were inevitably also reconstructing the world of their own childhoods. In fact, their methodological resistance to positivism in the social sciences led them to foreground precisely such subjective and biographical dimensions within their sociological narratives. And this leads to odd forms of parallax whereby sociological observations about parents at the same time refract the more intimate, personal dimensions of their own autobiographies. Sometimes these personal dimensions are consciously invoked; sometimes they are more complexly implicit, but can be reconstructed by cross-reading the official statements on 'the family' with more personal exchanges about inter-generational attachment in their correspondence.

What was also on Adorno and Horkheimer's minds in the early 1940s, when they were beginning work on *Studies on the Authoritarian Personality*, as well as having the discussions that would emerge as *Dialectic of Enlightenment*, was anxiety over their own parents, who were similarly experiencing exile in these same years, and who were often the subject of personal communications within the group. In 1938, for instance, Adorno's father spent some weeks in prison and lost the right to dispose of his own property, while Horkheimer worried about his parents who were enduring the winter in impoverished circumstances in Switzerland. There is then an intriguing overlap between their feelings of anxiety, guilt and loss (and also idealization) with respect to their own parents, and the shifts of tone entering into their sociological perspective on the bourgeois family and the superego in the later 1930s and 1940s.

Adorno's lines near the opening of *Minima Moralia* – 'Our relationship to parents is beginning to undergo a sad, shadowy transformation. Through their economic impotence they have lost their awesomeness' (1978: 22) – personalizes the sociological narrative, and by doing so entangles the historical critique with notes of personal regret, and something else, too, which has to do with the perennial rites of passage of children: 'Perhaps people have at all times felt the parental generation to become harmless, powerless, with the waning of its physical strength' (22). This puts the whole 1930s critique of the father temporarily on a different footing, because it raises the issue of a different kind of psychological investment in the attacks on fatherhood. Following this through as a psychoanalytic question: how might one distinguish the role which 'identification with the father' might play in an intellectual project aimed at dismantling patriarchal authority? Likewise, when Adorno in the same section writes that 'One of the Nazi's symbolic outrages is the killing of the very old' (22), it is complicated by the note that has already been sounded about witnessing, perhaps even waiting for, the waning of one's parents' strength. When his own father died in 1946, Adorno wrote to his mother (by then in New York) that he had two thoughts. One was about the awfulness of death in exile. The other was that 'when one's father dies, one's own life feels like theft, an outrage . . . the injustice of continuing to live, as if one were cheating the dead man of his light and breath. The sense of this guilt is ineffably strong in me' (Adorno, 2006: 259). To what extent then, did such feelings of guilt correlate with his revised sentiments on bourgeois life, shattered in the war, and now needing to be recollected rather than overcome? To what extent do they also recall the very Oedipal guilt, in which Freud locates the genesis of the superego?

There is something here, in the multiple crises over the experience and theorization of the father – psychological, social, historical and intellectual – which resonates through all the debates about the superego, back through Freud's work on loss and mourning, to some of the original insights about the Oedipus complex in the *Interpretation of Dreams*, which Freud himself envisaged as a response to the death of his father and the working through of *his* guilt and ambivalence about that relationship.[14]

There are similar passages in Horkheimer's writing, where an intensely personal note about his own father intersects with his more sociological pronouncements on the superego. In the letter he wrote to Adorno in January 1945, on hearing the news of his own father's death in Switzerland, Horkheimer poignantly records:

> The reunion with my parents was one of the dearest hopes of my life. I was bound to my father, not just through gratitude for the many personal traits, through which I've been able to enjoy life. But also, particularly recently, for the way in which the bourgeois attitude still preserved itself in him, even against the approach of death. Only now, with its disappearance, does this attitude take on a new relationship to truth.
>
> (Horkheimer, 1996: 623)

There's an extraordinary rendering here of Horkheimer's view of the waning of bourgeois patriarchy, running parallel to and brought to a head in the death of his own father. In the same lines, one sees emerging a revised perspective on the bourgeois family – he was lucky to have been brought up in a framework that preserved the pattern of bourgeois culture (precisely that which he had devoted so much energy to dismantling ten years earlier), which only now reveals its historical 'truth'. The 'now' seems to refer both to the death of the father, and the succumbing of bourgeois structures per se in the bitter conflict with Nazi totalitarianism. The intense personal investment in the significance of the father here merges with new tendencies in the ongoing socio-historical investigation of authority. It seems impossible to disentangle them.

Horkheimer went on to write, in moving terms, that he was sad that his father would no longer be able to rejoice over any of the things he himself was experiencing – 'even this Project in the Committee' (623) (referring to his nego-tiations with the American Jewish Committee over the authoritarian personality studies). One of the boons of the project was that he knew his father would have been proud about it. Adorno replied 'everything connected with our parents has become indescribably sad, and indeed at the same time conciliatory' (Horkheimer, 1996: 624),[15] which anticipates his line in *Minima Moralia*: 'Our relationship to parents is beginning to undergo a sad, shadowy transformation' (1978: 22).

The sentiments expressed in Horkheimer's letter were taken up in *The Eclipse of Reason*, published a couple of years later, in a passage in which, after point-ing out the deficiencies in modern father–son relations in America, he proceeds to give the 'good' version of how the adolescent can move beyond his distress at 'the gap between the ideals taught to him . . . and the reality principle to which he is compelled to submit':

> Rather than sacrifice truth by conforming to prevailing standards, he will insist on expressing in his life as much truth as he can, both in theory and in practice. His will be a life of conflict; he must be ready to run the risk of utter loneliness.
>
> (Horkheimer, 2004 [1947]: 76)

(This is surely in part a self-description of the experience of the émigré.) But 'the irrational hostility that would incline him to project his inner difficulties upon the world', that is, as a fascist might, 'is overcome by a passion to realize what *his father* represented in his childish imagination, namely, *truth*' (76–7, my italics).

In the earlier letter, the death of Horkheimer's father encapsulated a truth about the significance of the bourgeois order in the moment of its extinction; here, the kind of truth necessary to sustain the individual's critical autonomy in a quasi-totalitarian society is grounded in the adult's faithful adherence to the *image of the father he internalized as a child*. In a process not unlike the formation of the superego itself, it appears that the object of critique of the 1930s – and the psy-choanalysis through which it was articulated – in the late 1940s provided a basis on which to found critical theory and the social consciousness of the individual. Endured conflict with the father, implies Horkheimer, is that which has made the critical theorist what he is.

Notes

1 Based in part on Freud's seeming conflation of the 'ego ideal' with the 'superego' in his 1923 text, some sociological writers used these terms interchangeably (Adorno, 1991 [1951]: 133; Elias, 1994 [1939]). See also Jessica Benjamin's criticism (2007: 71) that 'Adorno is unable to distinguish between conscience and consciousness, superego and

ego, social control and self-control'. In marked contrast to this, psychoanalytic theory continued to differentiate and elaborate these terms as distinct entities, as well as further differentiating layers of superego formation (Laplanche and Pontalis, 1988).

2 For examples of how such inferences about the superego were translated into initiatives for dealing with antisocial behaviour, see Shapira, Chapter 6 in this volume, on Glover's work at the Institute for the Scientific Treatment of Delinquency.

3 During the 1930s and 1940s things were to shift, in the clinical psychoanalytic literature at least, as Klein, Bowlby, Winnicott and others increasingly prioritized the mother–infant relation as the formative one.

4 See Herzog (2005) for detailed commentary on the complexity, and contradictoriness, with which Nazi ideologues subjected the sphere of reproduction of families, physical and ideological, to ever more direct political manipulation.

5 The way in which representations of the father oscillated between tyranny and impotence was fleshed out in Siegfried Kracauer's writings on German expressionist cinema (Kracauer, 2004 [1947]).

6 For more context on this work, and on the psychoanalytic study of anti-Semitism, see Chapter 3 by Stephen Frosh in this volume.

7 See also Horkheimer (1941: 376): 'What previously served to promote man's development, the joy in knowledge, living through memory and foresight, pleasure in oneself and others, narcissism as well as love, are losing their content. Neither conscience nor egoism is left.'

8 See Riesman (1950) for a less polemical but contemporary account of the historical shift away from the superego, which Riesman identifies as 'inner-directedness'.

9 For more on the 'rackets' theory, and on Horkheimer's 'Rackets and Spirit', see Chapter 6 in *Max Horkheimer: A New Interpretation* (Stirk, 1992).

10 As Lowenthal wrote in the 1920s: 'Help and reconstruction for individuals and for society as a whole – that is the star that illumines Freud's life and work' (Lowenthal, 1989: 45).

11 The association here is again with Benjamin, in this case his observation that the 'aura' that once surrounded experiences – embedding them in the ritual contexts of daily life – has gradually been destroyed in modernity, so that they lose their narrative coherence, becoming reduced to isolated facts and incidental data.

12 For more information on these associations see Wheatland (2009: 153–8).

13 Their reading of Freud is aligned with that of the Frankfurt school, in that it centres on the father and reacts against modernity, attacking the optimism of post-war progressive liberal attitudes – the world of consumer culture, and the relaxation of authoritarian structures. Horkheimer's views on juvenile delinquency, for instance, brings him close to such conservative liberals: 'What they [youth] suffer from is probably not too strong and sound a family but rather a lack of family. In this respect the conservative statements on the cause of juvenile delinquency touch upon certain basic social factors frequently clouded by more differentiated and progressive psychological theories' (Horkheimer, 1949: 373).

14 See for instance the dream of 'Count Thun', in which rebellious thoughts about authority – in this case directed at the aristocracy rather than the bourgeoisie – become entangled with a counter-balancing guilty recollection of his ailing father (Freud, 1900: 208–18).

15 The word he uses is *versöhnlich* which also implies appeasement and atonement, as well as invoking *Vesöhnung*, the Hegelian word for the reconciliatory stage of the dialectic.

Part III

Precarious democracies

Psychoanalytic criminology, childhood and the democratic self

Michal Shapira

British psychoanalysts played a dramatic part in efforts to rebuild democracy after 1945. Indeed, they argued, with increasing influence, that understanding children and family relationships was key to a successful social and political future. Well-known clinicians and theorists like Anna Freud, Donald Winnicott, Melanie Klein and John Bowlby, as well as now-forgotten analysts such as Edward Glover, Melitta Schmideberg and Kate Friedlander, helped shape approaches not only to individuals but also to broader political questions in an age of total war and mass violence against civilians. Such analysts, who had witnessed first-hand the Blitz in Britain, contributed to the pressure for an increase in state responsibility for citizens' mental health. Moreover, they demonstrated many links between what they termed the 'war outside' and an emotional 'war inside' (inner battles and anxieties rooted in infancy and in family dynamics).

Yet despite its impact at the time, much of this historical contribution has been ignored or downplayed. It is important therefore to revisit this work and to revise the received view of psychoanalysis as exclusively an elite discipline, confined to individual work in the clinic. In both practical initiatives and numerous public declarations, in fact, psychoanalysts were influential in linking the psyche and the social, and in placing the problem of aggression and anxiety at the very heart of the interpretation of contemporary politics and history. Healthy family dynamics and normal childhood development, they argued, are central to the challenge of cultivating emotionally balanced and mature democratic subjects in an era bedevilled by totalitarianism.

This chapter concentrates on the little-known work of psychoanalysts in their roles as members of the Institute for the Scientific Treatment of Delinquency (ISTD) in London. These clinicians offered influential commentaries on the causes of crime at a time when debates about the fostering of non-violent citizenship were being widely discussed. The ISTD had a wider impact than has been previously recognized by historians. The Institute treated a high number of patients who had fallen foul of the law, and provided numerous public lectures and expert witness testimonies to the government. It had a profound effect on policy – influencing changes in child welfare legislation regarding the roles of parents – and on the formulation of regulations concerning juvenile delinquency and crime in general.

In the following pages I describe the historical context for the establishment and development of the ISTD before turning to look at its therapeutic records in more detail. Of central importance here is the psychological understanding of crime that was advocated in theory and practice by ISTD psychoanalysts, as well as the relationships forged between ideas of mental health and democracy.

In the post-war period, psychoanalytic ideas resonated with those of government officials and courts, and were also taken up in first-person descriptions by many of those deemed criminals. Indeed, such language became common parlance for a wider public. While many of the psychoanalytic ideas promulgated at the ISTD were already available before and during the war, they became far more important in political discussion after 1945, in the context of the welfare state and new analyses of the social causes of criminality.

The establishment and early work of the ISTD

Sigmund Freud himself rarely wrote on crime. However, in his few references to the topic, he developed the basic idea that criminals might well be suffering from unconscious guilt that made them seek punishment. The origin of this guilt, he wrote in Vienna in 1916, 'derived from the Oedipus complex and the two great criminal intentions of killing the father and having sex with the mother'. In comparison with these two imagined sins, the crimes committed in order to fix the sense of guilt came as a relief to the sufferers (Freud, 1916: 332). Importantly, for Freud, economic gain was frequently a superficial reason for criminal behaviour. The origins of such actions, he argued, were to be found in childhood (Freud, 1916: 333; 1931: 252).

Building on such leads, different analysts from the 1920s onwards contributed to developments in forensic psychoanalysis and new thinking about juvenile delinquency, amplifying Freud's view that criminals might wish to be punished for an offence that felt less offensive than their fantasized one (see Aichhorn, 1935 [1925]).[1] However, an important, yet hitherto largely unexplored, site through which psychoanalytic criminology would flourish was the ISTD.[2]

Established in London in 1931–2 by a group of experts influenced by the psychoanalytic work of the criminologist Grace Pailthorpe, the ISTD[3] was a multidisciplinary body whose membership increasingly included magistrates, Home Office officials, lawyers, police and prison staff, probation officers and social workers. The organization actively sought out expert advisers who were already committed to a psychoanalytic approach to crime. Freud was among its vicepresidents and members included the analysts Ernest Jones, John Bowlby, David Eder, Marjorie Franklin, Melitta Schmideberg and Barbara Low.[4] Its leading personalities were also analysts, notably Edward Glover, Denis Carroll and Emanuel Miller, along with the German émigré criminologist Hermann Mannheim. Although many of the personnel shared in this analytic identity, their career backgrounds were diverse: Barbara Low, for example, was a teacher, Glover a medical doctor. Bowlby, Jones and Eder had backgrounds in Britain while Schmideberg and others were Jewish refugees from continental Europe who joined the ISTD in the 1930s.

The Institute aimed to develop Freud's ideas, initiate and promote scientific research, advise lawyers, judges and magistrates, and promote wider discussion of crime and punishment. But psychoanalytic treatment was the ISTD's original forte and the focus of its work. Its first priority was to organize a clinic for delinquents, which would also serve the courts. In 1933, the Institute was able to open the Psychopathic Clinic,[5] and to admit its first patient, an adult woman of violent temper charged with assault on her female employer (Saville and Rumney, 1992: 7–8). Throughout the 1930s, the Institute dealt with many young criminals who were sent from courts, child clinics and hospitals. The ISTD also started offering public lectures both to experts from adjacent fields and to the general public.

ISTD psychoanalysts played an essential part in the interwar transformation of policy on punishment into 'welfare discipline', a process whereby the intention was to treat or readjust offenders, as well as, or even rather than, merely to chastise. Analysts, to be sure, were not the only ones to emphasize an individualized approach in the care of delinquents, nor was such an ambition for moral reform or character change in criminals new (see also Urwin and Sharland, 1992). Yet while some (like Cyril Burt) began incorporating psychology into environmental explanations, and others still emphasized poverty and unemployment, ISTD psychoanalysts above all emphasized unconscious aspects of the personality as a crucial factor in criminality, as they worked in tight collaboration with the legal, probation and prison systems (Garland, 1988; Hendrick, 2003: 113–17).

The question of continuity and change in theories of crime and punishment is a complex one; and the degree to which the Second World War transformed psychoanalytic criminology is open to debate. Certainly, the problem of how best to use psychological knowledge in order to foster non-violent and non-delinquent citizens, or to mould individuals into society, had already been widely considered in the interwar era. In fact, many of the anti-fascist and anti-totalitarian theories of the time, regarding the psychic determinants of violence and aggression, were already articulated in the 1930s, and thus pre-dated the catastrophe of the Second World War and the Holocaust. There is indeed an intellectual continuity between the interwar and war periods, regarding such psychosocial ideas about the nature and origins of Nazism (and Stalinism to a lesser extent), or the nature of interpersonal violence. Yet the Second World War clearly also made a major difference to this field, amplifying the case for psychological explanations of criminality, and the importance of the family and social 'nurture' to future well-being and security within a democratic polity. The ISTD received more public attention during the Blitz (not least given the experience of evacuation and the breaking up of families) due to an increased fear of a 'crime wave' among juvenile delinquents – a concern to which the ISTD itself contributed significantly as well.

Despite difficulties, the ISTD continued to operate and spread its ideas once the war broke out, and helped to maintain a certain vision of democracy that emphasized the importance of psychology in preventing violence, crime and social chaos.

This took on still greater urgency during the post-war period, as political divisions re-emerged now that the war was won, and efforts were made to consolidate the case for and viability of a British welfare state, developed first under the new socialist Labour government from 1945 to 1951, and later under different Conservative governments from 1951 to 1964 (Bailey, 1987; cf. Hendrick, 1990). The post-war realization of the hitherto unfathomed scale of the evils of Nazism in particular, along with the actual war experience in Britain, lent an ever more pressing urgency to the task of reinterpreting the basis of democracy and taming aggression and 'a-sociality'. Thus, despite a continuity in many of these ideas on violence, their currency in political debate was visibly rising in value at this point.

Juvenile delinquency was increasingly seen as a problem of 'maladjusted' citizenship. The welfare state was cast as the very antithesis of a Nazi model of society based on brute power and racism. Indeed, British ideas on the 'humane' treatment of juvenile delinquency were frequently contrasted with the 'authoritarian' German approach to crime and punishment, to say nothing of its treatment of those regarded as 'unworthy of life'. For example, witnessing the high post-war increase of youth-related crime in the British Zone of Occupied Germany, British officials tried to impose self-consciously British methods on the population, and criticized German institutions for being too harsh in their treatment of young people. The insistent declaration was that rehabilitation would take precedence over punishment. The nourishment of progressive psychological attitudes towards crime, such officers believed, would be an important means of re-educating German young people towards democracy and of eradicating Nazism (Smith, 1994). This wish mirrored mid-century British approaches (themselves, admittedly, contested at home) of treating delinquents as morally redeemable and reclaiming them for citizenship, while regarding prison as a last resort, most especially for the young.

British officials hoped that their welfarist policies would eventually also reshape the attitudes of German experts: authoritarian punishment, the brutal repression of 'undesirable elements of society', and the very frequent use of imprisonment were now seen to have the indelible hallmarks of Nazism (Smith, 1994).[6] The British authorities in occupied Germany thus pushed for the psychological treatment of crime (with emphasis on child guidance) and sought to cultivate the capacity for youth to be self-disciplined and self-reliant rather than blindly submissive in the face of authority (Smith, 1994; see also Lewis, 1988).[7]

Similar views about the proper handling of crime in a democracy were being advocated in Britain itself, a trend largely led by pronouncements from the ISTD.[8] The problems of children and young people continued to capture public attention in the post-war years, as did the question of rehabilitating delinquents and creating good citizens.

After 1945, ISTD psychoanalysts saw themselves even more than before as in the vanguard of reform, and as active, and at times interventionist therapists in the lives of patients who broke the law. The organization also challenged the stark division between notions of the normal and abnormal. State committees frequently called upon the ISTD to provide expert testimony on topics ranging from corporal punishment to homosexuality and prostitution. While some writings in this period referred back to the Blitz and total war to offer renewed humanist and Enlightenment perspectives that emphasized the belief in the good of humanity, what was striking about the ISTD literature was its insistent focus upon the role of negative and destructive emotions in the social order. Envisioning the success (and vulnerability) of democracy, psychoanalysts thus retained the idea that anxiety, aggression, hatred, sadism and guilt were all central to understanding the nature of social and political processes (Zaretsky, 2004; Makari, 2008).

As all of this suggests, the intellectual concerns of criminology at the end of the 1940s were dominated by psychoanalysis to an extent that may be hard to comprehend today. Indeed, for at least a decade, psychoanalytic principles were at the heart of the training of social workers and probation officers (Martin, 1988).[9] At the ISTD, the main body through which forensic psychoanalysis was disseminated, the immediate post-war period was to prove busy in the extreme, even if some attempts were made to restore more normal working conditions, after the inevitable disruptions and acute anxieties of the struggle against the Third Reich (Saville and Rumney, 1992: 19–20). As staff returned from army duties to civil life, the ISTD's Psychopathic Clinic was able to carry a heavier caseload and the Institute expanded its clinical and educational activities. For example, Kate Friedlander gave a series of student seminars, and a study group on 'Some Aspects of Freudian Theory Specially Relevant to Human Maladjustment' was conducted by Barbara Low. The Home Office furthered its close connection with the ISTD, seeking collaboration in arranging courses for probation officer trainees. The ISTD duly obliged, continually arranging lectures and case conferences for this constituency.[10] When the Ministry of Health expressed its wish to place the ISTD under the National Health Service Act of 1948, some feared that its identity would be diffused and lost. Eventually, the members decided that the clinic would fall under the purview of the Act, but that the non-clinical work done at the ISTD would not fall within the scope of the National Health Service.[11] In this same year, the caseload rose to 400 new patients (Saville and Rumney, 1992: 18).[12] A rebranding exercise around this time meant that it was known henceforth as the Institute for the Study and Treatment of Delinquency and its clinical facility became the Portman Clinic.[13] In 1949, Edward Glover was appointed Honorary Adviser in Criminal Psychiatry as part of a group of seven experts (including ISTD analyst Denis Carroll) convened by the United Nations to consider the problem of crime internationally.

The Institute's programme of lectures to both members and outsiders continued apace, along with teaching seminars for magistrates and prison officers, conferences, courses, and case-demonstrations to small groups of experts and students.[14] Low provided lectures to university students on 'Difficult and Delinquent Personalities – the Freudian Approach', and Glover addressed lawyers and magistrates on 'Psychopathic Personality'. Following a previous conference called by the Home Secretary and Minister of Education to discuss the increase in juvenile delinquency, a follow-up event was convened by different organizations, including the ISTD, to discuss the scientific implications of the problem.[15] By 1950, the ISTD reached the zenith of its productivity, with roughly 400 active members (Glover, 1950: 498).[16] In July that year the ISTD published the first issue of the *British Journal of Delinquency* (which would become the *British Journal of Criminology* in 1960), a leading, prestigious periodical that also provided a legitimizing stage for psychoanalytic ideas. An additional development took place in 1953 when the Scientific Committee of the ISTD formed a 150-member Scientific Group for the Discussion of Delinquency Problems. The group flourished (at times it was to become notably critical of psychoanalysis) and in 1961 was re-established as the British Society of Criminology. Among its members were several Home Office officials (Saville and Rumney, 1992: 19). The post-war years, as all these activities indicate, were a time of growth, extramural dialogue, and intensified influence for the ISTD. Its consistent call was for the state to extend its responsibilities towards citizens, to protect and regulate the lives of delinquents, and to intervene in family dynamics and in education. The ISTD influentially re-imagined parenthood, not only as a natural capacity but also as a social responsibility. What follows is a closer examination of the way clinical practices were transformed in the context of criminological work, and of the kinds of active interventions the ISTD staff characteristically sought to make in their patients' lives – not only clinically, but by engaging the support of the various social services concerned with those coming through the courts.

Psychoanalytic understanding of crime in theory and practice

Though individual ISTD members held slightly different, if often evolving, theoretical positions, common to all of them was the belief in teamwork or expert collaboration, a stress on psychological rather than economic origins of crime, and a wish to change public opinion and policy.

Glover, as noted, was one of the leading figures in the ISTD and, as its chairman for many years, he often articulated publicly its official stance. Glover was an esteemed psychoanalyst at the time, though he is now nearly forgotten (see Roazen, 2000). He had become an Associate Member of the British Psychoanalytical Society as early as 1921 and, alongside his work there, he developed his expertise on crime at the ISTD.[17] Writing after the war, Glover (and other analysts before him) believed that the main contributions of forensic psychoanalysis were in its application to the fields of diagnosis, prevention and the practical handling of delinquents, rather than in long-term treatment (Glover, 1960a; cf. Friedlander, 1943). Although careful to insist on the importance of cooperation among different experts, he believed that psychoanalysis added a crucial perspective that would help reconfigure data on delinquency across disciplines, and bring home the importance of emotional factors. Even poverty 'would be rated as an external emotional stimulus exerting its maximum force on constitutional sensitivities with a history of early instinctual frustration' (Glover, 1960b: 179).

The treatment work of ISTD member and refugee analyst Hedwig Schwarz with a juvenile delinquent she named 'Dorothy', did not refer to team research directly (Schwarz, 1950–1). Nevertheless, it reveals a psychoanalyst at work who, in the spirit of the ISTD, was in close communication with magistrates and probation officers, and who played a very active role in her patient's life. This treatment, which serves as a testimony to the hardships of war and its aftermath, and the flexibility of psychoanalytic work with delinquents, merits further scrutiny.[18]

Schwarz memorably described 19-year-old Dorothy, whom she treated from March 1945 until April 1946. Dorothy was on probation. We learn from Schwarz how Dorothy had been charged with a long list of offences involving stealing, the first of which had occurred when, aged 12, she stole a bottle of milk. She was evacuated during the war to a foster family at the order of the court, under the assumption that the poverty of her family was responsible for her stealing. Dorothy continued to steal, however, and was put in a hostel for difficult children. At 14 she insisted on going back home. After Dorothy's brother was killed in an air raid, both she and her mother were evacuated to the country. There, Dorothy stole again and was put back in a hostel. Dorothy's father, who had been wounded in the First World War, had become thereafter what Schwarz called a 'permanent invalid'. He died on Dorothy's seventeenth birthday.

After special permission had been secured, Dorothy was able to attend sessions with Schwarz once a week (at first accompanied by a probation officer). From the early days of the treatment onwards, Schwarz intervened in her patient's life to an extent well beyond what was conventional in classical Freudianism.[19] The analyst tried to make Dorothy feel that she was on her side, providing her with paints and knitting wool to counteract her boredom in the hostel. Dorothy's wish to return home and support her mother and youngest brother, while her two elder brothers were in the services, was not only registered in the session but also used by Schwarz in a direct bid to persuade the probation officer to let Dorothy go home on condition that she would agree to psychoanalytic treatment. Schwarz also convinced the official to find Dorothy a job in the vicinity of the consulting room. Schwarz explained that she chose to act as she might have done in the introductory phase of a child analysis, establishing a positive relationship and making the child aware of its problems, as well as securing the practical arrangements with the parents.[20] According to Schwarz, adult delinquents, who have a personality structure not unlike that of a child, cannot be expected to behave responsibly. She explained:

Very often, I think, we have to resort to unorthodox methods, e.g. bringing the delinquent into coming, or threatening him with possible consequences if he refuses, or again using both methods alternately so that we get a chance to begin treatment and to make the patient dependent enough on us to accept our help.

(Schwarz, 1950–1: 31)

She believed that probation conditions could be used to good effect to promote analytic work: especially when treatment is made a definite condition of continuing probation.[21]

After facilitating the treatment in this way, even pressing Dorothy directly to undergo such work, Schwarz was able to see her four times a week. Schwarz insisted, like other analysts before her, that Dorothy's stealing had to do with her childhood family dynamics, rivalry and envy towards her mother, and aggression and envy towards her siblings, followed by guilt and a wish for punishment. Dorothy's stealing served the purposes of gratifying a wish for retribution. She was therefore 'a criminal from a sense of guilt', as Freud had put it earlier in the century. This guilt was also expressed by the fact that Dorothy was always caught and succeeded in making people call in the police.

When Schwarz shifted into a more 'orthodox' analysis, Dorothy's 'resistance' grew and she began seeing her analyst as a person forcing her to continue.[22] When Dorothy inquired whether she would need to come for the whole duration of the probation, Schwarz urged Dorothy to see the treatment as an opportunity to understand her own behaviour so that she could finish her probation without a relapse. Schwarz also decided to intervene again and secure Dorothy's release from regular visits to the probation officer (Schwarz, 1950–1: 36). However, Schwarz was not yet aware that during that time Dorothy was already relapsing into crime by stealing copies of the *Picture Post* magazine from her analyst's waiting room.[23] Dorothy also made a train ticket collector stop her for travelling without a ticket on the eve of VJ Day when the whole town was celebrating. This later impressed on Schwarz again that Dorothy had a strong wish to be punished.

Shortly after, Dorothy went to the north of England to visit the mother of the man she was dating. Instead of coming back to her work and analysis, Dorothy decided unexpectedly to stay there. Schwarz's reaction was again unusually interventionist. Discussing the matter with the probation officer, Schwarz decided to visit Dorothy and persuade her to finish her probation. During the visit, Schwarz asked to meet the patient's boyfriend to make sure that he intended to marry her. Schwarz was able to come to an agreement with the probation officer that Dorothy would write regularly to her and would report to the probation service. Unfortunately, Dorothy again found herself in jail after stealing in her new place. Schwarz tried to help her by sending a report to the local bench, explaining the 'psychological aspect' of the patient's thefts and the promised marriage.

Despite this partial failure of treatment, Schwarz believed that it was of some help to Dorothy as it made her conscious of certain 'emotional conflicts'. Schwarz also believed that the analysis of Dorothy's childhood would make this young woman a better mother towards her own future children (1950–1: 43–4). Thus, perhaps more than demonstrating the effectiveness of analytic treatment, this reported case was a testimony to the extent to which psychoanalysts in the ISTD had an active influence on penal issues and worked in close alliance with the legal and probation system. It also shows that analysts such as Schwarz were willing to go far in influencing the life of patients who occupied vulnerable and economically inferior positions. Published in the *British Journal of Delinquency* (without noted reservations from editors, nor apparently any subsequent criticism from readers), it seems safe to assume that this case was not entirely exceptional.

An ISTD public pamphlet written for the mass consumption of non-specialists presents the same spirit of social intervention. In this publication, ISTD member Ethel Perry described the psychoanalytic treatment of a delinquent she named 'Josephine' in which unorthodox methods were again used.[24] Josephine was in psychoanalysis during the time she was on probation for attempted burglary. Previously, she had also been shoplifting. Before coming to treatment with Perry, she was briefly examined by different experts. A welfare officer reported that she never could hold a job and claimed, 'she revolted from any ordered life and just could not fit into the group'. Her psychiatrist believed that she had 'no affective roots' since she was an illegitimate child abandoned in an orphanage, and that beneath her façade of confidence and alertness was anxiety and apprehension.[25] Perry seemed to agree with this description and also suggested directly to her patient that she wanted to take revenge on authority and had aggressive and cruel traits resulting from intolerable feelings of her own unimportance. Perry proposed that the purpose of her delinquency was to keep her stimulated so that she would have no time to feel her anxious loneliness. Josephine's treatment had then to uncover unpleasant memories that delinquency had been used, hitherto, to repress.

Perry encouraged Josephine to talk about her life and then attempted to give her interpretations when she was least expecting it. Outside the clinic, Josephine was able to say more about herself, so Perry, in strikingly idiosyncratic fashion, chose to wander with her in the park. As Perry describes it, 'sometimes I managed to offer what I hope were words of wisdom between movements of a concerto at a lunch-hour concert or between mouthfuls of Argentine at a British restaurant'.[26] Perry believed that this 'peculiar form of therapy' was helping Josephine and made herself available to her patient even during the weekend, becoming a friend and a substitute mother to her.

Perry's descriptions of Josephine's problems are moving, providing a vivid picture of the troubles young people suffered through poverty and war. These descriptions showed how the patient needed to hide the fact that she lived in a hostel and did not have a real home like her work colleagues. In addition, she was terrified of feeling that she was alone in the world and without a family. Along with her fear of isolation, she also dreaded having an emotional relationship with others, and seemed beset by a cruelly depriving external reality, as well as the terror of her own possible mental disease. Josephine had a sense of injustice when she compared her life with that of those she served in her work.

At one point, Perry described how Josephine witnessed and then reacted to a discussion of the Beveridge Report, the key document for envisioning a new form of social democracy and framing a welfare state that would take care of all citizens 'from the cradle to the grave'.[27] Josephine 'had to wait at a meeting where the Beveridge proposals for Social Security were discussed. There she had to listen to people who had never earned their living denounce these as "unjust", and had been unable to say anything.'[28] During treatment, Josephine explored how routine at her childhood orphanage was deadening to her and 'made her mad'. Later in her life, she was put in a special place for delinquents whose purpose, in her words, was, 'to make a good honest citizen out of me working my guts out'. She added, 'I didn't agree so I made a little exit from there . . . then I got in with the crooks and learned how to dodge authorities.' She objected to what she saw as the 'normality' of her analyst, that is, the fact that Perry was holding a job and adjusting to a life with no change. This, Josephine thought, was 'unbearable' and 'limiting', and she said, 'I'd rather die than be normal if it means doing the same things at the same time every day.'[29] Indeed, Josephine's own adjustment to reality was tested when a V2 bomb fell near the hostel where she was staying, almost wounding her and reawakening her fear of mental disease. In her analysis, she told Perry that she hated her body and pleaded, 'if only my spirit could get away from it. I just can't escape from my body. It had to be fed and clothed and worked for at horrible jobs.'[30] Despite these difficulties, and Josephine's direct and poignant criticism of the treatment, of her analyst and of welfare policies regarding delinquency, Perry believed that psychoanalysis, here in its unorthodox forms, helped Josephine, since she had better insight into her condition and better adjustment to outside worka-day reality. Perry hoped for Josephine's further adjustment to reality by means of affording her the happiness that good social relationships provide.[31] Both Perry's and Schwarz's work resonated with the prevailing public post-war wish to con-tain asocial behaviour in juvenile delinquents. This desire linked with wartime anxieties that a wave of crime would follow from the break-up of families during the Second World War, as well as demonstrating a more general concern with strengthening the nature of democratic citizenry.[32] Their analytic work was also written in the context of changes in childcare policy, most significantly represented by the 1944 Education Act and the 1948 Children Act (Hendrick, 1990).

ISTD member Kate Friedlander's influential book, *The Psycho-Analytic Approach to Juvenile Delinquency*, published in 1947, provided a popular ver-sion of the Freudian stance in relation to crime and helped to develop a support-ive climate for interventions and reforms which the analysts were trying to make (Friedlander, 1960 [1947]). The book also explored connections between child-hood experiences, crime, and life in a democratic society between war and peace.

Friedlander started by claiming, 'delinquency is a disease of society, just as can-cer, for instance, is a disease of the individual' (1960 [1947]: vii). She called for further modifications to criminal law and changes in public opinion by advancing 'modern scientific methods' of dealing with delinquency and replacing punishment with the re-education and rehabilitation of the offender, by extending probation, pro-viding hostels and remand homes, and also centres of observation (1960 [1947]: vii).

Sociological research emphasizing the ways in which the environment con-tributes to the development of delinquency, Friedlander argued, is unable to answer why some people from the same place become delinquent while others do not (1960 [1947]: 7–10). In order to answer such a question, one must turn to psychoanalysis. Criminals, she claimed, are human beings who have failed to achieve social adaptation in their childhood and have been frustrated in their human relationships, especially their relationship with their mothers (1960 [1947]: 49).

Yet delinquency was more than just a social nuisance for Friedlander. Significantly, it had to do with the possibility of collaborative living in democracy. She argued, 'Our civilization is built up on the assumption that people are able to set their relationship to their fellow human beings above the gratification of their instinctive desires.' However, she added that delinquents share an 'inability to postpone desires because they cannot form good relationships with the people in their surroundings, and this results in their excessive self-love' (1960 [1947]: 70). Friedlander ended her book by warning that delinquency figures had risen due to the war:

> Let us meet this threat to our community by helping these young boys and girls to become useful citizens in the post-war world: they have suffered, through no fault of their own, in their emotional development by the insecurity of family life and a world at war. They are victims as much as the wounded soldier or the bombed-out citizen.
>
> (1960 [1947]: 286–7)

Friedlander linked the concern for children's mental care and stable democratic citizenship, saying:

> By realizing the emotional need of these boys and girls and by working out plans for their re-education on scientific lines, we shall not only prevent an increase in criminal careers but also increase the numbers of happy, socially adapted and therefore, useful citizens.
>
> (1960 [1947]: 287)

Similar ideas led ISTD analyst Melitta Schmideberg, better known as Melanie Klein's daughter and opponent in the theoretical controversies that had erupted at the British Psychoanalytical Society of the 1930s and 1940s, to question whether criminals are in fact amoral from a psychoanalytic perspective (Schmideberg, 1953–4). While law-breakers commit actions from which 'respectable' persons refrain, it is erroneous to claim that they commit them without hesitation, anxiety, guilt, or regret, she argued (Schmideberg, 1953–4: 272).[33] The feelings of anxiety and the process of forgetting, evident in criminals after the offence, she continued, bear comparison with those of civilians during the Blitz, who after the bombing forgot how scared they had been.[34] In treatment, Schmideberg found that criminals could be excellent husbands or loyal to their fellow criminals, and that the only difference between them and law-abiding citizens was that 'respectable society is their enemy, and they fight it as the underground French fought the Nazis, taking similar pride in the exploit' (Schmideberg, 1953–4: 274). Schmideberg offered the counterintuitive idea that there is in fact also, often enough, a moral drive behind crime. Paradoxically, she argued, moral impulses could sometimes make the criminal act amorally. For example, one patient, who felt guilty of rising above his parents, could not act in a respectable way and instead searched for 'bad company' (Schmideberg, 1953–4: 280).

Schmideberg, Friedlander, Glover and others were then willing to see themselves as social educators of public opinion, advocating certain reformist views in relation to crime. The years of total war had focused attention on new ways through which to manage the lives of citizens. Indeed, ensuring their mental health, happiness, and capacity for collaborative human relations became, for many politicians, a pressing pursuit of post-war government and, in this context, the campaign against asocial behaviour in the national community quickly became a priority.

Crystallizing many of these arguments – particularly the links between the prevention of crime and the success of democracy – was an ISTD article, 'The Enemy Within'. Published in *The Times* (6 March 1956), as part of a funding appeal for the Institute, it asserted that:

> Nations spent money on military defence, or for economic welfare, but they did not seem to spend enough on the study and correction of the enemy within. If they could not correct the enemies who were part of their own flesh and blood, it would seem to stand to reason that they would be remiss in their efforts to deal with matters outside their own boundaries.

In much the same spirit, child psychoanalysts suggested the myriad links between child mental health and democratic, or authoritarian, even totalitarian, political attitudes. In all of these ways, they and their colleagues eschewed the notion that psychoanalysis was an elitist science for the financially privileged. Indeed, the history of the ISTD shows how British psychoanalysis was an influential discipline committed to shaping the post-war order, transforming both public policy and individual experiences, working with citizens of diverse backgrounds, and advancing new concepts of self and mental health. The ISTD members' views of crime became popular and added to the call to treat rather than punish criminals, and they placed the family centre stage as the critical breeding ground, for better or for worse, of new citizens.

Notes

1 Aichhorn's work was mentioned with praise in the British Parliament (see Eissler, 1949: x; see also Klein, 1934: 312–15; Winnicott, 1958: 306–15).
2 Despite its influence, this institution has been neglected by historians. Note, however, that the ISTD has sought to chart its own history. See Saville and Rumney (1992).
3 In 1931 it was called the Association for the Scientific Treatment of Criminals and the Association for the Scientific Treatment of Delinquency and Crime, a title subsequently changed to the Institute of the Scientific Treatment of Delinquency and Crime. From 1948 it became the Institute for the Study and Treatment of Delinquency. I refer to it throughout simply as the ISTD.
4 Centre for Crime and Justice Studies, King's College, London, ISTD Archive (here after ISTDA): ISTDA/330DDDD: *ISTD Annual Report 1934.*

5 The Institute's use of the word 'psychopathic' differs from the way it is usually understood today. Glover (1950: 492) later defined as psychopathic 'a person who manifests,
   and has manifested from childhood, chronic disorders of his instinctual life, of the
   emotions, of thought processes (including absence of moral senses, feeling or thought)
   and of behaviour (including outbreaks of violence or sexual perversion, or both)'.
6 On prisons under the Nazis see Wachsmann (2004). Wachsmann shows that until
   1943 the number of inmates in the regular penal system exceeded the numbers of
   those held in concentration camps. Before the war, many Germans saw crime and
   delinquent juvenile behaviour as symptoms of societal disintegration. This fear continued after 1945, but was tied to various new social and political tensions and the
   development of consumer culture (see Poiger, 2000). For the French context, see also
   Jobs (2007).
7 For the shift from the welfarist approach during the 1960s and 1970s, see Garland
   (2001).
8 The Beveridge Report imagined a welfare state that would free citizens from the giant
   evils of want, squalor, ignorance and disease, as well as idleness.
9 For competing psychological theories see West (1988).
10 ISTDA/330BBBB: *ISTD Annual 1946*: 13.
11 The clinic then became the financial responsibility of the Paddington Group
   Management Committee of the North West Metropolitan Regional Hospital Board.
12 See ISTDA/330BBBB: *ISTD Annual Report 1947*. During the early years of the
   clinic, it treated an average of 144 criminal offenders each year. Following the war,
   the numbers rose to 170 in 1946, 272 in 1947 and 488 in 1949. Most of the cases were
   sent directly by magistrates. The three largest groups of offences were larceny, sexual
   offences and, in the case of juveniles, 'behaviour problems' or 'being out-of-control'
   (see Glover, 1950: 491).
13 In the 1970s, the Portman Clinic had moved to north-west London and the Institute
   moved to Croydon, Surrey (Saville and Rumney, 1992: 23).
14 The ISTD continued to collaborate with the London University Extension Lectures
   and gave courses with high enrolment (Saville and Rumney, 1992: 32).
15 ISTDA/330AAAA: *ISTD Annual Report 1949–1950*: 6.
16 See *ISTD Annual Report 1949–1950*: 3.
17 Glover resigned from the British Psychoanalytical Society in 1944 after the
   'Controversial Discussions' between Anna Freud, Melanie Klein, and their supporters
   (see King, 1991: xiii).
18 Hedwig Schwarz was also a member of the Institute of Psycho-Analysis, London.
19 Though it should be noted that, in practice, Sigmund Freud himself and other analysts
   of his generation were often 'unorthodox' themselves with their patients.
20 This approach was influenced by the work of Anna Freud, who believed in the usefulness of forming a connection with the patient and in the educative value of the treatment. Such ideas contrasted with those of Melanie Klein, who preferred to conduct deep
   interpretation of the patient's words and actions from the earliest possible moment.
21 Glover believed that next to social workers and educational psychologists, probation
   officers provided many of the strongest supporters of institutions like the ISTD. (See
   Glover, 1960c: 44.)
22 Denis Carroll (Caroll *et al.*, 1937) claimed that delinquent patients' unwillingness
   to attend sessions was connected to the fact that the therapy is identified with court-
   assigned punishment.
23 This was a popular anti-fascist photojournalistic magazine, supportive of the welfare
   state.
24 ISTDA/Pamphlet Collection (hereafter PMC)/330/DDDD: Ethel Perry, 'The Psycho-
   Analysis of a Delinquent: Interplay between Phantasy and Reality in the Life of a Law
   Breaker' (London: Psychological and Social Series, 1947).

25 Ibid.: 4–6. This conceptualization was influenced by the work of John Bowlby.
26 Ibid.: 9.
27 While promising greater equality to all and a new state commitment to citizens, the Report prescribed different gender roles to men and women. See Pedersen (1993).
28 ISTDA/PMC/330/DDDD: Perry, op. cit.: 13.
29 Ibid.: 14.
30 Ibid.: 15.
31 Ibid.: 16.
32 Indeed, pressure for good behaviour was high in the immediate post-war years. See ISTDA/PMC/ 330/DDDD: Joan Warburg, 'Play Therapy' (London: Psychological and Social Series, 1946): 1 and 16. See also Schmideberg (1948) and ISTDA/PMC/330/DDDD: Melitta Schmideberg, 'Folklore of Parenthood' (London: Psychological and Social Series, 1947).
33 Schmideberg wrote, 'we must study criminals, as anthropologists have studied the aborigines, against their own background, watching the sum total of their lives and reactions without being shocked by the actions we condemn' (1953–4: 272).
34 Indeed, in ways similar to those in which analysts turned away from the impact of real violence on British citizens during the Blitz and looked instead at their 'inner' emotions, so it was with crime, in which the environment played a secondary role in analytic explanations.

Chapter 7

'The aggression problems of our time'

Psychoanalysis as moral politics in post-Nazi Germany

Dagmar Herzog

I

In 1967, the physician and psychoanalyst Alexander Mitscherlich, with his wife Margarete, also an analyst, published what is still the most influential and internationally known product of West German psychoanalysis: *Die Unfähigkeit zu trauern* (The Inability to Mourn). The Mitscherlichs argued that what Germans had proven themselves unable to mourn was *not* the multiple millions of murdered Jews of Europe that had been killed in their name and in all too many cases with their assistance, but rather their own erstwhile passionate love for Adolf Hitler. Yet while this has not generally been noted, another persistent theme in the book was the question of how best to understand the phenomenon of human aggression. This included the need to develop a more complex theoretical framework than Sigmund Freud had produced – not least in view of the massive empirical evidence provided by Germans themselves, but also in light of the many further demonstrations of its ubiquity throughout human history.

Aggression, this second great vital force beside libido, had been seen by Freud variously – at least since the topic forced itself upon his attention with the events of the First World War – as: an equally powerful and parallel drive to libido; one at odds with libido and providing a countervailing pressure; one which got peculiarly mixed up with and fused with libido (or vice versa, as libido got fused with aggression); a phenomenon which grew in proportion as libidinal aims were thwarted (1915; 1920; 1924b; 1930). Subsequent to Freud's death in 1939, the topic went in and out of focus in the internecine debates roiling the global psychoanalytic diaspora that had been set in motion by Nazism's brutal ascent. Often it became relegated to the margins of the main arenas of debate. When the topic showed up at all, it was mainly in the interstices of discussions of early childhood – prompted not least by the controversial emphases of (by that point Britain-based) Melanie Klein on greed, rage, and envy in babies (Shapira, 2013). It also appeared, albeit in a stringently depoliticized form, in American ego psychologists Heinz Hartmann and Ernst Kris's efforts, together with those of Anna Freud, to systematize Freudian ideas about normative stages of development in *The Psychoanalytic Study of the Child*, the journal launched in the

US in 1945. But the topic resurfaced with peculiar force in post-Second World War West Germany.

In no other national context would the attempt to make sense of aggression become such a core preoccupation specifically for psychoanalysts and allied professionals. And, conversely, in no other post-war national context would the wider public reception of psychoanalysis as a whole, in its dual nature as a clinical and culturally critical enterprise, be so strongly shaped by debates *not* over sexual desire, or anxiety, or narcissism (the themes which would, in sequence, obsess the post-war American public in its ambivalent but titillated engagement with psychoanalysis), but rather over the vagaries and vicissitudes of human aggression (Lunbeck, 2014). Although the topic of sex did ultimately re-enter the West German debate about aggression as well, the main emphasis of the controversies remained on the subject of aggression itself. This, in turn, had everything to do with the unanticipated but absolutely tremendous excitement with which the work of a non-analyst, the Austrian-German ethologist and ornithologist Konrad Lorenz, was received in the West German media. Lorenz was a specialist particularly on parental 'imprinting' in greylag geese, but also devoted observer-reporter of the vast repertoire of behaviours of other animals, from monkeys to rats to fish to dogs.

From quite early on in the post-war years Lorenz was a household name in West Germany due to his beguilingly folksy tales of animal doings, published as *Er redete mit dem Vieh, den Vögeln und den Fischen* ('He Spoke with the Cattle, the Birds, and the Fish', 1949) and *So kam der Mensch auf den Hund* ('Man Meets Dog', 1950). And he was well known among research professionals, including among psychoanalysts on both sides of the Atlantic, for numerous scholarly essays on instincts, evolution, and behaviour. British and American analysts were particularly fascinated by what they saw as the implications of his research for demonstrating the importance of early mother–child bonding, but – often enough status-anxious and pleased to find support for their own claims about human nature – psychoanalysts followed many other aspects of Lorenz's work, and he was footnoted in a tremendous number of post-war psychoanalytic texts (Tidd, 1960; Vicedo, 2013). Yet it was the book appearing in 1963, *Das sogenannte Böse: Zur Naturgeschichte der Aggression* ('The So-Called Evil: On the Natural History of Aggression', published in the US in 1966 as *On Aggression*), that was the truly blockbuster hit which secured Lorenz's international reputation.

Both in the Anglo-American and in the West German context, Lorenz's book on aggression would often be read in conjunction with two further books exploring the animal origins of human behaviour published a few years later: the American playwright (and student of behavioural science) Robert Ardrey's *The Territorial Imperative* (1966) and the British zoologist Desmond Morris's *The Naked Ape* (1967). One strand of public fascination with these texts clearly had to do with a wave of interest in biological as opposed to sociological explanations of human nature – and not least with a desire to re-secure traditional notions of gender in an era of rapidly changing social roles for men and women (Bartlett and Bartlett, 1971; Schubert, 1973; Milam, 2010; Weidman, 2011). However, there was something distinctively post-Nazi German about the glowing appreciation and fervour with which Lorenz's specific contribution to the wider project of analogizing from animals to humans was embraced.

Das sogenannte Böse, after all, as the German title indicated, was a vigorous defence of aggression as by no means always a force for evil. The short take-home message – amidst all the witty, cheerfully chatty accounts of animal conduct – was welcome indeed. It had two main components: aggression was ubiquitous in animals and in people (i.e. it was not just a German speciality). And, more importantly: aggression was a force for *good*. All cultural progress and effective activity, as well as (and however counterintuitively) the treasured bonds of deep friendship and marital love, had roots in the aggressive instinct.

It was also Lorenz who did more than anyone else to introduce Freud into the national conversation on aggression. Lorenz had situated himself, at the very opening of *Das sogenannte Böse*, as someone who had long been resistant to psychoanalysis, not least because he could not agree with 'the concept of a death drive, which according to a theory of Freud's is a destructive principle which exists as an opposite pole to all instincts of self-preservation' (x). But then, as Lorenz reported, he had been delighted to find, in his travels across the US (these included, in 1960–1, a longer-term visit at the Menninger Clinic in Topeka, Kansas, but also time in New York), that many American analysts did not agree with the idea of its existence either. What Lorenz did find useful, however, was Freud's belatedly found conviction that aggression, like libido, *was* a drive. The difference was that Lorenz was eager to see the aggressive drive as life-preserving and life-enhancing ('in natural conditions it helps just as much as any other to ensure the survival of the individual and the species' (x)).

However unintentionally, what the publication of *Das sogenannte Böse* set in motion was an outpouring of debate in 1960s–1970s West Germany over whether or not aggression was indeed best understood as a drive (or 'instinct' – West Germans were alert to the confusions that had been caused by some early translators of Freud into English), and also, more generally, whether Freud was a useful resource or a problem. No other text caused more people to start wondering what Freud himself had actually argued. Not just Lorenz and his supporters, but also Lorenz's critics – and they were increasingly vociferous – contributed to the reformulation of what Freud was thought to stand for.

By the later 1960s and early 1970s, at least three new versions of Freud were circulating in the West German media and wider public discussion. One was a sex-radical version, which restored to public attention Freud's own erstwhile commitment to seeing libido as the force that explained almost everything in life. Another was the far more conservative Freud who had insisted that humans were not by nature good; this version, however paradoxically, was a co-production of Lorenz's supporters with those of his critics who could not accept the idea of aggression as a drive at all and instead proposed alternative models of human behaviour which more strongly emphasized social and political factors. And the third was the complex effort at compromise that Alexander Mitscherlich formulated. Mitscherlich never did succeed in developing a fully satisfactory theoretical framework, and his writings showed the strain of the effort to find middle ground. And yet ultimately Mitscherlich's strategic genius lay not least precisely in an ability to leave the theoretical questions open.

Henceforth, the public and professional arguments about Freud in West Germany would no longer be about whether or not to take him seriously. Rather, the question became *which* Freud would be promoted and invoked in order to advance a variety of political agendas. At the same time, all the previously assumed alignments between theoretical frameworks and political implications got scrambled. The controversies, in short, sparked both a repositioning of psychoanalysis within West German culture and a reconsideration of what exactly the content of psychoanalysis might be.[1]

II

Alexander Mitscherlich succeeded in his life project of returning psychoanalysis to post-Nazi Central Europe – and securing for it far greater social prestige than it ever had in Freud's own day – primarily by advancing a highly idiosyncratic version of psychoanalysis as a secular moral-political language. Mitscherlich became, on the one hand, *the* main West German representative of the psychoanalytic enterprise: through his editorship of the journal *Psyche*; his clinical and theoretical work especially in psychosomatics (psychosomatics in fact became the major pathway by which psychoanalysis eventually became integrated into German medicine); his activism in bringing emigrated psychoanalytic celebrities back to address the West German public; and, after an early post-war stint in Heidelberg, his directorship of the Sigmund Freud Institute in Frankfurt am Main. On the other hand, Mitscherlich also served as 'the conscience of the nation', a 'gentle repentance-preacher' (Freimüller, 2007: 8; Rutschky, 2006).

Mitscherlich managed to finesse this double role not least by creatively amalgamating elements of Hartmannesque American ego psychology with frankly left-liberal political commentary on current events with (what in hindsight may seem rather un-analytic and conceptually clunky) persistent enjoinders to West Germans to develop what he variously referred to as 'ego-strength' (*Ichstärke*), 'self-control', 'capacity for critical thinking', or 'the critical thinking-capacity of the ego' (1974a: 10–17; cf. A. and M. Mitscherlich, 1967: 171, 318; Bohleber, 2009). The contrast with someone like his French counterpart Jacques Lacan, whose baseline assumption was that there could be no such thing as a stable ego, could not have been starker (Lacan, 2002 [1966]). But for West German conditions, Mitscherlich's approach proved ideal. This was, after all, a culture in which contempt for psychoanalysis in the wider public and among medical professionals had been intensively fostered under the Nazis. Freud was said to have a 'dirty fantasy' and an 'Asiatic world view', and psychoanalysis was deemed both to contain 'nothing original' – for to claim otherwise would be 'to give too much honour to the unproductivity of the Jewish race' – and to be 'nothing other than the Jewish nation's rape of Western culture' (Anon., 1933; Hunger, 1943: 317). These attitudes hardly disappeared overnight in the war's aftermath. But despite this Mitscherlich succeeded spectacularly in convincing West Germans to think about psychoanalysis differently, not least through a distinctive style which mixed declared empathy for and identification with his fellow citizens with encouragement and coaxing injunction.

Mitscherlich's work was profoundly shaped by an irritated, albeit sporadic, engagement with the astonishing public success of Konrad Lorenz. In correspondence with mentors and friends, Mitscherlich declared his disdain for Lorenz and his sense of intellectual superiority to him. And in 1964 Mitscherlich organized a workshop – to which he invited Lorenz – whose express aim was to repudiate Lorenz's conclusions about aggression (Hoyer, 2008: 371–2; Krovoza, 2001: 917). The book resulting from this workshop eventually appeared in 1969 as *Bis hierher und nicht weiter: Ist die menschliche Aggression unbefriedbar?* ('Up to Here and No Further: Can Human Aggression Not Be Pacified?'). But actually his relationship to Lorenz's oeuvre was more complicated. It is not just that already in his earliest published writing on aggression (a two-part meditation, 'Aggression und Anpassung' [Aggression and Adaptation], in *Psyche* in 1956 and 1958) Mitscherlich had cited Lorenz favourably. In addition, the *magnum opus* of 1967, co-written with Margarete Mitscherlich, *Die Unfähigkeit zu trauern* – which actually contains eight essays, only the first of which is the title story, and the remainder of which return recurrently to the puzzle of human aggression – needs to be read not only as a repudiation but also as a partial incorporation of Lorenz's theses. So too Mitscherlich's marvellous speech in 1969 on the occasion of his winning the Peace Prize of the Frankfurt Book Trade – 'Über Feindseligkeit und hergestellte Dummheit' ('On Hostility and Man-made Stupidity') – remained in conversation with Lorenz's theses (and was indisputably understood that way by the media). The pre-eminent liberal news magazine *Der Spiegel*, for instance, in a reprint of the full text, plucked from the speech and chose as its headline the Mitscherlich remark that 'Aggression is a fundamental force of life', clearly positioning the speech within the ongoing national fracas over how to feel about the existence and value of an aggressive drive (1969a: 206).

Aggression thus became one of the central themes of Mitscherlich's public life. In addition to *Die Unfähigkeit zu trauern* and *Bis hierher und nicht weiter*, he published or co-published three further books on the topic: *Aggression und Anpassung in der Industriegesellschaft* ('Aggression and Adaptation in Industrial Society', 1968, with Herbert Marcuse and others); *Die Idee des Friedens und die menschliche Aggressivität* ('The Idea of Peace and Human Aggressivity', 1969); and *Toleranz – Überprüfung eines Begriffs* ('Tolerance – Verification of a Concept', 1974), which contained multiple essays on aggression, cruelty, and war, including a reprint of the Peace Prize speech. The timing was crucial. Mitscherlich was just – barely – succeeding in getting psychoanalysis to be taken seriously in West Germany when Lorenz's *Das sogenannte Böse* burst on the scene (Mitscherlich, 1964; Shabecoff, 1965; Kauders, 2014: 194–5, 207, 211).

In the West German context, Nazism and the Holocaust lurked behind nearly all the ensuing arguments. Almost no-one in the several rounds of debates over aggression that followed would use the terms 'totalitarian' or 'totalitarianism'.[2] But many phenomena with which those terms might be associated – from 'Big Brother' to 'brainwashing' to 'dictatorships' to the dynamic of mutual surveillance in 'an aggressive mass formation . . . in which the tiniest deviation of behaviour is no longer abided' (all mentioned by Mitscherlich) – were palpable reference points (1974a: 8, 11, 13–14, 28). At the same time, the debates would be filled with multilayered subtlety and innuendo, as within seemingly innocuous remarks there could be worlds of meaning. A new spate of violence and wars around the globe in the 1960s and after added a cacophonous diversity of possible resonances to what the Mitscherlichs had, in *Die Unfähigkeit zu trauern*, summarized succinctly as 'the aggression problems of our time' (172). The US's escalation of the war in Vietnam from 1965 on, the renewed outbreak of war in the Middle East in 1967, and eventually also the rise of violent leftist movements within the West whose actions were, in turn, met by state violence, provided countless occasions both to evade *and* to engage the actual intricacies of what had happened during the Third Reich. Current events complexly refracted the attempts to make sense of the national past.

III

Although the New Left student movement that reshaped the political landscape of West Germany after the mid 1960s liked to describe itself as antifascist, it is better understood as an 'anti*post*fascist' movement – in other words, a movement developed in opposition to the more conservative early postfascist settlement in West Germany (Herzog, 2005: 7, 139). Certainly there was something distinctively 'antipostfascist' about the fury with which members of the West German New Left would attack Lorenz from the later 1960s on. In the process, Lorenz and Mitscherlich were intermittently lumped together. In the pages of the venerable weekly, *Die Zeit*, one anti-Lorenz reviewer opined in 1969:

> One really has to call it tragic: Mitscherlich is the sole German psychoanalyst who is determined to pursue the sociopolitical responsibility of his discipline with full earnestness and whose voice carries weight with the public . . . But he hardly ever gets concrete . . . Mitscherlich's thinking is paralyzed by the unresolved contradictions of Freud's drive-dualism. In the final analysis, then, the decisive evils are after all only secondarily caused by society, because 'evil', hate, and pleasure in destruction are ineradicably biologically anchored in human nature.
>
> (Krieger, 1969)

Others were yet harsher. The editor of an anthology entitled *Zur Aggression Verdammt?* ('Condemned to Aggression?', 1971) blasted both Lorenz and Mitscherlich, but pointedly urged:

above all the psychoanalysts to spend the next decades on research and otherwise – remain silent. Whoever reads psychoanalytic texts, always again runs into the same, old hypotheses (of Oedipus-, of castration-complex, of the death drive, etc.), that get passed on in a kind of ignorant 'inbreeding', without a single convincing bit of empirical proof being provided.

(Selg, 1971: 147)

The escalation of the conflicts over the value and causes of aggression, however, had another effect as well, for they inadvertently triggered a sarcastic backlash in the mainstream media against what rapidly came to seem like the New Left's severe naïveté about the dark sides of human nature.

This second round of nationwide debate about the source and function of aggression drew in many further passionately eloquent commentators. In and around the generation of Lorenz (born 1903) and Mitscherlich (born 1908), there was also: the Freudian Marxist Frankfurt School philosopher and beloved mentor to the New Left Herbert Marcuse (born 1898), the German-British psychoanalyst Paula Heimann (born 1899), the neo-Freudian social psychologist Erich Fromm (born 1900), the émigré philosopher Hannah Arendt (born 1906), and the Viennese-Los Angelean analyst and specialist on terrorism and hostages Friedrich Hacker (born 1914). In the intermediate generation (born 1928–33), there was: the philosopher and publicist Arno Plack, the philosopher Rolf Denker, the historian Hermann Glaser, and the poet and journalist Hans Krieger. And in the younger generation there was Mitscherlich's assistant at the Sigmund Freud Institute, the social psychologist Klaus Horn, as well as the psychologist Herbert Selg, the education specialist Hanns-Dietrich Dann, the sociologists Wolf Lepenies and Helmut Nolte, and the political artist Hans-Georg Rauch, among many others.

The debate also drew in new advocates for Lorenz, including Lorenz's student, the ethologist-anthropologist Irenäus Eibl-Eibesfeldt, the author of *Liebe und Hass* ('Love and Hate', 1970), which asserted early on in passing that *both* ethology and psychoanalysis 'have established that man has an innate aggressive drive', took sideswipes at Lorenz's left-wing critics, and later in the book mocked the New Left's sex-radical communal experiments (13, 265–7). In subsequent writings, Eibl-Eibesfeldt took aim at the gullibility of the New Left's 'educational optimism' and expressed doubt 'that one can prevent the development of undesirable tendencies simply through appropriate childrearing and somehow thereby create a society without pecking order and without aggression' (quoted in Horn, 1974a: 192).

Strikingly, some of Lorenz's critics fussed a great deal over whether or not Freud himself had really been committed to the notion of a death drive, with some pointing out that Freud had conceded the idea was speculative, others that Freud had, after all, resisted it for twenty years, and yet others noting the incoherencies that had ensued for Freud as he explored the idea and how he had subsequently contradicted or modified the notion once more (Denker, 1966: 97; Krieger, 1969; Lepenies and Nolte, 1971: 104–5). Others, like the historian Hermann Glaser, author of the widely acclaimed *Eros in der Politik* ('Eros in Politics', 1967), simply side-stepped the problem by accepting without complaint a dualist drive theory that saw aggression as a drive comparable to libido, while nonetheless spending the bulk of his text accumulating evidence that a culture based in sexual repression exponentially fuelled the prevalence of aggression. Precisely *because* Freud had been alert to 'the dark pull of evil', Glaser ventured, it was all the more important to attend to what Freud had said about the damage done by sexual repression and to work toward an 'eroticized' society in which human beings lived 'in freedom', and in which 'reason is no longer oppressive, but open to sensuality' (28, 258–9).[3] But many who were unsettled or disgusted by Lorenz – and even more alarmed by 'what great popularity is enjoyed in Germany by the aggression-drive hypothesis' – actively sought substitute models to explain human behaviour and were adamant that there could be no such thing as a non-libidinal drive; they emphasized instead that aggression was above all a *learned* behaviour, and that there was much that could practically be done to discourage its spread (Selg, 1971: 9).

Among the most ardent critics of Lorenz were also those who strove to combine a recovery of the work of the Freudian Marxist Wilhelm Reich (who had famously contended in the 1920s and1930s, in numerous variations, that aggression was the result of a lack of sexual satisfaction) with an updated version of the 'frustration-aggression' theories of inter- and intra-group violence and scapegoating developed by psychologist John Dollard and his team at Yale, which had grown out of Dollard's fieldwork on race relations in the US South. The philosopher Arno Plack, for example, was outraged by what he diagnosed as Lorenz's feat in making not sex but aggression 'the *Ur*-drive, the drive of all drives, that moves everything that is living' (1967: 249; cf. Lepenies and Nolte, 1971: 117). Plack's book, *Die Gesellschaft und das Böse: Eine Kritik der herrschenden Moral* ('Society and Evil: A Critique of the Dominant Morality', 1967) was meant – as was made clear by both the title and the cover format (which had the words *DAS BÖSE* repeated over and over in huge black letters against a hot pink background) – as a definitive rebuttal to Lorenz. For Plack, the enthusiasm for Lorenz and the public scepticism about the New Left's efforts at sexual liberation were all part of one big package of misconceived morality. It was the dominant morality, in Plack's view, that repressed and thereby perverted the sexual drive and made pleasure in brutality and killing pervasive. As Plack reductively but fervently declared: 'It would be wrong to hold the view that all of what happened in Auschwitz was typically German. It was typical for a society that suppresses sexuality' (1967: 309).

Yet another variation, meanwhile, involved the reflections of Herbert Marcuse. He remained an unapologetic advocate, as he had been since the 1950s, for a radical and utopian understanding of the Freudian inheritance. However, simultaneously he continued to mull over a puzzle that had long preoccupied many members of the Frankfurt School: how the increasing powerlessness experienced by individuals in a competitive-technological society exacerbated aggression and diminished individuals' capacity for political resistance (Marcuse *et al.*, 1968: 7–29).

Mitscherlich's younger associate Klaus Horn also repeatedly built on Marcuse, Mitscherlich *and* Freud in order to push beyond the stalemated terms of debate. Horn persistently challenged the Lorenzians' instrumental concept of 'the biological', referring to their 'ideological', 'ontologized' or 'reified' approach, as they strove to trump the New Left. He regarded it as no coincidence that in the US as well, under the impact of the 'Nixon restoration', there was an increasing backlash against Cold War liberal social engineering projects – a backlash based upon the pretext that there was, as an article in *Fortune* magazine had put it, a 'basic intractability of human nature' (Horn, 1974a: 190–1, 193; Horn, 1974b: 62; Alexander 1972: 132). Horn had given a lot of thought to just how extraordinarily tractable human nature had proven to be under Nazism, and found this argumentative appeal to intractable 'human nature' repellent. The whole point of sophisticated psychoanalysis, he contended, was to understand not just the continual interaction of the biological and the cultural, but also, quite literally, their mutual constitutiveness.

IV

Nonetheless, already by the early 1970s, a new version of Freud gained ascendancy in the West German media and among a wider public, finally securing his status as august authority. It did so, however, by portraying Freud as a conservative and a pessimist. As late as 1968, the inventor of psychoanalysis had been celebrated in *Der Spiegel*, at least, as one of the great liberators of humankind from centuries of hypocrisy around and hostility to sexuality. (Here Freud was placed, rather startlingly, in a lineage with the actively anti-psychoanalytic but certainly pro-sexual Alfred Kinsey and William Masters (Anon., 1968).) By 1971, however, the very same periodical was explaining that Freud was increasingly being understood to lend gravitas to the downbeat idea that human nature irretrievably tended toward mutual unkindness: 'Freud's teaching about aggression and the behaviour research of Lorenz are ever more frequently being enlisted for the development of a conservative theory of society' (Anon., 1971b, 90). Again in 1972, *Der Spiegel* published an interview with the psychoanalyst Friedrich Hacker focused upon his tome *Aggression: Die Brutalisierung der modernen Welt* ('Aggression: The Brutalization of the Modern World', 1971) that addressed him 'as a Freudian [*als Freudianer*]' and in the same breath invoked 'Freud's view, delivered in the wake of the First World War, that a potential for aggression resides in the human being, that has to find expression, one way or another' (Anon., 1972). While Hacker considered himself as rather more balanced, *Der Spiegel* placed his volume, along with a new one by Robert Ardrey (*The Social Contract*, 1970), among 'the recently constantly swelling ranks of books in which the conservative conception of a hierarchically organized society is being defended against the New Left' (Anon., 1971b, 90). Perhaps this was not surprising, since Hacker's volume was graced with a foreword by none other than Lorenz. Here and elsewhere, Lorenz was blatant in his disdain for the young rebels (Lorenz in Hacker, 1971: 11; Lorenz, 1970; cf. Rauch, 1973).

To twenty-first-century eyes, the idea of accepting the existence of a drive for aggression might seem uncontroversial and banally, if sadly, obvious – or it could seem wrong but inconsequentially so. The pivotal point here is that under the very specific circumstances of a culture only a quarter-century away from (what had been at the time a wildly popular) mass-murderous dictatorship, the claim seemed, to many people, not just wrong, but emphatically and menacingly so – even if not all commentators critical of Lorenz invoked the Holocaust, but rather pointed to current events unfolding in their present. *Der Spiegel* surmised at one point in 1972 that 'The heatedness of the debate about this is most likely explained by the fact that people use the Freudian teaching of an inborn drive-potential in order to deduce a kind of legitimation of war' (Anon., 1972: 127). Indeed, some of Lorenz's fiercest critics put their case in these terms: 'The talk of an aggression-drive is perilous; it encourages the further spread of aggressive behavioural tendencies and heightens the danger of war in international relations' (Selg, 1971: 9). Critics also took issue with what was perceived as Lorenz's endorsement of a society based on constant competition and striving for higher status in the social pecking order (Plack, 1973: 10). Meanwhile, Erich Fromm sought to explain the appeal of Lorenz's 'simplistic' 'instinctivism' by suggesting it must be 'welcome to people who are frightened and feel impotent to change the course leading to destruction'. He added that a more 'serious study of the causes of destructiveness' would force a 'questioning of the basic premises of current ideology'. In other words, it would force an analysis of:

> the irrationality of our social system and . . . the taboos hiding behind digni-fied words, such as 'defence', 'honour', and 'patriotism'. Nothing short of an analysis in depth of our social system can disclose the reasons for the increase in destructiveness, or suggest ways and means of reducing it. The instinctivist theory offers to relieve us of the hard task of making such an analysis.
>
> (Fromm, 1973: 2–3)

In fact, however, there was even more to it. Many of Lorenz's critics on the left were convinced his entire purpose was to provide exoneration for the elder generation of Germans. A group around the young psychologist Herbert Selg explained – as *Der Spiegel* summarized it – the 'great public resonance' of Lorenz's book in West Germany by the way it 'seems to exculpate all those "whose slate did not stay completely clean", in accordance with the motto: "If we have an aggression drive and this drive must be expressed, then we actually can't really help ourselves, that . . . "' (Anon., 1971a: 109; ellipsis in original). This was an obvious gesture back to the past of the Third Reich. Already in 1966, the phi-losopher Rolf Denker had bluntly proposed as a reason for Lorenz's 'bestseller' status 'no doubt, for one thing, the ongoing discussion of the gruesome deeds of the Third Reich . . . One looks for an answer to the question, how something like that was possible.' However:

the way the book has been discussed until now will not galvanize people to actions against aggression or for its more sensible channelling, but rather is more likely to lead to disposing of the topic in a trivializing and affirmative way. For many the expositions will have a reassuring effect . . . Who knows how many aging, publicly unknown fascists who received this book as a Christmas present have acquired a relieved conscience from reading it.

(Denker, 1966: 94–5)

Along related lines – summing the tone of the debates retrospectively in 1978 – the New Left literary and cultural critic Klaus Theweleit, in his *magnum opus* on proto-fascist and fascist patterns in German history, *Männerphantasien* ('Male Fantasies'), meditated on 'the immense popularity of theories of human beings as intrinsically aggressive' and deliberately associated these theories with the self-exculpatory manoeuvres of the high-ranking Nazi Hermann Göring, who from his Nuremberg prison cell in 1946 had fatuously and self-servingly informed the American psychologist G.M. Gilbert that 'there is a curse on humanity. It is dominated by the hunger for power and the pleasure of aggression' (268). The analyst Paula Heimann was more careful, and made no presumptions about Lorenz's motivations. But she was at pains to emphasize the profound non-comparability of Lorenz's findings about animals, in which intra-species aggression could serve 'the preservation of the species, for which the preconditions are the possession of territory, food, mating, brood-behaviour, and which is limited in its ferocity by innate inhibitory mechanisms', and the kind of brutalities that were unique to humans. What distinguished the human from the animal was twofold: on the one hand, 'the feeling of pleasure that is derived from the tormenting and destruction per se' and, on the other, the human being's tendency to *rationalize* that pleasure in cruelty and 'to invent noble goals with whose help he disguises and implements his delight in destruction'. As she pointedly added: 'Our memory of the human concept of "*Lebensraum*" is still fresh; and with it the sluices to unlimited and calculated cruelty were opened wide' (1969: 105–7).[4]

V

One of Mitscherlich's most characteristic moves was to declare the insolubility of the theoretical questions. Already in *Die Unfähigkeit zu trauern*, the Mitscherlichs announced that:

We do not know for certain whether there is such a thing as primary destructivity (a genuine 'death drive') or whether the natural pleasure of aggression is transformed into the pleasure of inflicting pain only by experiences of impotence, humiliation, and loss of self-esteem.

(1967: 197)

Similarly, in 1969, in *Die Idee des Friedens*, Mitscherlich included a footnote repeating a point he had already made in his earliest *Psyche* essays on aggression (reprinted here with slight modifications), which summarily remarked that 'the difficult drive-theoretical question about a primary drive-pair (Eros-Destrudo) or a reactive origin of aggressivity can hardly be answered on the basis of our current knowledge' (80). Nonetheless, Mitscherlich undermined this agnostic stance at other points, frankly expressing his commitment to Freud's concept of a 'death drive', acting dismissively towards what he (interchangeably) referred to as the 'behaviourist counter-theory' or 'frustration theory', voicing objection to 'the doctrine that man's hostility is simply a reaction to the disappointments and the suffering which society has meted out to him', and distancing himself specifically from the idea he ascribed to Wilhelm Reich – that aggression and destruction derived from 'inhibited urges'(1956: 183; 1969b: 8; 1969a: 209; 1969c: 80).

At other moments, however, Alexander and Margarete Mitscherlich also freely incorporated ideas that sounded a great deal as though they came from Wilhelm Reich. For example, in *Die Unfähigkeit zu trauern*, they noted that 'The conclusion can hardly be avoided that aggression has to make up for missing and unattainable libidinal satisfaction.' And later in the book, meditating on how the phenomena of 'brutal excesses – such as torture to promote morality – contain an element of perverted libidinal gratification', they remarked that 'the fact that throughout long periods of Christian history sexual lust was damned, forced the individual to repress sexuality and to find partial substitute satisfaction in acts of destruction' (106, 198). Similarly in the title essay from his anthology on 'Tolerance', Mitscherlich entered into the Reichian spirit when he wrote about the possible causal relationships between sexual frustration and misdirected violence. He noted at one point that:

> The role of pleasure in cruel acts – or more precisely: the libidinization of cruelty – is often chosen as an escape in the attempt to satisfy inner tensions wherever pleasure as such is treated by the superego and from the heights of the civilized value-world as sinful, culture-less, animalistic and thereby is soured and ruined for the individual.

Or at another moment, but with the causation reversed, he argued: 'Tolerance contributes to the strengthening – the development and differentiation – of the libidinous side of world events. It relaxes and thereby subdues aggressive inclinations' (14, 30–1). And in yet another essay from 1970, this one on 'sexual enlightenment for grown-ups', Mitscherlich, in his inimitably awkward but moving phrasing, channelled a combination of Marcuse and Hartmann when he reminded readers that 'Eros' could only do its needed work in 'generating compassion . . . in countless interpersonal as well as global-political matters' if it was permitted 'access to the ego, to its shaping in conscious insight' (1970: 146–7).

Ultimately, Mitscherlich found the language he was looking for. In 1974, in an essay entitled *Zwei Arten der Grausamkeit* ('Two Kinds of Cruelty'), Mitscherlich – perhaps taking his cue from Paula Heimann, who had been his own training analyst (in 1958–9 in London) – expressed what had been missing, and tellingly so, from the ethologists in their obsession with proving the evolutionary origins of human aggression. The human animal differed from the others because it was not just aggressive but *cruel*. Holding fast to his conviction that 'the only psychological theory that, neither moralistic nor anxious, keeps in focus the time-transcending phenomenon of cruelty, is Freud's death-drive thesis', Mitscherlich offered his most thoughtful comments yet on 'cruelty as pleasure' versus 'cruelty as work'. Both were uniquely human. But 'cruelty as work' was the far more prevalent problem – and, in his view, the strongest evidence that the death drive was real. Cruelty as work was cruelty that was approved by a collectivity, rather than arising from a private predilection; cruelty as work was characterized by an absence of subsequent remorse; cruelty as work almost always depended on the absolute helplessness of the victims; and cruelty as work was 'asexually destructive'. As Mitscherlich put it:

> Cruelty as *work* knows no orgasm; instead it is about piece-rate labour, about managing one's daily allotment of tormenting and murdering . . . The destruction-worker goes home in the evening like others do with the feeling of having had a busy day.
>
> (1974b: 175)

Yes, this 'destruction-worker' might well experience pleasure, but it was in very few cases a sexual pleasure. Instead – and here Mitscherlich borrowed both from the survivor of Gestapo torture Jean Améry and from the narcissism theories of the Austrian-American analyst Heinz Kohut – it was an 'unhindered omnipotence-experience' – 'the realization of fantasies of a "grandiose self"'. These were the dynamics, Mitscherlich believed, that had been most in evidence at Treblinka and Auschwitz, but also in the forest at Katyn, among the Brazilian death squads, at Con-Son (the penal colony at which US soldiers tortured communists), and at My Lai. The Marquis de Sade's elaborate fantasies had attracted at best a handful of followers through the centuries. 'Eichmann, by contrast, was of a different sort. He provided the killings the way one provides a supermarket with wares' (1974b: 181–8).

It could be argued, looking back, that Lorenz's provocation pushed some rather productive theorizing into view that was unlikely to have happened otherwise. Mitscherlich, at least, had found himself in a continual double argument – on the one side with the market competitor Lorenz, but on the other with the often overly simplistic but indisputably morally passionate anti-Lorenz New Left. All through the post-war decades, Mitscherlich had worked on multiple fronts at once: striving to shore up psychoanalysis' cultural authority; channelling directly or creatively repurposing potentially interesting ideas from other disciplines; continually finding common ground between warring factions while with disarming graciousness appreciating insights from each; and endlessly circling around knotty, insoluble puzzles of human behaviour while coaxing his fellow citizens to think along with him.

Mitscherlich was a crucial contributor to a much larger, worldwide, post-1945 reorientation of the psychoanalytic venture. Psychoanalysis became accessible and emotionally involving for a wider lay public and for multiple neighbouring disciplines. The field turned its attention to many more themes beyond familial dynamics and sex, as the possible cultural-critical uses of Freudian thought were also updated and expanded. Meanwhile, and inevitably, in the course of these many developments, the 'it' that was psychoanalysis was changing.

Notes

1 The Frankfurt School re-émigré sociologist-philosophers Theodor Adorno and Max Horkheimer were significant figures in the effort to return psychoanalysis to the residually anti-Semitic culture of post-World War Two Germany. They were instrumental in promoting and encouraging Mitscherlich – even as they were not consistently impressed with him and sometimes found his work to be derivative of their own ideas (Freimüller, 2007: 213, 242; Hoyer, 2008: 324). Certainly Horkheimer cooperated closely with Mitscherlich in bringing prominent emigrated analysts back to West Germany to speak. But as late as 1965, Horkheimer was lamenting the West German public's ongoing indifference to psychoanalysis (Shabecoff, 1965). Not least due to the polemical stimulus provided by Lorenz and then to the rise of the New Left, that situation would soon change.
2 The one exception was the historian Herman Glaser, who first described Freud's view of sadism as being the result of the death-drive becoming defused from libido and directed at an external object and then elaborated on Adorno et al.'s theories about 'the authoritarian personality' (characterized by conventionalism and fierce adherence to bourgeois sexual norms, authoritarian submissiveness, uncritical behaviour toward idealized moral authorities within the in-group, and the suppression of ambivalent feelings towards those in power) before moving on to discuss 'the totalitarian personality', 'the totalitarian state', and (what he called) 'totalitarian sadism': 'The roots of sadism are always the same – the Inquisition is not structurally different from the Judeocide of the SS-henchmen, even if the latter could intensify the extent of the mass extermination due to technological options' (1967: 115, 121, 124–5).
3 'Mass murderers', those who engaged in 'tormenting and slaughtering innocent people, for example in concentration and extermination camps, in "cleansings", in expulsions', were, in Glaser's view (and in the view of countless of his contemporaries), 'product[s] of a repressed society' (1967: 122). For comprehensive discussion of the West German New Left's ardently held convictions about the causal connection between the repression of sexuality and the propensity to brutality – and the impact these convictions had on their assumptions about both Nazism's popular appeal and the causes of the Holocaust, see Herzog, 2005: 2–3, 6–7, 132–40, 156–62, 171–83.
4 Although rumours had circulated in professional circles in the 1960s that Lorenz had been a Nazi (and Paula Heimann for one had suspected), the height of the debates about Lorenz's ideas about aggression (1963–73) occurred without any public mention of the possibility. Not until 1973 when it was announced that Lorenz would be winning the Nobel Prize jointly with his fellow Austrian Karl von Frisch and the Dutch-British Nikolaas Tinbergen for 'their discoveries concerning "organization and elicitation of individual and social behaviour patterns"' in animals – and Lorenz's achievements, in particular, were hailed as proving that 'fixed action patterns appeared as reactions to key stimuli without any previous experience, i.e. without any learning' (Karolinska Institutet, 1973) – were journalists spurred to investigate, and find, Lorenz's (initially vehemently denied) NSDAP affiliation, as well as nasty eugenicist remarks he had put in print in 1940 about the degeneration purportedly caused by domestication (of humans as well as of animals) and in which he had unabashedly called for 'a sharper eradication of the less ethically valuable [*eine noch schärfere Ausmerzung ethisch Minderwertiger*]'

(Anon., 1973). Lorenz subsequently declared his own phrasing unfortunate and claimed that his use of the word 'eradication' had never meant murder, making semi-apologetic remarks in the autobiography produced for his Nobel acceptance (1973). Scholars in the 1970s and into the present disagree about the significance of his Nazi sympathies, some seeing him as at worst a badly naïve opportunist, while others are convinced not only of his malice but of the corrupting influence of racist and eugenicist perspectives on the quality of his science; further eugenicist writings produced between 1938 and 1943 were found later (Thimm, 2001). Lorenz remained rather uninhibited in his views, at the occasion of his 85th birthday in 1988 remarking in an interview about his annoyance that 'Humanity has done nothing sensible about overpopulation. One could for this reason develop a certain sympathy for AIDS [*Man könnte daher eine gewisse Sympathie für Aids bekommen*]' (Lorenz, 1988). An important subplot involves the impact on Lorenz's career development of the (Jewish) best friend of his youth, the ethologist Bernhard Hellmann, later murdered at Sobibor (Taschwer, 2013).

Chapter 8

Totalitarianism and cultural relativism

The dilemma of the neo-Freudians

Peter Mandler

Freudian psychoanalysis was, for reasons amply and richly covered across the chapters in this volume, particularly well suited to a war against a totalitarian enemy.[1] It was capable of offering a universal yardstick of 'normal' mental health that produced a rich language of reassurance for 'healthy' allies and an even richer language of pathology with which to stigmatize 'sick' enemies. However much Freud's own desire was for psychoanalysis to become an instrument of cultural critique, in the hands of American medical men it was already, by the late 1930s, working to shore up Americans' sense of themselves as a model (psychologically as well as politically) for the world, and in the 1940s it worked even better to brand Americans' enemies as an anti-model. Psychoanalytic diagnoses of the Germans and the Japanese during the Second World War illustrate vividly how well designed for propaganda purposes the Freudian language of pathology proved to be.[2]

Thus Henry Dicks, the Tavistock Clinic psychiatrist, though far from an orthodox Freudian, drew heavy-handedly on the technical language of Freudian psychoanalysis to stigmatize the German personality when recruited by the British authorities during and after the war to perform enemy analysis. He described the German personality as dominated by 'mother-seeking tendencies . . . banned from personal awareness', repressed aggressive feelings projected onto authority, nonconforming aggressive trends dealt with by further identification with authority and by 'counter-cathexis' or 'reaction formation', the 'surrender of the ego' in favour of authority and 'externalising the super-ego', an over-compensatory stress on 'secondary narcissism', repressed aggression taken out on the weak, masochistic longings exhibited in stereotyped idealization of loyalty and conformity, repressed anti-paternal tendencies in adolescent revolt often through gangs with older brother leaders, and the yearning for freedom transferred to the national group (through id projection); overall, 'an ambivalent, compulsive character structure with the emphasis on submissive/dominant conformity, a strong counter-cathexis of the virtues of duty, of "control" by the self, especially buttressed by re-projected "external" super-ego symbols' (Dicks, 1951: 100-61, esp. 104; and cf. Dicks 1950). And that was the ordinary German – the Nazi personality was far worse: 'likely to be men of markedly pregenital or immature personality structure in which libido organization followed a sado-masochistic pattern' with 'increased secondary ("defensive") narcissism' and 'tendencies toward hypochondriacal and schizoid or hypomanic features' (Dicks, 1951: 100-61, esp. 136-40; and cf. Dicks 1950). Herman Spitzer (1944) argued at about the same time that: 'The Japanese civilization pattern seems to be most closely akin to the clinical view of an obsessional neurosis. Even a superficial view shows the concern with ritual and avoidance, the masochistic elements, the intensely violent reaction to frustration and the general rigidity of behaviour'. Because aggression was 'much less securely controlled in the Japanese than in other civilizations', unfused with libido and given no healthy outlet, the Japanese were a nation of 'compulsive neurotics', and in wartime when they were finally given authorized outlet for their aggression against foreigners were capable of depths of cruelty simply impossible for other varieties of human being (Spitzer, 1944, see also Spitzer, 1947). Little wonder that in a war of all against all, when ordinary Americans were pitted against ordinary Germans and Japanese, Freudian psychoanalysis was immediately attractive to wartime propagandists as providing new ways to polarize good allies and evil enemies.

It was, however, less immediately attractive to those who wished to distinguish among allies – to develop propaganda or diplomatic strategies suited distinctively to different varieties of people without normalizing or pathologizing any of them – or for that smaller group who wished to separate ordinary, presumably healthy Germans and Japanese from their militarist leaders.[3] For these purposes a much more relativistic and less normalized psychoanalytic typology was necessary, and this was supplied between the 1930s and the 1950s principally by that group loosely dubbed the 'neo-Freudians', who had already in the early 1930s begun to dissent from orthodox Freudianism by arguing for a much more culturally constructed and thus more various psychodynamics. This dissent got most of them thrown out of the mainstream psychoanalytic organizations during the so-called psychoanalytic civil wars, when 'formal credentials, theoretical purity, loyalty to Freud, and generational dynamics' were paramount (McLaughlin, 1998).[4]

Ironically the neo-Freudian movement was partly inspired by the comparisons that émigré analysts drew between the German personality structure with which they had been most familiar in their earlier careers and the American personality structure they encountered after 1933 (though also by their assessment of change over time in the American personality structure brought on by the Great Depression). As Abram Kardiner, a non-émigré neo-Freudian, put it, 'even the most conservative and reactionary of the psychoanalysts had to recognize that the changes in the external environment had something to do with how people felt, because this was the first time they had ever seen it, black on white, and it was new to America'.[5] Discussions in these circles about social and cultural variation – among émigrés such as Erich Fromm, Karen Horney, Erik Erikson, Max Horkheimer and Herbert Marcuse, and sympathetic non-émigrés such as Kardiner and Harry Stack Sullivan – were (again in Kardiner's words) 'not permitted to continue . . . because [the Freudian establishment] said this was Adlerian, and by labelling it Adlerian they put the same stamp of disapproval on it that one does nowadays by calling somebody a Communist'.[6] Accordingly, most of the members of this circle who had been members of the New York Psychoanalytic Institute had left it before the start of the war.

It would have been perfectly possible for these neo-Freudians to have adopted the same polarized view of the German and the American personalities as did the orthodox, but simply on a less universalistic basis. That they did not had something to do with the Marxism embraced by many though not all of them. But it also had something to do with their creative engagement in the late 1930s with cultural anthropology; that this was important is evident in the fact that this engagement occurred semi-independently more than once, in the partnership of Kardiner with Ralph Linton, for example, or of Fromm and Horney with Ruth Benedict and Margaret Mead, or of Erikson with Scudder Mekeel and then later with Mead again.[7] These encounters represented a timely meeting of minds between psychoanalysts who were getting more interested in cultural variation and anthropologists who were getting more interested in psychological variation (the so-called 'culture and personality' movement). What the anthropologists brought to the table, most of all, was their unwavering commitment to cultural relativism – the idea that human plasticity under differing environmental conditions had led to an almost infinite variety of distinctive 'culture patterns', each with its own integrity, that the scientist's job was not to judge or rank these patterns but to show how they fitted the choices and experiences of the people who made them – and that this applied also to the distinctive personality patterns that could now be identified for each culture pattern. On the whole they disapproved of what they called 'abstract terms from psychoanalysis, such as guilt, sadism, masochism, etc.', which they denied had 'cross-cultural validity' and which they associated with Western imperial attempts to stigmatize peoples different from themselves.[8] This degree of relativism would prove useful for the discrete tasks I've already identified – diagnosing differences between allies, and distinguishing the culture of the German and Japanese people from their militarist leaders – but it would also prove highly difficult to sustain as an ideological project in wartime.

When war broke out, the neo-Freudians and their anthropologist allies found themselves on the horns of a dilemma. On the one hand, they wanted the Allies to win the war and they wanted to do everything they could to bring that about; they had a culturally specific tool that they could apply to the Germans, for use in prisoner of war (POW) interrogation, propaganda and black operations, and they had plenty of customers in various government and military agencies (the State Department, the Army, the Office of War Information, the Office of Strategic Services [OSS], and so on). On the other hand, their cultural relativism caused them to want to apply their tool to *all* cultures, in a neutral rather than in a hostile mode, and from the beginning of the war they were keenly aware of the danger that stigmatizing enemies psychologically might only confirm Americans in their burgeoning sense of the universal application of the American way. Different people adopted different strategies to deal with this inherent tension. Erich Fromm's *Escape from Freedom* (1941), probably the single most influential war-time book in a psychoanalytic mode, provided a devastating diagnosis of the 'authoritarian character' of the Germans, but didn't let the Americans off the hook, suggesting that the Germans were just a special case in a general psycholog-ical crisis of capitalism.[9] Erik Erikson, more empirically, undertook an in-depth study of German POWs; his diagnosis looked much like Dicks', but he stressed the short-term historical specificity of German character defects, brought on by military defeat and the failure of democracy and above all by the unique figure of Adolf Hitler. He was hopeful that after Hitler's downfall the Germans might be brought back to their senses by generous social and economic policies (Erikson, 1942; see further Hoffman, 1993–4; Friedman, 1999; Mandler 2013). Similarly, Ruth Benedict's study of the Japanese for the Office of War Information – which made the famous distinction between Western 'guilt' and Japanese 'shame' cultures – historicized the aggression that the Japanese had displayed in the war.[10] 'Japan has a history of peace and non-aggression that cannot be matched in the Western World', she wrote, and its recent reputation as 'one of the most aggres-sively warlike nations of the world' had come about only as a result of conflict with the West (Benedict, 1942: 10–11). She was even more hopeful than Erikson had been about the Germans, that in a post-war world, stripped of their militarist leadership, the Japanese could play a peaceful role in forging a brotherhood of man, while retaining their great cultural difference from the West.

Margaret Mead chose a different tack, eschewing enemy work almost entirely and focusing her efforts on offering psychological analyses of allies in order to support intercultural cooperation and provide a foundation for that desired post-war order of united (albeit different) nations. She spent most of the war anato-mizing the American and British personality structures in neo-Freudian terms, working closely with Erikson and her most psychoanalytically inclined collabora-tor, the British writer Geoffrey Gorer. Mead consciously distanced herself from enemy work precisely because she was keenly aware of the dangers of stigmatiz-ing whole peoples psychologically and of likewise privileging the peoples of the Allied nations, especially the Americans, thereby warranting a kind of psycholog-ical imperialism in the post-war world. But it is striking how few of her colleagues were able to maintain a similar self-denying ordinance, because of the urgency they felt about winning the war first. Even Ruth Benedict, who was as aware of the hazards as Mead, and spent most of the war working on allies or neutrals – the Dutch, the Norwegians and the Romanians, the Burmese and the Thais – ended up in the last year of the war as the principal psychocultural analyst of the Japanese for the Office of War Information (Mandler, 2013: chs. 2–4).

The dilemmas faced by cultural relativists when doing 'enemy work' came to something of a climax in two conferences held, as Allied victory appeared increasingly inevitable, to discuss psychiatric approaches to the post-war recon-struction of Germany and Japan. The first was held in spring 1944, jointly organ-ized by Margaret Mead and the psychiatrist Richard Brickner (not an analyst), to discuss psychiatric approaches to the reconstruction of Germany.[11] Brickner had been the author of a book published in 1943, *Is Germany Incurable?*, which had diagnosed the entire nation of Germans as 'paranoid' and prescribed for it an army of psychiatrists to identify the psychiatrically 'clear' Germans and treat everyone else.[12] Mead denied the applicability of a diagnosis such as 'paranoia' to an entire people, and in any case thought culture patterns were sufficiently sticky and cohesive that they couldn't (and indeed shouldn't) be 'treated' in this way; nevertheless, she liked the idea of a 'therapeutic' peace as opposed to a punitive one, and sought to work with the psychiatrists to reach a consensus on what was both possible and desirable.

Perhaps predictably, the conference was riven by deep acrimony about how fundamentally flawed was the German character and how much outside agents could do about it. The analyst Lawrence Kubie took up Brickner's hard position that Germany was sick and needed to be 'cured by the imposition of outside force', preferably a UN occupation that would re-educate and re-socialize an entire people.[13] Another analyst, Thomas French, took the opposite, 'soft' position, essentially 'hands off', which was more to Mead's taste but which threatened a PR disaster by seeming to exculpate the German people at the height of the war.[14] Mead, together with the sociologist Talcott Parsons, had to engineer a delicate compromise, arguing as Erich Fromm had done for the 'situational' nature of the Germans' current problems and for a post-war regime that would repair the damage of Nazism without denying the Germans' essential Germanness, which neither could nor should be erased. Above all, Mead insisted in the conference's concluding report, Americans should not be 'cocky': any post-war occupation must 'not mean that we shall be imposing our own particular way of life upon the Germans. It will mean that we shall be helping to build attitudes that are essential to the continuance of a peaceful world.'[15] But the consequence of such rhetoric was that the conferees did get a reputation, in the febrile atmosphere of the closing months of the European war, for being 'soft' on the Germans.[16]

Later that year a parallel conference was held on the Japanese, sponsored by the Institute for Pacific Relations. Many of the same figures reassembled, including Kubie, French, Mead, Parsons and Brickner, now augmented by Japanese specialists. But some of the Japanese specialists, including Benedict, were even more shocked by the application of a universal (and they thought inappropriate) psychiatric language to the whole of a people – 'pathological', 'adolescent', 'neurotic'. When one participant read out Karen Horney's description of 'the neurotic personality of our time' and commented that it gave 'the most perfect description of the Japanese that he had ever read', another rejoined, 'the same results would be achieved by substituting the word "American"'.[17] And this dispute then went public when one participant wrote a blistering critique of the conference for the *American Anthropologist* journal, denying bitterly that:

> because of our enemy's undesirable character structure and our own desirable virtues in this regard (plus better firearms), we have the moral right to walk in

and reform, by force if necessary, the family life, education, and religion of peoples different from ourselves.

(Embree, 1945: 635–7)

Ruth Benedict agreed. It was partly to counter this suggestion that she published her wartime research on the Japanese as *The Chrysanthemum and the Sword* (1946), which became a post-war bestseller, arguing as Mead had done for Germany that a culture pattern could *not* be reformed by force, that an American occupation ought to adopt the minimal measures necessary to help the Japanese re-establish their own equilibrium, and that above all Americans ought to be alert to the dangers of imagining other peoples to be psychologically just like themselves.[18]

In the end, Mead was probably right to feel that advocates of cultural diversity ought to concentrate their energies on friends and neutrals during the war, in the hopes that this could provide a foundation for cultural relativism to flourish in the post-war order. In the immediate post-war years, she was able to use her wartime capital to establish a number of influential projects for the 'orchestration of cultural diversity'; one of these, the World Federation for Mental Health, was a continuation of her wartime collaboration with psychiatry, aimed at thwarting 'Psychiatric Imperialism', as she called it, 'an attempt . . . to impose Western standards of behaviour on cultures whose character patterns stem from different "internalizations"', and aiming to find instead patterns of 'good human relations' that recognized cultural diversity (Calder, 1948: 148; 'The World Federation for Mental Health', 1950). Unfortunately, as we know, the war didn't end in 1945. Within a few years of 1945 hot war had been succeeded by cold war. Cultural relativism might still, just about, be of interest in mediating relations between Western allies but, increasingly, policymakers and public opinion were obsessed with relations between West and East – and once again, 'understanding' was not the goal, nor was a relativistic assessment of personality differences between (for example) Americans and Russians thought to be at all helpful in pursuing Western interests.

The problem that the neo-Freudians faced in confronting the Cold War was that the psychological differences they posited between national cultures were too great, too unbridgeable, for the purposes of policymakers seeking to fight and win an ideological war. It was not only that their goal of understanding (and 'orchestrating') diverse national cultures to make a multi-polar post-war order was seen as 'soft' on enemies – the problem they had faced towards the end of the war in advocating what was perceived as a 'soft peace' with Germany and Japan. It was also that the Cold War was shaping up to be a war between two universalisms – capitalism and communism, or two versions of modernization – in which neither side wished to create a multi-polar order; rather, they sought to convert the new world order to their own ideological position. For this purpose, the assertion of deep-seated psychological differences was seen as counter-productive. (It suited rather better non-aligned cultures; hence the continuing interest in 'culture and personality' approaches to national difference in emerging 'new nations' as a result of decolonization, in Africa, South Asia and Southeast Asia.)[19] In this altered context, even a 'hard peace' based on psychological assumptions, such as had reared its head among psychiatrists at the 1944 conferences, was unacceptable to ideological Cold Warriors. The universalist claims of both sides in the Cold War had to appeal to and be easily assimilated by all peoples of all nations. Peoples who were failing to adopt the 'correct' position could not be disabled by intrinsic psychological dispositions; they must be suffering from oppression or false consciousness, and must thus be ripe for 'liberation'. Economic, political or ideological factors thus took the place of psychological factors in Cold War thinking, both among policy elites and in public opinion.[20]

This shift was already in evidence in the immediate post-war years in the British and American Zones of Germany, where neither the 'soft' position of Mead and her allies nor the 'hard' position of Brickner and the psychiatrists proved attractive to the occupation authorities. Despite some early moves towards the use of psychiatric testing to identify 'Nazi personalities', who might on this basis be excluded from positions of authority, and the application of psychological methods to post-war reconstruction in education and religious affairs, already in the first year of the occupation there was a shift away from 're-education' to 'reorientation', on the practical grounds that the West needed as many German allies as possible, whatever their psychological make-up. Even Henry Dicks, the man whose wartime researches had successfully pathologized not only Nazis but the whole of the German population, in Freudian terms, had concluded as early as the end of 1946 that 'the experience of defeat and the disintegration of German society had profoundly modified the average German personality'. There was, it turned out, no need for re-education; the pathological traits Dicks had detected in wartime might not have been so deep-rooted after all, or at least exacerbated by derangements incited by the pathological state of war. He recommended that the Allies 'pay less attention to the negative qualities of their subjects and seek rather to find positive characteristics, to reject more and more the policy of excluding the unfit in favour of one which would direct the energies of the "greys"' – the vast majority of Germans who were neither pathological Nazis nor completely 'healthy' by psychoanalytic standards – 'into useful channels'.[21] This sudden change of heart chimed magically with Western policy: instead of psychological re-engineering, Germany needed only Western aid and propaganda to turn it into a loyal ally. And the push was on to hand over authority to an independent (and Western-aligned) Germany, with a minimum of psychological screening (Schwartz, 1991; Torriani, 2005).

A similar tale can be told about the Japanese occupation, though the handover was more protracted. Certainly psychological thinking about Japanese difference was at a discount, the quest to find the maximum number of 'good Japanese' made urgent first by the practical demands of occupation and then by the Cold War. As early as November 1945, the War Department was making efforts to cast off stereotypes of Japanese character it had been eagerly peddling a few months earlier; its account of 'Our Job in Japan' was ideological *rather* than psychological:

Our problem's in the brain inside of the Japanese head. There are seventy million of these in Japan, physically no different than any other brains in the world, actually all made of exactly the same stuff as ours. These brains, like our brains, can do good things or bad things, all depending on the kind of ideas that are put inside.

(Dower, 1999: 214–17)

In the end, Douglas MacArthur, the Supreme Commander for the Allied Powers in occupied Japan, was more optimistic about his own ability to rebuild Japan in his own image, and his personal policy, drawing on American optimism about the universal applicability of Western norms in 'modernizing' backward countries like Japan, won out (Dower, 1999: 220–4). By the mid 1950s Western social scientists were discovering, as Dicks had done for the Germans, that the Japanese character framework was neither as malign as the 'hard peace' faction had made out, nor as benign as the 'soft peace' advocates such as Benedict had claimed, but much more situational; under beneficent Western oversight the younger generation were 'evolving towards personal independence' and 'ready to assume leadership', again magically in line with American hopes and wishes (Stoetzel, 1955: 148–9, 202–6, 232–4).

The most startling evidence of this sudden de-psychologizing of the Cold War understanding of national difference can be found in the 'swaddling controversy' of 1949–51, which had the effect of first highlighting and then suddenly and permanently discrediting neo-Freudian approaches to the 'new' enemy of the Cold War, the Soviet Union. Even before the war was over, Benedict and Mead had understood that the future of their 'culture and personality' approach to international relations would depend on its applicability to the Soviet Union, as well as to their more familiar and comfortable subjects, the US and Britain. With funding from the Navy and the Air Force, they launched a series of enquiries into the Russian national character, which Mead fatefully entrusted to her close collaborator Geoffrey Gorer. Gorer's more orthodox Freudian language – and his uninhibited use of its vocabulary of orality and anality and polymorphous sexuality, even in formal reports to starchy military men – went down poorly enough. But it was the political implications of the neo-Freudian approach that now caused most offence. Gorer's depiction of the Russian people – from childhood fated to subservience and passivity, as evidenced by the peculiar Russian practice of the tight swaddling of infants – seemed to doom them to communist enslavement forever. At a time when American policy was shifting from 'containment' (suitably, a policy compatible with the 'swaddling' theory) to 'liberation', this diagnosis of the psychological incapacity of the 'captive nations' for freedom was ideologically unacceptable to public opinion, and instantly repudiated – indeed, ridiculed – by policy elites of both parties in the State Department.[22] The 'swaddling controversy' closed the door almost entirely on neo-Freudian understandings of international relations in the Cold War. Decades later, the only memory of neo-Freudianism that lingered in the minds of surviving policymakers from this era was the preposterous idea, basically traceable to Gorer, that you could explain Japanese or Russian behaviour by reference to their methods of toilet-training.[23]

Both orthodox Freudian and neo-Freudian understandings of national difference were hit by this shift; but the neo-Freudians were hit harder, because their unique selling point had always been their emphasis on the cultural foundations of personality difference, whereas orthodox Freudians (mostly clinicians) were more oriented to individual cases of pathology. In their place developed a set of theories about Russian (and, later, Chinese) difference based on economic and political systems, the most notable of which, the central focus of this book, was the theory of totalitarianism. While there had been a widespread desire in wartime among ordinary Americans to pathologize the Germans and Japanese as innately evil – leading to the neo-imperial dangers against which Mead, Benedict, Fromm and Erikson warned – during the Cold War ordinary Americans did not want to think of the Russians as evil at all, simply oppressed, and thus susceptible to liberation. They came to think of the Russians – as, after the war, they had quickly come to think of the Germans and the Japanese – as people just like them, but suppressed by aberrant leaders or political conditions. What theories of totalitarianism offered was an explanation for the victimization of the Russian masses and their successful control by an evil elite. The shift of emphasis from psychological to political factors offered the consolation of 'good Russians' (like good Germans and good Japanese) who were only rendered 'bad', temporarily and artificially, by unusual methods of top-down control. As David Engerman has pointed out, many Cold War Sovietologists viewed the party elite as the *only* thing that was radically different about the Soviet Union; they viewed the Soviet Union as a modern 'industrial society', whose people lived their lives more or less normally, though under the suzerainty of a dictatorial political system. This proved a congenial view to many policymakers, though ideological public opinion preferred a view of totalitarianism that placed even more emphasis on the malign effects of dictatorship on 'captive nations' struggling to be free (Engerman, 2009: esp. 182–6, 204–5, 222–4, 329–30; see also Hixson, 1997; Lucas, 1999).

There was, of course, a neo-Freudian version of the theory of totalitarianism too – Adorno's 'authoritarian personality' (Adorno *et al.*, 1950), which could be applied to the Americans under the spell of McCarthy as well as to the Russians in the grip of Stalin – but for that very reason the 'authoritarian personality' thesis fared badly in Cold War conditions. While Western audiences had proved surprisingly open at the outset of the Second World War to the similarly self-critical account of authoritarianism in Fromm's *Escape from Freedom* – in which monopoly capitalism led to 'compulsory conformity' even in liberal societies, though for class and cultural reasons very much more so in Nazi Germany – the polarization of the Cold War did not allow for a similar opening to parallels between conformism in the US and the USSR (1994 [1941]: 111–39, 207–10). As David Riesman noted at the time, 'the campaign against "psychologizing"' limited the purchase of the authoritarian personality thesis among 'self-styled realists' even in the social sciences, who liked to think that 'only power matters', and that power is 'a thing, a commodity, not a relation: Stalin's question, "How many divisions has the Pope?" is also asked in the social sciences' (Riesman, 1961: 437–8).

The only 'psychologizing' that seemed permissible in this context was that applied exclusively to the Soviet elite, rather than to the Russian people, aligned with the view that 'only power matters'. Thus the figure from the neo-Freudian circle who met with greatest success in the Cold War policy environment was Nathan Leites, a strong ideological anti-communist, who tried to steer Mead's post-war projects away from diagnoses of national character and towards psychological analysis of the Communist Party elites in both Russia and China. In his influential book *The Operational Code of the Politburo* (1951), written for the Air Force think tank RAND, Leites based his analysis almost entirely on the works of Lenin and Stalin to show what psychological characteristics were demanded by communist ideology, and thus differentiated the convinced party elite from the detached masses. *The Operational Code* was hailed as 'the most challenging and decisive analysis of the Kremlin's techniques' since the early post-war writings of George Kennan, and used during the Korean War as a 'tactical manual' for negotiations with Communist leaders. As the sociologist Daniel Bell pointed out at the time, it revived the 'great man' theory of history, exculpating (or excluding) the mass of the people, and focusing attention on the psychological make-up of a small handful of leaders (Leites, 1951; Rosten, 1951; Bell, 1962 [1958]; Robin, 2001: 131–43; Kuklick, 2006: 32–52).

With Leites's theory of elite psychology we have come closer to the clinical ideal of individual pathology and certainly far from the culturally based diagnoses of the neo-Freudian 'culture and personality' school.[24] The kind of cultural relativism espoused by Leites's former allies in that school had no place in a Cold War world of competing universalisms. But, interestingly, neither did the pathologizing language of psychological difference generated by psychiatrists and psychoanalysts for enemy propaganda in the world war. The lessons of the post-war reconstruction of Germany and Japan had been learnt: the flaws lay not in 'national character', but in the abuse of power and leadership. The 'enemies' of the Cold War were not whole peoples, but bad leaders and their oppressive tools of control. Psychological difference was neither a blessing nor a curse; it might only be a personal quirk. For this reason, neo-Freudianism fared rather better in the post-war world as a guide for understanding individual differences *within* rather than *between* cultures.[25]

Notes

1 A version of this chapter was given as the Jacob Talmon Memorial Lecture at the Hebrew University of Jerusalem in June 2014. I am grateful to my host, Dror Wahrman, to the Talmon family, and to the audience for their generous and perceptive criticism, and also to the editors of this volume for helpful comments on an earlier draft.

2 For the application of specifically psychoanalytic thinking to 'enemy' propaganda during the war, see, on Germany, Hoffman (1982: 68–87) and Pick (2012); on Japan, Dower (1986 esp. 123–36).

3 I discuss the case of the Boasian anthropologists, whose strong cultural relativism made them generally less interested in pathologizing either ally or enemy cultures, in *Return from the Natives: How Margaret Mead Won the Second World War and Lost the Cold War* (Mandler, 2013).

4 My thinking in this chapter owes a great deal to McLaughlin's prescient study of neo-Freudianism.

5 Interview with Abram Kardiner, 171–3, 180–5: Columbia University, Oral History Research Office, Psychoanalytic Project, No. 590.

6 Ibid.

7 On the Linton–Kardiner partnership, see Ibid., and also Manson (1988: 27–72); on Fromm, Horney, Benedict and Mead, see Birnbach (1962: 45–83), Caffrey (1989: 248–53), Banner (2003: 296–312, 342), Brick (2006: ch. 3); on Erikson, Mekeel and Mead, see Friedman (1999: 134–9, 165–98).

8 Geoffrey Gorer to Lt Col. G.R. Hargreaves, War Office, 27 Apr. 1945: Gorer Papers, Special Collections, University of Sussex, Box 32.

9 Fromm's *Escape from Freedom* was published in the US in 1941 and in the UK as *The Fear of Freedom*; see further Alpers (2003: 104), Gitre (2010: 17–18) and Moore (2010: 183).

10 The wartime study was eventually published as *The Chrysanthemum and the Sword: Patterns of Japanese Culture* (Benedict, 1946).

11 On the so-called 'Brickner conferences' – though it was really one long conference, that met in stages – see Gerhardt (1996: 297–324), Moore (2010: ch. 8) and Mandler (2013: 144–55).

12 The book was edited by Geoffrey Gorer, at Mead's behest, though they found it intellectually and rhetorically crude.

13 Margaret Mead to Talcott Parsons, 12 May 1944: Talcott Parsons Papers, Harvard University Archives, HUGFP 15.2, Box 11.

14 'Conference on Germany after the War'. Second Day, 30 Apr. 1944: Margaret Mead Papers, Library of Congress, M31.

15 A version of the final report was published in 1945 at the war's end: 'Germany After the War – Round Table – 1945'. *American Journal of Orthopsychiatry* 15: 381–441; quotes from 427–31, 439.

16 On critics of the 'soft peace' option, see Casey (2005: 62–92). The classic statement of the 'hard peace' option, the Morgenthau Plan, emerged directly after the Brickner conferences.

17 Margaret Mead, 'Provisional Analytical Summary of IPR Conference on Japanese Character Structure', 16–17 Dec. 1944: Mead Papers, M36.

18 Ruth Benedict, 'Problems in Japanese Morale Submitted for Study by Psychiatrists', n.d. (1944): Mead Papers, M36.

19 See, for example, the work of Cora Du Bois and Claire Holt on Indonesia in this period, which was popular with Indonesian nationalists, and which was carried on later in Cornell University's Modern Indonesia Project (Burton, 2000: 156–75).

20 See Engerman (2003: 273–85) on the shift to 'universal theories of society, economics, and politics' in the understanding of Russia, although Engerman sees the Boasian anthropologists as playing more of a role in this shift than I do.

21 'The German Personnel Research Branch: A Brief Historical Sketch and Summary of Findings', 31 Dec. 1946: Gorer Papers, Box 32; and see further, Mandler (2013: 152–4).

22 I discuss this episode fully in Mandler (2013: ch. 6).

23 This is my impression gleaned from interviews with a few surviving members of Cora Du Bois's circle who had moved with her from the OSS to Asian desks at the State Department after the war.

24 Yet even Leites's approach was too psychological to attract many followers (see George, 1988: 3–4).

25 For example, in the post-war writings of Erik Erikson, Erich Fromm, C. Wright Mills and David Riesman.

Chapter 9

D.W. Winnicott and the social democratic vision

Sally Alexander

War aims

'If we are better than our enemies then we are only a little better', Donald Winnicott (1896–1971), paediatrician and psychoanalyst, observed in 'Discussion of War Aims', written in the summer of 1940 – a vital turning point in the war against Nazism, between the popular anger and disillusionment of Dunkirk and before the beginning of the London Blitz on 7 September 1940 (Calder, 1969). It would be rash to claim superior qualities that our enemies lack, Winnicott continued, as human nature was the same throughout Europe, despite differences in behaviour. 'Total behaviour' included recognition of historical responsibility. It took into account hitherto obscure factors in human psychology, such as unconscious identification with the enemy – including sometimes identification with aggressive or cruel ideas and the relief that comes when these are shared and acted out among a group. In Winnicott's view, Germany was not solely responsible for making use of 'Hitler's peculiar qualities'. Before condemning entire enemy populations, the individual must acknowledge the greed, destruction and deceit in 'himself if he is to appear civilized'; failure to do so resulted in projection, 'seeing the unpleasant parts of [ourselves] only when these appear in others'. Total behaviour 'includes this badness' which is often externalized and displaced onto others. One reason for Hitler's power over his enemies, Winnicott ventured, was that, 'he lures them into a position of righteousness which breaks down because it is false' (Winnicott, 1986 [1940]). Denial of the 'badness' inside was no basis for self-government – whether of individual, group or nation; denial was as dangerous to future peace as warmongering, or deliberate cruelty. Civilization depends on nations and individuals accepting 'historical responsibility'.

'War Aims' was a direct response to Winston Churchill's first speech to the House of Commons as leader of the wartime coalition government in May 1940. We 'fight to exist': Winnicott endorsed Churchill's rhetoric with a characteristic appeal for life and what might be gained from war.[1] 'We are doing no very extraordinary thing if we fight because we do not wish to be exterminated or enslaved' (212). It is enough to want to survive. But 'War Aims' was more than an argument for war – military victory – against the 'impotence' of pacifism. It was a contribution to the debate conducted in Parliament, among the armed forces, the media, in factories, homes and streets – everywhere in Britain – about the value of democracy and freedom and how they might spur a demoralized, impoverished population into the war effort (Todd, 2014: 124); a debate shaped in the aftermath of universal suffrage and the First World War, that 'fierce . . . indecisive war' (Greene, 2002 [1934]): 170), which underpinned post-1945 reconstruction and the building of the welfare state – the project of liberal nations throughout the Cold War (Mazower, 1999: 186). What – as well as life – was worth fighting for, Winnicott asked. Liberal nations must 'aim at a more mature stage' of emotional development in their citizens; 'we are trying to feel . . . as well as be free' (Winnicott, 1986 [1940]: 214).

It was dangerous to assume that people simply wanted and enjoyed freedom, Winnicott warned. People feared freedom and 'tend at times to be drawn towards being controlled'. Freedom from physical excitement or tension, for instance, was brief – 'interim' – and much less gratifying ('orgiastic') than erotic fantasies of slavery and cruelty that held many in thrall; while the freedom to live without external constraint – that is, solely according to one's own 'strict conscience' – was exhausting. It brought 'the free man . . . no relief from any ideas he may have of being persecuted' and he is 'left with no logical excuse for angry or aggressive feelings except the insatiability of his own greed'. War brought temporary relief for those who wanted to obey orders and created ample opportunity for small dictators – 'we have to hope they will relinquish their power when peace eventually comes' (212–16 and see also Freud, 1933: 212–13).

Democracy is the exercise of freedom, Winnicott continued. Freedom to vote, to take responsibility for changing leaders, means tolerating the 'eclipse' of our own opinions by the will of the majority – an achievement that involved 'much pain and strain'. But the 'feeling' of freedom, which 'confers dignity on the human animal', is 'too much to expect except of a few . . . valuable men and women of each era, who do not necessarily achieve fame' (219). 'War Aims', however, does not explain how 'mature sharing of responsibility' might come about. Ten years later, in a paper on democracy (addressed to psychiatric social workers in 1950, two years after the creation of the National Health Service), Winnicott suggested that infants are born with a potential for democracy which 'good enough environments', 'good enough homes' might nurture (243–58).[2] Work with 'unplaceable' evacuee children, the treatment of psychotic and borderline patients during the war (Winnicott, 1958 [1945]: 145), deepened his understanding of unconscious feeling and the environment – maternal or if necessary institutional – which might strengthen or repair the potential for democracy by developing concern and the capacity for creative living in the child.

'War Aims' was the first of several papers, written between 1940 and Winnicott's death in 1971, for a lay audience, which explored the relationship between politics and personal feeling, historical event and unconscious motivation.[3] These papers contain Winnicott's strongest convictions about psychoanalysis (Phillips, 1988: 98); they also reveal his deep engagement with the philosophical and political issues of the time. Winnicott's ethical reference points – 'historical responsibility', mutual dignity of victor and defeated, trade unions, 'negro' slavery as the measure of freedom – were touchstones of liberal democracy and international human rights in the aftermath of the Great War. His individual, besieged from within and without by the lure or threats of others or ideas, echoes St Augustine and John Stuart Mill, except that Winnicott's individual was driven by neither spiritual redemption nor educated reason but feelings and compulsions unknown to himself – man was no longer, in Freud's famous phrase 'master in his own house'. John Maynard Keynes' warning issued in *Economic Consequences of the Peace* (1919), which had galvanized 'middle' opinion between the wars, runs through 'War Aims'.[4] The Treaty of Versailles' vengeful treatment of Germany, Keynes argued, rendered central Europe's devastated populations vulnerable to demagoguery and violence – a 'new Napoleonic domination' arising from the ashes of Europe's 'cosmopolitan militarism' (Keynes, 1919: 272). For those willing to be 'educated' during the 1930s, Winnicott argued in 'War Aims', Mussolini's claim that possession's only justification was 'physical force' had been clear enough (212).[5] As Jewish analysts fled Nazism, culminating in the Freud family's exile from Vienna to Hampstead, London, in the summer of 1938, the brutalities of the dictators came closer to home.

Historians of social democracy and the welfare state usually overlook psychoanalysis's contribution to their making. Practising analysts in Britain were few (perhaps 40 or 50) between 1919, when the British Psychoanalytic Society (BPAS) was founded, and 1940; its focus on the individual unconscious and infantile sexuality seemingly at odds with the ethical demands of social need identified by collective movements.[6] Yet European and British psychoanalysts pioneered child analysis and the treatment of shell shock; the BPAS included many feminists, opened a free London Clinic in 1926 and, by the late 1930s, the pressure to comprehend the unconscious roots of fascism made the BPAS a bulwark of democracy whose most radical members, in particular the European émigrés, believed their work reached into the structures of the family and sexual reform – they saw themselves as 'brokers of social change' (Danto, 2005: 6).

Winnicott himself – born into a wealthy, non-conformist, Plymouth merchant household, with a 'depressed' mother, two sisters, several (female) servants, educated at Cambridge and Bart's (St. Bartholmew's Hospital, London) – fits exactly between Stefan Collini's Edwardian 'public moralists' and Richard Titmuss's 'thinking minority' of the 1940s (Collini, 1991; Kynaston, 2007: 55). Classical education, empirical science and an enthusiasm for scouting, athletics, music hall, verse and comparative religion – these shaped his English masculinity. Darwin and Freud were his mentors.

The first paediatrician to train as a psychoanalyst, Winnicott worked in voluntary, Poor Law and local authority London hospitals as well as private practice from 1920, 'settings' among the mosaic of institutions and research from which the Welfare State was formed (Harris, 1992: 116–17, 140). He and his audiences – psychiatric social workers, midwives, GPs, child guidance workers, teachers, free thinkers – *were* the expanding professional classes (many of whom read psychoanalysis) which by the 1940s included more civil servants, more women – a more 'listening, gentle public opinion' in historian David Kynaston's optimistic reading. They brought the post-war settlement into being and made it work (Kynaston, 2007: 231).

Winnicott – like William Beveridge and Keynes – was a liberal not a socialist. He opposed the 'nationalization of doctors' while supporting the face-to-face encounter between doctor and patient in an equal relationship of respect. He pioneered child analysis in outpatient clinics as well as private practice, explored infant feeling while advocating the need for public institutions (nursery schools, child guidance centres, foster homes) run by people, not bureaucracies – bureaucracies can't think. Rejecting his father's municipal liberalism, the First World War proved his social awakening. While a Cambridge undergraduate, he volunteered as an orderly in the colleges transformed into hospitals; then served as surgeon probationer on a destroyer for ten months in the final year of war. He never lost the feeling, he wrote towards the end of his life, that his being alive was 'one small facet' of something – some 'huge crystal' – of which his friends' deaths were other facets (C. Winnicott, 1989: 4, 12). Winnicott's political generation was perhaps the first and last in the wake of world war (1918) and universal women's suffrage (1928) to believe that everyone who had a vote was a ruler.

From his first reading of Freud as a Cambridge student in 1919, Winnicott knew that he wanted to communicate psychoanalytic ideas so that, as he famously wrote to his older sister Violet, 'who runs can read' (Rodman, 1987: 2). If his BBC broadcasts between the late 1940s and early 1960s almost realized this dream, it was because they met a willing audience – exhausted by war and death, longing for homes, employment, health and hope; we felt, Betty Harrison, a young trade union officer remembered, on the threshold of a new world with 'such a feeling of a new beginning' (Harrison, 1977: 6). The 'rhapsodist' of maternal devotion, in Anne Karpf's phrase, Winnicott made every mother emotionally matter – a vital often forgotten component of 'Never Again' (Karpf, 2015: 105). Winnicott's idiom of intimate life for the nation – good enough mothers, ordinary homes, protective environments, home as the factory/workshop of democracy – spoke to that yearning. Social workers, nurses, doctors gave him the most 'valuable' insights (Winnicott, 1989 [1967]: 577). But his patients 'paid to teach him'. Through listening, 'history-taking' and writing up case notes, Winnicott digested (to use his preferred metaphor for Melanie Klein's processes of introjection and projection) their words and thoughts, tapping into a reservoir of common experience in peace and war made up of unconscious fantasy including daydreams and nightmares.[7]

Unconscious feeling overflows the self in 'War Aims'. It fuels the jealousy that power arouses, the 'cruelty and stupidities' of petty rules and regulations, the fears that underpin slavery and emancipation, which he regards as one, (215), and the love of fighting (Bourke, 1999). Love of freedom will not 'beget freedom', Winnicott argued; it has to be forced on people. Yet nothing in the human environment was fixed (Keynes again). Change comes as each new generation, seeking 'solutions to difficulties in their own way', discovers that they have to fight, if necessary to die, for freedom themselves. Hope, paradoxically, resides in unconscious feeling itself. Acknowledge the force of greed in human affairs, he observed, writing at a moment of necessary hope, and 'we shall discover that greed is love in primitive form' (213–20). Love and aggression have the same human source.

Winnicott's ideas were formed in the matrix between paediatrics and his training analyses in the BPAS between 1927 and 1940. Nowhere were the 'cruelty and stupidities' of petty rules and regulations more vexed than in the BPAS at war with itself in the 1940s (in the wake of Freud's death) over child analysis and what it meant. These arguments and Winnicott's war work with difficult evacuees exposed a darker dimension of 'maternal devotion'. In people's unconscious fantasy, he wrote in 1950, 'the most awful ideas cluster around mother and infant'; the almost ubiquitous fear of 'woman' stems from the fear of 'absolute dependence' on the mother into which every child is born and which if unacknowledged is the source of the dictator's will to power (Winnicott, 1950: 248–55). The rest of this essay traces the emergence of those fears and the link he made between deprivation in the mother/child relation and the most lethal forms of mental intransigence – the most disturbing aspect of Winnicott's thought.

Psychoanalysis in London

The British Psychoanalytical Society (BPAS) was on the brink of division in 1939 for two reasons. The tight grip of the founders – a small group around Ernest Jones and Edward Glover – on the administration of the Institute, training programme and free clinic of the BPAS was one source of rivalrous conflict. The first series of meetings of the Controversial Discussions in 1942–3 was about democracy within the BPAS itself. Winnicott was a constructive presence in this phase. The more potent division, brewing since Klein's arrival in London in 1926, was between Melanie Klein and her critics over the method and meanings of child analysis (King, 1991).

Klein's analysis of children (including her own three from 1910) had aroused disapproval if not hostility from colleagues in Vienna and Budapest. She worked through the transference, using play in place of free association as the revelation of unconscious phantasy. Klein's insights – that the greedy, destructive infant experienced unconscious guilt and anxiety in the first weeks if not days of life; that the weaning process invoked the Oedipus complex; and that the maternal body was the source of omnipotent, phallic fears in the infant midway through her first year – mirrored and made sense of Winnicott's clinical observations of infant anxiety and fantasy. But Klein's London critics, who included Barbara Low (educationalist and founder of London's free clinic in 1926), Marjorie Brierley (an organiser of the Controversial Discussions, later an independent), and from the mid-thirties Edward Glover, co-founder of the BPAS, believed they broke with Freudian thought. They advocated a pedagogical approach to child therapy, sought the cooperation of parents, and questioned whether the infant or child's ego was sufficiently established to enable analysis of unconscious fantasy. The arrival of Anna Freud and her Viennese colleagues in London in 1938 strengthened this critique whose emotional intensity was heightened when Klein's own daughter, Melitta Schmideberg, turned on her mother's ideas, impugning her motives from 1933 (Groskurth, 1986: 200–300).

Child analysis had been practised in London before 1914, its path prefigured by the erotically ambivalent figure of the child which had surfaced in English law and culture for a century before Freud recast human subjectivity (Steedman, 1995). Freud's ideas about infantile sexuality were first applied, as far as is known, in the medical examination of the 'starved little bodies' of children in London County Council (LCC) schools between 1907 and 1914.[8]

Educated women were attracted to psychoanalysis; a new, open, profession in close proximity to philanthropy, teaching and social reform. Psychoanalysis and feminism shared a fascination with family relations, hauntings and self-realization (Raitt, 2000: 134–5); and mother and child were the icon of feminist campaigns for maternity services, family allowances, slum clearance, the abolition of home-work, minimum wage, and national insurance for married women (Rowbotham, 2010: 103–24; Thane, 1991). Feminists Jessie Murray and Julia Turner founded and ran London's first outpatient clinic, the Medico-Psychological Clinic (1913–20) in Brunswick Square, which offered eclectic therapies for anxiety, depression and shell shock for low fees during the First World War, five years before Freud advocated free treatment for the poor at the International Congress of Psychoanalysis held in Budapest just before the Armistice in 1918, and thirteen years before the BPAS opened its London clinic in 1926 (Freud, 1919: 167; Danto, 2005: 167). Leading members of the BPAS from 1919 received their first analysis at the Brunswick Clinic before they travelled to Berlin, Vienna and Budapest after the First World War (Alexander, 1995; Marcus, 2012).

The first two papers presented to the BPAS in 1919 were studies in child analysis, given by Nina Searl and Mary Chadwick. Barbara Low, Susan Isaacs and Ella Sharpe also worked with children (Paskauskas, 1995: 627–9). When Melanie Klein settled in London in 1926 at the invitation of Ernest Jones, and Alix and James Strachey, she counted Nina Searl and Susan Isaacs (both training candidates with Winnicott) and Joan Riviere (founding member of the BPAS and Winnicott's future training analyst) among her friends.

Paediatrician to psychoanalyst

Winnicott qualified as a physician in 1920. After a spell as houseman and casualty officer, in 1923 he was appointed child physician to Queen's Hospital in Homerton, London's East End, physician of rheumatology for the LCC, and child physician in Paddington Green Hospital.[9] He hired rooms close to Harley Street, the doctors' quarter since the 1870s, and sometimes referred families from his clinic there. In the same year he married his first wife, Alice, a potter and close family friend. Her father was a Methodist and gynaecologist – the latter being the qualifying exam that Winnicott failed three times (Rodman, 2003: 40). In 1923 he read *The Interpretation of Dreams* and began analysis because he could not remember his dreams, nor could he make love to his wife. Ernest Jones, founder and president of the British Psycho-Analytical Society (1919–42), whom he consulted, sent him to the heart of Bloomsbury, to James Strachey, Freud's translator and editor of the *Standard Edition* (*SE*).

Strachey, Winnicott's 'favourite example of an analyst', had spent months in Vienna with Freud engaged in 'something between a conversation and analysis'. He came from 'a very definite grouping in English society, the Indian Civil Service' (Caine, 2005). Erudite, sophisticated, apparently unaggressive (not with his wife, Winnicott noted), he 'was brought up in the cultural life' which Winnicott encountered only at Cambridge and which he believed should be available to everyone. Winnicott took from Strachey his trust in the development of a process in the patient which he could then make use of, a process initiated by what Strachey named 'mutative interpretation' made at Klein's 'moment of urgency' in treatment (Winnicott, 1969; Strachey, 1934: 9).

When Winnicott described his method of history-taking, his attempts to apply what he learned in analysis to his child patients – especially those suffering from nightmares – Strachey sent him in search of Klein because he (Strachey) knew nothing of children.[10] For ten years Winnicott moved 'in the learning area of Mrs Klein' who 'took the trouble to try to help me with cases and tell me about her own work' (Winnicott, 1989 [1967]: 575–6). 'Overnight' he 'changed from being a pioneer into being a student with a pioneer teacher'.

Winnicott's analysis with Strachey ended in 1934. He qualified as a psychoanalyst the year after, with a paper presented to the BPAS that explored manic defence as a form of omniscient fantasy (Winnicott, 1958). In it he distinguished between fantasy and inner reality. Daydreams and adventure stories, for instance, were forms of omniscient fantasy that escaped the fear and anxiety aroused by the sadism and cruelty of the infant's inner world – the 'badness' inside. Winnicott's excitement, his eagerness to demonstrate the idea of fantasy as flight, to grasp the unthinkable destruction and greed of the inner world – ideas gleaned from Klein – and to make these ideas his own, to add, as he put it, his own 'splash of paint', is palpable (greedy even) and he wanted Klein to supervise his training analysis. But Klein had already supervised at least one of his training cases and she wanted him to analyse her son, Eric (Winnicott, 1989: 4).[11] Lineages of transference and counter–transference make objectivity – so valued by empiricism – impossible. 'With our minds we are studying the very minds we are using', he explained to trainee doctors in 1945, 'and with our feelings we are examining feeling' (Winnicott, 1996: 4). Joan Riviere, a fluent translator of Kleinian thought, who had her own knotted history of transference with Jones and Sigmund Freud, became Winnicott's training analyst in 1935. Riviere 'wouldn't have it', Winnicott later recalled, when he expressed his interest in 'environment' (Winnicott, 1989 [1967]: 576).

'Clamour of need'

Winnicott meant different things by environment – from womb, breast, maternal body to house, street, institution. He had always needed to feel the 'social pressure', he wrote in the 1950s, meaning the queues at his outpatient clinics, as well as the stimulation of private practice and therapeutic consultations (Winnicott, 1958: ix). It took him about five years as a paediatrician to realize that the infant was a human being (Winnicott, 1989 [1967]: 574); not until 1942 did he 'blurt out' to a meeting of the BPAS that wherever there's a baby there's a mother (or her equivalent) – his most famous formulation of the 'facilitating environment' (Winnicott, 1989 [1967]). Whereas Klein had confirmed his understanding of the infant's capacity for feeling and that fantasy's energy derived from the pre-oedipal pre-genital drives, his emphasis on the bodily power of fantasy or 'illusion' (his word for the infant's earliest hallucinatory imaginings of the breast, the maternal body and its insides), on muscle, rhythm, breath, the indwelling of the self, the idea that the mind was built up through the psyche-soma – continued to differentiate his work from Klein's (Winnicott, 1984 [1962]; Winnicott, 1988: 7–10).

His first book *Clinical Notes* (1931) is usually read as pre-psychoanalytic. Based on the 'clamour of need' he encountered in outpatient departments, it was addressed to doctors – 'young and ambitious' – who embarked on general practice expecting diseases for which their training had prepared them, only to be presented with 'common disorders and symptoms' of patients, three-fifths of whom had nothing physically wrong with them. The 'vast mass of indefinite and chronic unwellness' which child patients presented – fidgetiness, itchiness, frequent micturition or defecation, projectile vomiting, fainting, joint aches, sleeplessness, loss of appetite (the list is as long as Anna 'O''s (Freud and Breuer, 1895)) – rarely fitted pneumonia, chorea, TB or rheumatic fever, common childhood illnesses of the time.[12] Their origins were psychological. They were symptoms of anxiety registered at different psychic depths which stemmed from emotional development that is 'normally difficult and commonly incomplete' (4). Children fell 'ill in feelings' (Winnicott, 1958: 38).

Events of everyday life – mother's pregnancy, the sight of a naked parent, two or three to a bed, birth of a sibling, use of a strap, death of a parent – might precipitate symptoms of anxiety which compelled the parent to bring the child to see him. Peggy aged 10, for instance, highly intelligent, a mimic and performer, lost all her confidence and vivacity when someone shouted at her in the street that she was not her parents' child. She lost her memory for facts, developed night terrors, remembered nothing before the age of 6. Peggy's story was common to many twentieth-century London children (Alexander, 2009). Adopted (the daughter of her mother's sister), Peggy spent two years in a Dr Barnado's home before her mother reclaimed her. Her parents had a child who died before she was born and she knew about this child. The 'complicated home life' did not make her ill, nor did the fact of illegitimacy. Winnicott saw her 'twice a week for about six weeks'; from this he learned something of her unconscious fears which had to do with 'the origin of babies . . . conception and coitus' – a gesture to Freud perhaps. The parents' well-meant inhibition might have 'played a part' in her distress, he thought; but Peggy's fantasies of anxiety and shame at being jeered at about who she was and how she had come into being needed time and a calm presence to act as a 'blackboard'. By listening and waiting, Winnicott found that Peggy was able to 'deal with the material which was already present in her mind', until eventually she was able to remember, 'hold her own in invective' and to do well at school again (107). She was better able to think.

Clinical Notes describes the visceral feelings which Winnicott's intense focus on the mother/infant relationship revealed. Parents, in particular mothers, were listened to with respect; their words and phrases and those of their children – 'dreadful dreads', 'night terrors', 'wee-wee', 'twittering limbs', 'creeping pains', 'nerves' – revealed a common sense of health and bodily feeling he incorporated into his prose. A word like self, he wrote, knew more than the physician.[13] He used drawing, conversation, dream analysis and play in therapeutic consultations or short treatments with children, filtering their terrors and fantasies through nonsense rhymes and magical thinking – the Opies' *Dictionary of Nursery Rhymes* (1951), or the Brothers Grimm rather than the *Golden Bough*.[14] Above all the doctor's desire to 'cure' must be curbed – he or she was not there to force knowledge on a child. Whenever possible, the doctor might leave things alone, keep only 'a watching brief', act as a special sort of friend, let time take its course because 'present struggle not future cure is life' (127). The clinician who can 'feel a child's feelings' fosters the desire to live.

Empathy was never enough, but Winnicott's identification with infants and children was swift and spontaneous.[15] Sometimes describing a baby he described himself:

> As I came into the room the baby (seven months) fixed me with her eyes. As soon as she felt I was in communication with her she smiled . . . I took an unsharpened pencil and held it in front of her. Still looking at me, and smiling and watching me, she took the pencil with her right hand and without hesitation put it to her mouth where she enjoyed it . . . saliva was flowing. All this continued in one way and another until, in the usual way, she dropped the pencil by accident. I returned the pencil and the game restarted.
>
> (Winnicott, 2006 [1965]: 172)

Watching the infant play with the pencil or spatula – the toy or prop always to hand in his weekly clinics – he caught glimpses of the child's inner world like a 'film strip' (Winnicott, 1958 [1936]: 47). The spatula stands for the breast or the penis, or bears the weight of the infant's fantasy 'of what a man might have', Winnicott suggested in 1941.[16] He went on, complicating the imaginary capacities and mobile libidinal power of sexual difference in the infant's mind:

> The truth is that what the baby later knows to be a penis he earlier senses as a quality of mother, such as liveliness, punctuality at feed times, reliability . . . a hundred other things about her that are not essentially herself. It is as if, when a baby goes for the breast and drinks milk, in fantasy he puts his hand in, or dives into or tears his way into his mother's body according to

the strength of the impulse and its ferocity, and takes from her breast whatever is good there . . . this later is known as penis.

(Observation, 1941: 63–4)

In the 1950s, Winnicott reiterated – in more sober language for the BBC – how the father (of unconscious fantasy) gathers up residues of infant feeling for the mother, or rather the two mothers of infantile fantasy – the object of libidinal desire, and the facilitating, protecting mother.[17] The mother yields up with relief the 'dead, uncompromising' elements of authority which the father (magically?) transforms into law, the glamour of the outside world and the 'rock of sexual union' for the child to 'kick against' (Winnicott, 1964: 113–17). Feminists in the 1960s kicked against this same rock of sexual difference – 'the heterosexual imperative' – breaking it like Humpty Dumpty into pieces, with the help of the pill, women's and gay liberation (Winnicott, 1986).[18]

Reliance on and respect for the mother's intuition, whether spontaneous or – as he sometimes recognized – cumulative generational experience and memory, was in place by the 1930s. Leaving things alone, letting time take its course, laid the seeds for his emphasis on moments of calm, the 'unexcited' states in which the child, through an object or thing – not itself – could find what they already knew, as Peggy did. But the mother's capacity for kindling inner aliveness is implicit not elaborated. Being alone in the presence of another (Winnicott's later formulation) enabled the emergence of the capacity to think; creative living depended on the mother's sensitive adaptation to infant need (Winnicott, 1965 [1959]).[19]

Towards the end of his paper on 'Appetite' (1936) Winnicott ponders the gap between fantasy and reality in feeding disorders. Anna Freud was the stimulus here. She had mentioned to Winnicott that there might not be a 'direct correlation' between inhibition in play (with the spatula) in the clinical setting and the actual feeding relationship at home. Acknowledging the need for research into this gap Winnicott suggested that the doctor's – his own – presence with mother and infant in the outpatient clinic might represent the father's place at home (a rare instance of identification with the father). After the war, increasingly the mother, not the father, was the model for the psychoanalyst's counter-transference. Mental health in the infant, he wrote in 1948, was 'laid down by the mother', her attributes being devotion, adaptation, disillusion, in summary anticipation of his important paper on primary maternal identification in 1956 (Winnicott, 1958 [1948]: 160).

1940 was a turning point in Winnicott's life and work. Aged 44 with seventeen years' clinical experience in London hospitals and private practice behind him, he embarked on war work and a new love with a 'ruthless' (his word) determination to strike out as a thinker using his own clinical work (Green, 2013 [1975]). War work, its setting another public institution, provided him with the opportunity to meet 'difficult' children aged 11–14 (excluded from his Paddington Green clinic), whose 'environment' had, for the while, failed them. 'Deprivation' made him realize the power of the maternal environment.

War work

British analysts were eager to enlist on the outbreak of war, 3 September 1939 (Roazen, 2000: 142–3).[20] Private practice dwindled. Many left London or signed up for military service, others were employed by voluntary societies, local authorities, the War or Home Office; others established wartime nurseries, schools, homes for evacuated children, institutions and activities, some of which were integrated into the institutional framework of the welfare state inaugurated by Clement Attlee's Labour government after 1945 (Shapira, 2013; King, 1991).

Between 1940 and 1945 Winnicott was employed as visiting consultant psychiatrist to advise on the treatment of 'unplaceable' evacuees in Oxfordshire.[21] Margery Franklin, a psychiatrist and psychoanalytic colleague, approached him on behalf of the Quaker-run 'Q Camps' (Fees, n.d.).[22] The billet was the condemned Bicester Workhouse, built to house 345 unemployed homeless men, 162 of whom lived there until March 1939. Long corridors, dormitories with blacked out windows, rows of beds and baths, proved entirely unsuitable for difficult boys. David Wills was the director, a Quaker and New York-trained psychiatric social worker, whose aim was to bring boys to a sense of responsibility by providing a vigorous and democratic institutional life. From Wills he learned that listening was more important than interpretation, Winnicott remembered. In this way, he 'grew smaller' (Winnicott, 2012 [1984]: 190–1).

In 1940 Oxfordshire County Council took over the organization of evacuation, including 'unplaceable' children, and employed Winnicott as consultant psychiatrist for the five hostels eventually set up.[23] Clare Britton, the psychiatric social worker responsible for his visits, organized him, liaised between him – the 'eccentric doctor' – and the nurses, psychiatric social workers, and other workers in the scheme. Winnicott, with the Board of Governors for each hostel, communicated with the Ministry of Health. His methods were unorthodox and improvised. He visited once a week, took the boys for walks, talks, played with them, encouraged their drawings, and interpreted their dreams, but he refused to instruct the other hostel workers.[24]

Winnicott treated 285 children who 'were difficult to billet' (Winnicott and Britton, 2012 [1984]: 64). Most he saw over a period of years. Bed-wetting, minor thefts, running away, petty violence – typical forms of antisocial behaviour – were a nuisance to be tolerated, they did not amount to a psychopathology. In the child or adolescent removed from home, such behaviour was a 'sign of hope', a message to 'the environment' that something good had been lost, which, with help from a reliable, sympathetic therapist or carer, might be remembered and start a process of self-recovery before deprivation became entrenched. The degree of deprivation depended on the depth of loss, its aftermath, and the length of time in which the memory can be sustained, which varies with the age of the child (Winnicott, 2012 [1984]: 152–3).

In 1939 Winnicott (with John Bowlby) had warned of the emotional risks of separating the child aged between 2 and 5 from its mother – something which 'most mothers knew' – in a letter to the *British Medical Journal*. A break in continuity did not just bring sadness, it might produce 'black-outs' with severe consequences for the child's mental development. The child under 5 was less able to keep the idea of a loved one 'alive in his mind'.[25] He also wrote about a mother's deprivation, how her own sense of unworthiness to hold something so precious as her own child, led her to cooperate with the scheme (Winnicott, 2012 [1984]: 28). Evacuation was a series of 'tragedies', he wrote in 1941; the best he could imagine for the scheme was that it should fail (Winnicott, 2012 [1984]: 21).[26]

In spite of his doubts, Winnicott discovered through the evacuation scheme that sympathetic foster homes and hostels could be of help. Some children gained from separation from a mother or family. He made twelve placements himself from his London practice. In 1970, shortly before his death, he described how the institution itself – its buildings, regular routines of meals and baths, having someone there – might provide a reliable, holding environment, a therapy for a child 'dumped' in one (Winnicott, 2012 [1984]: 191). The 1948 Children Act, which accepted his and Clare Britton's recommendations that care and foster homes should be responsible for a few children looked after by wardens who were parental figures, preferably husband and wife, who made their own rules, would 'stay put' and 'possess a genuine love of children', Winnicott judged an achievement (Winnicott and Britton, 2012 [1984]: 56–61).[27]

Families and homes as the building blocks of mature democratic citizens reached a crescendo in his writings in the mid 1940s, in tune with the wider mental climate post-war. 'Home Again', a BBC talk addressed to foster parents in 1945, filled London's streets with the sight and sound of children's games – hopscotch, cricket, gangsters (the Gestapo almost a benign presence); two or three rooms, with parents, siblings, perhaps a cat, a shelf for toys, signified the 'ordinary decent home' – the reward of citizenship for parents who managed to raise the child in the 'hard life' ahead (Winnicott, 2012 [1984]: 45–8). But however deeply his thought affirmed 'ordinary' families or incorporated the social environment, Winnicott's focus was always the human unconscious. He says nothing about racial health, 'racial suicide' nor biological 'natural selection', aims which punctuated even the most sympathetic social science of the time (Slater, 1944). All his social policy recommendations were humane, whether hospitals permitting daily parental visits (attributed to Bowlby, begun patchily in the 1940s), resistance to neurosurgery (the surgeon gets caught up in the patients' fantasies about the location of pain) (Winnicott, 1958 [1949]: 253), or ECT (in which the patient's suicidal masochism met the doctor's unconscious hatred of insanity) (Winnicott, 1989: 539–40). He consistently opposed eugenics, whether proposals for compulsory sterilization (1931), or genetic inheritance as an explanation of mental illness or personality. Heredity mattered but it was less significant in mental life than the relationship with the mother and the early environment.[28]

Winnicott's war work with antisocial children confirmed the value of 'therapeutic consultations', of short psychotherapies and psychoanalysis (when feasible) 'on demand' (Winnicott, 1991 [1977]: xv). Like Freud and Jones before him, he believed psychoanalysis was appropriate only for the few with time, money and inclination (Paskauskas, 1995: 342). Nevertheless, whatever 'therapy' a good institutional home might provide for the child with antisocial tendencies – emotional behaviour manifest in most healthy or 'normal' adolescents in his experience – severe deprivation was more obdurate. A child whose mother, or her substitute, had been unable to provide devotion and adaptation to need in the first weeks of life, or a 'child who had been bandied about', might suffer catastrophic deprivation – a sense of inner chaos, disintegration, persecution, a source of an inequality difficult to eradicate (Winnicott, 2012 [1984]: 160). The absence of, or even a break in, a 'good enough' environment could lead to the child developing a 'false self' based on 'compliance'; or worse, the child might break down or go mad (he disliked the term 'maladjusted'). Psychiatric illness could feel like confinement (Winnicott, 1986 [1969]: 230).

Winnicott's first wife, Alice, an occupational therapist at London's Maudsley Hospital during the war, took one difficult nine-year-old boy into their Hampstead home for three months – 'a most maddening, lovable child, sometimes stark staring mad'. This child's persistent truancy, disobedience and minor acts of violence 'engendered hate' in Winnicott such that he was compelled to lock the child outside for fear of beating him. From this experience, echoed in some of his patients, he reconstructed the mother's hatred as the harbinger of hate in the child (Winnicott, 1958 [1947]: 199–200). Complex feelings like hate, pity or envy were neither innate nor instinctual as he inferred from Klein; prefigured by maternal feeling they depended on some degree of 'ego organization' or integration in the infant.

Winnicott's Paddington Green clinic continued after the war; it was twice threatened with closure in 1948–9 when 8,000 mothers' signatures were gathered (Anon., n.d.), and 1955. After his father's death in 1951 Winnicott divorced Alice and married Clare Britton, who taught social work at the London School of Economics and later the Home Office.[29] In 1953 she began training analysis, on Winnicott's recommendation, with Klein. Winnicott, despite a weak heart, was twice president of the BPAS in the 1950s and early 1960s, produced the remarkable essays elaborating his understanding of maternal devotion, spelled out the foundations of creative life in the transitional space, the capacity to be alone, and explored play and regression as methods of treatment – work which brought him an international reputation (audiences for both his clinic and, after his retirement in 1964, his weekly seminar held at home, had long waiting lists).[30] Nevertheless, he felt excluded from the Institute's training programme, split in two after the 'Ladies' Agreement' established a cold war between the Kleinians and the 'Viennese' inside the BPAS (Steiner, 1985: 59). 'I have never been a mother', he wrote to Joan Riviere in 1956, asking her to intervene on his behalf with Klein, 'but still I believe I have a positive contribution to make however small' (Rodman, 1987: 96).[31]

Feminists in the 1960s and 1970s rebelled against social democracy's vision of home and family as the basis of national life. Raised on orange juice, free milk, and secondary schools (1944), they were children of the welfare state and impatient with its limits. Combining Winnicott with Bowlby and more generally 'British object relations', women's liberation charged them with confining women to marriage and home (and economic dependence), making separation trauma the ethic of social democracy.[32] Never – as far as I remember (I was one of them) – was the connection between the 'democratic way of life' and maternal deprivation reconstructed. Maternal devotion, ordinary families in good enough homes as the basis for government, had become an orthodoxy – the maternal superego – of the post-war settlement; the political context in which they had been advocated (total war against fascism and Nazism, the need to strengthen the child's inner aliveness and creativity as the foundation of mature independent citizens capable of withstanding totalitarian or dictatorial forms of thinking) forgotten or never known.

In fact primary maternal preoccupation was never 'destiny' for Winnicott; it was simply a state of mind – a 'fugue' – inaugurated in the final weeks of pregnancy (or not), sustained for the first weeks or months of life by some mothers but not all of them and not for ever (Winnicott, 1958; Alexander, 2011). Devotion was necessary at the beginning of life when the infant was absolutely dependent on the mother, or her substitute, for the meeting of infant need, and the development of the inner world, the ego and feeling (hate, greed, envy, pity). The infant's mental activity turns the good enough mother into a perfect mother, he wrote in 1945 (Winnicott, 1958 [1949]: 245). As the infant grew and learned to distinguish between the me and the not-me, to hallucinate the object, necessary disillusionment (an idea that had affinities with Klein's depressive position, though Winnicott never could 'think' with the death-drive) was established, and with it the capacity for despair. He supported mothers' right to work after the war (and urged Bowlby to do the same), advocated maternity provision, nursery schools, supported the recommendations of the WHO in 1950, and stressed the historical diversity of families (Winnicott, 1986 [1948]: 155–6). Mothers' own stories, words and insights drive the case-history narratives which underpin his writings – an archive of everyday life.

Afterword

Winnicott always knew the unconscious was unwelcome knowledge. By the 1960s his sense of people's resistance to psychoanalysis had deepened. 'Badness inside' was not 'everyone's cup of tea' – a signature phrase; 'no-one wants to know what close examination of personal feeling reveals'. Unconscious motivation was 'frightening', it 'disturbed' those new to psychoanalysis because it spelt determinism (Winnicott, 1986 [1965]). People feared psychoanalysis's potential violation of the private innermost self which was 'sacred', never meant to be known (Winnicott, 1990 [1963]: 187). When rebellious libertarian adolescents in the 1960s (their slogan 'make love not war') provoked the re-emergence of the authoritarian wish to condemn and repress, the irony was not lost on him. We had wanted to give children a good start, he noted ruefully; student revolt, race riots (feminism he might have added) provoked harsh measures which might 'eventually lead up to dictatorship' (Winnicott, 1986 [1969]: 228, 230). His political generation had lived and worked through two world wars, two periods of 'reconstruction', they never ceased to be vigilant in the pursuit of freedom and democracy. The price of ignoring unconscious feelings for the value of war, he believed, 'was no less than the disaster of a third world war' (Winnicott, 1986 [1965]: 176).[33] He came down on the side of hope – just.

Winnicott's insistence that 'we are no better than our enemies', on not falling into a false sense of righteousness by imagining that all the greed and guilt in the world is lodged in other people's hearts and not our own, injects the dimension of unconscious fantasy and inner reality into political thinking. His claim that dictators are everywhere, and that few are 'mature' enough to take responsibility for democracy, muddies the water between totalitarianism and parliamentary democracy. Mussolini's declaration of possession as violence, anti-Semitism, the Gestapo were manifestations of a common European legacy which led some to Nazism, others to liberal democracy. No-one is innocent in this description of human nature. Winnicott's insights follow Money-Kyrle's 'we are like people who go about not knowing their pockets are full of dynamite' (Money-Kyrle, 1978: 132); they anticipate Hannah Arendt, for whom the devastating conditions of totalitarianism include democracy's illusions about political participation and judgement (Arendt, 1973 [1958]: 312–18). Historical responsibility includes unconscious motivation – the deep recesses of the mind where greed and violence dwell, yet which is sometimes just below the surface and is what everyone knows but has forgotten.

Klein has been claimed as the psychoanalyst for the welfare state (Zaretsky, 2004) and celebrated for her belief in the right of every child to an unconscious inner life (Steiner, 1985). Winnicott too deserves that recognition. Working in outpatient departments, using the minds of mothers and children from the early 1920s, he argued for public provision and good enough environments consistently in talks, bestselling books, medical journals and BBC broadcasts, and for 'therapeutic consultations' in paediatric psychiatry. Aggression and destruction, the longing for subjection to others (erotic appeal of sadistic violence) is situated in ourselves, in the distortions, gaps and blanks of inner reality (Winnicott, 1958 [1935], 131). The dictator's will to power is rooted in 'fear of loss of control over disordered elements, fear of chaos', but above all fear of absolute dependence, on 'woman': 'the dictator can be overthrown . . . but the woman figure of primitive unconscious fantasy has no limits to her existence or power' (Winnicott, 1986: 253).

Unconscious fantasy is both creative and destructive. It will (and does) sabotage the democratic tendency in the individual as in government; it subverted social 'norms' embodied, for the post-war era, in William Beveridge's 'cradle to the grave', or Aneurin Bevan's council housing with 'inside bathrooms'. Ordinary homes and families, good enough mothers, sometimes fail. The 'tragedies' of the early evacuation scheme, petty bureaucratic rules, the attempts of elements in the BPAS to impose a rigid grid of thought and clinical practice, were the subsoil of totalitarian thinking. Winnicott was no egalitarian. Emotional deprivation was both more arbitrarily cruel and potentially more damaging than poverty. Nevertheless, his understanding of environmental provision – which might protect the vulnerable – extended from the mother, to community, street, police state and law (Winnicott, 2012 [1984]: 107). Economists and planners ignore the unconscious at their peril, Winnicott warned. 'Listen to the unconscious, not the planners' might have been his watchword. 'Human nature is almost all we have' (Winnicott, 1988: 1).

Notes

1　Churchill replaced Neville ('Peace in our time') Chamberlain as Prime Minister in May 1940, with Britain in action in Norway and the Mediterranean, the 'air battle continuous' (Churchill, n.d.).

2　'Good enough' comes from J.S. Mill, 'On Liberty', ch. 3 (Mill, 1910 edn).

3　They include: 'Thoughts for the Times on Democracy' (1950); 'Berlin Walls' (1969); 'The Pill and the Moon' (1969); 'On Feminism'(1964); 'Freedom' (1969).

4　Psychoanalysts in the BPAS who remained independent after the division of the training programmes between the Kleinians and 'the Viennese' in 1944 were named the 'middle' group.

5　Mussolini's invasion of Abyssinia in 1934 put paid to the League of Nation's policy of collective security, abandoned in 1937.

6　Michal Shapira, *The War Inside: Psychoanalysis, Total War, and the Making of the Democratic Self in Postwar Britain* (Cambridge University Press, 2013), is the important recent exception. See also Danto, 2005; Brooke, 1996.

7　Winnicott completed 70 full analyses, and collected 60,000 case histories. His archives (at the Wellcome Institute Library) contain unpublished papers and case notes.

8　Hobman, 1945: 95. School medicals were introduced by the Liberal Government 1906–11. For a detailed critical reading of the origins of British psychoanalysis, see Kuhn, 2014, 2015.

9　Rodman, (1999 [1987]): xv–xiv lists all of Winnicott's public appointments.

10　James Strachey's correspondence with Alix in Berlin in fact includes several references to child observation, and his own wish for a child with Alix (Meisel and Kendrick, 1986: 40, 125).

11　The fragment of analysis in 'Notes on Time Factor' is from Klein's son (Winnicott, 1996).

12　Winnicott believed that rheumatic fever had disappeared by the early 1960s.

13　For a valuable discussion of 'self' see (Abram, 1996: 268–89).

14　Winnicott conducted at least one internal examination with the child under anaesthetic (Winnicott, 1931: 30).

15　Children understood Winnicott, Tizard, colleague and friend, said at his memorial (Rodman, 2003: 40).

16　See also the discussion of pen on paper in the Controversial Discussions (King, 1991: 704).

17　Winnicott makes these two elements in the maternal relation a bridge between Klein and Anna Freud in Winnicott (1958: 239).

18　*The Child, the Family and the Outside World* was given to me on the birth of my first child in October 1965. I relied on Dr Spock.

19 The capacity to be alone, the third (transitional) space of creative living, and maternal ambivalence are Winnicott's strongest legacy in contemporary thought.

20 Three weeks later Sigmund Freud died of cancer of the jaw, from which he had suffered for seventeen years, in Maresfield Garden, Hampstead.

21 He had assisted Glover's research into the early effects of air raids on the civilian population (Glover, 1941, 1942).

22 Winnicott excluded very disturbed children from his Paddington Green clinic; they were too disruptive. Those he thought he could help he referred to his private clinic, sometimes deferring fees. Only two or three child analysts were in training in the 1930s.

23 For the transition from voluntary to local authority funding and management, see Daunton, 1996; Thane, 1991.

24 Lisa Farley's 'squiggle evidence' uses the war work to explore memory, silence, the unthought (Farley, 2013).

25 In 1972 my 4-year-old niece died of encephalitis despite three resuscitations. A child under 5 doesn't know to fight for life, her parents were told; she simply falls asleep.

26 More than one million children were evacuated during the London Blitz (White, 2008: 37–45).

27 For a more complicated account of the effects on the child of both deprivation – 'broken homes' – and institutions, see Winnicott, 2012 [1984]).

28 Freud had noted the absence of heredity in Ernest Jones' thinking (Paskauskas, 1995).

29 They lived in Belgravia; a plan of his consulting rooms appears in *The Piggle* (Winnicott, 1991 [1977]: 2).

30 For Henry Karnac's complete bibliography, see Rodman, 2003: 419–37. Lesley Caldwell with Helen Taylor Robinson is joint general editor of the Winnicott Trust's *The Collected Works of D.W. Winnicott* project (12 vols., forthcoming).

31 Conversation with Klein runs through his essays, but see Winnicott (1984 [1962] and 1989 [1967]).

32 Denise Riley puts maternal deprivation in its wartime context (Riley, 1983).

33 As well as the value of war, Winnicott in 'The Price of Disregarding Psychoanalytic Research' (1986 [1965]: 172–82) advocated the need for research on the 'idea of black' as it appeared in dreams and play, the bomb, and population explosion.

Part IV

Writing the history of psychoanalysis

Chapter 10

Totalitarianism and the talking cure
A conversation

John Forrester and Eli Zaretsky

This is the edited transcription of a discussion that took place at the London conference, 'Psychoanalysis in the Age of Totalitarianism', 2012, between Eli Zaretsky and John Forrester, chaired by Daniel Pick.

DP: Let me suggest we begin this conversation about psychoanalysis and its history in the context of 'totalitarianism' by thinking about geography. To look at this question from an American or European vantage point, I expect, might be very different.

EZ: That is a very interesting question; I was often criticized for *Secrets of the Soul* [Zaretsky, 2004] being too oriented to the North American experience. I was criticized in many different countries for this and I thought about it a lot. But it was only in the email exchange that John and I began in preparation for this dialogue that I realized the way in which that was a fair criticism and the way in which it was not. I think America is central to the history of psychoanalysis. All I ask you to do is just consider what this history would look like had there been no America. Psychoanalysis would be a very interesting side current of twentieth-century European intellectual history; it would be like structuralism or something like that. It would have been fine, and it might have had a kind of unity around the issue of the father, the role of the father and a resonance with the rise of fascism.

Earlier in the conference I criticized the use of the term 'totalitarianism', since it buys into the Cold War framework, which sought to equate fascism and communism. In doing so, I wasn't advocating that we go back and use the language of fascism versus communism that characterized leftist rhetoric from the 1930s through the 1960s. But we do have to recognize that that was the organizing discourse in the period when psychoanalysis flourished, or at least the latter part of that period. So psychoanalysis had something to say to what I would prefer to call the general crisis of the twentieth century, meaning the European crisis of the two world wars, the mass killing and so forth. And incidentally, I thought it was really extraordinary that, according to an earlier contribution at the conference,[1] Jeffrey Masson asserted that Freud never wrote anything about

Nazism [see Masson, 1992: 154–5]. What does Masson think *Moses and Monotheism* was about? Freud was not someone who would wave a flag and say 'Hey, this is about Nazism', but he wrote that book in 1938 in Vienna, and it is full of reflections on contemporary history. I think it is really very interesting that we then deal with the whole history of the Second World War and the Jews and the question of anti-Semitism and whether the Judeocide is unique and so forth but we do not refer to *Moses and Monotheism*. We do not recognize that *Moses and Monotheism* is one of the fundamental texts reflecting on the coming of war, in the way that we recognize that Polanyi's *Great Transformation*, or Auerbach's *Mimesis* are great reflections on the war. But we should.

JF: So my response to the question is to imagine the history of psychoanalysis without America. I am going to imagine twentieth-century history without America. Is that possible? The more you think about it, the more difficult it might get. But here is a go for the bit concerning psychoanalysis. Psychoanalysis was a fashion, and a very successful one at that, in America from about 1945 to 1970, because it took over the psychiatry departments of medical schools and other institutions, higher education institutions, and became identified with psychiatry (which was the last thing in the world that Freud wanted it to be). So American psychoanalysis, as one understands it historically, is the big mistake, from the point of view of the history of psychoanalysis.

EZ: Right.

JF: But mistake or not, be that as it may, this American psychiatric psychoanalysis between 1945 and 1970 was a very extraordinary episode, but not necessarily of great importance for the overall history of psychoanalysis. To help consider in proper proportion an outrageous claim like that, you want to add that whenever you look at psychoanalysis in *any* culture it is going to turn out that way – each episode is extraordinary in a different way. What about psychoanalysis from 1968 to 1995 in Argentina? That is an extraordinary story as well. What about psychoanalysis from 1953 in Paris to 1981, when *Le Maître* [Lacan] dies? That is an extraordinary story as well.

DP: Not everybody's master (audience laughter).

JF: I take it back (audience laughter). So immediately I want to say: yes, you could tell the story of psychoanalysis as the accumulation and contingent interaction of these local stories. That's the way I like to do it nowadays. So the American story will be just one of them, a truly extraordinary one I agree, but it is definitely local and specific. And would it have anything to do with totalitarianism in the sense that we are talking about today? Well, the most immediate source of contact is with the émigrés who come from Europe, who take over the institutes and societies of most of North America, in a rather surprising way, given the fact that they come in and have to change language, but they do so seamlessly. It is not the same in nuclear physics (where the requirements of the Department of Defense were so important) nor in in organic chemistry (where anti-Semitism played a significant role in excluding the émigrés from top American universities and industry leaders).

DP: Was it so seamless as that? Wasn't there actually a good deal of anxiety in the American psychoanalytic world about how to deal with this influx of European colleagues? Worries about unemployment, for instance? And wasn't there actually quite a lot of misery and hardship? It wasn't quite as frictionless perhaps as this story suggests.

EZ: No, right, Karl Menninger, who was a leading figure in mainstream United States psychiatry, said I never saw a group that had so many strange birds, referring to the psychoanalysts. I agree that, compared to other émigré phenomena, like Gestalt psychology, it was a fantastically successful process of assimilation. But I think you need a much bigger picture to deal with the story of psychoanalysis in these years because it was such an extraordinary episode. We need a picture of the twentieth-century world, if we are to explain psychoanalysis and, peculiarly, we need psychoanalysis to formulate an adequate picture of the twentieth century. The best history we have now, the *Age of Extremes*, Hobsbawm's great book (Hobsbawm, 1994), is an inspired beginning. Still, we need a conceptual history that includes, on the one hand, what I like to call the general crisis of the twentieth century – the two world wars, the hundreds of millions of people who were killed, on both the fascist Nazi side of it, and the Soviet side of it and so forth – and, on the other, Americanization, mass culture, the American century. We need to see these two sides of the century as related, not simply contrasted as the totalitarianism thesis does, before we can adequately situate and comprehend psychoanalysis.

So when I say that the United States had an incredible impact on psychoanalysis, I'm not so much thinking about the fantastic success that these analysts had in the 1940s and 1950s, which was really quite brief. Rather, I'm thinking about the integration of Freud's ideas into film, TV and culture, and the way that the US spread this kind of consumerist idea about what I call personal life throughout the world. This was achieved to such a degree that there really is no place in the world that has not been touched by psychoanalytic ideas. But how were they touched? They were mostly touched through American mass culture.

I think you have to understand why America picked up the talking cure with such enthusiasm, used it and then dropped it, so easily, as if it was never part of American culture in the first place. They talk about it now, and they talk about brain research and they say it is just fantastic, we are learning that not all of our thoughts derive from the conscious mind (audience laughter). This is how they talk in America, as if they didn't have this latest fad fifty years ago of psychoanalysis. It has to do with certain characteristics about America, about American history, about consumer culture and society, and the way these swept the world. But that is why I think this conference is quite wonderful: it brings in the questions of fascism and violence and so forth, which are centrally connected to the spread of mass culture, even though they are of course different. This overlap between mass culture and fascism – crucial though the differences are – was something Freud understood, as did of course such Freudian-influenced thinkers as Adorno and Marcuse.

JF: Okay, let me try another hypothesis. This is stimulated by Joel [Isaac]'s wonderful talk this morning.[2] He talked about the two phases of liberalism and fascism, and we might add Bolshevism and communism, as being in response to the failure of liberalism. And he said that, after the crisis of totalitarianism, liberalism came back – did you notice? – but it comes back in a different form: with a theory, a reconfigured theory of the self in particular, which may itself owe something to psychoanalysis.

So one version of twentieth-century history would then be that there is essentially a liberal consensus for politics at the beginning of the century, which is in crisis – for many reasons: capitalism but also the First World War puts it in crisis in an acute way. Then these other parasitic political discourses move in – principally communism and fascism. And then liberalism comes back. Now the interesting sociological observation to make about psychoanalysis is that it can only survive in a liberal society, because of the emphasis it gives to free speech, to freedom of speech, to free association: the fundamental rule of psychoanalysis requires that you can't think 'Am I being recorded? Am I going to be reported to the police?' The mandatory reporting laws introduced in some states in the US from the late 1980s on (legally requiring, on pain of imprisonment or fines, professionals – doctors, priests, teachers, therapists and many others, but not lawyers – to report to the police any information concerning illegal acts that their professional interaction with clients reveals), complicate this matter importantly, but let us leave those to one side for the moment. My hypothesis would then be that psychoanalysis, in some sense, is an ideological flowering of liberal society, both at the beginning of the twentieth century and then throughout the second half of the twentieth century, with these huge holes – the Soviet Union, where psychoanalysis could not survive, and Nazism where it was specifically expelled. Psychoanalysis is in some sense very closely tied to the fate, to the rise and fall and rise again, of liberalism.

EZ: I agree, but the difficulty with liberalism, as Joel said, is that it's procedural and formal, and liberalism was in crisis at the end of the nineteenth and the beginning of the twentieth centuries. And psychoanalysis was, in some sense, a way of complicating liberalism, by not presupposing the social contract, innate rationality, self-interest, *homo economicus* and so forth. In this respect, the relation of psychoanalysis to liberalism can be likened to the relation of feminism to liberalism, or at least the more radical versions of feminism. In both cases, we see an immanent critique of liberalism; in both cases, too, the relation to liberalism was mediated through social democracy. The whole of twentieth-century reform – I mean trade unions and collective action and the welfare state – is liberal; it is part of the history of liberalism.

So we should look at psychoanalysis in that context. There is a difference between something that's critical and something that's complex. Critical is always complex. Complex is not always critical. Such often praised values as irony, indeterminacy, pluralism – these 'liberal' values can contribute to the general obfuscation. If you look at the history of psychoanalysis overall as part of this whole transformation of liberalism, liberal values, liberal society and so forth, you see how it lost its critical capacities – largely, incidentally, in the same time and as part of the same process by which the 'totalitarianism' discourse gained hegemony. Psychoanalysis no longer is, in my view, a critical discipline; psychoanalysts no longer understand what is meant by critical.

I'll give you an example: if you read Freud's essay (Freud, 1928) on Dostoyevsky and parricide, he says, here is perhaps the most brilliant man of the nineteenth century and yet he winds up with the oppressors (meaning Tsarism and the Orthodox Church in Russia). How did this happen? Freud doesn't want psychoanalysts running around waving political flags; he takes for granted that there is a struggle in society between oppressors and people on the side of emancipation.

In the 1950s, in the creation of the whole discourse on totalitarianism, you see this in the way that the anti-communist liberals described the authoritarian personality because the concept described so-called right-wing authoritarianism and not left wing. That whole tradition that Stephen [Frosh] talks about [see Chapter 3] was red-baited out of existence in the 1950s. In that process Cold War liberals said: what liberalism is about is not being critical, because that's communism, that's what the Soviets do. What liberalism is about is being complex; it's having a view of how complex things are, of the need to be on the centre, of pragmatism and so forth. When psychoanalysts – at least in the United States – were absorbed into that framework they wound up, to use Freud's own words, being in the service of the oppressors, saying: 'We are liberal; they are totalitarian, therefore, we are going to bomb them.' Projection does not advance critical thought. Critical thought, by its nature, is self-reflective. And projection, now directed at so-called Islamo-fascism, is still going on in the United States.

DP: What you say reminds me that tomorrow we are going to have a paper about the collusion between some analysts and the CIA [see Chapter 11 of this volume by Knuth Müller]. But at this point I want to return to the idea that John raises about psychoanalysis flourishing in liberal, pluralistic societies.

Obviously, that's mostly – and preferably – the case; it presupposes the kind of tolerance and freedom of speech and so on that he is talking about. But I wonder, John, if you might say something about psychoanalysis under pressure? Where it has existed against the grain. For instance in the Soviet Union in the 1920s, before Stalin completely held sway, or at times in Latin America under military regimes.

JF: Well I think the difficulty about South America is that it might be a very uncomfortable truth for psychoanalysts to recognize that it can survive under some circumstances if the liberal professions are protected. And in that case you are not living in what you might call a total fascist state, you are living in a partial fascist state. There is the word 'total', which is crucial in totalitarianism. And I have always understood that totalitarianism means the obliteration of 'civil society' (this useful but tricky term, developed since the 1970s and 1980s).

In other words, under totalitarianism, all the semi-independent institutions in society (the classic examples – universities, guilds for an earlier era, unions for the modern era, all professional organizations) come under direct control from some higher authority: that can be the central committee, the politburo, or it could be the leader, in Hitler and the apparatus that reports directly to him. This is the sense in which the 'total' in totalitarianism covers both communism and fascism. In the ideal of liberal society there are many centres of authority. There is political authority; there may also be religious authority; there is legal authority, which is different from, or complexly intertwined with, the political – the last is one of the crucial ones obviously. But then there is also cultural, pedagogical and scientific authority: all the universities are in principle autonomous in liberal societies (which they are not in totalitarian societies). So there might be a kind of sliding scale here, in which some of the free institutions, the separate institutions, are being brought under the control of the state.

DP: Of course, it is painful that Freud, Anna Freud and Ernest Jones all hoped, well after 1933, that some sort of psychoanalysis could be salvaged within Nazi Germany. They mistook the situation at that point; even after the exodus of the Jewish analysts they thought it might be worth continuing to deal with the increasingly beleaguered, and also increasingly compromised organization in Germany. Is that picture right? What I have read of the secondary literature of psychoanalysis in the Third Reich suggests they had great difficulty seeing the writing on the wall: hence they went on corresponding until quite late on, hoping to keep something going.

JF: But they weren't sure that Nazism was going to go the whole hog, you might say.

DP: No.

EZ: Psychoanalysis has absolutely flourished under dictatorships. It flourished – I mean this is my point about it losing its connection to critical thought.

You give the example of Freud and Anna Freud and so forth in the 1930s, that shows the weakness already of psychoanalysis. They didn't know that Hitler would go the whole way but they knew that 80 per cent of the psychoanalysts in the Berlin Psychoanalytic Institute were Jewish and that they had been expelled. And they still thought, well into 1936 and 1937, that you could expel all the Jews in your institute, 80 per cent, and still go on with psychoanalysis. So Freud thought that, and I think that shows a really profound weakness in Freud's thought.

DP: Mightn't we put it less harshly and say it was a predicament for him?

EZ: No, it was a tragedy. And my heart goes out to Freud and to all of them. It was a horrible thing.

DP: Another point one might make about psychoanalysis in an authoritarian society, like in some of the Latin American states, concerns the profoundly different existential choices that were available, in terms of collusion or protest. We would need to look not just at the scandalous moments of cooperation with such regimes, but also at the history of resistance, a tradition of analysis that stood in opposition to such states.

EZ: There is the Marie Langer tradition and various attempts to meld Marxism and psychoanalysis in Latin America. When I was in Latin America I interviewed a lot of psychoanalysts in Argentina and Brazil and they said that it just flourished under the dictators because the dictators wanted to have a certain kind of cultural furbishing, as a sign of how up to date and modern they were. They're not like the dictators of the 1930s, they're the dictators of the 1980s (audience laughter). And they had psychoanalysts and so forth.

So I understand perfectly well that in an analytic situation you don't share politics with a patient. That in psychoanalysis we are dealing with the intra-psychic life of an individual and we are not reducing that to any social thing. But that is completely different from having an organization whose leaders think that you could still proceed after they are expelling Jews. Those are two different questions.

JF: Can I just complicate matters a little bit by distinguishing psychoanalysis as a practice and psychoanalytic institutions? A lot of people who are critical in your sense think that psychoanalytical institutions are irremediably anti-psychoanalytic, and that you can't have honestly psychoanalytic institutions, since they are deeply corrupting of the fundamental ethos of psychoanalysis. The French analyst François Roustang (1982) offers the clearest example of that argument, so that you could imagine undercover psychoanalysis going on alongside institutions that have been taken over or partially taken over. And that leads one to the suspicion that maybe psychoanalysis is always undercover, even within the most liberal psychoanalytic institutions. It is in its essence to be undercover because it is surrounded by an extraordinary set of barriers inherent in its practice. As Winnicott said: you have to close the door to do psychoanalysis. Both on the side of the patient and the analyst you have all sorts of constraints on what can leak outside. And so that is what I mean by a liberal society, in which you have things like liberal professions and rules of confidentiality, being the traditional home base for psychoanalysis. And whether or not you have corrupt left-wing or right-wing psychoanalytic institutions is maybe neither here nor there.

EZ: Of course, I understand that what goes on between a patient and a doctor or analyst is sacred, and that we need the liberal idea of the sanctity of the conscience or the individual mind – what Freud called '*Freilichkeit*' – for any analysis to exist. This is a value for liberals and for any conceivable left in my view. Of course, politics per se has no place in analytic treatment. This does not mean that psychoanalytic thought – among the most epochal thinking of our time – has no place in understanding politics and history. I need only mention such figures as Wilhelm Reich, Frantz Fanon or Juliet Mitchell to remind us of how central Freudian thought has been to the twentieth century. Now it is a fact that the general influence has been on the left. In fact, the one time psychoanalysis was appropriated by the right was during the 1940s, when the Cold War liberals painted it as anti-radical, for example in trying to psychologize the American abolitionists or other radical and revolutionary currents. When the analysts – like Bettelheim – bought into that, the fate of analysis was sealed. It lost its connection with human progress.

DP: Perhaps I can add another link here – I was thinking of bringing in the tradition of French analysts to which you, John, referred very briefly earlier on, and I want to ask how that fits into the bigger historiographical story of psychoanalysis and totalitarianism. And one could also take up something that Lyndsey Stonebridge said earlier [see Chapter 4], regarding ego psychology and what it was anxious about, or what it was trying to shore up the ego against. There is a familiar critique made of American ego psychology in terms of its focus on adaptation, which many read as an injunction to social conformism in the 1950s – its acceptance of so much of the American dream. But might this kind of critique have underestimated the terrible anxiety that ran through ego psychology concerning the potential return of fascism? That émigré generation which came from Europe and wanted to shore up the ego against something they regarded as grotesque? Perhaps what they were haunted by was the idea of so powerful a relation between fascism and the unconscious. So what they were seeking to entrench was not necessarily the post-war American dream, but rather to protect the 'normal' ego from something much more terrifying. In short, I want to get at the fact that the spectres of fascism were still around, in the post-war culture of analysis in the US.

EZ: I don't think I have to tell this audience that Freud is the creator of ego psychology and I think the theory of the ego is the high point of psychoanalysis. And I just think that the whole Lacanian and French attack on it was a travesty – it was ridiculous (audience laughter). I debated with Elisabeth

Roudinesco on this point.[3] Ego psychology was a moment when they were trying to turn psychoanalysis into a more general psychology. Not that it would be turned into a general psychology, but I still think that it has relations to neuropsychology and other areas of psychology and so forth.

So the American ego psychologists were trying to bring out the connection of the ego to society, the side of the ego that faces toward the external world and so forth. I just wanted to say, going back to my point about America and consumerism and the local versus the international, global character of psychoanalysis, that when I debated with Elisabeth Roudinesco on this point she asked: Why do you link the spread of psychoanalysis in the twentieth century to consumer capitalism? Why not link it to the rise of the state, the twentieth-century state? A question that is sort of related to this conference. But if you look at psychoanalysis in France, and how it entered there, you find it did so as part of mass consumption; it was the moment when France got television and automobiles and the sexual couple and the second industrial revolution and so forth, after the Second World War. That's how psychoanalysis entered France. And that's how ego psychology came into the United States; it was a fantastically liberating thing, and it had to do with consumer society and everything that is liberating about consumer society.

JF: Modern psychoanalysis linked to consumer society? I am uncertain about that claim. One of the things that may be wrong with it is that I am not sure it works for thinking about the history of psychoanalysis in Britain. British psychoanalysis has the peculiar character of being generated by a very closely interlinked small group: for the first twenty-five years, it was very un-Jewish, unlike nearly every other psychoanalytic culture. It was theoretically productive, a tradition that continues to this day, but also, strikingly, throughout its existence, even from its beginnings, very well embedded in the upper middle-class elites: that's where psychoanalysis has always belonged in Britain, unlike most other countries, including France. That's partly what the story of *Freud in Cambridge* is about.[4] Why did Cambridge go overboard about psychoanalysis in the 1920s? Well, psychoanalysis was perfectly formed for the upper middle-class elites who were working in Cambridge.

DP: Why? Can you just explain why it was perfectly formed?

JF: Briefly, as it's dangerous to ask me to start talking about my own research, since I may find it difficult to stop. In Cambridge in the 1920s, the upper middle-class elites in the making were wide open to the appeal of a scientistic 'banner' under which to advance a technocratic solution to social and epistemic problems: a new science to replace religion, a science-based morality, like Darwinism, in the form of Darwinism, to answer the crises presented by the Great War – the collapse of Christian morality and of capital, simultaneously. In the 1930s they were to look for the answers in Marxism and the ideal of social planning; but in the 1920s it looked as if psychology would supply the answer. In addition, these were elites that also often took on the liminal position of bohemian lifestyles and moral codes and outlook – these were anti-establishment elites (the Bloomsbury Group, J.D. Bernal, Lionel Penrose, Geoffrey Pyke and others). More generally, beyond the English example, the story of mass psychoanalysis, if it is going to be a mass movement, begins as a bohemian mass movement in the first thirty years of the twentieth century. And then in the later period you are talking about, maybe it is a consumer form of psychoanalysis, but everything was consumerism back then. But even here England may be different, since it remained an elite practice probably well into the 1980s. France receives its major psychoanalytic expansion as part of the post-war economic expansion. Germany gets it back, rediscovers it through Alexander Mitscherlich and others. But as to why French psychoanalysis suddenly becomes so interesting? That question is more complicated and has little to do with its sudden market success.

EZ: Of course psychoanalysis is different in different locales, Israel and so forth, and I do think that England doesn't really fit the model of consumer society that has been developed in regard to the United States. The history of psychoanalysis in Britain is different, just as the history of modernism is different. Modernism in the visual arts, for example, developed later in Britain than it did on the Continent.

DP: Can I raise another question before we open it up to audience discussion? Which is how far either of you think psychoanalytic thought has itself been reshaped by these issues? How far was its own history affected by attempts to reckon with fascism and communism, or to think about totalitarianism? There are numerous ways one could explore the linkages between the most dramatic and terrible events of the fascist period or the Cold War to analysis, either individually or collectively. To take one example, I gather Lacan got reports from the Nuremberg trials, I think via Jean Delay the psychiatrist who was there. Lacan had an interest in Sade, and sadism, and also in Nazism, but how these issues related to one another isn't clear to me. I was wondering if you had thoughts about how Lacan's thought, or for that matter some of Klein's concepts, or those of other major pioneers, registered or resonated with fascism and Nazism or with totalitarianism? One could also explore how Freud's concept of the death drive was taken up in relation to these political questions – for instance, how it was used by the Frankfurt School and others in attempts to explain the pathologies of politics, and how such work in turn may have affected models of the mind, or even clinical discussion.

JF: Here is the easy case for that kind of argument – and if the argument doesn't run for the easy case, we will realize how tricky it will be for the difficult cases. Jean-Paul Sartre writes *Being and Nothingness* bang in the middle of the war: in that book the fundamental concept is negation. What has *Being and Nothingness* got to do with totalitarianism, the massacres and the genocides going on at the time? On the face of it, nothing. It is very difficult to prove, even though he famously uses scenes directly drawn from the experience of war (in the section on 'The existence of others', soldiers under the watchful gaze of a hilltop farmhouse's windows). Well, if you can't prove it with Sartre you are not going to prove it with most of the others.

But what I am often most tempted to say about French psychoanalysis is that it does move into a ready-made ecological niche in the post-war economy, which is that of French philosophy and existentialism. In the period I am most familiar with, French psychoanalytic culture in the 1970s and 1980s, it was quite clear that psychoanalysis was in some sense taking over from philosophy. And, as a result, everyone educated since 1970 in France learns their Freud, the last of the philosophers, the culmination of the 'French' philosophical tradition, in the *baccalauréat*. Now is that a response, is French psychoanalysis, and before it existentialism, its direct predecessor you might say – is that a direct response to the Second World War? These arguments are not strong, however attractive they are.

Notes

1 Editors' note: a paper entitled 'National Socialism on the American Couch', by José Brunner at the Wellcome Conference in London, referred to earlier, 2012.
2 Editors' note: the basis for Chapter 2 of this book.
3 Editors' note: Elisabeth Roudinesco, the author of several books *inter alia*, on Lacan, and the major history of psychoanalysis in France, *La Bataille de cent ans*. The discussion referred to here took place as part of a series entitled 'Rencontres à la Villa Gillet', 3 March 2009, at the Villa Gillet, Lyons, France.
4 Editors' note: the title of a forthcoming book by John Forrester and Laura Cameron.

Part V

Mind control, communism and the Cold War

Psychoanalysis and American intelligence since 1940

Unexpected liaisons

Knuth Müller

Introduction

'You know that wars make psychiatry, but wars especially make psychoanalysis', stated the former president of the New York Psychoanalytic Society, Charles Fisher, in an interview with psychoanalyst Arnold D. Richards in 1985 (Richards, 1985).[1] Psychoanalysis had contributed to military psychiatric efforts to deal with 'shellshock' during the First World War, leading its proponents to hope that Freud's reputation would be secured and its fortunes enhanced. But as Freud wrote in 1918:

> No sooner does [psychoanalysis] begin to interest the world on account of the war neuroses than the war ends, and once we find a source that affords us monetary resources, it has to dry up immediately. But hard luck is one of the constants of life.
>
> (Freud, 1918: 311)

Although the end of the war was a relief to many (Freud included), for the political fortunes of the psychoanalytic movement it seemed a mixed blessing.

Two decades later another world war renewed the need for qualified medical personnel to deal with the vast numbers of military casualties whose ailments had been re-named by military psychiatrists as 'war neuroses'. This time psychoanalytically oriented expertise and treatment techniques were much sought after and a number of psychoanalysts were appointed to high-ranking senior positions within the armed forces. Their efforts not only fostered the growth of psychodynamically oriented treatment for US service men, but also gave psychoanalysts an influential standing within the psychiatric and military professions, as John Millet, a member of the New York Psychoanalytic Society, recalled in 1963: 'William Menninger revolutionized the conduct of affairs in the office of the Surgeon General of the United States Army during the war, recommending for important positions of command some of the leading young psychoanalysts in this country' (Millet, 1963). The rise of Nazism and the Second World War savaged the Continental European psychoanalytic movement but, at the same time, transformed the position and standing of American psychiatry: it gained unprecedented acceptance by the military services, intelligence agencies and the medical profession (Menninger, 1945).

As part of this trend, from 1940 various psychoanalysts in the United States began to collaborate with the US Intelligence Community (IC). Early activities (1940–5) of analysts in this field primarily focused on the immediate threat of Nazi Germany, fascist Italy and their imperial Japanese ally, and included studies of home front radio broadcasts and domestic morale, analysis of enemy propaganda messages, accounts of the enemy's 'national character', and psychobiographical studies of Adolf Hitler. A number of additional tasks that also originated in the Second World War continued and expanded during the Cold War years, for instance research into and operational use of potential 'truth drugs' such as THC, mescaline, sodium amytal, LSD and PCP. The aim here was to optimize intelligence interrogation techniques and to evaluate so-called 'brainwashing' methods by communist-ruled countries. Largely funded by intelligence agencies and branches of the military services from the early 1950s to mid 1970s, medical and psychological research projects also combined drug research with studies of sensory deprivation, isolation, hypnosis and stress (Marks, 1988 [1979]; McCoy, 2006). Such experiments were conducted mainly on unwitting subjects, such as students, soldiers, prisoners and mental patients – in one documented case with deadly consequences (US Army, 1975). A particular area of focus and experiment concerned 'regressive' processes; these were incorporated into various techniques of modern psychological torture that were summed up in the CIA's *KUBARK Counterintelligence Interrogation Manual* of 1963.[2] This chapter outlines the history and consequences of this particularly under-explored episode in psychoanalytic history.

Beginnings 1940–5

In 1940, almost two years before the United States entered the war, various proponents of Freudian psychoanalysis, some of them exiled from their European homelands, were developing collaborations with US intelligence in order to combat Nazism. Walter Langer, for example, worked for the Office of the Coordinator of Information (COI), a precursor of the CIA, then headed by Colonel William 'Wild Bill' Donovan. As a lay psychoanalyst,[3] Langer first served as a consultant to the COI (established in 1941) and to the Office of Strategic Services (OSS) between 1942 and 1945. Erik Erikson wrote several reports for the COI on subjects such as Nazi mentality, submarine psychology and psychological observations of prisoners of war in Canadian and US internment camps between 1940 and 1943 (Erikson in Schlein, 1987: 431–5).

In October 1941, the American Psychoanalytic Association (APsaA) wrote to its members with an enthusiastic endorsement of such contributions to the war effort: 'An exceptional opportunity has been offered the Association to show its mettle through the appointment of Dr Walter Langer', now head of the 'Psychoanalytic Field Unit' (PFU) within the COI, who was 'charged with the specific responsibility of mobilizing these resources of our membership'.[4] A note added that Langer would be assisted by an Advisory Committee, selected by him, drawn from members of the various constituent societies.[5]

A newly formed Committee on Morale of the American Psychoanalytic Association (APsaA MC) had already gathered in New York on 25 May 1941 tasked with facilitating contributions to national morale ('Notes and News', 1941: 555).[6] One of its first tasks was to gather material from analytic patients who held 'fascist, communist or similar attitudes' in order to 'discover and tabulate all mechanisms typical of such cases' ('Notes and News', 1941: 555). The aim was to identify patterns deemed typical of anti-democratic attitudes and to counteract these through psychoanalytically informed propaganda strategies. Soon a joint APsaA/US-intelligence-led programme of 're-education' by means of domestic and overseas propaganda was also envisioned. The Chicago Psychoanalytic Institute, under the directorship of Franz Alexander, began a '[p]sychoanalytic study of civilian morale through pooling of observations made on about 150–200 patients while under daily observation'.[7] This microscopic study was to be completed by more extensive observations made via social agencies and other clinics. The raw data would be gathered from the material of patients treated by Alexander and other colleagues, and then sent to the Office of Facts and Figures (OFF) of the COI, along with a preliminary report prepared by Alexander.[8]

The data collection focused especially on morale issues in relation to the war. Michael Grotjahn, for example, wrote about a 19-year-old patient code-named 'Michael Boy' who suffered from several traumatic events, including the occasion when, as a young child, he had accidentally shot and killed his younger brother with his father's gun. Grotjahn concluded that the killing was rooted in a neurotic animosity against his mother, 'who confesses that she preferred the younger brother'. Fraught with guilt and shame, the patient was utterly fearful of going to war, believing that he would pay for his earlier actions:

He is terribly afraid that he will be drafted and he is absolutely sure that he will not come back. [. . .] The more, in the course of analysis, the patient's traumatic neurosis is worked through, the more real is his attitude towards the war. He forgot to register when the sugar rationing started. He is not going to forget the coming draft registration.[9]

This passage illuminates in a disturbing manner how analysts like Grotjahn dealt with 'the problem of adaptation' during wartime. In other analytic societies similar initiatives were underway. David Levy of the New York Psychoanalytic Society also prepared nine papers for the OFF, containing material about patients he treated. They bore such titles as 'Psychoanalytic Study of a Communist', 'Psychoanalytic Study of an "Almost" Bundist' or 'Analysis of a Potential Nazi'.[10]

In addressing the role of psychoanalysts in relation to sociopolitical activism during the Second World War, Ernest Jones stated at the Sixteenth International Psychoanalytic Association (IPA) congress in Zürich in 1949:

The temptation is understandably great to add sociopolitical factors to those that are our special concern, and to re-read our findings in terms of sociology, but it is a temptation which, one is proud to observe, has, with very few exceptions, been stoutly resisted.

(in A. Freud, 1949: 179)

He feared that 'emotional short cuts in our thinking' and the resulting urge 'to follow the way of politicians' could lead the analyst to lose 'faith [. . .] in personal integrity and complete honesty' (in A. Freud, 1949: 179), which he considered benchmarks of psychoanalytic identity. In reality, psychoanalysts were far from being apolitical. In October 1941 Langer, by this time head of the PFU of the COI, member of the APsaA Committee on Morale and independent consultant to the OSS between 1942 and 1945, wrote two memoranda reporting that about 100 of 204 members of the APsaA were cooperating with his unit. So by this point, almost half of all APsaA members were, according to him, engaged, directly or indirectly, in intelligence work.[11]

Within the Committee on Morale there seemed to be a consensus that 'revolutionary political attitudes' are a sign of 'psychopathology' and thus suitable cases for psychoanalytic treatment.[12] Radio propaganda was thought to be an important treatment tool at the level of mass behaviour. Meanwhile, Ernest Simmel, the former director of the first psychoanalytic clinic in Berlin during the years 1927–31, penned a 1941 report for the COI, 'A Psychological Radio Offensive against Germany from a Psychoanalytical Viewpoint' (Simmel in Cavin, 2006: n. 45). This émigré psychiatrist and analyst, now better known for his editing of a substantial publication on anti-Semitism in 1946 (Simmel, 1946), proposed to the COI implementing 'shortwave psychotherapy' for the German people. The task of US propaganda, as Simmel understood it, was not to 'demoralize a mentally well-integrated population, but on the contrary to re-integrate the mental condition of a population already suffering from the demoralizing effects of a psychological offensive staged against them by their own leaders' (Simmel in Cavin, 2006: n. 47). Since psychoanalysts are specialists in fostering 'a process of maturation into the mind of mentally disintegrated individuals, and this by means of the spoken word only', he advised making the German people 'conscious of the psychological technique employed' by Hitler's regime:

> Nazi propaganda aims directly at the emotional forces of the irrational unconscious and tries to exclude any critical interference of the super-ego, either by paralyzing it (through dread) or by bribing it (by narcissistic premiums). We are able to counteract this 'technique' by diverting the attention of the individual from the content of propaganda messages to the mechanisms of their presentation. In this way, we block an immediate emotional reaction.
>
> (Simmel in Cavin, 2006: n. 47)

The Committee eventually formulated the steps to be taken. Langer proposed to Donovan that US propaganda could best undermine this attitude of distrust and suspicion within the German population towards US news broadcasts by strictly adhering to the truth in news programmes:

> If the communication is an established fact, present it as a fact; if it is a conclusion drawn from conflicting data, present it as such with appropriate qualifications; if only a rumour, present it as such with whatever sources are known but disclaim any responsibility for its validity.[13]

Langer's suggestions on how to apply psychoanalytic principles to US propaganda techniques included adherence to 'complete objectivity', aiming at 'creating trust above the news value', fostering 'an atmosphere of confidence and trust in the listener, in the subject-matter, [and in the] person who is doing the broadcasting'.[14]

In short, a trustworthy working alliance had to be built up, 'on the premise that he [the enemy listener] is not going to believe everything we are going to tell him and we do not expect him to'. Propaganda should be an empathic endeavour from a neutral point of view, not a weapon of assault, directed at people who already harboured doubts about their government. Finally, with respect to the timing of broadcasts, an interesting equivalence was supposed with the timing of interpretations during psychoanalytic treatment. This broadcast strategy, Langer hoped, would serve to supply information that the listener was consciously or unconsciously seeking, while at the same time 'we do our utmost to absolve him from any feelings of guilt arising from his doubts'.[15] Thus, psychoanalysts saw their particular contribution to the fight against totalitarian structures as lying in their ability to formulate an understanding of the unconscious dynamics at work in the German, Italian and Japanese population. Easing possible feelings of guilt in these populations was thought likely to lead to a more open reception of Allied propaganda efforts. Through analyses of enemy propaganda, Langer and his colleagues also hoped to identify unconscious motivational factors that might be exploited for Allied use. By regarding enemy nations as if they were psychiatric patients suffering from paranoid and omnipotent delusions, psychiatrists like Richard Brickner in his 1943 book *Is Germany Incurable?*, or psychoanalysts such as George Devereux, Henry Murray and Ernst Simmel,[16] suggested that that 'treatment' of an enemy population by mental health specialists, who took note of the 'illness', would be more helpful in the long run than punishments simply meted out by military or civil courts set up by the occupying powers.[17]

Langer's paper on 'Psychoanalytical Contributions to Psychological Warfare' shows how clinicians saw themselves as being able to contribute quite particular technical skills to the analysis of propaganda materials. It proposes, for instance, an approach that would analyse enemy radio propaganda by focusing on:

> the choice of a peculiar word, the repetition of a phrase, the recurrence or treatment of a particular topic which reveals to a reader, experienced in the manifestation of unconscious processes, the existence of an underlying trend which the speaker or writer is trying to conceal. Speeches and writings of the leaders are particularly fruitful from this point of view.[18]

Langer listed an array of tasks for clinicians within the intelligence realm and proposed that both enemy nations and individual leaders should become a focus of inquiry.[19] Analysis was apparently required of the enemy's literature, philosophies, religious tendencies, music, art, myths and superstitions, not to mention historical trends, heroes and national aspirations, in order to 'understand their behavior, attitudes and ideals in terms of unconscious conflicts and mechanisms'. He also recommended the 'comparative study of case histories of members of the various nationality groups who have been psychoanalyzed' in order to discover common unconscious conflicts, tendencies, emotional reactions, defence mechanisms and frustrations. This would be particularly important in connection with the Nazi character 'since many American youths in analysis at the present time show similar tendencies very clearly'.[20]

The plan was to 'frame a comprehensive psychograph of each group in which both conscious and unconscious factors and their dynamic interrelationships are represented'. By evaluating enemy manoeuvres, both on the military and psychological fronts, using psychoanalytic means, Langer argued that US intelligence would eventually be able to predict enemy reactions under specified conditions and circumstances, and so develop 'the type of psychological attack to which a given people is most vulnerable'. He urged the case for arousing, modifying, diverting, or in other ways manipulating the expression of 'unconscious needs to our own purposes', and for generating plans to deal 'with the respective nationality groups during and after the war'.[21]

As part of this envisaged campaign of psychological warfare under psychoanalytic auspices, he further suggested paying close attention to the psychology of women in enemy nations: 'Here, again, the arousal and manipulation of unconscious and irrational forces should supplement our rational approach.'[22] Somewhat tantalizingly Langer did not elaborate further on his gender plan.

The OSS Truth Drug Committee

When the COI became the OSS in June 1942, a variety of new intelligence-related fields opened up for the psychoanalytic profession. In October, the Psychological Warfare Branch of the Military Intelligence Service (MIS) 'activated a committee to investigate the feasibility of using drugs in the interrogation of Prisoners of War'.[23] The OSS Truth Drug Committee was chaired by Winfried Overholser, head of St Elizabeth's Hospital in Washington, DC.[24] Other members included OSS-affiliated psychiatrists John Whitehorn, Professor of Psychiatry at the Johns Hopkins University,[25] Edward Strecker, Professor of Psychiatry at the University of Pennsylvania,[26] and psychoanalyst Lawrence Kubie, Associate in neurology at the Neurological Institute in New York City.[27] Human experiments were conducted, for example, under the directorship of Kubie at the Neurological Institute in New York.[28] But those who hoped that under the influence of cannabis subjects would begin to 'sing like a bird' were to be disappointed.[29] A final summary report prepared by the OSS Special Assistants Division, Research and Development

Branch in 1945 reiterated the view that uninhibited truthfulness could not be obtained by this method.[30]

Evidently there was wider US military and intelligence interest in finding a suitable truth drug, but the subject was also of particular interest to various clinicians, including analysts such as Kubie. In an article published in 1945, he and Sydney Margolin (at that time a psychoanalytic candidate, who was to continue his training at the New York Psychoanalytic Institute after his military duties) specified their interest in drugs such as sodium pentothal, nitrous oxide and cannabis derivatives (Kubie and Margolin, 1945). In this more clinical, rather than military, context, they argued that, just as an analgesic drug makes it possible for an individual to allow his hand to be operated on, so a psychically 'analgesic' drug, which lowers the intensity of the reactions to such unpleasant emotions as rage, anxiety and guilt, might allow 'a patient to explore painful areas of experience without immediate psychic withdrawal at the first warnings of discomfort'. Perhaps drawing on his work for the OSS, Kubie argued, rather questionably to say the least, that:

> Under drugs the relationship of patient and therapist may contain in overt forms everything which in a veiled form occurs in what is known in psychoanalysis as the transference relationship. A full understanding of the dynamics of transference made the therapeutic utilization of this phenomenon possible.
> (Kubie and Margolin, 1945: 148)

But he added the caveat 'it is important that such procedures as these should be under close supervision by men who are trained to deal with powerful unconscious forces' (1945: 149) – in other words making it clear that qualified psychoanalysts were in a privileged position to carry out this work.

Kubie and Margolin claimed that drugged patients are more tolerant to interpretations and subsequent emerging emotions; apparently interpretations also became more emotionally significant and patients could incorporate them 'into [their] intellectual and emotional process so as to use them in the resynthesis of [their] psychic functions' (1945: 147–8). But what they did not address was whether such interpretations resulted in more accurate reflections of the patient's emotional experience, or whether the analyst's interpretations were simply more easily accepted, since the subject, in a drugged state, was less able to evaluate them or think about them.

This pursuit of drugs (and hypnosis) as a means to speed up transference processes and 'circumvent resistances' (1945: 149–50), as Kubie and Margolin summarized in their findings, resonated with old fears of analytic abuses (the patient, without free will, at the mercy of the clinician who could simply implant ideas or draw out a confession), but also with various controversial or abandoned techniques from earlier periods in the history of analysis that also sought to speed up treatment or to bypass the patient's resistance. In this sense various American psychoanalysts and intelligence specialists found themselves on shared ground: in each domain, attempts were made to advance a science that could get at the truth, and in which so-called 'truth drugs' might serve as useful allies. The fact that the 'biographical truth is not to be had', as Freud wrote to Arnold Zweig in 1936, seemed to have made little impact on the thinking of some exponents of analysis, and of intelligence work, during this period (E.L. Freud, 1984 [1968]: 137). What the members of the OSS Truth Drug Committee strikingly failed to discuss, as far as we know, were the ethical implications for conducting clandestine human drug experiments on behalf of the US Intelligence Community.

Cold War years

When the hot war turned cold, many of these early forays by practitioners of psychodynamic psychiatry found a new lease of life. Fuelled by their alleged successes in treating psychiatric casualties during the Second World War,[31] many analysts were in a strong position to take on leading positions in psychiatric hospitals throughout the country, and many institutions appointed psychoanalytically trained psychiatrists, often with ongoing or former military and/or intelligence backgrounds.

The Cold War, as is well known, led to a diminution in the various denazification measures that had been installed at the point of Allied victory. Indeed, with the new struggle for intercontinental power against the Soviet Union, former Nazis were sometimes recruited if they could contribute to national scientific development. Being interested not only in technological but also in medical and pharmaceutical advances, US intelligence experts scanned through documents produced by Nazi officials that detailed human experiments in Auschwitz and Dachau. These involved the very same drugs (e.g. mescaline, various barbiturates) that the OSS had also been investigating during the war.[32] The manipulation and induced 'regression' of captives through drugs and other means, in order to break psychic resistances and alter perception and behaviour, continued to be an object of investigation by the CIA and other agencies during the Cold War years. Such inquiries were also thought to provide an essential means of understanding, exploiting and countering brainwashing mechanisms. Some of these experiments seem to have involved the witting or unwitting participation of psychoanalysts.

The argument for conducting experiments with mind-altering drugs can be found in various intelligence memos during the late 1940s and 1950s. A CIA document from 1949, for example, speculates on techniques that the communists might have used in order to extract confessions from dissidents which would later be used as evidence against them during the infamous show trials held by the USSR and its satellite nations:

> Suffice it to say that all points toward the application of . . . hypnotic and/or hypno-analytic [techniques], the confessions being elicited either by virtue of post hypnotic suggestion with resultant trance state, or by means of accelerated psychoanalytic techniques with post hypnotic behavior.[33]

In the context of the 'brainwash scare', US intelligence funnelled billions of dollars into private and government institutions, universities, penitentiaries and hospitals in order to study ways and means of manipulating and controlling the human mind and behaviour (McCoy, 2006: 7).[34] This CIA-led inquiry into the human mind ran under various code names such as BLUEBIRD, ARTICHOKE and MKULTRA. Operating from 1953 until 1963, MKULTRA ultimately formed the nucleus for a range of CIA mind-control programmes during the Cold War. Renamed MKSEARCH in 1964, it continued until at least 1972. As part of these programmes thousands of human experiments were conducted at army bases at home and abroad, as well as at psychiatric institutions, and correction and inter-rogation centres.

Between 1955 and 1963, a number of psychoanalysts were discussing mind-control techniques as well. Some linked the process to the models of ego psychol-ogy, illustrating how brainwashing could be understood as an assault upon the ego's autonomy. For example, David Rapaport, a Hungarian-born lay psychoana-lyst and well-known theoretician of ego psychology, described in 1958 how he thought such brainwashing process was achieved:

> Thus, the outstanding conditions which impair the ego's autonomy from the environment are: (1) massive intrapsychic blocking of the instinctual drives which are the ultimate guarantees of this autonomy; (2) maximized needful-ness, danger, and fear which enlist the drives (usually the guarantees of this autonomy) to prompt surrender of autonomy; (3) lack of privacy, deprivation of stimulus-nutriment, memorial and verbal supports, all of which seem to be necessary for the maintenance of the structures (thought-structures, values, ideologies, identity) which are the proximal guarantees of this autonomy; (4) a steady stream of instructions and information which, in the lack of other stimulus-nutriment, attain such power that they have the ego completely at their mercy.
>
> (Rapaport, 1958: 22)

For various military and intelligence specialists, these techniques offered poten-tial explanations of the mysterious 'brainwashing' process, but also suggested what might ultimately be achieved, in terms of attaining full control over a person. However, at the same time in the clinical arena, some psychiatrists and psycho-analysts (or candidates) wondered if such methods might be used to help free patients from maladaptive relational patterns causing various mental illnesses. To be sure, most analysts took the mainstream view that ego psychology should be in the service of 'classic' psychoanalytic treatment. Some, however, resorted to the idea that if the ego is weakened to such an extent that the patient behaves more or less like a baby – mainly through techniques of accelerated and excessive regression – old maladaptive relational patterns could be erased more quickly and reliably, and more radical therapeutic changes achieved. The utopian and dys-topian prospect of refashioning the mind *tout court* was shared, in this sense, between various exponents of intelligence and therapy. As a result, certain clinical and experimental projects were implemented with financial aid from the IC. In the context of the early Cold War, these formed part of what Allen W. Dulles in 1953 termed 'brain warfare' ('Soviet Brain-Washing', 1953: 8).

The case of Harold Blauer provides a graphic example of how badly things could go wrong in the search for mind-manipulating techniques and substances. This patient at the New York State Psychiatric Institute (NYSPI), who died in 1953, had been put under the medical care of the Department of Experimental Psychiatry as a test subject. Between 1951 and 1960 the US Army Chemical Corps (ACC) collaborated with the NYSPI and later with a NYSPI-associated private organization, the Research Foundation for Mental Hygiene, in order to conduct human experiments in a search for suitable substances. Declassified US Army documents show that on 8 January 1953 a fatal dose of MDA, furnished by the IC, was injected into Blauer's vein.[35] According to the Army Inspector's General Report, the drug was administered by psychiatrist and psychoanalyst James P. Cattell, a member of the Association for Psychoanalytic Medicine since 1951 ('New Members', 1951: 47). Cattell later claimed that 'we didn't know whether it was dog piss or – [. . .]. This was secret. This was a secret we weren't in on.'[36] Paul Hoch, psychiatrist and affiliate member of the Association for Psychoanalytic Medicine in New York, and principal investigator of the ACC/NYSPI programme, later claimed that these experiments were for diagnostic purposes. But, in 1987, Sidney Malitz, a former NYSPI psychiatrist who had trained at the Columbia University Psychoanalytic Clinic between 1954 and 1960, claimed in an auto-biographical sketch the true purpose of these experiments. They were aimed at 'developing a weapon that would immobilize but not kill an enemy'. He also recalled the purpose of assorted LSD experiments: 'We did do some experiments with normal paid volunteers who were asked to do one of the following: deliberately lie after having ingested LSD or attempt to withhold disclosing the most embarrassing secret of their lives' (Malitz, 1987: 29). Due to the sensitive nature of these experiments, psychoanalyst Nolan Lewis, director of the NYSPI until the end of 1953, Paul Hoch, James Cattell and various other NYSPI staff members had all received security clearances 'up to and including "Secret"'by the IC.[37]

Another site for IC-related human experiments was the Allan Memorial Institute at McGill University in Montreal, under the directorship of psychiatrist Donald Ewen Cameron. New procedures were tested out here, in part financed by the CIA and the Canadian government in the late 1950s and early 1960s (Marks, 1988 [1979]: 141–51), beginning with a technique that Cameron termed 'psychic driving' – this was the repetitive (up to 500,000 times) and forced exposure to certain verbalized psychodynamic statements issued to patients via earphones, built into – for example – non-removable football helmets (Cameron, 1959). To this were added various other experimental processes developed or carried out by colleagues who were psychiatrists and analysts (or candidates), such as Raúl Vispo, Hassan Azima or Hector Warnes.[38] Thus patients undergoing psychic driving were typically also immobilized, using variants of Azima's 'prolonged sleep treatment' in which patients were heavily sedated with barbiturates in order to foster regressive processes (Azima, 1955; see also Müller, 2013: ch. 4).

Cameron assembled various combinations of these techniques under the heading of 'depatterning', where the goal was to put patients into states of total regression by the use of various physical and psychopharmacological means until he or she eventually lost control of their physical and mental capacities, including control over bowel and bladder functions.[39] The ultimate aim was to 'depattern', that is, destroy the personality 'patterns', which were considered to be malfunctioning or maladaptive, and to 'drive' into the brain new and 'normal' traits with a technique he called 'psychic driving' (Cameron, 1956; 1959). While at McGill, Azima developed Margolin's 'anaclitic therapy' along similar lines, as another attempt to arrive at an accelerated psychoanalytic technique. He described this form of treatment in 1961 as a process of 'rapid and massive regression', in which he hoped he could evoke uninhibited 'pregenital, particularly oral modes of object-relations . . . in action or in fantasy', thus inducing an anaclitic transference in order to allow 'an experimental, non-verbal, and "primary" working-through of these pre-genital vicissitudes'. The theoretical expectation was that the events evoked 'are more than "as if" or "instead" experiences, and *are* identical in their intensity and lived quality with their genetic origins' (Azima, 1961: 1071 ff.). Azima further argued that the deeply regressed and absolutely dependent patient would eventually be able to re-introject a more benign model of mother–child relations by experiencing the therapist as a new, more reliable and loving mother 'in vivo'.

Such techniques assumed, of course, the authority of the psychiatrist to decide what kind of 'healthy' patterns were to be implanted into the helpless patient. Or at least, this was the fantasy. In an interview with Cameron, published in the Canadian *Weekend Magazine* in 1955 under the heading 'Beneficial Brain-Washing', journalist Jacqueline Moore outlined the similarities between brainwashing and the psychiatric experiments conducted at the Allan Memorial Institute. Here Cameron stated: 'Any technique . . . that can leave a persisting imprint on one's mind, even if it is only used in treatment, can certainly cast light on what we presume is done under the heading of brain-washing' (in Moore, 1955: 7). The work of Cameron and his staff did indeed have affinities with what was elsewhere labelled a 'brainwashing' process, and bears comparison with overt interrogation or torture techniques also explored in the years after 9/11 by the notorious CIA torture programme.

Another major field of 'ego autonomy impairing' procedures was also shaped by a CIA-funded project at McGill University. Beginning in 1951, under the leadership of psychologist Donald Hebb, this explored the effects of total sensory deprivation (SD). Volunteer subjects suffered from devastating reactions, such as hallucinations, broad cognitive impairments, restlessness, anxiety and panic attacks, visual disturbances, derealization, depersonalization, confusion, headaches, nausea and fatigue (Bexton *et al.*, 1954; Heron *et al.*, 1956).

Hebb was not himself a psychoanalyst, but there was considerable interest in these techniques amongst various American analysts in this period. With substantial financial aid from an equally enthralled military intelligence community, several psychiatrists and psychologists tried to replicate the McGill findings, through a multitude of experimental variations, and researched various psychological effects triggered by isolation/SD experiences.[40] Azima and others explored the SD effects by adding hallucinogens like LSD or by adding large doses of barbiturates to the subject's isolation experience.[41] This experimental work had a number of different aims: the comparison of hallucinogenic occurrences during SD and LSD; the study of isolation experiences arising from candidate evaluation techniques for the Mercury human space programme or the testing of Air Force pilots; and the pursuit of the therapeutic rationale of radically disintegrating ego functions down to the most basic instinctual drives, from which new ego structures were to be generated, as modelled on the visions of (psychoanalytic-oriented or trained) psychiatrists and psychologists (Goldberger and Holt, 1961; Lilly, 1997 [1988]).[42]

Psychologist Leo Goldberger, who began his psychoanalytic training in 1963, had participated in SD/LSD experiments two years earlier. These were also funded by the military, but as Goldberger pointed out in 1970, SD research was born not only out of the brainwashing scare but also from the space programme. However, it also served a further aim – the exploration of how it was possible to evoke major behavioural and physiological changes by merely psychological means. 'To induce a phenomenon experimentally is to get close to understanding its causation. That was the promise held out by research on sensory deprivation', Goldberger (1970: 710) explained. A similar rationale was used by experimenters who worked on psychotropic substances: if a drug caused phenomena akin to mental disorders, then it promised to shed light on the causation. CIA- and military-financed SD and drug research, on the other hand, was seen at the time as being crucial for creating a 'Manchurian Candidate' (Marks, 1988 [1979]), that is, bringing 'an individual to the point where he will do our bidding against his will and even against such fundamental laws of nature such as self-preservation'.[43]

In this context, it became hard to distinguish between behavioural theories of manipulating learning and certain techniques to speed up the process of reshaping internalized objects through psychodynamic therapy. Both, it seemed, according to at least some of the protagonists in this debate, could serve to delete maladaptive learning processes and implant (hence Cameron's 'dynamic implant') new ones – a 'social engineering' process by those who claimed to hold 'the truth'. As with the OSS Truth Drug Committee's miscarried attempt to find a serum that would guarantee the production of reliable confessions, the search for a 'Manchurian Candidate', as envisioned by the IC, in fact utterly failed. What was gained, however, was a multitude of psychological techniques to break a person for interrogation purposes, known today as 'white torture' (Mausfeld, 2009). In 1963 the CIA's *KUBARK Counterintelligence Interrogation Manual*, followed in 1983 by the *Human Resource Exploitation Training Manual*, summarized the findings of mind-control programmes such as MKULTRA. As the historian Alfred McCoy (2006; 2012) has shown, some of these techniques, which constituted a form of torture, eventually became 'standard operating procedures' at US camps such as Guantánamo Bay, Bagram, Abu Ghraib, USS *Bataan*, and various CIA black sites throughout the world. *KUBARK* refers back to research previously undertaken by a number of psychoanalysts and psychiatrists, some financed overtly or covertly by the military-intelligence complex.[44]

What the various participant clinicians gained through their IC collaboration included, no doubt, prestige, power, influence, dominance in the mental health field, sometimes also funding too, or direct career advancement. Hopefully they also gained a greater awareness that real, or at least beneficial, psychic changes in a patient take time, and rely on a safe environment and a trusting and secure relationship that has to develop slowly between two human beings. The changes effected by drugs, physical acceleration techniques or an 'Automation of Psychotherapy' (Cameron *et al.*, 1964) are all, to say the least, dubious and controversial. Cameron's brutal physical and chemical techniques can hardly be said to have unlocked the mysteries of mental illness. After having engaged in numerous human experiments that now seem, surely, ethically indefensible, both the skilled interrogator and the psychoanalyst seem to have gained one major moment of enlightenment: it is always and only the quality of the relationship within a trustful, secure environment and untouched by third-party interests that will yield sufficient and lasting changes. In the light of the collaborations between analysts and intelligence agencies documented in these pages, one might recall the old but utterly important virtues of psychoanalytic work:

> Nothing takes place between them except that they talk to each other. The analyst makes use of no instruments – not even for examining the patient – nor does he prescribe any medicines.
>
> (Freud, 1926: 187)

Concluding remarks

The recently published study of Wilhelm Reich by the German psychoanalyst Andreas Peglau is but the latest of many works to show that during the Third Reich the German psychoanalytic community was anything but apolitical (Peglau, 2013). The American psychoanalytic community proved to be heavily politically motivated too. But in their case it was primarily in order to fight totalitarianism, not to adhere to a totalitarian regime. An apolitical psychoanalytic community, such as the one Ernest Jones proclaimed in 1949, never existed (A. Freud, 1949: 179).

On the one hand, the US psychoanalytic community can be proud of having engaged in the fight against fascism and Nazism during the Second World War. At the same time, it is lamentable that some analysts seem to have lent their services so uncritically to the US military and intelligence community by using analytic material for intelligence purposes. The reputation and influence of analysis rose to unprecedented heights in the US between the late 1940s and early 1960s. In receiving continued financial aid from the IC for Cold War-related research on topics including SD, stress, sleep deprivation and psychoactive drugs, aspects of their work – sometimes undertaken in utter disrespect for the Hippocratic Oath and the Nuremberg Code of 1947 – contributed to the development of modern psychological torture techniques, thus in some ways supporting the totalitarian structures that they were originally committed to counteracting.

This history serves as a reminder to the psychoanalytic community that the original concept of 'making the unconscious conscious' needs to be understood not only as a purely clinical task, but also as a guide in the reassessment of its own history. I conclude with these remarks by a British psychologist, David Harper, in the course of reflections on the complicity of psychology with the Security State:

> There are, therefore, three reasons for focusing on these topics. Firstly, the discipline of psychology positions itself as a science, but there is often scant discussion of the ethics and politics concerning the use of this knowledge. Secondly, psychologists show a remarkable ignorance about the history of their discipline, particularly the application of psychological knowledge by the military and security agencies. Thirdly, because of this ignorance, the discipline runs the risk of repeating previous mistakes. [. . .] It is important that we continually revisit this history, and do not forget our complicity in its abuses.
>
> (Harper, 2007: 16)

Notes

1 For a detailed account of this collaboration, see Müller (2013). A thoroughly revised and updated German version is currently in preparation.
2 For parallel experiments on unwitting subjects, with radiation, see Kutcher (2006; 2009).
3 Langer became an official candidate of the Vienna Psychoanalytic Society in 1936 and was analysed by Anna Freud. In 1938 he followed the Freud family to London and continued his training with Anna Freud. Having finished his training in late 1938 he went back to the USA to settle in New York. Although fully trained as a psychoanalyst he was not offered official membership status by the New York Psychoanalytic Institute due to his non-medical background. Soon after opening his independent psychoanalytic practice in New York, he had to resettle in Cambridge, Massachusetts, due to health issues. It was not until 1949 that the Boston Psychoanalytic Institute awarded him membership status as a lay psychoanalyst ('Events in the Psychoanalytic World', 1949: 5; 'List of Members of the International Psycho-Analytical Association', 1950: 303; Langer and Gifford, 1978).
4 Minutes of Meeting of Committee on Morale of the American Psychoanalytic Association, New York, 5 December 1941, Oskar Diethelm Library (ODL), American Psychoanalytic Association Collection, US Government, Committee on Morale 1941–1942, RG 14, S1.
5 Committee on Morale of the American Psychoanalytic Association, newsletter, to Membership of the American Psychoanalytic Association, 20 October 1941, ODL, David Levy Papers, Box 5, Folder 5.36.
6 See also: Minutes of the First Meeting of the Committee on Morale of the American Psychoanalytic Association, New York City, 25 May, ODL, American Psychoanalytic Association Collection, US Government, Committee on Morale 1941–1942, RG 14, S1: '[W]e were laying the foundation for what we hoped would be an advisory committee to the Government on all matters concerning the development of morale in the various services of Government and in the civilian population at large.'

7 Franz Alexander to Allan Gregg, 4 February 1942, Rockefeller Foundation Archive, RG 1.1, Series 216A, Box 4, Folder 40.

8 Other analysts involved included Therese Benedek, Edward Eisler, Michael Grotjahn, Helen McLean and George Mohr.

9 Data Sheet 'Michael Boy', NARA II, RG 44, Entry 149, Box 1716, Folder: 'Psychiatric Reports'.

10 David Levy to John Millet, 18 February 1942, ODL, Levy Papers, Box 5, Folder 5.36. Despite several archival inquiries, I have not yet been able to locate the reports by Alexander and Levy. What kind of clinical data was used, how it was presented to the COI/OSS, and how the COI/OSS interpreted the material are questions that remain unanswered at this point.

11 Walter Langer to Mr Johnson, Coordinator's Office, Subject: Memorandum on Budget of Psychoanalytic Field Unit, October 6, 1941, NARA II, Wash-R&A-OP-17, RG 226, A1 Entry 146, Box 129, Folder 74/1837; Walter Langer to Col. Donovan, October 20, 1941, Subject: Report on Progress of Psychoanalytic Studies, NARA II, WASH-R&A-OP-17, RG 226, A1 Entry 146, Box 129, Folder 74/1837.

12 Minutes of the Forty-Fourth Meeting of the American Psychoanalytic Association, Boston, 17–20 May 1942, ODL, American Psychoanalytic Association Collection, Annual Meetings, Agendas and Minutes 1911–1954, RG 08, S1, S. 35; Samuel Atkin to John Millet, 1 December 1941, ODL, American Psychoanalytic Association Collection, Committee on Morale 1941–1942, RG 14, S1.

13 Langer to Donovan, 31 October 1941, Tentative Findings and Recommendations. NARA II. URL: http://www.bbk.ac.uk/thepursuitofthenazimind/NYP.php (Retrieved: 18 January 2014).

14 Ibid.: 3–5.

15 Ibid.: 7–9.

16 See also Chase (2003); Devereux (1953: 631); Murray (1943). On Simmel, see Cavin (2006).

17 Other analysts such as Ernst Kris, who was based at the New School for Social Research, worked on a broad array of propaganda-related topics throughout the Second World War. Seven lengthy reports resulted from the 'Totalitarian Research Project' of the New School, with topics such as 'German Radio News Bulletins. Problems & Methods of Analysis', 'Data on German Defeat Situation', or 'A Typological Analysis of Stereotypes in German News Broadcasts'. See: Research Paper No. 1–7, New School for Social Research Library, New York City, NY, Totalitarian Research Project, Box 1.

18 Langer to Donovan, Psychoanalytical Contributions to Psychological Warfare, 1 January 1943, NARA II, WASH-R&A-OP-17, RG 226, A1 Entry 146, Box 129, Folder 73B/1836: 3.

19 Ibid.: 1.

20 Ibid.: 3–6.

21 Ibid.: 6–7.

22 Ibid.: 7–8.

23 Allan Abrams, Acting Director, Research & Development [R&D] to Donovan, Subject: Report on T.D., 4 June 1943, NARA II, RG 226, A-1 Entry 210, Box 34b. Located at URL: http://www.bbk.ac.uk/thepursuitofthenazimind/NYP.php (Retrieved: 18 January 2014).

24 Ibid.; see also Marks (1988 [1979]: 6).

25 Whitehorn became honorary member of the Washington–Baltimore Psychoanalytic Society in 1944 (see 'List of Members of the International Psycho-Analytical Association', 1944: 196).

26 In 1958 Strecker became honorary member of the Philadelphia Association for Psychoanalysis ('News and Proceedings of Affiliate Societies and Institutes', 1959: 373).

27 Abrams, to Donovan, op. cit.

28 Albarelli (2009): 219.

29   CIA-Mori ID: 184373, Development of 'Truth Drug' with Attached Memorandum [2 June 1943], 21 June, 1943, CIA MKULTRA Document Collection: 2.

30   CIA-Mori ID: 144767, 6 September 1945, Final Summary Reports with Attached Reports Titled 'Final Summary Report of K Table' and 'Final Summary Report of T.D.', 5 and 6 September 1945, CIA MKULTRA Document Collection: 4.

31   In a 1985 interview with Arnold Richards, past president of the New York Psychoanalytic Society, Charles Fisher stated that psychoanalysts 'showed more understanding and sympathy for war neurotics and managed to get them medical discharges more rapidly than other doctors' (Richards, 1985; see also Pols and Oak, 2007: 2135).

32   US Naval Technical Mission in Europe. Technical Report no. 331–45, 'German Aviation Medical Research at the Dachau Concentration Camp', Oct. 1945, Harvard Medical Library/Francis A. Countway Library of Medicine, H MS c64. Box 11, folder 75.

33   CIA-Mori ID: 144891, Communist 'Confession' Techniques, 17 May, 1949, CIA MKULTRA Document Collection: 1; CIA-Mori ID: 184374, An Analysis of Confessions in Russian Trials with Attachment Titled 'Mindszenty', Estimated Pub Date: 1 January 1943, CIA MKULTRA Document Collection: 2.

34   McCoy estimates that the costs for 'psychological warfare and secret research into human consciousness [. . .] reached a cost of a billion dollars annually – a veritable Manhattan Project of the mind' (2006: 7).

35   US Army, 1975 Inspector General Report of Inquiry into the Facts and Circumstances Surrounding the Death of Mr. Harold Blauer at the New York Psychiatric Institute (NYSPI) and Subsequent Claims Actions. US-Army IG Report DAIG-IN 27–75, 28 October 1975 [henceforth: DAIG-IN 27–75]. Washington, DC (Department of the Army. Office of the Inspector General); see also Marks (1979: 71 n.); Scheflin and Opton (1978: 170–6).

36   US Army, 1975, DAIG-IN 27–75, op. cit., Exhibit B-2: List of Witnesses, Dr. James P. Cattell: 14.

37   US Army, 1975, DAIG-IN 27–75, op. cit., Exhibit E: NYSPI Second Quarterly Report, 26 August 1952: 1.

38   Hassan Azima, a psychiatrist, was a candidate at the Canadian Psychoanalytic Institute during his time at the Allan Memorial and his time with Cameron. Shortly before his death on 26 June, 1962, he graduated as one of the first candidates of the Canadian Psychoanalytic Institute; Rául Vispo is mentioned in 1958 as a member of the Argentine Psychoanalytic Assocation; Hector Warnes became a member of the Canadian Institute of Psychoanalysis in 1968, so after his time with Azima and Cameron.

39   The term 'depatterning' characteristically described the use of a combination of high doses of drugs, including LSD and PCP, sensory deprivation, extensive use of ECT, along with additional procedures such as psychic driving and Azima's sleep techniques.

40   For example, Hassan Azima, Bernard Bressler, Sanford I. Cohen, Leo Goldberger, Robert R. Holt, Edwin Z. Levy, John C. Lilly, George E. Ruff, Jay T. Shurley, Albert J. Silverman, Philip Solomon, Rául H. Vispo (see Müller, 2013: ch. 4).

41   Contributing colleagues included Goldberger, who trained at the New York Psychoanalytic Institute between 1963 and 1968 (*Bulletin of the American Psychoanalytic Association* 19, 835–52: 847); Holt, then a candidate at Topeka Psychoanalytic Association (*Bulletin of the International Psycho-Analytical Association* 29, 260–73: 267), and Lilly, who trained in Philadelphia (Goldberger and Holt, 1961; Lilly, 1997 [1988]: 73, 104, 230ff.).

42   Note that Lilly used LSD and SD only on himself.

43   CIA-Mori ID no. 144686, Project Artichoke, (Deleted) Evaluation of ISSO Role, 25 January 1952. CIA MKULTRA Document Collection: 1–2.

44   *KUBARK*'s annotated literature list mentions, for example, Louis Gottschalk, John Lilly, James Moloney and Philip Solomon.

Chapter 12

Therapeutic violence

Psychoanalysis and the 're-education' of political prisoners in Cold War Yugoslavia and Eastern Europe

Ana Antic

> The Romanian tanks are on their borders, the Bulgarian tanks are on the Bulgarian borders, on the Hungarian borders stand and wait the Hungarian tanks, and at that very moment, when the Party needed you the most, you stabbed it in the back. That's not nice, that's treason, and you need to realize that. We shall try to help you to get yourselves out of that quagmire.
>
> (Simic and Trifunovic, 1990: 228)

This is how, in 1950, Marija Zelic, Yugoslav state police investigator, greeted one of the first groups of political prisoners who were about to undergo years of brutal physical torture and political 're-education' because they were suspected of pro-Stalinist ideological leanings and activity. In 1948, Yugoslavia, a newly socialist, revolutionary country which had just emerged from the most devastating conflict in its brief history, experienced yet another exceptionally turbulent international episode: its close military, political and ideological relations with the USSR crumbled within a few months, and Yugoslavia fell out of the Soviet sphere of influence. In June 1948 the Yugoslav Communist Party (CPY) was expelled from the Cominform (Communist Information Bureau, an international forum of communist and workers' parties, founded in 1947). This followed the Cominform's damning resolution which accused the CPY of deviating from Marxism-Leninism, and promoting openly anti-Soviet policies and viewpoints (see Dedijer, 1969; Gibianskii, 1997; Jakovina, 2003; Kullaa, 2011). The Tito–Stalin split ultimately benefited Yugoslavia: the country went on to receive extensive Western material and political support and, even more importantly, developed its own, much more liberal and internationally open brand of socialism. The Yugoslav regime's unique position within the Eastern bloc allowed its leaders to pursue experimental policies, and to encourage rich exchanges with both the Eastern and the Western worlds. However, this political break had serious social consequences; Yugoslavia's falling out with Moscow was further complicated by its dangerous geographical position: as Zelic noted with great alarm, the state was surrounded by Soviet satellites, and the prospect of foreign invasion as well as internal treason was a real possibility for years. Moreover, the intimate ideological bonds between the Yugoslav and Soviet Communist

Parties could not be broken off so easily, and many committed communists' loyalties remained hopelessly confused.

The country's dangerous departure from the increasingly oppressive Soviet zone sparked, in turn, the most authoritarian and Stalinist-like political episode in Yugoslavia's entire history. Afraid for its survival and fearing popular defection to the Soviet side in case of invasion, the Yugoslav regime embarked on a long and thorough purge of its most esteemed cadres (Banac, 1988). Thousands ended up in political prisons, and the regime devised a programme of 're-education' for all those former comrades who 'failed' to understand the true meaning of the Soviet–Yugoslav split. The most notorious of the several 're-education' camps established was the Goli Otok labour and prison camp complex. Here, a brutal psychological experiment was conducted with tens of thousands of inmates incarcerated on a secluded island off the northern Croatian coast. While much has been published on Goli Otok, the psychiatric aspect of its regime remains completely unexplored. This chapter sheds light on how certain psychiatric as well as psychoanalytic ideas shaped the conceptualization and realization of this experiment, and discusses the central role of these disciplines more broadly in East European authoritarian political projects. In so doing it explores how elements of the psychoanalytic toolkit could be employed, along with certain behaviourist techniques, and put to use in the service of so-called political re-education, rather than as a therapeutic practice. In this respect, although the Goli Otok camp also relied on the input of individual analysts and therapists, this chapter is primarily concerned with how Freudian ideas and techniques were appropriated as a form of overt political control, where 'the patient' in fact had no choice but to participate in this 'talking cure'.

Wartime origins of 're-education' experiments

In the aftermath of the unprecedented violence of the Second World War and the socialist revolution of 1945, psychodynamic and psychotherapeutically oriented approaches became quite influential in post-war psychiatry in Yugoslavia. This was quite unlike developments in other countries of the socialist bloc. Psychiatry underwent a radical transformation during the war, challenging an almost exclusively organicist, German-influenced, hereditarian scientific outlook and developing into a mental health discipline, notably shaped by psychoanalytic ideas, and with a new focus on environmental influences. However, the origins of this lasting change did not lie in the radical socialist overhaul of 1945 but in the war years themselves. When Yugoslavia's communist psychiatrists argued that a socio-economic transformation and psychological healing could free society of mental woes, they echoed views already promulgated by a unique institution in wartime Yugoslavia: the Institute for Compulsory Re-education of Communist Youth in Serbia. The latter, which had been founded and run by the Serbian collaborationist government (1942–4), openly accepted various psychoanalytic principles, notably transference, and seriously considered the role of psychological and environmental factors in the emergence and therapeutic treatment of mental illness (Borkovic, 1966: 97–8). Moreover, the institute provided a model for the application, in a most peculiar form, of psychodynamic therapies. Its techniques aimed to erase the dire psychological effects of the 'national trauma' of the country's humiliating defeat and occupation in 1941.

The institute was important for post-war socialist psychiatry and served more specifically as a model of sorts for the labour camp which the Yugoslav state established for suspected pro-Stalinists in its own ranks in 1949 – the aforementioned infamous Goli Otok (Naked Island, or Barren Island). At the institute, sustained efforts were made to try to persuade the pro-communist young to abandon their ideological beliefs and support the pro-fascist government of Serbia. The institute combined elements of psychoanalytic thought with a behaviourist interpretation of human psychological development, accompanied by violent physical punishments. Goli Otok used the same approach but significantly increased the intensity of physical violence. In fact, one of the leading men of the wartime collaborationist Belgrade Special Police's Anti-Communist Section (which co-organized and co-ran the institute, which was otherwise under Gestapo auspices), Bozidar Becirevic, was co-opted by the post-war Yugoslav state police, and kept alive in order to share his 'expertise' regarding the techniques of questioning and 're-educating' communist prisoners (Kostic, 2012: 72).

The head of the wartime institute, Milovan Popovic, believed that his educational philosophy was centrally informed by the theory and practice of psychoanalysis. In a statement that explicitly referred to Freud, Popovic explained:

> It is necessary to establish between us and them a relationship full of closeness and trust. Freud could only use psychoanalysis to treat the ill if he succeeded to develop in his patients true love, of [a] sexual nature, towards himself. Only then did they open their souls to him and allowed him to see their wounds. We must observe similar rules. The children must first believe in us, that we will defend and protect them like the closest of kin, and only then can they reveal their souls to us.[1]

In other words, Popovic protested against the brutal police treatment of young political prisoners before they were sent to the institute, claiming that such violence and cruelty could only exacerbate the ideological delusions of the offenders. However, although there were important commonalities between the institute and the post-war Goli Otok prison camp, the latter integrated violence with certain psychoanalytic ideas and re-education techniques much more forcefully.

The continuity of expertise across 1945 ensured that there were important affinities between the two experimental projects. The wartime institute had developed an internal structure similar to the one at Goli Otok, and encouraged self-management among the inmates; young inmates were expected to participate in decision-making processes wherever possible. An internal spying structure was also fostered; inmates were incited to report on one another's suspicious or dissident behaviour to the instructors, and to view the latter as their true allies and friends, even ersatz parents. At the same time, the institute's instructors provided modified individual therapeutic sessions. These were then also adopted at Goli Otok and turned into regular, compulsory confessional sessions. The instructors might be staff members, police investigators or indeed 're-educated' prisoners who had already climbed the camp's ladder. Just as at Goli Otok, the institute leadership insisted that the inmates produce elaborate narratives about themselves. Along with personal testimonies, they were also required to produce confessional essays on a number of different topics. This coerceive form of self-exploration and introspection was regarded as key to the process of re-education.[2]

Post-war, Yugoslav psychiatry and psychoanalysis became the most liberalized and westernized of those professions in the region, but even some of the most seemingly progressive members also contributed crucially to the operation of the violent and repressive re-education programme at Goli Otok. Psychoanalysis and psychiatry can thus provide a lens through which to study the complicated and unexpected political alliances of the Cold War. Yugoslavia was unique among the socialist countries in providing a political and medical culture in which particular versions of psychoanalysis could thrive. The mental health professions received generous material and logistical support from the state, and became the most internationalized of all medical professions. But Yugoslav psychoanalysts and progressive psychiatrists were also closely – and centrally – involved in violent anti-Stalinist processes, purges and 're-education' projects, and in the subsequent East European psychiatric and pedagogical networks.

In rethinking the role of psychoanalysis in a Marxist society, a leading Yugoslav analyst and military psychiatrist Vladislav Klajn[3] proposed and then implemented a curious combination of techniques, which significantly decreased the length of analysis, and sought to give the analyst a more direct and powerful leadership role in the process. It is likely there was an intellectual link between this more authoritarian version of psychoanalysis and the psychological re-education that was implemented in the Goli Otok camp. Klajn proposed that when it was applied to 'primitive', 'undereducated' or 'intellectually less elevated patients', the psychotherapeutic method needed to be more active, more 'authoritative'; in short, the therapist had to lead patients and 'force them to active cooperation' (Klajn, 1958: 531). This was a novel take on the old idea of psychiatrists as teachers and the need for enlightenment. For Klajn, Freud's insights constituted an invaluable contribution to understanding the psyche and mechanisms of mental illness. However, Klajn soon developed into a rather unorthodox 'socialist psychoanalyst', attempting to devise an approach appropriate to Yugoslavia's particular profile. He mostly shunned long-term sessions in favour of shorter, more intense treatments, in which the importance and strength of consciousness and ego were emphasized over the unconscious, and he conceptualized the therapist as akin to a tutor who directed his patients in a firm, disciplined and, if necessary, heavy-handed manner, while dispensing 'guidance' much more straightforwardly than an orthodox psychoanalyst would have done (Klajn, 1989: 78–83).

Klajn famously defended psychoanalysis at Party meetings, and claimed that, in his soul, he could combine Freudianism with Marxism, while expressing his admiration for the work of Karen Horney (Klajn, 1989: 109). Importantly, Klajn was also a high-ranking officer in the Yugoslav state police and a lecturer at the Federal State Police's Polytechnic. Due to his tight connection to police and military structures throughout the 1950s, recent research has related him and another psychiatrist from within the state police, Dr Svetislav Popovic, to experiments and developments at Goli Otok (Kostic, 2012: 41–2). Moreover, Klajn himself worked as the head of the neuro-psychiatric ward at the Belgrade hospital Dragisa Misovic, whose director was the senior physician for the Goli Otok prisoners and whose doctors regularly treated the camp's inmates as well as the Yugoslav regime's highest functionaries (in his ward, Klajn introduced and supervised analytic psychotherapy for neurotic patients). But even if Klajn was not directly connected to the Goli Otok experiments – and the exact nature of his involvement remains unclear as the relevant archives have so far been unavailable to researchers – his conceptualization of 'socialist psychoanalysis' as a more authoritarian version of psychotherapy informed by certain analytic categories probably influenced the formulation of violent 'therapeutic' techniques at the camp, especially since he regularly lectured to state police employees.

'Goli Otok': the pedagogy of self-management

The Goli Otok camp's psychological outlook was eclectic, complex and contradictory, and characterized by a melange of theoretical and methodological approaches. The leadership insisted on immediately and brutally modifying their inmates' behaviour, through endless repetition, reinforcement (dispensation of life-saving privileges) and severe punishments (Kostic, 2012: 102). Such insistence reflected the camp's behaviourist approach to re-education, the belief that a structured adjustment of acts – especially public acts – was the precursor to the acquisition of new habits that would transform personality traits and shape choices, most notably political behaviour and convictions (Perucica, 1990: 63). By contrast with the tenets of leading behaviourists, however, the camp authorities did not disregard the relevance of internal mental states. Indeed, its leaders and ideologues were also concerned with uncovering and transforming deeper layers of the psyche. Even behaviourist techniques were often applied with the aim of achieving a deeper – psychoanalytic – transformation of personality, and reworking the subject's personal motivations. This 'therapeutic' ambition bizarrely co-resided, as noted, with techniques of terror and humiliation, an aggressive atmosphere, and the constant possibility of torture. Indeed, 'therapeutic sessions' themselves routinely included a violent component. Introspection and self-analysis played an enormous role in this process, and their application in the violent context of the camp constituted Goli Otok's unique culture of 'therapeutic violence'.

The Goli Otok camp came into operation at approximately the same time as Chinese forces were testing certain 're-education' methods on their American prisoners of war during the Korean War (1950–3). While there were common features between the Yugoslav and Chinese approaches (most likely stemming from their common Soviet pre-history), the former's re-education experiment introduced the original method of 'self-management' of the inmates, so that the presence of the state, though overwhelming, was not immediately visible in the camp (see Bidermann, 1963; Robin, 2001). The Chinese–Korean re-education programme included some elements of the Goli Otok experience: there was a clear prisoner hierarchy, and a particular system of rewards and punishments. The 're-educable' and 'incorrigible' cases were clearly demarcated, so that solidarity within the prisoner community was discouraged and sabotaged. Moreover, the 're-educated' prisoners sometimes surpassed their instructors in their expressions of loyalty to the new cause of communism. They were also soon involved in spying networks inside the camp, and reported on their co-prisoners (Watson, 1978). Around this time, a wide-ranging and all-pervasive ideological campaign engulfed Chinese society in the early 1950s, aiming at the deep psychological reconstitution of Chinese citizens as well as foreigners living there. This complicated 'thought reform' – as Robert Jay Lifton labelled it – affected prisons, universities and factories. The Yugoslav attempts at re-education, although much more modest and targeted, strikingly involved techniques that similarly focused on participants' intense self-exploration and guided self-analysis.

Since Goli Otok mainly held Communist Party members who had been affiliated with the cause for decades, the system of re-education aimed to convey the message that the imprisoned comrades finally understood the magnitude of their past mistakes and confusions, and led themselves and their colleagues out of the blunder, with the generous help of the CPY. As former inmate Emilijan Milan Kalafatic testified, those who had 'revised' their attitude had to repeat daily at various local political meetings and classes, in front of other prisoners, that 'Yugoslavia is the only socialist country in the world'. They were required to 'celebrate the theory of the withering away of the state, although it was clear to everyone that the state apparatus of violence remained in its entirety, and was even augmented'. This was the cornerstone of Yugoslavia's theory and application of workers' self-management after the 1950s, and it was first formulated and discussed in the violent context of Goli Otok (Kalafatic, 1990: 525–6).

Indeed, many former inmates testified that the lower the level of the camp's organization, the less visible became any representatives of state authority (such as policemen). One could get a strong impression that it was in fact the most 'advanced' and 're-educated' prisoners who mostly ran the affairs and conceptualized the camp's programme. As Dragoslav Mihailovic remembered, the increasingly porous boundary between the inmates and their keepers (policemen, guards, police investigators) further complicated the situation, making the experience of incarceration even more difficult to handle, since no real community of the imprisoned, no internal moral code of behaviour, could develop (Mihailovic, 1990: 105).

With its elaborate hierarchical prisoner structure, the camp's unique 'apparatus of compulsion' rested on the core idea that prisoners were constantly expected to survey and 'read' one another. Furthermore, all inmates were led to believe that 'those ... who saw and understood their own betrayal ask and force the others to do the same' (Stojanovic, 1991: 185–6). Each camp within the complex had its own centre for prisoners' self-management (albeit under the watchful eye of police investigators), with their leaders, deputies, foremen and officers in charge of cultural affairs. This pattern was then replicated in the cells and barracks, each of which was organized into a collective (similar to communist front organizations), and within which there were always the 'actives', those who made up the 're-education' vanguard. Barrack heads (room wardens), tasked with ideological leadership roles, were again composed of prisoners who had proved to the police investigators the authenticity of their political 'revision'. What happened in the barracks, the site where all inmates would return each night, determined the prisoners' future (Perucica, 1990: 134–44).

Finally, each barrack had its own share of 'bandits' – those who still failed to comply, self-criticize and admit their own dangerous past, and who were then subjected to 'boycott'. This included various degrees of physical and psychological torture, and complete isolation from other inmates. Nobody was allowed to communicate to the 'bandits' and they were allocated the hardest, most exhausting and often most meaningless forms of labour. Those who were higher in the ranks – members of the collectives or activists – were tasked with attending to the 're-education' of the bandits, while ensuring that their time at the camp was kept as miserable and psychologically devastating as possible until their reform. In fact, in order to remain an activist, one had not only to fully 'revise' one's attitudes, demonstrate a complete and accurate understanding of the Yugoslav position in its conflict with the USSR, and so on; one also needed to prove one's 'revision' in practice, by using any means available to 'persuade' the bandits to change their orientation and join the collective. In reality, this meant that all the activists had to excel in 'chasing up' recalcitrant inmates, in exerting 'psychophysical methods of compulsion' – cursing, yelling at, even hitting the bandits (Popovic, 1989: 112–13). This was indeed the true test of the validity of their 'rebirth' as honest communists. If they were suspected of faking their pressure on the bandits, activists were likely to be demoted and relieved of previous privileges or even severely punished. In fact, Goli Otok prisoners experienced most of their physical and psychological traumas at the hands of their fellow inmates and often former comrades.

Psychotherapeutic techniques

In a rare analysis of the psychiatric aspects of Goli Otok 're-education', psychiatrist Todor Bakovic proposed that psychiatrists and psychoanalysts who advised the state police regarding the organization of the camp's internal mechanisms should draw upon the psychoanalytic concepts of ambivalence and projection. The very nature of the Yugoslav–Soviet split, according to Bakovic, created conditions for such psychic states and mechanisms. He argued that the passionate ideological and personal loyalty of most Yugoslav communists to Stalin and the Soviet Union, and the uncritical adoration of Stalin in the post-1945 Communist

Party of Yugoslavia, meant that the ensuing conflict between Tito and the Soviet leadership came as a dramatic psychological blow. What used to be an idea and an allegiance worth sacrificing one's life for turned into a source of shame, suffering and even imprisonment. People who proved themselves as war heroes were now humiliated, excommunicated and branded as backstabbers. Bakovic's retrospective interpretation of the techniques applied at the camp, therefore, argued that the notion of ambivalence was deliberately fostered on two levels: first, it was Party members who arrested their own comrades, colleagues, friends, co-warriors, and accused them of treason, lack of patriotism, disloyalty; second, within the camp itself, the differentiation of rank occurred among co-prisoners and co-sufferers, with the police keeping their apparent distance: 'the immediate performers of torture were the inmates themselves, and they mostly suffered from each other' (Bakovic, 1998: 212–13).

Bakovic suggested that psychoanalysts such as Klajn himself, who advised the police on these matters, must have been aware of the powerful defence mechanism of projection, which then inevitably developed from such complex psychological circumstances: if 'revisers' felt any remorse for their humiliating 'revision', if there was any self-contempt or self-recrimination on their part, if they felt the need for self-punishment as a result of their collaboration with the police investigators at the camp, these feelings, he argued, were then probably projected onto the 'bandits', leading to further tendencies towards brutalization: 'They see their punishment of their comrades as a punishment of themselves . . . The greater the remorse, the harder the blows. The harder the blows, the greater the relief' (Bakovic, 1998: 213). According to Bakovic, this ensured the spontaneity, the efficiency of the system, as well as its notorious cruelty in requiring the enactment of physical and psychological abuses by one prisoner upon another. Milovan Popovic, a former inmate who had spent most of his incarceration at Goli Otok as a 'bandit', confirmed Bakovic's points, insisting that the re-educated torturer of his co-prisoners always hated the victim, and this was the result of the complex and painful psychological processes that accompanied his transition to an upper level within the hierarchy: 'a torturer with conscience hated his victim because of the guilty conscience itself' (Popovic, 1989). It was as though, were it not for the victim, there would not have been any guilty conscience either:

> Through his very existence the victim put him in a situation where he had to push and pull him, to scream at him, to treat him, a fellow man, a former comrade, now a co-prisoner, like he never thought anybody would treat [another human being].
>
> (Popovic, 1989)

For those reasons, it was suggested, the conscientious prisoners grew into the worst torturers, and actively strove to sink 'ever deeper in the disgusting earth of evil'. It was this capacity to induce such projections of self-hatred onto the victims, Bakovic argued, that kept Goli Otok ticking so successfully. However, although Bakovic's identification of particular psychoanalytic processes at work at the camp was very revealing, his interpretation of the Goli Otok mechanisms provides no evidence that psychoanalysis was intentionally applied there. In the rest of the chapter, I will demonstrate that psychoanalytic and psychotherapeutic categories did play a central role in the very organization and conceptualization of the camp.

Although this appeared to be a process entirely run from below, almost all Goli Otok convicts agree that the collective's treatment of those making public declarations in their barracks was in fact carefully planned by the police. Yet, as we have noted, the barracks meetings and 'investigations' were set up as though they were collective therapeutic sessions, with inmates obliged to reveal their innermost thoughts, emotions and quandaries, to confess and discuss their life histories, present and criticize their motivations, and dissect their past political and social engagements in front of 'healed' comrades.

Goli Otok, no less than the contemporaneous Chinese re-education experiments, drew considerably upon early Soviet jurisprudence and its conceptualizations of punishment as an opportunity for rebirth and rehabilitation. While the Gulag largely dispensed with the idea of self-managing rehabilitation of prisoners, the 1920s Soviet prisons and labour colonies that had emerged earlier had applied a striking set of measures in order to try to re-educate political offenders, common criminals and juvenile delinquents – as could be seen, for instance, at the Solovetsky labour camp, the Bolshevo camp for juvenile delinquents, and Anton Makarenko's Gorky colony for delinquent, orphaned and/or homeless children in Kharkov. All of these had highlighted – more or less cynically – the goal of re-education and political and moral rehabilitation, and vehemently insisted on the principles of prisoners' self-government inside the camps. Similar to Goli Otok, these early Soviet prisons paid substantial attention to organizing cultural, artistic and educational programmes, as well as compulsory political discussion classes. Moreover, self-criticism sessions were regular and compulsory, while prisoners' tribunals were common, and they served to force prisoners publicly to acknowledge their own past mistakes and wrongdoing (see Applebaum, 2003; David-Fox, 2012; Soloman, 1980; Tolokontseva, 2012). However, the Goli Otok camp was exceptional in its heavy emphasis on psychotherapeutic and analytic techniques and concepts, and its attendant and almost exclusive focus on introspection, self-exploration and self-knowledge. It was as though the entire process of investigation, confession-writing and interrogation primarily served as a basis for personal, psychological growth, as the following examples show.

In former inmate Rade Panic's book based on his memories of Goli Otok, the room warden utters the following introductory words before the ritual 'declarations of attitude' by a group of prisoners:

> To revise or not to revise, this seems to you a small difference. It's not. It's everything. It's your life. It's up to you what you will do with it. Until yesterday, I was just like you, a bandit, a stubborn foreign hireling, maybe not

personally but certainly objectively speaking, an agent of the Comintern. Then I saw the light. This should be your starting point, this realization that you are all bandits and traitors.

(Panic, 1997: 41)

Confessions thus did not serve to reveal the truth to the police – the police had already discovered it. Former inmate Vera Cenic testified that, even though the Goli Otok investigators always claimed that 'the Party already knew everything', she had been constantly pressed to 'spit out everything, absolutely everything, and the Party would then ascertain how honest and prepared [she] was to revise [her] position' (Cenic, 1994: 121). Unlike in the Soviet show trials, the confessions also did not have any public, propagandistic or political function, given that the fate of Goli Otok's prisoners was hidden from the eyes of the wider population, and the inmates were never tried or convicted but only received 'administrative sentences'. But the purpose of inmates' public declarations and self-criticism was precisely this self-realization, guided self-knowledge – that, even though they might not have been conscious of it or purposely engaged in treason and malicious endeavours, every single person arrested was harbouring negative dispositions towards his or her own Party and state, and was in need of a political and ethical 'rebirth'. Goli Otok then served to make each prisoner conscious of these malevolent traits in his or her own personality.

Even though it was a physically brutal labour camp, Goli Otok allotted its inmates more than enough time for such self-reflection. The very living conditions, in a setting of bleak isolation, were supposed to induce introspection. The infamous investigation (*istraga*) never ended here: as there was no trial or conviction, there could be no end to such intimate, soul-searching investigations. On average, every inmate wrote and submitted between 20 and 30 statements in the course of their *istraga*, and the very process of statement-writing and revision was central to the re-education programme (Radonjic, 1995: 76).

These life narratives were not focused on particular (real or imagined) crimes; they had to encompass the inmate's entire life, both rational and irrational spheres of his or her personality, and always started in early childhood. Women's camp commander Marija Zelic Popovic, whom most remember as an extremely physically brutal figure, would herself later recall how she strove to help the inmates realize and understand their 'true' nature, of which many had not even been aware – that they were traitors and unreliable, that they had harboured negative and pernicious thoughts against their own Party and enmity towards the state – and to assist them to 'unburden' themselves of such orientations and potentials. Although Popovic had no medical, psychiatric or psychoanalytic training, she approached her task of restructuring the inmates' personalities in explicitly medical terms: 'With each inmate I get her file, just like each patient is accompanied by a medical case history . . . Now I see who I am really dealing with.' The files also contained a 'diagnosis', or at least an opinion of the police investigator in the first instance. Popovic then adopted the role of a stern and authoritarian analyst, who pressed the inmates to tell and retell, to reconstruct and examine their past decision-making until they realized the underlying source of their betrayal. She suggested how 'they were sometimes not even aware of the path they had started walking down' and related her own traumatization as a result of this process, because she had to deal with the inmates' 'resistances' to this process of self-realization.[4] In most cases, this relentless search for 'hidden' treacherous thoughts implied a purely fictional reconstruction of such ideas, which likely never existed but had to be spelled out as unconscious.

It was in order to help this process of 'unearthing' and self-discovery that the camp relied on a set of analytic or quasi-analytic concepts and techniques concerned with intimate self-discovery. During such exercises, the confessing inmate would occupy the centre of the room, while emotionally prodded by the room warden and activists to admit 'what you did, what you used to think, what you are thinking now'. On occasion, encouragement was given to focus on the deepest, most hidden (real or invented) thoughts, dreams and affects. Even the investigators and camp guards at times confirmed that the perfidious and treacherous thoughts which sometimes existed may not have been entirely known to the inmates themselves, and therefore needed to be 'recovered' and would prove to be a revelation of sorts to the subjects themselves:

> First of all, you will tell your investigator all your . . . dirty thoughts. Every single one of your betrayals you will pour out to the investigator, every hostile activity and intention . . . All your thoughts. You need to throw up all your filthy thoughts and to re-examine them in the hot light of the sun.
>
> (Panic, 1997: 44–5)

It is precisely the idea of 'filthy hidden thoughts' which were unknown to the inmates themselves and had to be forcibly dug up and confronted that most resembled – and was most likely inspired by – the Freudian notion of the 'unconscious'. Former inmate Eva Nahiri described in her interview with famous writer Danilo Kis, in 1989, that she was instructed to sit for days and write a report (*zapisnik*), in which she was to reveal 'everything [she] knew and didn't know, everything [she] dreamed about', her entire internal life from the moment she 'sucked in her mother's milk' until the time of incarceration. The investigators would then decide what was relevant, and, even more importantly, whether she was lying or not. Others were asked to write up all of their impressions of the Goli Otok camp and any associations they had in relation to it – if they mentioned anything remotely negative, they were placed back in isolation and 'under boycott' (Simic and Trifunovic, 1990: 36–7). Soon after his imprisonment, Kosta Perucica was subjected to unspeakable tortures in order to force him into an intimate account of his political development and philosophy: in his report, he was instructed to recount his wartime and post-war doubts about the Party, confusions at certain political developments, to write 'about things that had always been very unclear to me', but also to remember every single letter he drafted, every, even passing, conversation he had had with his colleagues, and the reactions and feelings such conversations elicited in him (Perucica, 1990: 70–1). Although books, paper and pencils were sorely lacking at other times, the camp provided willing inmates with all the necessary equipment to 'pour their soul and their feelings out in writing' (Stojanovic, 1991: 231).

Former inmate 'Caca' remembered a particular form of self-criticism (*raskritikovanje*), practised in the female prison camp, in the course of which 'bandits' were required to sit in the centre of a circle made up of other, re-educated inmates, and to discuss the minutiae of their sexual lives, feelings and fantasies, and to describe physical relationships and experiences with husbands, boyfriends, colleagues. In a strongly patriarchal setting, this 'exercise' inevitably served further to humiliate and mortify those considered recalcitrant. Again, there seems to have been a warped application here of the psychoanalytic insistence upon the central role of sexual experiences and drives in the constitution of human personality.

The prisoners had little choice but to engage, therefore, in re-evaluations and re-assessment of their own motives, desires and longings, and to reinterpret their past relationships with their family members and others close to them, in the service of this entwined political and psychopathological model. Even ostensibly trivial inclinations and acts were to be 'poured out' and examined, searched as indicators of particular personality traits. This was meant, so it was claimed, to lead to:

> sharpening the criteria, a true transformation, into a man more conscious and more awake than before. Being at Goli Otok creates new people out of us. That new man realizes how naïve and blind he was before. Old facts are re-evaluated in a new light. That's why it's normal for the investigation [*istraga*] to be renewed [and open] all time.
>
> (Panic, 1997: 44–5)

The road of self-discovery was supposed to lead ultimately to a more satisfying and self-conscious form of living, and to overcome inner alienation.

> Your entire previous life was one large mistake. You looked around, you saw nothing. You listened superficially, you understood nothing. For some this will be the end, for others real life is only just starting. Life full of clear and sharp views, full of meaning.
>
> (Mihailovic, 1990: 243)

The camp authorities regularly incited – often violently forced – the inmates to 'remember' events from their past lives, communications, relations and encounters with certain people, their impressions, feelings or reactions to particular ideas or news. Partly, the purpose of constantly revisiting these reports and confessions was to achieve this 'remembering' of crucial events that the inmates may have omitted on purpose, forgotten or repressed (inmate 'Jelka', quoted in Simic and Trifunovic, 1990: 159–60; Stojanovic, 1991: 87). Moreover, each new 'remembered' and revealed element indicated a set of relationships and psychological connections which the inmate in question needed to acknowledge and include in a revised self-image:

Some of you think they had said all they knew. They did not. What looked like everything yesterday, is not sufficient today any more. [Goli] Otok will sharpen your criticism and you will once again speak of all of that from a much sharper point of view.

(Panic, 1997: 45)

In the end, all inmates had to share their new realization that they had always been 'spineless, cowards, without any memorable merits for the broader community'. As one inmate reportedly declared:

My greatest disappointment in the conflict between our two parties was not the break between them but a division in my own soul. I believed my entire life that I had been brave . . . but only after the Resolution was declared did I understand what a coward I have always been.

(Ibid.)

At Goli Otok he realized that he became a traitor to the Party because he had been afraid of the Red Army's invasion. Moreover, he was stunned to discover yet another hidden motive: 'My next big weakness is my enormous thirst for power. I was hoping to become an editor-in-chief when the Russians arrived' (Panic, 1997: 60–1). In a similar vein, Cenic felt no other choice but to admit that it was only in prison she finally understood that writing her diary, in which she noted some critical thoughts about Tito and which then proved to be the most incriminating evidence against her, had been an act of political betrayal (Cenic, 1994:124).

According to some of the inmates' testimonies, the ultimate result – and possibly one of the aims – of Goli Otok's measures was not so much reintegration, but in effect the disintegration of the prisoners' personality through self-analysis:

this perfidious, destructive self-analysis [led to a] demolishing of all life motifs. Convinced of the power of time they have, gradually and patiently they will take [the prisoner] from a rational critical attitude to the self, to pathological contempt for both his own personality and his closest environment.

(Mihailovic, 1990: 16)

A modified, violent and humiliating version of drama therapy also played a crucial role, and was no less perverse in its formulation than the versions of 'psychotherapy' already described. In fact it will already be evident enough how much performance and publicity were required of the inmates anyway in such sessions. But, in addition, the camp's inmates would sometimes have to stage, before audiences of their peers, a largely pre-arranged scripted theatrical performance of their political declarations and public repentance for past crimes. The camp's management insisted on the carnivalesque nature of such theatre performances; they pressured inmates to produce plays and collages which ridiculed Stalin, the Soviet Union and the Yugoslav 'bandits', while they celebrated Tito and the CPY. A frequent theme here was the staged 'burial' of the 1948

Resolution of the Informbureau. These burials were always organized at night, after all prisoners had returned from their physical exertions. A makeshift wooden coffin was prepared, and some of the most stubborn and 'unre-educable' of the inmates forced to carry it throughout the camp, between all the barracks, while the rest of the prisoners and guards observed and often laughed. Other 'bandits' were instructed to perform the roles of the dead Resolution's bereaved relatives, to wail and cry, bending their bodies in mock suffering. They were supposed to yell: 'Our Aunt Resolution died, what shall we do without it, poor us without the Resolution', while the activists spurred them on, ridiculing and beating them (Kosier, 1991: 388–91). In fact, while there was no particular script prepared for this particular elaborate performance, some inmates with professional backgrounds or experience in film or theatre were co-opted to be directors. The burials of the Resolution thus involved all the prisoners at the same time. They were also instituted as further humiliation and punishment for those who refused to participate in 're-education' programmes. With these scorned inmates cast in the ludicrous roles of the Resolution's 'family', such performances served to force them to start reinterpreting their own political orientation in similarly negative terms, as absurd and laughable choices, while they demonstrated to all the others the pathetic and ultimately impotent character of the Soviet attack on the Yugoslav state and of some Yugoslavs' support for the Soviet side. Goli Otok dramas were also quite an efficient way to force such recalcitrant prisoners finally and explicitly to adopt the role that the camp and the police authorities had prepared for them but to which they had difficulties adjusting. In 1953, after the news of Stalin's death was received, a similar procession was organized, in which several prisoners were painted black and dressed in priestly gowns, and led like cattle and with crosses on their necks around the courtyard of the prison.

Conclusion: 're-education' in context

The use of such varied 'therapeutic elements' was not confined to the Goli Otok camp. As we already saw, the wartime institute for compulsory 're-education' of young communists took the first steps in the direction of a combined psychoanalytic and behaviourist experimentation, although its applications were mild by comparison. But another socialist country, Romania, adopted similar and equally brutal psychological methods in the infamous Pitesti prison, which mainly incarcerated university students accused of anti-communism and support for the Iron Guard. While there is still, to my knowledge, no evidence regarding potential exchange and transfer of experiences between the Yugoslav and Romanian security police departments, the similarities were striking. The Pitesti experiments in 'depersonalization', which ran from 1949 until 1952, remain unmatched in the history of Romanian communism, and, like Goli Otok, seem to have drawn on a complex combination of ideas derived from psychoanalysis, behaviourism, reflexology and Makarenko's pedagogy (Bacu, 1971).[5] It is indeed both fascinating and tragically ironic that very similar torture and brainwashing techniques were applied and developed at roughly the same time on both sides of the Yugoslav–Soviet split in 1948. In the spring of 1950, Veselin Popovic, who had since 1949 been head of the first two female prisons for those accused of supporting the Informbureau Resolution in Serbia (many inmates of these prisons soon ended up at the Goli Otok complex), successfully organized his escape to Romania, where he was long held under the surveillance of the Romanian state police and may have shared with them some of the re-education techniques practised in Yugoslavia (Mihailovic, 1990: 216).

Although psychoanalysis originated in Central Europe, this region soon disappeared from the discipline's intellectual geography. But there is still a significant lacuna in scholarship when it comes to the position and history of psychoanalytic thinking in East Central Europe, and the assumption appears to be that socialist regimes eliminated psychoanalysis entirely, and that such ideas and practices could not survive or prosper under the conditions of authoritarianism and repression. It is thus critical to explore the role that psychoanalysis and psychiatry played in these repressive, authoritarian projects of the East European socialist regimes, along with an ensemble of other beliefs and practices derived from experimental psychology and other 'psy' disciplines, However unsavoury, it is important to include such evidence within the general history of the discipline.

Notes

1 Archive of Serbia, Zavod u Smederevskoj Palanci, 3/3–1, 50: 1.
2 On the psychoanalytic aspect of the institute's programme, see Antic (2014).
3 Klajn was a veteran partisan fighter with the rank of colonel of the Yugoslav army and a high-ranking Communist Party functionary as well as a practising psychoanalyst. Following his medical studies and specialization in psychiatry, Klajn underwent two years of training analysis with Nikola Sugar between 1938 and 1940, and was a permanent member of Sugar's psychoanalytic circle in interwar Yugoslavia. In turn, Nikola Sugar, the first Yugoslav psychoanalyst who supervised the first generation of post-war analysts in the country, was a member of the Viennese and Budapest psychoanalytic societies, and completed his own training analysis with Felix Boehm, and also worked closely with Paul Schilder.
4 Iskaz Marije Zelic, II Programme of Radio Belgrade, 3 May 1990.
5 On the Romanian case, see also Ierunca (1990), Merisca (1997), Stanescu (2010) and Segel (2012). The Romanian authorities referred to the prison as 'the Centre for Student Re-education', and it also involved elaborate techniques of inmates' 'self-management' and a hierarchical construction of committees run by the most reliable 're-educated' students. The Pitesti inmates were forced to perform humiliating forms of torture upon each other, and were subjected to long and violent interrogation sessions and 'external and internal unmasking' procedures, in the course of which they had to continuously retell and rewrite their own life histories.

Part VI

Colonial subjects

Spectres of dependency

Psychoanalysis in the age of decolonization

Erik Linstrum

In the theoretical imagination of decolonization, Frantz Fanon today stands as the indispensable figure. Both chronicler and participant in the Algerian War of Independence, he rose to fame with the publication of *Black Skin, White Masks* (1986 [1952]), drawing on phenomenology, existentialism, and Lacanian psychoanalysis to describe the alienation of the colonial subject in metropolitan Europe. Almost a decade later, in *The Wretched of the Earth* (1990 [1961]), Fanon shifted attention to the trauma inflicted by imperial rule, challenging the Orientalist essentialism of the Algiers School of psychiatry while arguing that violent rebellion was the inevitable fate of violently oppressive regimes.[1] Canonized by the postcolonial theorists of the 1990s, his writings have since become standard texts in history and literary criticism.[2]

While anticolonial conflicts still raged in the 1950s, however, Western intellectuals and officials preferred the theories of a rival thinker. Octave Mannoni, the French psychoanalyst and author of *La psychologie de la colonisation* (1950) who lived on Madagascar for more than two decades, drew a spirited attack from Fanon for his theory of a 'dependency complex' among colonized people. Attempting to rehabilitate Mannoni's reputation in recent years, psychoanalytic thinkers have turned to his other, less controversial writings to establish a portrait of the analyst as anticolonial theorist (Combrichon, 1999; Lane, 2002). Yet it was the 1950 text, translated into English as *Prospero and Caliban* (1956) and judged problematic even by many of Mannoni's latter-day defenders, which intrigued so many readers at the time. Heralded as the key to the colonized unconscious, the idea of 'dependency' attracted attention across national boundaries. While *Prospero and Caliban* alienated French leftists by failing to emphasize the economic underpinnings of empire, the book commanded favourable attention across a wide swath of the ideological spectrum in Britain and the United States.[3] Taking Mannoni as a point of departure, this chapter explores the strange career of psychoanalysis as a political language in the age of decolonization.

If the totalitarian unconscious described by the Frankfurt School revolved around the desire to exact obedience and impose conformity, ideas about the relationship between leaders and followers in the colonies took inspiration from that model while also diverging from it. The always looming, increasingly tangible threat of rebellion suggested a very different dynamic from the fascination with authority which seemed to characterize European fascism. Confronting nationalist uprisings across the world, defenders of empire repeatedly took refuge in the belief that unconscious forces – rather than rational calculations or ideological commitments – fuelled indigenous resistance. Amid the late colonial and Cold War imperative to win 'hearts and minds', the promise of defeating revolt through therapeutic insight as well as force was a powerful one (Pols, 2011; Warne, 2013; Linstrum, 2016). While *Prospero and Caliban* implicitly assumed that Western powers should continue to guide the fate of indigenous people, however, it simultaneously expressed pessimism about their ability to do so effectively. By portraying overseas rule as a tangled family romance, Mannoni's critique delivered an unsettling message for the colonizer as well as the colonized. Could Western officials and settlers, accustomed to exacting obedience as a matter of right, ever adapt to a world in which their authority was no longer unquestioned? Tempering deep-seated paternalism with a sense of powerlessness, the ambiguity of *Prospero and Caliban* was well calculated to appeal to Western readers in the post-war years.

Fanon came to psychoanalysis by way of Lacan – a debt especially evident in *Black Skin, White Masks*, with its racialized interpretation of the mirror stage and attack on the emptiness of subjectivity defined through perceptions of others.[4] Although Mannoni entered analysis with Lacan in 1947 and remained close to him for decades, *Prospero and Caliban* owed far more to Alfred Adler. The book's portrait of a neurotic embrace uniting colonizer and colonized did not hinge on the concepts of misrecognition or symbolization; on the contrary, Mannoni stressed that the problems of each group were accurately perceived by the other, opening the way to a pathological relationship of mutual exploitation. Long before the advent of European rule, according to Mannoni, a rigidly hierarchical Malagasy culture organized around ancestor worship and authoritarian patriarchs produced the 'dependency complex'. When these indigenous father figures appeared impotent in the face of European conquest, the Malagasy did not abandon their submissive and juvenile attitudes but simply redirected them toward a new set of paternal rulers. When the French colonial order threatened to collapse during the Second World War, the resulting fear of 'abandonment' incited them to lash out with violence. Citing a number of dream narratives in which the figure of the French *colon* loomed large, Mannoni concluded that the Malagasy were addicted to the emotional rewards of a paternalistic relationship but also plagued by ambivalence – childlike but sullenly so. 'Feelings of hostility' lurked beneath the surface of subservient behaviour, Mannoni argued, suggesting that true psychic independence would remain elusive for Madagascar even if formal political independence were granted (Mannoni, 1990).

Where Fanon valorized the therapeutic possibilities of violence, then, Mannoni portrayed it as a symptom of dysfunction. Branding anticolonial movements as products of inchoate emotion and questioning their capacity to organize functional societies, *Prospero and Caliban* has unsurprisingly been described as 'psychoanalysis to the rescue of colonialism' (Bloch, 1997). Crucially for Mannoni's analysis, however, colonial rulers were afflicted with a disorder of their own: the inferiority complex and the 'urge to dominate' which came along with it. Threatened by the competitive pressure of modernity, resenting their expulsion from the protective embrace of the family, some Europeans sought satisfaction in an exaggerated sense of superiority over others. Mannoni here followed Adler closely: the aggressive and self-serving behaviour of the inferiority complex emerged as a by-product of the passage from infantile dependency to adulthood and independence. These frustrated cast-offs of European modernity played an outsized role in the making of settler culture: 'the mediocre . . . are the most rabid racialists . . . They gain more from it because they are more hungry for compensation.' In thrall to their neurotic compulsions, colonizers encouraged the dependency of the colonized 'by instinctively adopting a paternalist attitude, with too much affection and too much punishment' (Mannoni, 1990: 66, 120). For Mannoni, the confused feelings provoked by parental abandonment explained everything – the Western drive for self-aggrandizement as well as the violence that roiled indigenous society at the first sign of retreat.

Although Mannoni was writing in the late 1940s, his chief theoretical influences dated to a much earlier period. He drew not only on Adler, but also on Lucien Lévy-Bruhl, adopting the model of the 'primitive mentality' with few apparent qualifications. Other elements of his argument were likewise far from novel. The claim that colonized populations exhibited a psychological predisposition to acquiesce in European rule, for instance, had a long genealogy in the British Empire. In the 1930s, Freudian thinkers advanced the theory of 'traumatic weaning', which held that breastfeeding until age four – with babies constantly at their mother's side – fostered feelings of weakness and dependence and thus permanently warped the African personality. The 'great, godlike' father who kept his distance in those early years, then abruptly usurped the child's position when infancy ended, served as the template for an 'irrational fear' of 'every man, black or white, in authority' (Sachs, 1947: 147–8). South African psychoanalyst Wulf Sachs is usually credited as the leading theorist of traumatic weaning. [5] But British officials, including J.F. Ritchie of the Colonial Education Service in Northern Rhodesia and Cicely Williams of the Colonial Medical Service in the Gold Coast, advanced strikingly similar arguments (Vaughan, 1991: 116–17; McCulloch, 1995: 93–8; Linstrum, 2016). Because the state represented 'the parent-surrogate *par excellence*', as Ritchie put it, childhood trauma caused Africans to 'either turn away from politics altogether' or 'ardently and blindly support every pronouncement of authority' (Ritchie, 1968: 46, 61).

This strand in the rhetoric of dependency – the suggestion that pathologies of the colonized mind pre-dated European conquest, and even invited it, rather than arising after the fact from the experience of oppression – lay at the heart of Fanon's dispute with Mannoni. It also elicited some of the most enthusiastic responses to *Prospero and Caliban*. For defenders of imperial authority, Mannoni's theory reinforced an already widespread sense that decolonization was unfolding as a generational drama, with rebellious subjects cast as restive adolescents who had to be coaxed back into the family fold (Bailkin, 2012). Some officials took this metaphor quite literally. Explaining the growth of discontent in late 1940s Kenya as a response to government restrictions on land use, colonial governor Philip Mitchell found a parallel 'in our feelings when, as children, we are first sent to school, compelled to keep regular hours and learn things out of books, instead of running about in the garden or on the beach, and playing with our friends'.[6]

Like Mannoni, however, most British observers employed the trope of the childlike subject in subtler ways than this. Anticolonial unrest was not simply a rejection of paternal control but a sign that paternalism was already breaking down; it was the difficulty of *internalizing* discipline on the path to independence, rather than the *imposition* of discipline by external authority, that triggered a violent reaction. Educators at Makerere College in Uganda read Mannoni for insight into the stresses confronting their elite students; 'caught between two worlds', as a commonplace phrase went, this transitional generation seemed to offer a test case for the pathologies of modernization (Mills, 2006: 250). The prominent daughter of Kenya's White Highlands, Elspeth Huxley, hailed *Prospero and Caliban* as confirmation of psychiatrist J.C. Carothers's *The Psychology of Mau Mau* (1954) and its stress on the dangers of 'detribalization' in particular. 'To adopt without disaster everything from Parliamentary institutions to automation and scientific humanism,' she argued, 'what has to change is not the institutions of a society, but the personality of the men and women who made it' (Huxley, 1956). Tory MP Edward Wakefield, recommending 'a book by M. Mannoni' to his House of Commons colleagues in 1954, portrayed the grievances of the incompletely modernized subject as the driving force of anticolonial revolts from the Indian Rebellion to Mau Mau. Citing his service decades earlier as an Indian Civil Service official, Wakefield recalled that 'in the remote parts of that continent . . . the Westerner was still looked up to. The district officer was regarded as "Man-Bap" – the father and mother of his people.' Because education, Christianization, and other forms of Western influence had sapped the vitality of indigenous traditions, the colonial subject willingly 'transferred his allegiance to the white man's magic'. As the transition to a rational, modern outlook proved more difficult than expected, however, the result was 'a sense of frustration and failure to develop one's full individuality.'[7]

If apologists for empire found much to admire in *Prospero and Caliban*, however, these tendentious interpretations were not universal. On the contrary: many British observers balanced the image of volatile and ungrateful *indigènes* with stinging indictments of imperial arrogance. In these accounts, it was not only benevolent projects of modernization, but pathological assertions of dominance by the colonizer, that provoked the colonized to respond with violence. Anthony Sampson's review in the *Times Literary Supplement*, pointedly titled 'White Settlers on the Couch', stressed the colonizer's 'urge to escape from his own society, to dominate others, to expect gratitude and childlike love' (Sampson, 1956). Others agreed that *Prospero and Caliban* laid bare the origins of a distinctly colonial type: the mediocrity puffed up with a false sense of importance. According to historian A.P. Thornton, Mannoni belonged in the company of Graham Greene, Joseph Conrad, and Robert Louis Stephenson because he managed to explain why so many burnt-out cases ended up in the colonies. By taking refuge in a place 'where his superiority will not be questioned', Thornton mused, the insecure personality could find solace in the colonies as he could not in Europe (Thornton, 1965). Signalling the need to raise awareness about that danger, former Indian Civil Service officer Philip Mason commended Mannoni's book to 'every administrator, missionary, and business man in the colonial world'. Mason wanted the ruler of empire to prepare for the moment of reckoning: the day when it became necessary to 'go back to a world where he will no longer be the sole authoritarian, where he will have to argue with people who can answer back, and will have to persuade them that he is right before they will do as they are told' (Mason, 1957). Indeed, that day had already arrived in many parts of the world, with the consequence that old justifications for racial hierarchies were crumbling. One consequence of reading Mannoni was that Mason felt compelled to apologize for not taking a stand against racism during his service in British India. Holding the privileged position in a colonial society, he reflected, had an 'anaesthetizing effect' on his sense of justice (Mason, 1954).

Here too, post-war theories of imperialism showed more continuity than change from the interwar era. A generation of British leftists inspired by Freud and Adler had challenged the legitimacy of colonization by locating its origin in irrational and unconscious forces. A retired Indian Civil Service administrator named Bernard Houghton lent support to the nationalist cause with polemics like *The Psychology of Empire* (1921), which blamed imperial expansion on 'a desire to dominate, to appear important . . . the Narcissus complex . . . a reversion to the infant stage of auto-sexuality'. Given virtually unfettered power to rule, Houghton argued, the imperial proconsul 'regresses to the infantile stage, himself alone real, all the world centred on him' (Houghton, 1921). For John Hoyland, a Quaker missionary in 1920s India, feelings of inferiority rather than narcissism warped colonizing minds, but the result was the same. In Hoyland's view, compensation for childhood feelings of weakness and dependence took shape in feelings of 'acquisitiveness and possessiveness', and these in turn explained 'the profit-motive in industry', the 'grab for Africa', and 'the attitude of the average Britisher towards the Indian and the negro' (Hoyland, 1937). The closest Anglophone analogue to Mannoni may have been Wulf Sachs, who balanced his diagnosis of African dependency with a diagnosis of European racial neurosis. Tracing the 'idea of superior "races"' to the frustrations of the economically marginalized, Sachs described aggression toward Jewish and African 'others' as an irrational displacement of class conflict (Sachs, 1943; Sachs, 1944).

By the 1950s – with the Raj relegated to history and European control of Africa looking increasingly unstable – the idea that decolonization required a recalibration of the emotional bonds between ruler and ruled had an especially powerful appeal in Britain. A central assumption of the Commonwealth, after all, was that sentimental ties forged in the imperial era might undergird a continuing political union. The establishment of the Institute of Race Relations in London in 1951, often remembered in the context of Commonwealth migration at home, was in fact closely tied to anxieties about the future of British influence with postcolonial populations overseas (Bailkin, 2012). The inaugural director of the Institute, Philip Mason, worried that a colonial legacy of racism risked alienating Third World populations from the West and thus making them susceptible to communism. Mason never accepted Mannoni's theory without qualification: above all, he questioned the implication that indigenous minds dwelled endlessly on white authority figures. But his conviction that pathologies inherited from empire remained virulent shaped the Institute's research agenda in its early years.

One researcher sponsored by the Institute of Race Relations in those years was psychologist Gustav Jahoda. Doing fieldwork with attitude questionnaires on the eve of Ghanaian independence in the mid 1950s, Jahoda noticed a belief among some older Africans that only European rule could bring progress. Did these lingering feelings of awe and deference provide an opening for the British to exercise influence in the postcolonial era? Drawing explicitly on Mannoni, Jahoda arrived at a more pessimistic conclusion. The transitional period from dependency to independence once again appeared fraught and unpredictable; among semi-educated Africans, Jahoda warned, a newly emergent inferiority complex encouraged outbursts of magic, criminality, and 'fantasy compensation'. Like Mason, Jahoda registered many qualifications to Mannoni's theory: the veneration of British officials as godlike figures was no longer commonplace in West Africa; the brute reality of a European monopoly over economic and political power, rather than innate pathology, produced those feelings in the first place; a healthy, secure sense of self was not merely possible but already a reality for some Ghanaians. But this sunny prognosis applied mainly to the 'small elite' of Africans who enjoyed the privileges of post-secondary education and the ability to work alongside Europeans in prestigious positions. For the vast majority with limited access to education, Jahoda painted a darker portrait: 'aggressive attitudes', 'fanciful hopes', and 'identification with figures that are "power-symbols"', most notably Kwame Nkrumah. While the Ghanaian personality would achieve stability in the long term, Jahoda implied, the period of decolonization threatened to be tumultuous (Jahoda, 1961: 107–35).

This particular conflation of the personal and the political – identifying the psychology of dependency as an explanation for the emotional intensity of anticolonial movements – also shaped Colonial Office-sponsored research in the human sciences. The incompletely modernized, therefore frustrated and radicalized, subject was a recurring trope in these studies. A pair of American psychologists stationed at the East African Institute of Social Research in Uganda found that Africans attending the most 'acculturated' schools – those close to cities, staffed by European teachers, and using English as the language of instruction – gave questionnaire responses which expressed the greatest hostility toward white people and the indigenous chiefs who collaborated with them. Proceeding from the assumption that Western education involved more 'training for self-discipline, responsibility, etc.', they concluded that the pressures of individualism were pushing Africans toward radicalism (Ainsworth and Ainsworth, 1962a; Ainsworth and Ainsworth, 1962b).

This conclusion dovetailed with the assumption, widely shared by British officials and intellectuals in the 1950s, that the passage from dependency to inferiority explained the emotional volatility of decolonization. Training the next generation of overseas administrators at Oxford, Colonial Office adviser Margery Perham taught that the 'inferiority complex' among African leaders represented 'a force of great, of dangerous, of still incalculable power – a mental atomic energy'. Humiliated by the consciousness that their states, economies, and schools bore the imprint of European conquest, they resorted to the 'projection of guilt', blaming Britain for all their problems and seeking independence before they could realistically hope to stand on their own. A veteran of the colonial service in Nigeria agreed that the 'pathology of wounded self-esteem' was fuelling nationalist demands. So did the governor of the Gold Coast, Alan Burns, who also cited the 'inferiority complex' and described educated Africans as suspicious, touchy, and aggressive. Psychologist Robert Thouless described Colonel Nasser as a candidate for psychiatric treatment; political scientist William Gutteridge identified 'anti-white emotion' as the motive force of West African nationalism; legal scholar Ivor Jennings labelled Indian nationalism as 'not rational in its essence'; and psychoanalyst Alix Strachey saw 'the child's desire to be equal to his elders' as the motive force of anticolonial and postcolonial politics (Linstrum, 2016).

Of course, researchers did not always distinguish phases of dependency and inferiority as clearly as Mannoni did. One of the most ambitious Colonial Office projects, the West Indian Social Survey carried out in Jamaica in 1946–9, uncovered evidence that symptoms of both complexes were widespread on the island. The psychologist who analysed results from thousands of Rorschach inkblots and other projective tests, Madeline Kerr, saw signs of a 'retreat into neurosis' and a 'lack of integration in the Jamaican personality'. Like Mannoni, Kerr perceived a delicate moment of transition in the post-war era. Even as a limited form of self-government had been introduced to Jamaica after decades of authoritarian rule, 'the mental and emotional hang-overs' of colonization and slavery showed few signs of receding. Textbooks valorized a distant and unreal British culture while black culture remained in thrall to myths of white superiority. The weakness of the father in Jamaican families – a consequence, in part, of scarce opportunities for wage labour – left an opening for less healthy forms of authority. Echoing the theorists of traumatic weaning, Kerr pointed to the dominance of matriarchs as an explanation for the supposed absence of drive and initiative in the Jamaican personality. 'This dependence on the woman', she argued, 'does lead to an adult attitude of expecting some substitute mother to look after, provide and make things easy for you' (Kerr, 1952: 69). At the same time, Kerr wondered whether Jamaica's 'odd choice of leaders is due to the fact that boys have not experienced male leadership'. The combination of racial resentment and obedience to authority gave an opening to 'demagogues' like labour leader and future prime minister Alexander Bustamante, who made 'meaningless speeches' and promised to 'take on his shoulders all your troubles'. Kerr worried that 'dangerous situations would result' if the aggressive impulses of the Jamaican crowd ever found a scapegoat (Linstrum, 2016).

Since Kerr published her conclusions about Jamaica in 1952 – four years before *Prospero and Caliban* appeared in English – it is unlikely that Mannoni figured as a significant influence. But her diagnosis of the Jamaican mind helps to explain why the notion of a 'dependency complex' subsequently found a warm reception in Britain. Whether couched in terms of weak fathers, domineering mothers, or both, theories about the psychology of colonized populations repeatedly located the origins of political behaviour in the dynamics of the family. With remarkable consistency across the imperial arenas of Africa, Asia, and the West Indies – and across the conventional dividing line of the Second World War – British thinkers argued that the dependent mentality fostered by indigenous child-rearing complicated efforts to exercise authority overseas. Habits of deference, which might seem useful from an imperialist perspective, were always shadowed by less desirable forces: passivity and emotionalism, self-loathing and resentment, frustration and aggression.

Acknowledging the psychological importance of the mother-child bond was, of course, a longstanding feature of Freudian thought. But the claim that healthy personalities could only be forged through particular child-rearing practices reached new prominence with the post-war vogue of 'Bowlbyism'. Although John Bowlby's attachment theory has long figured in debates about the domestic politics of the welfare state, it is less often noted that his influence extended far beyond the metropole, fostering a global ideal for family life across cultures.[8] The frontispiece of Bowlby's *magnum opus*, *Attachment and Loss*, pointedly featured a photograph of a naked Amazonian woman cradling her infant son, the only image to appear in three volumes. The universality of attachment behaviour was documented by near-simultaneous observational studies in Scotland and – thanks to Bowlby's American collaborator Mary Ainsworth – in Uganda. The WHO supplied an imprimatur of global authority: Hargreaves commissioned Bowlby to write a report on *Maternal Care and Mental Health*, which eventually sold 400,000 copies in an abridged edition. Within the WHO, Hargreaves emerged as a vociferous advocate of the idea that children deprived of continuous maternal care in early life suffered 'a degree of permanent damage of personality development – damage particularly to the capacity to form relationships with others and to the cognitive capacity we call abstraction' (Linstrum, 2016). The appeal of Bowlby's theory came in part from its description of emotional deprivation in terms analogous to the ubiquitous post-war problem of nutritional deficiency, suggesting that targeted intervention by experts could correct the personality disorders that thwarted progress in the world beyond the West (Duniec and Raz, 2011).

One consequence of the Bowlbyist moment was a resurgence of warnings about the trauma of weaning in other cultures. Paradoxically, in these accounts, dependency emerged from a breakdown of the mother–child bond. At a time when Western apostles of modernization stressed that transforming societies required psychological transformation as well, many of them identified maternal care as a key force for moulding personalities capable of making decisions, embracing change, and tolerating uncertainty.[9] According to Kenneth Soddy – another Tavistock psychiatrist and a leading figure in the World Federation of Mental Health, which was founded after the war – the central problem in the psychology of economic development was 'how a climate of change may be created in the individual'. Like Bowlby, Soddy portrayed the 'standard nuclear family' as a prerequisite for emotional adaptability. By establishing a 'warm and secure relationship' through breastfeeding and then gradually training the child to feed independently, the ideal mother taught her offspring 'to gain satisfaction from the very acceptance of new things'. In the sprawling extended families of many non-Western cultures, however, this critical shift never materialized. Because a profusion of siblings, grandparents, aunts, and uncles weakened the intensity of emotional connections, the experience of growth into adulthood lacked the sense of joy that only a mother's love could impart. As a consequence, Soddy argued, adaptation to 'change may be no more than a passive conformity'. The supposedly 'rigid form of relationships' in a clan governed by status hierarchies translated into lack of enthusiasm for change in the world outside the family (Linstrum, 2016).

In postcolonial India, too, research seemed to demonstrate that child-rearing habits impeded social progress. Like other proponents of traumatic weaning, Morris Carstairs concluded that the generous, undisciplined style of mothering he observed in a Rajasthan village prevented the youngest children from learning how to manage frustration. Thanks to the untrammelled affection they briefly enjoyed, Indian babies could entertain visions of omnipotence until the harsh experience of maternal deprivation shattered this idyll. As Carstairs saw it, 'the underlying mistrust which seems to cloud so many of my informants' adult personal relationships may well be derived from the fantasy of a fickle mother who mysteriously withholds her caresses.' This sense of insecurity had implications for economic development because, according to Carstairs, it encouraged conformity and passivity rather than ambition and risk-taking. In the late 1950s and again in the mid 1960s, psychologists advising the US government cited Carstairs as an authoritative explanation for the resistance to change which supposedly characterized the Indian personality. An American psychologist working in India speculated in 1965 that the emotional impulse to cling to authority rather than challenge it explained the 'stagnation and immobility' which thwarted development projects. 'Even today', Harvard researcher David Winter observed, 'the Western scholar meets Indians who will say, "Ah, you know, *sahib*, it was all better under the British."' The Punjabi villager who suggested that economic progress depended on the Municipal Board cleaning up drains and the Department of Agriculture supplying better farming tools exemplified this lack of initiative (Linstrum, 2016).

The dependency diagnosis enjoyed such wide currency, in part, because it met the ideological needs of the moment. As imperial rule waned, it offered a rationale for continuing to intervene in other societies while casting blame for any failures on the disordered state of indigenous minds. At the Council on Foreign Relations in the 1950s, American scholars were reading Mannoni as they debated whether the 'territorial status of dependency' in newly liberated colonies had merely given way to the 'psychological status of dependency'.[10] But dependency theory also suggested a new orientation for Western authority: aiming at the cultivation of autonomous, emotionally well-adjusted subjects rather than attempting to impose policies by fiat. With old-fashioned displays of dominance now discredited – both because they satisfied suspect emotional needs and because they provoked ever more impassioned resistance – thinkers on both sides of the Atlantic agreed on the need to exercise overseas influence in subtler ways.

Under the influence of Kurt Lewin's theory of group dynamics, the Americans pioneered the idea of 'community development' in the Third World: education for democratic citizenship which attempted to demonstrate the virtues of non-authoritarian leadership through a carefully choreographed process of consensus-building. Identifying the sentiments, opinions, and 'natural leaders' of the indigenous population, then mobilizing the collective on behalf of a tangible objective such as the construction of a school or hospital, was its essence. Defined in opposition to the impersonal technologies of mass society as well as traditional hierarchies of caste, tribe, and village, this approach played an especially prominent role in State Department and Ford Foundation initiatives in India in the late 1940s and early 1950s (Immerwahr, 2015; Hull, 2010; Hull, 2011).

In Britain, too, human scientists and government officials after the war converged on the belief that exerting influence indirectly, by posing as the instrument of collective sentiment, was preferable to relying on explicit assertions of authority. Drawing on Lewinian techniques of group therapy developed during the war by Wilfred Bion, the shift from compulsion to self-motivation was especially pronounced in British psychiatry (Torres, 2013; Harrison 2000). These intellectual currents also left their mark on imperial policy. At the University of London in the early 1950s, officials who underwent training in community development were reading Lewin's *Resolving Social Conflicts* (1948) as well as British texts, such as James Halliday's *Psychosocial Medicine* (1948) and Alex Comfort's *Authority and Delinquency in the Modern State* (1950), which touted therapeutic techniques as tools of governance. Because 'people will move forward only so far as they have the inward compulsions', colonial secretary Arthur Creech Jones declared in 1948, the 'fundamental problem' of governing colonized people was 'breaking down their resistance and stimulating their desires'. One administrator argued that overseas rule after the war should be guided by 'the psychology of disengagement . . . a gradual freeing of the people from the invisible ties which bind them to [their rulers].' The ideal district officer now invited people to discuss 'their problems, their difficulties and differences, with a view to giving all his assistance to effect a change of heart and attitude'. Lessons in civic education, ubiquitous across British Africa in the 1950s, blended old-fashioned exercises in character-building with warnings about the dangers of the 'inferiority complex' and 'the 'aggressive instinct'. In these visions, the familiar model of the official as father figure was increasingly overlaid with another template: the official as psychoanalyst. The emotional bond between ruler and ruled now functioned as a means of stimulating introspection rather than exacting obedience (Linstrum, 2016).

Mannoni's *Prospero and Caliban* mattered not because it single-handedly inspired anxieties about dependency in the colonized populations but because it made the connection between decolonization and the unconscious mind more explicit than ever before. The emotional disorders perpetuated by father figures in politics and biological mothers in the family had preoccupied British thinkers, in particular, for decades. These worries assumed new urgency as imperial authority began to break down after the Second World War. Psychoanalytic explanations that encompassed colonizer and colonized in the same pathological web appeared to account for the suddenness, and the disruptiveness, of empire's end. They also suggested the remedy – a paradoxical one – of cultivating independent habits in thought and feeling through the guidance of Western experts. In navigating this tension between coercion and autonomy, the psychoanalysis of decolonization was perhaps not so different from the psychoanalysis of totalitarianism after all. The democratic subject – self-reliant yet law-abiding, distinct from the mass yet socially conscious, nonconformist yet ultimately manageable – furnished a rough but recognizable template for the decolonized subject.

Notes

1 On the Algiers School, see Keller 2007.
2 See especially Bhabha 1994.
3 For a sample of the French reception, see the reviews by Georges Balandier (1950) and Robert Boudry (1950). Even favourable responses took a defensive tone, stressing that psychological explanations complemented accounts of economic exploitation rather than substituting for them: see the review by Francis Jeanson (1950).
4 David Macey (1999) has suggested that the mirror stage was the only psychoanalytic concept that played a significant role in Fanon's work.
5 On Sachs, see also Khanna 2003: 236–68; Dubow 1996; and Rose 1996.
6 See Philip Mitchell, circular letter, 1949, CO 537/6569, National Archives of the United Kingdom, Kew.
7 See 350 *Parl. Deb.*, H.C., 5th ser. (1953–4), 1611–14.
8 On Bowlby and welfarism, see Shapira 2013: 203–14; Mayhew 2006; and van der Horst 2011. For the classic criticism that Bowlby encouraged a conservative view of the family, by implying that mothers who pursued careers outside it risked damaging their children for life, see Mitchell 1974. For more sympathetic interpretations which attempt to distinguish the nuances of Bowlby's thought from the orthodoxies of 'Bowlbyism' in the public sphere, see Riley 1983; Thomson 2013; and Holmes 1993.

9 On the psychological dimension of overseas development, see Rothschild 1994; Ekbladh 2010; Cullather 2010: 77–94; Latham 2000: 33–41; Latham 2011: 46–8.
10 See Edwin J. Cohn to William Diebold, 27 August 1957, Council on Foreign Relations archive, series 3, box 164, folder 5, and Discussion Group on Economic Development in Africa minutes, 8 March 1956, Council on Foreign Relations archive, series 3, box 159, folder 4, Mudd Manuscript Library, Princeton, NJ.

Chapter 14

The vicissitudes of anger

Psychoanalysis in the time of apartheid

Ross Truscott and Derek Hook

Introduction[1]

Apartheid, as is well known, is the slogan under which the Afrikaner National Party (NP) came to power in South Africa in 1948. It ended, at least officially, in 1994 with South Africa's first democratic national election. In grappling with a history of psychoanalysis in South Africa in the years leading up to and during apartheid, and doing so within the context of this edited volume, *Psychoanalysis in the Age of Totalitarianism*, it is worth asking at the outset whether South Africa has a totalitarian past of which to speak. Was apartheid totalitarian?

It has certainly been stated that apartheid operated 'as a totalitarian, repressive state' (Wolpe, 1989: 17); it is still common for contemporary writers to refer to apartheid as a 'totalitarian regime' (Gobodo-Madikizela, 2008: 39), to speak of 'a country newly emerged from the tyranny and totalitarianism of apartheid' (Swartz, 2006: 552). At least according to Hannah Arendt's (1973) *The Origins of Totalitarianism*, these renderings of apartheid would seem overstated. Arendt suggests that the term be used 'sparingly and prudently' (xxviii). While she refers to white rule in South Africa as a 'tyrannical minority' (xxi), she is also clear that 'totalitarian government is different from dictatorships and tyrannies' (xxvii). [2] Jon Hyslop (2007) perhaps gets it right when he states, 'If the more committed apartheid ideologues had totalitarian aspirations, they were never able to impose them in an unrestricted way' (125). Highlighting opposition to the state by liberal politicians, journalists, academics and artists, Hyslop takes apartheid to have been an 'authoritarian' rather than a fully 'totalitarian' regime (125).

The standard story about the origins of psychoanalysis in South Africa is of a single, long, progressive – though interrupted – struggle by analysts and academics against apartheid and the racial segregation that preceded it, and for International Psychoanalytic Association (IPA) affiliation. In this narrative, particular weight is given to the liberal Johannesburg intellectual circle, of which Wulf Sachs and I.D. MacCrone were a part, and within which psychoanalytic ideas were fostered, processed, institutionalized and questioned (see Hayes, 2008).[3] Indeed, if apartheid was an authoritarian regime, as Hyslop suggests, it was MacCrone (1937) who first diagnosed the obsessional features of this authoritarianism in psycho-analytic terms, discerning them in the race attitudes of white South Africans in the 1930s.[4] The very presence of not only liberal, but also psychoanalytic critiques of both apartheid and the racial segregation of the Union of South Africa, then, would seem to support Hyslop's claim.

It is, however, precisely the distance between liberalism and totalitarianism that Arendt refuses in *The Origins of Totalitarianism*. In imperial rule, as Arendt understands it in the context of a South African history underpinned by lib-eral ideas, 'were many of the elements which gathered together could create a totalitarian government on the basis of racism' (1973 [1958]: 221). As Adam Sitze (2013) remarks, for Arendt, 'the colony is the very origin of the bureau-cratic rule so radicalized by the totalitarian regimes' (336, n. 80). South Africa's imperialism may not have escalated into full totalitarian rule, Arendt argues, but its cardinal features contained the kernels of totalitarianism. It is here that our objective comes into focus; we aim to explore how psychoanalysis was set to work within the orbit of what Arendt calls – in marking one of the origins of totalitarianism – 'imperialism'. The present discussion investigates the deploy-ment of psychoanalysis in a markedly authoritarian context that had, as it were, 'regressed' to one of the underlying kernels of totalitarianism, namely that of racist colonial administration. A further crucial issue also comes to the fore: while the struggle against racism has figured large in the narration of the his-tory of psychoanalysis in South Africa, a more critical reassessment, of the type that we propose here, entails exploring the relationship between psychoanalysis and the very apartheid thinking against which it has frequently been pitted (see Swartz, 2007; Parker, 2004).

Two interestingly distinct examples – the writings of Wulf Sachs and Chabani Manganyi – can serve to illustrate the complexities of psychoanalytic thinking and practice during the era of apartheid (Hayes, 2008; Hook, 2011). There are notable differences in the approach and background of these two proponents of psychoanalysis, not the least of which was their different racial designation (Sachs as white, Manganyi as black) under the apartheid system. Sachs, who worked in South Africa in the 1930s, was the representative of European and (at least initially) orthodox Freudian psychoanalysis. Manganyi, a South African by birth, began publishing some forty years later, in the 1970s, and developed a vernacular form of psychoanalysis informed by the objectives of black con-sciousness. Despite such differences, there are intriguing lines of convergence in their work: both men were obliged to engage with the question not only of anger, but also of violent revolt. These themes have considerable importance in grasping the political role of psychoanalysis under apartheid, certainly inas-much as anger is – at least as David Macey (2003) so persuasively argues – the basic political emotion, particularly so in contexts of marked oppression. Anger is, of course, a perennial psychoanalytic topic, one which was put to work in psychoanalytic writing in South Africa from the 1920s to the present (see Sitze, 2013). Moreover, anger has been at the heart of much postcolonial writing since

Frantz Fanon's (1967) call to the calculated violence of decolonization, Jean-Paul Sartre's (1967) affirmation of his approach and Arendt's (1972) subsequent dismissal of it.

In this brief survey of the psychoanalytic responses to anger offered by Sachs and Manganyi, we hope to extract lessons about the political role of psychoanalysis during apartheid more generally. We begin with *Black Hamlet*, which was first published in 1937, and renamed *Black Anger* in its US 1947 edition. This was Sachs's psychoanalytic biography of John Chavafambira, an *nganga* (healer-diviner) living in South Africa in the 1930s. The second section turns to Manganyi, who used psychoanalytic theory to explore black experience under the conditions of apartheid, perhaps most strikingly in the essay of 1977 we focus on here, 'The Violent Reverie'.

Black anger

Wulf Sachs, a Lithuanian-born Jew, settled in Johannesburg with his family in 1922 after finishing his medical training in London. He analysed John Chavafambira for roughly two and a half years. As is frequently pointed out, however, this was not an analysis in the strict sense. Having left his home in Manyikaland for South Africa in the early 1920s, Chavafambira was living with his wife, Maggie, in the slums of Rooiyard, Johannesburg. Sachs met Chavafambira in 1933 through the anthropologist, Ellen Hellman, who was conducting research on Rooiyard. After treating Maggie as a patient at Hellman's request, Sachs began to chat with Chavafambira at his house, 'speaking to him as one doctor to another' (73), conveying to him the importance of self-knowledge in being a good doctor, as well as the concept of the unconscious. '[W]hen I offered to help him discover this hidden part of himself,' Sachs observed, 'he accepted willingly' (73).

The idea of 'Hamletism' emerges in a chapter outlining Sachs's and Hellman's visit to Chavafambira after he and other black residents had been evicted from Rooiyard. Such evictions were nothing new: they had taken place in South Africa since at least the end of the nineteenth century. As Maynard Swanson (1977) argues, state racism could be mobilized around the threat of bubonic plague: the Public Health Acts of 1893 and 1897 served as legislative instruments to wage war against 'infection', 'equating black urban settlement, labour and living conditions with threats to public health and security' (410). The 1930s witnessed an intensification and proliferation of such policies by the South African state (Dubow, 1996).

This 'sanitation syndrome', as Swanson calls it, was met with anger and revolt in the Cape in the early twentieth century; it was anger, too, that Sachs encountered in Chavafambira after his eviction, 'his voice loud and trembling with passion' (234), irritated with these visitors' persistent questions, and suspecting their collusion with the authorities. Rather than seeking to subdue this rage, Sachs took it to be a sign of Chavafambira's latent vitality. On Sachs's account, Chavafambira had faltered, withdrawing from this anger impotently: 'Renunciation and flight', as Sachs put it, 'were John's choice in any situation requiring strength of will or endurance of pain' (234). The problem of symptomatic rage, therefore, is central to the plot of *Black Hamlet*.

Hamlet has, of course, been linked in the psychoanalytic literature to the Oedipus complex. If the drama of Oedipus exemplifies the crucial importance of the incest taboo and the murder of the father, Hamlet is one step removed from this, immobilized by a conflict caused entirely by fantasy, unable to avenge his father's death and kill his uncle because he sees in the latter the fulfilment of his forbidden wishes to kill his father and marry his mother (Freud, 1900; Jones, 1945). This is what Hamlet's uncle had done, and so he could not avenge his father's death because he was mortified, as Sachs (1934) puts it in an earlier text, by 'someone usurping this place, exactly as he had longed to do' (203). Like Hamlet, Chavafambira's father, a famous *nganga*, had died, and his mother had married her husband's brother, Charlie. Like Hamlet, Chavafambira suspected that his father had been poisoned by his uncle, who had been entrusted by his brother with initiating Chavafambira into the profession when he came of age, forbidding him to practise before then. Though his mother was dead, Chavafambira retained a loving image of her and dreamed of sleeping with her. These familial details, in Sachs's view, suggested a variety of resonances between the fates of the son of a Danish king and the son of a famous Manyika *nganga*. Most of all, though, Chavafambira was, according to Sachs, as indecisive and immobilized as Hamlet.

Hamlet has also been linked in psychoanalytic theory to loss and melancholia. Hamlet, having lost his father, was unable to mourn him. He was haunted by his dead father, indeed had incorporated him in melancholy fashion (Freud, 1917). Chavafambira's Hamletism is said to relate to a knot of intertwined losses, not only of his father and mother, but also of his homeland. This was the place he had left and for which, according to the narrative, he pines, along with lost traditions – traditions that authorized, however, the marriage of his mother to his uncle. As to the melancholic dimensions of Hamletism specifically as it relates to his parents, Sachs notes that, while Europeans erect strict boundaries between the living and the dead, in Africans it is 'normal' to communicate with the dead. He refers to this in Chavafambira's case as a particular kind of 'introjection of an object', which enabled him to 'retain his lost father and mother who were so dear and important to him' (83).

Reading Chavafambira's conflicts as a form of Hamletism may strike contemporary readers as glaringly Eurocentric. It is, however, the key to Sachs's strategic political intervention (Khanna, 2003; Bertoldi, 1998; Dubow, 1996; Rose, 1996). Colonial ethnopsychiatry had conceived melancholia as a supposedly refined psychopathology that 'natives' were, on account of their more 'primitive' psychic make-up, incapable of experiencing (Vaughan, 1991). Hamletism, in Sachs's (1937) view, was an affliction 'common to all of humanity', affecting 'men of all races and nations' (236–7), an assertion that contradicted ethnopsychiatric discourse, but also the policy of separate development being advanced in apartheid and pre-apartheid South Africa (Sitze, 2007). Bertoldi (1998) particularly stresses this facet, namely the oft-criticized 'universalizing' categories of the Oedipus complex and related theorizations, as what made psychoanalysis potentially radical and non-discriminatory in the apartheid context. In disputing the validity of differential racial categories in relation to the function of the Oedipus complex and melancholia, Sachs went against the grain of accepted psychoanalytic wisdom (Hayes, 2008; Manganyi, 1985) even while using psychoanalytic thinking to do so.

It has been suggested that in the reworking of *Black Hamlet* in *Black Anger* the reader bears witness to Sachs's emerging self-reflexivity. It seems difficult to contest that Sachs's growing awareness of the causes of psychic malaise of black South Africans is here projected onto the subject of his study, as Chavafambira's growing awareness (Hayes, 1998; Dubow, 1996). If ethnopsychiatry could be said to be the target of *Black Hamlet*, *Black Anger*, published ten years later, appears to undermine the very text it revises. The shift in emphasis, while it has been the subject of much commentary, is worth revisiting, specifically with regards to the issue of anger.

In the 1937 text, Sachs had earlier perceived Chavafambira as a kind of immobilized Hamlet, whom he sought to educate into the necessity of 'Revolt' (as the final chapter of *Black Hamlet* is entitled). As Rose (1996) puts it, the point of the encounter is 'to induce in its subject the imagined capacity to kill' (44). A key event in the narrative occurs when a distraught Chavafambira, en route to Manyikaland with Sachs, relates how he had the previous night poisoned Maggie using some of Sachs's medicine. As it turns out, he had only succeeded in sedating her, inducing heavy sleep. Sachs, though, was delighted, as 'there was steadily growing within him self-assertion and the instinct to fight his own way through life. Unnoticed by himself and others, John had become ready for revolt' (Sachs, 1937: 240). Sachs sought to induct Chavafambira into a more mature articulation of his aggression rather than continuing to put himself and others at risk in infantile melancholic rage or equally immature flights. Sachs thus aimed to encourage in Chavafambira an understanding of his tragic fate as a first step towards the redirection of his aggression. While for Hamlet, overcoming a state of inertia consisted in avenging his father's murder by killing his uncle, for Chavafambira it was more a matter of 'the spiritual murder of Charlie' (240), becoming an *nganga* like his father, usurping his uncle.

In *Black Hamlet*, anger is located in Chavafambira's unconscious conflict with paternal authority; it is at once his symptom and the sign of a shared humanity (Khanna, 2003). In *Black Anger*, specifically in the final chapter, anger is generated not as a symptom of an internal melancholic ambivalence, but as the product of a political situation, towards which Sachs seeks to redirect Chavafambira's emotions. This is a political situation in which psychoanalysis seems, at best, ineffectual. Sachs (1947) eventually questioned the very basis of his initial invitation to Chavafambira to undergo analysis: 'John's greatest need was not to know his repressed unconscious, but to know the society he lived in, to recognize its ills and to learn how to fight them' (275).

Chavafambira is said to have stated to a group gathered at his house, 'for months and months I would talk to him lying on the sofa and he would just say, "Yes" . . . "Very interesting" . . . "Tell me more" . . . "What do you think of it?" It would make me so angry, so angry! I wanted to leave him so many times and never come back, so angry he made me with all this silence' (Sachs, 1947: 304). To understand Chavafambira's fury as transference is in itself a political act. If 'primitive people' in psychoanalytic theory are those without history, the corollary is that the figure of the 'primitive' is seen to be unanalysable, incapable of a transferential relation that both holds and withholds a repressed history. To take Chavafambira's anger as transference – or, properly speaking, acting out – is to render him a universal subject of history. And it is precisely the emergence of anger in the transference – anger at psychoanalysis itself – that has facilitated the emergence and vocal expression of a type of passion that could not otherwise be voiced in such terms. Indeed, one might well ask: what other clinical treatment in the South Africa of that time would allow the expression of such sentiments of anger and rage to be directed by a black patient toward a white doctor? Then again, one might remark, in psychoanalytical fashion, upon a feature of this anger which has apparently been redirected at the psychoanalytic treatment itself. Critics of the depoliticizing qualities of psychoanalysis might well argue, and not without reason, that clinical treatment risks redirecting, even dissipating properly political anger, ascribing a psychical impetus and location to that state of mind, and all too easily transforming the question from the social to the intra-subjective, or at most, the dynamics of a family.

It pays here to offer a brief meta-theoretical reflection on the notion of desire as it has been developed and mobilized in Lacanian psychoanalysis. The idea here is that desire, in its multiple forms, should be prioritized in clinical interventions such that a variety of subsidiary affects, relations and diagnostic indicators come into view (Bailly, 2009). In the present context – considering the political role of psychoanalysis in an authoritarian, even (quasi-) totalitarian, state, it could be argued that anger plays a similar role. As soon as one prioritizes an analysis of the vicissitudes of anger, a variety of political relations are brought powerfully into view. This is borne out by a range of ostensibly clinical phenomena, such as symptomatic rage, impotent rage, melancholia, familial rivalry, chronic indecision, deferred or transferential anger – all of which can also be understood as psychopolitical effects, the result of apartheid's grievous asymmetries of power. As is evident below, this observation also has an important bearing upon Manganyi's psychoanalytic theorizations of anger, revolt and violence.

Violent reverie

Manganyi's significance as a scholar owes as much to his role as a psychologist as to his devotion to the cause of the Black Consciousness Movement (Hayes, 2011; Couve, 1986). The type of black consciousness that emerged in apartheid

South Africa, and that is typically embodied in the charismatic figure of Steve Biko, was essentially a youth movement, a form of cultural and political activism that endeavoured to foster bonds of solidarity between those considered 'non-white' by the apartheid state. It aimed to engender not only a sense of pride, self-reliance and agency, but to oppose both the condescending paternalism of white liberals, and the racist structures of apartheid South Africa (Biko, 1978; Mzamane, Maaba and Biko, 2006; Nengwekhulu, 1981). Black consciousness began 'as a campus movement in 1968' (McClintock, 1995: 340) – although the tradition of thought and anticolonial struggle it deployed has a long genealogy (Mangcu, 2012) – and it ended with the state's ban upon all black consciousness organizations in 1977 following the Soweto uprising in 1976 (Howarth, 2000).

The Soweto uprising was in part a revolt against Afrikaans being made the language of instruction in black schools for non-language subjects. As Anne McClintock (1995) puts it (329):

On the winter morning of June 16, 1976, fifteen thousand black children marched on Orlando Stadium in Soweto, carrying slogans dashed on the backs of exercise books. The children were stopped by armed police who opened fire and thirteen-year-old Hector Peterson became the first of hundreds of school children to be shot down by police in the months that followed.

It was in the aftermath of this event and the rapidly spreading revolt that Manganyi penned 'The Violent Reverie: The Unconscious in Literature and Society', originally published in 1977.[5] 'Negritude, theories of the African Personality and Black Consciousness', taken together, Manganyi wrote, are 'symptomatic of some profound need in the inner world of the black collective psyche to materialize a new identity to harness all the resources of its cultural and historical unconscious' (8). This was, for Manganyi, a personal demand: 'So overwhelming were the fantasies of revenge, so terrifying in their stark clarity, that it became important for me to arrive at some internal resolution of the diverse impulses which were constantly invading my consciousness' (Manganyi, 1977: i). It was also, however, a psychic predicament he recognized all around him:

Anger, resentment, ambivalent feelings and the impulse to violence must present themselves under diverse situations in the lives of members of subordinate groups. In between these primarily unconscious themes which occasionally seek objective expression in social action such as a politically motivated assassination or a terrorist blood-bath . . . is to be found the 'mask' or what I prefer to call . . . *false consciousness*.

(Manganyi, 2011: 15–16)

Manganyi's conceptualization of false consciousness is indebted to Fanon. It involves 'unconscious collusion with super-ordinates in [one's] dehumanization' (16), and it can be seen in 'the proverbial smile of the colonized . . . [their] expressionless face in the wake of intense provocation' (16).

The 'unconscious', for Manganyi, is, on the one hand, a wellspring of primitive drive impulses to be marshalled for revolt. Yet it is also – here echoing Fanon (1952) in *Black Skin, White Masks* – marked by identification with 'prevailing white images of the people of colour' (8), an internalization of an image of inhuman savagery used to rationalize apartheid policies of separate development. It is an immanently political entity inasmuch as we may witness there an 'unconscious collusion' with the white authorities (12). The unconscious refers, then, to those aspects of psychic life at once more unruly and more docile than the conscious attitudes of blacks would allow. One understands, then, why Manganyi cautioned against violent revolt, urging, rather, for a 'frontal attack on the legacy of the unconscious so as to appreciate most fully the consequences of servitude and its companion – the false consciousness' (9). Political anger, that is to say, must be dealt with in terms of its psychical consequences. This is not an unreasonable clinical imperative – one which could be said to harmonize with black consciousness thought – and yet it is one which once again poses the question of the deferral, or re-routing, of genuinely political anger.

Manganyi nonetheless succeeds in joining the sociopolitical and cultural concerns of black consciousness, of consciousness-raising, with the theoretical resources of psychoanalysis, by finding an analogy between 'the child's encounter and internalization of authority relationships with its parents' (10) and black experience in South Africa, that is, racialized superordinate-subordinate relations, dramatized in the master-slave relation. On the one hand 'the child encountering parental authority', and on the other 'the slave face to face with the authority of his master'; two relationships, Manganyi argues, characterized by 'anxiety about talion', the fear that objective violence to the loved and hated other will be met with retaliation (12).

'In the face of powerlessness and dependency', Manganyi states of the child, 'the emerging self is forced in the interests of its own survival and to cope with anxiety to initiate adaptive measures' (10). That is to say, the child is forced into, and rewarded for, 'losing some of the battles with parental authority' (11). In sacrificing omnipotence before the Law, one assumes an ambivalent attitude to authority, an ambivalence figured, Manganyi suggests, in the attitudes of subordinates in revolt against superordinates. For Manganyi, then, 'the slave does protest too much', and 'the reactionary character of such protest becomes apparent since its form is always benign enough as to ensure that the self-sustaining symbiotic relationship is left intact' (12). Manganyi's argument is that rebellion must be more calculated, more precise; it must demand a new position from which to be addressed. Such rebellion amounts, more often than not, to an acting out that remains unconscious of its real motives and that cannot as such be properly transformative. One is tempted to read in Manganyi's argument an echo of Jacques Lacan's observation, in *The Other Side of Psychoanalysis,* that student protesters in May 1968 risked, in their hysteria, reinstalling a new master. If violent revolt issues from what Manganyi calls 'false consciousness', then it is better to traverse, so to speak, these 'fantasies of revenge'.

The writer or the artist, Manganyi argues, 'responds at a more primitive level by placing his whole weight behind ritualization on a symbolic level in the place of a real murder as a social act' (17). Such, it would seem, is the role of sublimation. As an instance of violent reverie as working through, Manganyi has in mind a passage by Aimé Césaire that Fanon (1952) quotes in *Black Skin, White Masks*. The slave enters the master's bedroom and kills the master, 'a murder represented creatively', as Manganyi states, 'with almost clinical precision' (15). Césaire's scene of literary murder, a creative representation of murder accompanied by understanding, becomes for Manganyi paradigmatic of a process of working through, tracing these fantasies back to their origins, understanding them rather than acting them out. And the crucial point here is that this is a scene of murder not of the white man himself, but of 'the white man in himself' (175), that is, in the black man. It is, in Césaire's words, 'an unexpected and beneficent *inner* revolution' (cited in Fanon, 1952: 175, emphasis added).

Given that Manganyi posits a surrender of omnipotence, for which ambivalence and rage are the legible traces, it is fair to assume that what he is theorizing here, in the political realm, is castration, specifically – given that the Soweto uprising centered on being made to learn in the Afrikaans language – symbolic castration and the rage it can produce. Manganyi's argument may as such find support in more recent psychoanalytic thinking on anger, inasmuch as working through rage means getting to grips with elements of castration (Gherovici, 2003; Pommier, 2001). To the vicissitudes of anger already named – anger that is as both psychical phenomenon and political effect – we can add several further examples: infantile anger, acting out, anger in relation to castration, anger and sublimation.

Three related objections to Manganyi's argument can be raised. First, that Manganyi underestimates the effect of the Soweto uprising. It is true that the violence of the protest was met with a devastating intensification of military force across the country, but this was, arguably, a sign of the crisis that the uprising produced for the State (Howarth, 2000). Second, Manganyi's strict separation between aesthetic revolution and violent acts of protest is not – particularly in this instance – as clear-cut as he might have thought. On the one hand, the uprising was inspired in large part by the ideas of black consciousness. On the other, although black consciousness organizations were banned in 1977, the aftermath of Soweto, as McClintock (1995) notes, saw new forms of artistic creation inseparably linked to the uprising itself. Third, not only is Manganyi's conceptualization politically conservative, it may also be accused of being theoretically untenable. To problematize organized mass political action on the grounds of individual metapsychology surely entails the risk of infantilizing the black subject in revolt against apartheid. It should be noted that Manganyi was not comparing European children – or the childhood of a European neurotic analysand – with black adults, as has been the custom in so many psychoanalytic case studies. Rather, he was addressing black youths who, like himself, were overwhelmed by fury, finding in psychoanalytic theory a way of responding to a political situation, the stakes of which at the time were death.

The risk of infantilization, however, haunts the text and it is interesting to note how Manganyi circles back on psychoanalysis in a paper delivered at the Essex Sociology of Literature Project in 1984. In 'Making Strange', Manganyi (1985) not only deploys psychoanalysis, but is also sharply critical of it, specifically of its role within the colonial discourse of ethnopsychiatry. He especially singled out J.C. De Ridder's (1961) *The Personality of the Urban African in South Africa*. According to Manganyi's reading, De Ridder envisages the personality of the 'urban African' as 'dominated by the Id – which is to say, by the most primitive and pleasure-seeking system in the entire pleasure-seeking matrix as formulated by Freudian theory' (162). Thus, for De Ridder, 'the African is still a child who is not only sexually potent and mischievous but is also prone to violence, immature, anxious, insecure and naïvely exhibitionistic' (Manganyi, 1985: 162). Manganyi makes the crucial point that this 'Id-dominated' image of the 'urban African' produced by the likes of De Ridder – 'the African as childlike, as innately inferior, as dangerous sexually, and as a violent being' – was appropriated by the apartheid regime to advance its programme of separate development (162–3). Rather than an argument for psychoanalysis, Manganyi here presents the possibility that a 'frontal attack on the legacy of the unconscious' will have to reckon with the image of blackness produced by psychoanalysis, even as it might use psychoanalysis to do so.

This is not to dismiss all of Manganyi's argument. As in the case of transference anger discussed above, there is a politically progressive reading that can be offered of Manganyi's theorizations. The instances of cultural expression that Manganyi describes are crucial, illustrating how the prospect of acting out can be bypassed and how the route of literary sublimation can be taken instead. We have already suggested – perhaps contrary to Manganyi's conceptualizations – that symbolic and material violence are not always so easily separated. Such ostensibly sublimated forms of anger, certainly in the forms Manganyi discusses, do not cease to be political. In fact we can turn this argument around: the apparent sublimation of political anger – whether partial or not – allows for political emotions and grievances to be conveyed to ever wider populations, by endowing them with cultural and symbolic transmissibility. What was true of Chavafambira's transference anger is true also of Manganyi's category of sublimated rage. Although in both cases the anger has been subjected to the defences and evasions characteristic of all (partially) unconscious material, it is also true that this anger retains the prospect of re-politicization, and that psychoanalysis as both theoretical and clinical tool may help in the facilitation of this transformation.

Conclusion

We have employed two differing strategies in this brief foray into the history of psychoanalysis in the time of apartheid. We have focused on a couple of distinct strands in the history – the work of Wulf Sachs and Chabani Manganyi. Not only are these two strands representative of crucial trends in psychoanalysis of the period, they reveal much about the broader potential and limitations of psychoanalysis itself in the apartheid context. A further strategy concerns our specific focus on anger. Despite clear differences in perspective and orientation, both Sachs and Manganyi were forced to engage with and psychoanalytically theorize various vicissitudes of anger. Anger, we have argued, may well be treated as a meta-concept, a point of thematic unity from which to explore the history of psychoanalysis in South Africa. This provides a promising starting point for future work on the topic.

In their attempts to grapple with and theorize anger, the writings of Sachs and Manganyi also manifest the political ambiguities of psychoanalysis. Along with other contributions to this volume, this chapter has suggested that psychoanalysis has often leaned towards a politically conservative vision, even, in some cases, towards the outright reactionary, as we saw in Manganyi's critique of De Ridder's (1961) work. We should not be surprised by the fact that psychoanalysis as such has often survived surprisingly well in countries under authoritarian rule (Damousi and Plotkin, 2012; Plotkin, 2013). That being said, this chapter has sought to discern the capacity of psychoanalysis both to accommodate itself to the structures of a (quasi-totalitarian) authoritarian regime and to gesture beyond the horizons of such an authoritarian society, or even to invite revolt against it. Although there are moments in both Sachs and Manganyi where psychoanalytic theorization appears to result in the inhibition of political anger, it is also true that their interventions indicate how this anger, once realized in the transference and symbolized, has the prospect to be powerfully re-politicized.

The role and status of psychoanalysis within political discourse also suggests a problem much akin to that faced within the clinical environment: how to escape the endless self-replications of the past and aim instead to engender something new? This Janus face of psychoanalysis, its dual ability both to conduct and contest prevailing relations of power, is not surprising. Psychoanalysis is a practice based on tracing the unconscious, an unconscious that is often both more unruly and more docile towards authority than we may have expected. This is an unconscious that both continually transgresses social laws and that nevertheless takes obscene superego enjoyment in reinforcing them. Given that this polarity is, according to psychoanalytic theory, inherent in the unconscious, and that the unconscious is psychoanalysis's *raison de 'être*, then a multifarious role is perhaps inevitably to be expected of psychoanalysis itself, politically. And yet this overlooks the possibility, upon which clinical psychoanalysis stakes its reputation, that under the right conditions, the unconscious – like institutionalized, ideological psychoanalysis itself – might be set to work, interrogated, such that its own unspoken assumptions and historical antecedents might be brought to light.

Notes

1 Ross Truscott wishes to acknowledge and thank the Centre for Humanities Research at the University of the Western Cape for financial support, in the form of an Andrew W. Mellon Foundation postdoctoral fellowship in the Programme for the Study of the Humanities in Africa, which he held during 2014.

2 Arendt's text was first published in 1951, a mere three years after the NP came to power. Though these quotes are taken from Arendt's prefaces written in the 1960s, it could, of course, be argued that apartheid became increasingly totalitarian.

3 Exemplary in this regard is the account given by the South African Psychoanalytical Association (SAPA) of its own formation. Mark Solms (2010) offers the following abridged history: 'Although Freud had already proudly announced the establishment of a South African Psychoanalytic Society in 1935 (in the Postscript to his 1924 "Autobiographical Study"), the advent of apartheid and the death of Wulf Sachs put a premature end to the Society's fledgling training programme. Thereafter, South Africans wishing to undertake accredited psychoanalytic training of any kind had to do so abroad' (Solms, 2010).

4 Foster (1991) argues that MacCrone's later writing on the 'puritanical Calvinist personality' prefigures Adorno's (1950) *The Authoritarian Personality* (Foster, 1991: 69–70, 74).

5 The text was republished in 2011 (Hayes, 2011) in *Psychology in Society (PINS)*. Manganyi doesn't mention Soweto, he says only that it is a time of 'tyranny and militant terrorism' (7).

Part VII

Why psychoanalysis?

Chapter 15

Total belief

Delirium in the West

Jacqueline Rose

Was Hannah Arendt a psychoanalytic thinker? She obviously thought not. But in this chapter, I want to suggest that there is a psychoanalytic dimension to her thought, notably in relation to the dangers and perfection of totalitarian logic. One of the ways we can access that dimension most productively is through the question of how people come to invest themselves in their identifications, that is, through the category of belief. In the process I hope to show how the capacity for passionate, mind-controlling and bewildering identifications cannot be assigned exclusively to 'other' cultures (identified as 'extreme'), but have also been at the heart of some of the most delirious historical moments in the West.

The category of belief is at the heart of Arendt's analysis of totalitarianism. 'It cannot be doubted', she writes in the section 'Totalitarianism' that concludes *The Origins of Totalitarianism*:

> that the Nazi leadership actually believed in, and did not merely use as propaganda, such doctrines as the following: 'The more accurately we recognize and observe the laws of nature and of life . . . so much more do we conform to the will of the Almighty. The more insight we have into the will of the Almighty, the greater will be our success.'
>
> (Arendt, 1973 [1958]: 346)

As Arendt comments in a footnote, such formulations, which can be found repeatedly in the pamphlet literature issued by the SS for the ideological indoctrination of its cadets, are no more than variations on phrases from *Mein Kampf.* Hitler knew that his movement would only succeed by 'awakening a sacrosanct conviction in the heart of its followers' (Hitler, 1988: 339). He described the basic postulates of the movement as 'a covenant' and 'profession of faith' (1988: 415). He knew, that is, that Nazism had to be a total *Weltanschauung* that marshalled unconditional – passionate and visceral – allegiance: 'Experience teaches', he writes, 'that the human being fights only for something in which he believes and which he loves' (1988: 493).

To this end, Hitler did not hesitate, as is known, to draw on the powers of the Catholic Church: 'The mysterious artificial dimness of the Catholic churches also serves this purpose, the burning candles, the incense, the thurible, etc.' (1988: 430). The propositions of Nazism, writes Arendt, had the status of 'sacred untouchable truths' (1973 [1958]: 384). If such divine blather was aimed at the youngest cadets of the party, Hitler was also clear that only a few would be equal to the psychological task. The highest echelons of the party would be composed of a type of spiritual elite. Only a minority would be willing and able to fight for their convictions. 'The more radical and exciting my propaganda was,' he wrote, 'the more did it frighten weak and wavering characters away' (1988: 523). You do not need to be a psychoanalyst to know that the most effective mechanism of psychic subordination is fear. Writing on what binds us to our social identities, whose germ is to be found in the merciless rule of the superego over the child's mind, Freud comments simply: 'Fear [or in the German *Angst*] is at the bottom of the whole relationship' (Freud, 1930: 496).[1]

It is central to Arendt's argument that the Nazis were arch-manipulators of the precarious border between lying and truth. One way of thinking about belief in relation to Nazism, therefore, would be as a set of deranged conjugations of the proposition 'I speak the truth', which always, for Lacan, contains the lie as the inverse or perverse support of any utterance. 'Please stop lying, I already believe you', is the statement by a patient which analyst Theodor Reik (1975 [1948]: 173) invokes in order best to capture the radically exasperated, self-defeating claim to truth-hood of any human subject (what Wallace Stevens describes as the 'nicer knowledge of/Belief, that what it believes is not true' [in Kermode, 1966: 34]). 'Did he believe or disbelieve?' asks Reik. 'So much lives in us – wishes and their denials, faith and mistrust, appetites and distastes' (1975 [1948]: 173). To this extent, Nazi totalitarianism was playing on an old tune. According to Arendt (1973 [1958]: 384), it organized itself around a strict 'graduation of cynicism expressed in a hierarchy of contempt', with sympathizers despising their fellow citizens, party members despising fellow travellers, the elite formations despising the party membership. What was above all despised was the gullibility shown by the group that was the object of contempt. Each group considered itself to be the possessor of a different, superior, level of truth. To that extent, the higher you moved up the hierarchy, the more fervent – fearless, Hitler would say – your belief, but also the closer you would get to knowing that the whole system was based on a web of deceit (this is Slavoj Žižek's [1989: 28–30] version of cynicism way before its time).

Of course the leaders do not admit this to themselves. If they did the whole system would have crumbled. Right at the top are a group of men who live – who will always live and who will die – in a state of dissociation. After the war, there was not one who admitted to full knowledge of the atrocities that had taken place. As well as self-defence – legally ineffective of course – this was clearly a way of preserving an inner ideal. 'I had the highest ethics and the highest aims', Goering stated to American psychiatrist, Leon Goldensohn, who was given access to the Nuremberg defendants at the time of their trial – he had been entrusted with monitoring their mental health – 'I was not to blame for these horrors . . .

He was a genius . . . a great leader and I subscribe to his programme completely'
(in Goldensohn, 2006: 115, 121). (The interviews were conducted in May 1946;
after being condemned to death in October, Goering committed suicide in his
cell.) What of course could not be admitted was that he knew the whole system
was fraudulent but went along with it regardless.

For Arendt, the consequence of the system was a type of national and international mental pandemonium which also had a strict inner logic. 'The result',
she writes:

> is that the gullibility of the sympathizers makes lies credible to the outside
> world, while at the same time the graduated cynicism of membership and
> elite members eliminates the danger that the Leader will ever be forced by the
> weight of his own propaganda to make good his own statements.
>
> (1973 [1958]: 384)

The main delusion of the outside world was to misread this system – to trust, on
the one hand, that the enormity of its lies would be the undoing of totalitarianism,
and, on the other, that the Führer could be held to his word (Neville Chamberlain's
big mistake). Viewed from the outside, it was impossible that a people could be so
duped, or, if they were, that their leader could not be trusted. As well as a wish-
fulfilment, this is of course a type of kettle logic, as Freud famously defined the
(il)logic of the unconscious (1900: 119–20) – the people know and will ultimately
be guided by the truth; leaders – even or perhaps especially the Leader who so
misguides them – must be honourable men. That these two propositions cancel
each other out does not in any sense limit their combined power. Underneath the
problem of knowledge that has been so much at the forefront of discussion of
Nazi Germany – who knew, who did not know? – lies a strange, twisted, fabric of
belief. The question should perhaps therefore be: not who knew, but who believed
and how?

If, in Arendt's account, the elites are the ultimate cynics – 'not even supposed
to believe in the literal truths of ideological clichés' – they nonetheless occupy in
even more sinister fashion the domain of fiction (1973 [1958]: 384). It is their role
to transpose belief into evidence, to make the world conform to, mirror, fulfil, the
Nazi mind. The elite do not consist of ideologists. Instead their whole education
is aimed at 'abolishing their capacity for distinguishing between truth and falsehood, between reality and fiction' (1973 [1958]: 385). Theirs is a peculiar, unique
form of superiority which consists in their ability 'immediately to dissolve every
statement of fact into a declaration of purpose' (1973 [1958]: 385). Thus, while
the membership need to be persuaded of the inferiority of the Jews before it can
be safely asked to kill them, it is the characteristic of the elite formations to understand without question that 'the statement, all Jews are inferior, means that all
Jews must be killed' (1973 [1958]: 385). No 'mere mass phenomenon', this mentality requires a very particular form of cultivation. The whole effectiveness of
the programme depends on it. Without this mentality, which was the object of the

most careful indoctrination by totalitarian schools of leadership, the programme would not be able to bring itself to life. It would remain pure fiction. 'Without the elite,' writes Arendt, 'and its artificially induced inability to understand facts as facts, to distinguish between truth and falsehood, the movement could never move in the direction of realizing its fiction' (1973 [1958]: 385).

The elite are the guardians of a hallucinatory, delirious world – Arendt does not use the word 'psychotic', although she does use the word 'borderline', which has since become a key diagnostic term in psychoanalysis (1973 [1958]: 478).[2] Delirium always carries a risk, however. It is therefore central to this machinery that no-one must be capable of seeing the world through different eyes. For the masses to be carried, a protective wall has to be built to separate them from the outside world. Without such a wall, they would feel too acutely the discrepancy 'between the lying fictitiousness of their own and the reality of the normal world' (1973 [1958]: 366). I am less confident than Arendt in the concept of a 'normal world', and indeed in its reality. But note how the masses are the bearers of a form of knowledge that both knows and doesn't know itself. If the system never stops working, it is because the masses must be endlessly protected from the spectre of disbelief. Disbelief haunts the system, the other side of the delirium to which it is inextricably wed. This goes beyond the dimension of complicity, but it is not covered either by the idea of false consciousness or indeed by that of bad faith. It is as if Nazism constructed itself with the most painstaking attention to an order of belief that it knew only too well was beyond belief – '*incroyable*', as Julia Kristeva (2007) has put it (she argues that it is Freud's forays into this domain of belief that is at the core of the hostility against him). Provided we add that the element of unbelievability is not a threat to belief, but one way that belief operates, how – clearly at historic moments such as this one – it most effectively protects itself. For Kristeva we are touching on an order of necessity or compulsion – hence the title of her book: *This* Unbelievable *Need to Believe* (my emphasis).

It is not therefore simply the divine grandiosity of Nazism that is at issue, but the way the propositions of Nazism moved into the realm of incontrovertible, sacred fact and thereupon were immediately bound to fulfil themselves. The difference between a statement and a programme, Arendt observes, is that only the former can be contested – it is because the gap between the two was abolished that the Nazis could believe themselves to be the agents of a divine will. To say that the belief is delusional (which of course it was) is not therefore enough. What matters is how the form of the delirium – its mental enactment – turns the Nazi, and above all Hitler, into the agent of God. Remember this quotation:

> It cannot be doubted . . . that the Nazi leadership actually believed in, and did not merely use as propaganda, such doctrines as the following: 'The more accurately we recognize and observe the laws of nature and of life . . . so much more do we conform to the will of the Almighty. The more insight we have into the will of the Almighty, the greater will be our success.'
>
> (1973 [1958]: 345–46)

This is why Hitler announced his political intentions in the form of prophecy, of which the most famous example is his announcement to the Reichstag in January 1939: 'I want today once again to make a prophecy: In case the Jewish financiers . . . succeed once more in hurling the peoples into a world war, the result will be . . . the annihilation of the Jewish race in Europe' (1973 [1958]: 349).[3] This sounds like speculation – 'in case the Jewish financiers' – but it is in fact prediction, or rather two predictions bound by a hidden relation of causality: the Jews *will* succeed in precipitating world war, the Jews *will* be killed. It is a type of double apocalypse: the Jews are already guilty of the end of the world, from which the world must, and will, be saved.

Belief in the system therefore hangs on a strict order of time. The movement produced a mentality which 'thought in continents and felt in centuries' – Himmler described it as working 'for a great task which occurs but once in 2,000 years' (speech on 'Organization and Obligation of the SS and the Police', in Arendt, 1973 [1958]: 316). 'There is hardly a better way to avoid discussion,' Arendt wryly noted, 'than by releasing an argument from the control of the present and by saying that only the future will fulfil its merits' (1973 [1958]: 346). You cannot argue with a form of belief that has already secured its own future (this is not belief *in* the future, but belief *as* the future). 'All debate about the truth or falsity of a totalitarian dictator's prediction', she comments, 'is as weird as arguing with a potential murderer whether his future victim is dead or alive – since by killing the person in question the murderer can promptly provide proof of the correctness of his statement' (1973 [1958]: 350). As well as being a declaration of intent, Hitler's prophecy abolishes the distance between today and all the potential tomorrows of the world. It seizes the future according to a law or chain of fatality whose latent, sometimes explicit, nature is divine. 'Man only does or suffers,' wrote Arendt, 'what, according to immutable laws, is bound to happen anyway' (1973 [1958]: 349). It was de Toqueville, she reminds us, who wrote of the appeal of 'absolutist systems which represent all the events of history as depending on the first great causes linked by the chain of fatality, and which, as it were, suppress men from the history of the human race' (de Toqueville in Arendt, 1973 [1958]: 345).

Working on this subject, I found myself rereading *The Sense of an Ending* (1966) by Frank Kermode. I was struck by how central the question of belief, and indeed apocalypse – hence the title of the book – is to his deservedly famous study of fiction and time. The lines already cited from Wallace Stevens – 'the nicer knowledge of/Belief, that what it believes is not true' – form one of the epigraphs to Kermode's second chapter on 'Fictions'. For Stevens, 'the last and greatest fiction' is 'the fiction of an Absolute' (1966: 41). Kermode tracks this fiction throughout the book but he is also concerned – indeed at moments he struggles – to wrest the domain of literary fiction, whose only validity is its inventiveness or effective force, from what he calls its other 'dangerous relations' (1966: 37). In this discussion, totalitarianism is central precisely because of its power to bend the world to the mind. Nietzsche's argument that the only relevant question is how far an opinion is 'life-furthering, life-preserving, species-preserving' (in Kermode, 1966: 37) might be seen as in danger of encouraging people who believe that death on a large scale can also be a way – is in fact the only way – of preserving a species, of preserving life. This is not, as I read it, a bland critique of relativism (nor the even blander suggestion that Nietzsche has some affinity with, or in its strong version, responsibility for, Nazi atrocity). It is far more precisely an attempt to come to grips with what fiction can do, its internal grip or authority, and, specifically in relation to Nazism, the brutality and unseemly haste with which fiction tipped into the register of fact – the problem with delirium being not that the belief is false but instead that it becomes real so fast: 'If the value of an opinion is to be tested only by its success in the world,' writes Kermode echoing Arendt, 'the validity of one's opinion of the Jews can be proved by killing six million Jews' (1966: 38).

'There might even be a relation,' Kermode writes, 'between certain kinds of effectiveness in literature and totalitarianism in politics' (1966: 39). Thus, 'the consciously false apocalypse of both *King Lear* and the Third Reich force us to recognize that "it is ourselves we are encountering whenever we invent fictions"', fabrications *in extremis* both (1966: 38–9). There is, however, a crucial difference. Unlike *Lear*, Nazism tells us 'nothing about death' as universal, shared experience, but instead projects it onto, enacts it by means of, others. We could say that perversely Nazism never really countenances the death it performs (belonging rather, committing the other, to the realm of 'non-existence'; in Arendt's words, it knows 'neither birth nor death' [1973 (1958): 473]). And Nazism, as we have seen Arendt describe it, abolishes the distinction between fiction and reality, or statement and programme – Kermode calls it a 'degenerate fiction' – by presupposing, as he puts it, 'a total and adequate explanation of things as they are' (an irony given Nazism's preoccupation with what it termed degenerate art) (1966: 39; see also Peters, 2014). Kermode's is not therefore a positivist account of reality but reality as the endless capacity and openness of words. It is precisely because it loses its sense of belonging in time that Nazism starts its climb back up to the world of the gods. In literature, uncertainty hovers over time. Unlike the 'equivocally offered' futures of Shakespearean tragedy, the Third Reich was the disastrous consequence of trying 'to impose limited designs on the time of the world' (1966: 88). In tragedy, on the other hand, 'the great crises and ends of human life do not stop time' (1966: 89).

I had forgotten how important Arendt was to Kermode's argument, as well as how central Jewish thought was to his vision of the critic. What prevents apocalyptic grandiosity – the means of the world careering to its end – is the ceaseless interpretability of things which it is the task of the critic to cultivate. The sole 'myth' of Jewish thought is that there are as many interpretations of the text 'as may be found in the created world with which the book is coextensive' (Kermode, 1985: 90). Insisting that the world is a book that 'can be exfoliated into the universe', and that this process is endless, becomes then a, if not the, key counter-myth to the belief that time can be halted, world and word perfectly aligned, that 'the validity of one's opinions of the Jews can be proved by killing six million Jews' (Kermode, 1966: 38; 1985: 90). In this light, Nazism is an anti-hermeneutic. The aggressiveness of totalitarianism, Arendt insists, does not spring from lust for power but simply from the ideological drive 'to make the world consistent' (1973 [1958]: 458). On this too Hitler was explicit: 'The essentials of a teaching,' he wrote in *Mein Kampf*, 'must never be looked for in its external formulas, but in its inner meaning. And this meaning is unchangeable' (1988: 416).

I want now to push this a little further in psychoanalytic terms. Although it is rarely explicit, whenever I read Arendt, I am struck by this aspect of her writing. To her surprise, she was awarded the Sigmund Freud Preis of the Deutsche Akadamie für Sprache und Dichtung in 1967 (her biographer, Elizabeth Young-Bruehl, who herself went on to become a psychoanalyst, comments that Arendt would have won no prizes for sympathy with Freud). It is, however, central to her understanding of totalitarianism that it involves the inner domination of the human spirit, an 'inner coercion whose only content is the avoidance of contradictions' (Arendt, 1973 [1958]: 478) (the 'inner meaning' in Hitler's terms). What distinguishes totalitarianism from all other political movements is its demand for the 'total, unconditional, and unalterable loyalty of the individual member' (in Hitler's words, the problem of 'influencing the freedom of the human will') (Arendt, 1973 [1958]: 323; Hitler, 1988: 430). It achieves this deathly allegiance because it has discovered 'a means of dominating and terrorizing human beings from within' (1973 [1958]: 325). Everything outside the movement is dying (1979 [1958]: 381). This, one could say, is why Frau Goebbels murders her five children in the last days of the regime (a moment shockingly rendered in Oliver Hirschbiegel's 2004 film *Downfall* based on Hitler's final ten days in his Berlin bunker). In all of this there seems to be, for the participants themselves, something inexplicable involved. Looking back on his life, Albert Speer describes the inner compulsion that drew him to Hitler before he knew, but when, as he acknowledges in his interviews with journalist Gitta Sereny, he already should have known: 'The truth is that for a reason I still cannot explain to myself, perhaps like the thief who feels impelled to return to the scene of his crime, something very deep inside myself drew me towards the Chancellery' (Sereny, 1995: 526).

Totalitarianism is external coercion but it works above all through the inner life, relying, in Arendt's words, 'on the compulsion with which we can compel ourselves' (1973 [1958]: 473). It relies, that is, on our inner attraction to force – to what Freud will describe in his analysis of the superego as the cruelty which regulates the traffic between the different agencies of the mind. (As Arendt also remarks, cruelty can also feel like a liberation from a society's liberal and humanitarian hypocrisy – a warning first the 2010–15 coalition, and now Conservative, governments in the UK, with their mixture of social liberalism and economic cruelty, might do well to heed.) Cruelty, as Freud describes it, is the last resort of the humiliated (the superego wreaks on the defenceless ego all the subjugated child's wrath against its parents). The law of ruthless expansion, Arendt writes, was therefore a 'psychological necessity before it [was] a political device' (1973 [1958]: 330). The front generation which emerged from the humiliation and violence of the First World War, she suggests, 'read not Darwin but the Marquis de Sade' (1973 [1958]: 330). As we know, there were then strictly no limits to what could take place. Faced with the mentality of the SS, it would become the almost impossible task of the next generation to take the measure of the psychically destructive powers of a form of conviction so intense that it seems to have the power to destroy the mind itself, to grasp that 'the psyche can be destroyed even without the destruction of the physical man; that indeed, psyche, character, and individuality seem under certain circumstances to express themselves only through the rapidity or slowness with which they can disintegrate' (1973 [1958]: 441).

If totalitarianism wipes out the mind, however, it does so only by plunging its roots so effectively into the worst of what the mind is capable of. The reality of the camps was unbelievable precisely because the image of that reality could be found in the hidden echo chambers of the human heart. 'Everything that was done in the camps,' Arendt writes, 'is known to us from the world of perverse, malignant fantasies' (1973 [1958]: 445). At moments like this, as I see it, Arendt raises the psychological stakes of her discussion of the lies, deceit, and false actualization of the Nazi world. Nazism made its dreams come true (one definition of the psychotic is that their dreams come true). If it colonizes, destroys, the mind, it does so by breathing life – actual, concrete life – into the unconscious. We should then be sceptical about the Nazi claim that the only private individual in Germany was someone who was asleep (1973 [1958]: 339). Under such forms of coercion, nobody was ever free, not even – I would add especially – when they were asleep.

As I read this account, what it evokes most powerfully for me is the world of Daniel Paul Schreber, the Leipzig High Court Presiding Judge, whose deranged 1903 memoirs were the object of one of Freud's few forays into the realm of psychosis. In her 2004 study of the meta-psychology of belief, *Le Besoin de croire – métapsychologie du fait religieux*, French psychoanalyst Sophie de Mijolla-Mellor gives central place to Schreber (in a chapter called 'Ivresses Sacrées' or 'Sacred Intoxications'). Schreber believed that he was to be inseminated by God, in order to repopulate the earth with a new race. This makes him the carnal embodiment of God's will and futurity whose more abstract version – although abstract is not quite the right word – we have already seen at the heart of Nazism. His solution to the problem of suffering (and we should never underestimate the extent to which Nazism presented itself as a solution to the suffering of the German people) is to try to think, as Mijolla-Mellor puts it, 'from the point of view of God' (2004: 157). For Mijolla-Mellor, belief always contains this potentially delirious element, as it tries to counter the collapse of the child's faith in her or his own narcissistic omnipotence and in the parental capacity to restore the child's lost infantile ideal. Belief rises out of that melancholy recognition, as its most fervent denial (which is why, for Kristeva, belief is the privileged domain of the adolescent). If psychoanalysis then inspires its adherents to a type of faith in turn, it is at least in part because it allows the analyst, not just a new creed, but to make her or his way back to the mainspring of belief in the infantile mind, to play in the psychic forecourts of conviction (much of Mijolla-Mellor's book is devoted to analysing this dimension of belief in Freud's early psychoanalytic movement).

Freud was contemptuous of religious passion from which, as we know, he did all he could to distance himself (although, as I have written elsewhere, and as others have more fully documented, his relationship to his own Jewishness was complex – see, for example, Said, 1993; Yerushalmi, 1991). In doing so he also underestimated the wider social force of delusional systems, like Schreber's, which elevate the subject to an ecstatic, albeit tortured, relation to God. And by brushing aside longing for paternal protection as the regressive component of faith, he also sidestepped the potentially delirious tie that binds man to the divine. This is to make of Schreber – as Mijolla-Mellor does – a demonstration or test case of the unconscious element of belief. What Schreber then allows us to see so graphically is how this whole system relies on a systematic and interminable invasion of the realm of thought. Although Mijolla-Mellor does not make the link, the similarities to Arendt's account of totalitarianism is striking. That link is also historical – Schreber's father, as we now know, was at the heart of the new late-nineteenth-century Gymnasium project, unsurpassed in its physical exactions, that laid down some of the educational foundations for Hitler (the cruelty of these exactions – the belts, chin, head and backstraps to which Schreber was subjected – is well known).[4] This is from Schreber's *Memoirs*. He is describing his penetration by the divine rays:

> This influence showed itself relatively early in the form of *compulsive thinking* – an expression which I received from the inner voices themselves and which will hardly be known to other human beings, because the whole phenomenon lies outside human experience. The nature of compulsive thinking lies in a human being having to think incessantly; in other words, man's natural right to give the nerves of his mind their necessary rest from time to time by thinking nothing (as occurs most markedly during sleep) was from the beginning denied me by the rays in contact with me; they continually wanted to know what I was thinking about. For instance I was asked in these very words: 'What are you thinking of now?'; because this question is in itself complete nonsense, as a human being can at certain times as well think of *nothing* as of *thousands of things at the same time*, and because my nerves did not react to this absurd question, one was soon driven to take refuge in *falsifying my thoughts*. For instance the above question was answered spontaneously: 'He should' scilicet think 'about the Order of the World';

that is to say the influence of the rays forced my nerves to perform the movements corresponding to the use of these words.

(Schreber, 1988: 70, italics original)

Compulsive thinking obliges you to falsify your thoughts. Real mental freedom
consists in the freedom to think nothing (to drift off), or to think a thousand
things at the same time (another kind of drifting). This is the opposite of thinking
about the 'Order of the World', which requires above all that the mind be self-
present and consistent (an 'unchangeable inner meaning' in Hitler's [1988: 416]
terms). Under totalitarianism, Arendt writes, 'the self-coercive force of logicality
is mobilized lest anybody ever start thinking' – by which she means, not compul-
sively but on their own terms (1973 [1958]: 473). Unlike authoritarianism, total
domination does not aim to restrict freedom but to abolish it completely, including that of 'spontaneity in general', including, we might say, the capacity of the
mind to drift and roam (1973 [1958]: 405). There must be no secrets. Schreber's
instructions are precise. As if his tormentors had understood only too well that
the human mind makes its best bid for freedom simply by losing itself, by changing tack, by being open to the confused bits and pieces of mental life. This could
be a definition of the unconscious – which consists in the ability of the mind to
double and escape itself.

Arendt then comes very close to suggesting – after Lacan we might say – that
deception is the very kernel of human thought. 'Simply because of their capacity
to think,' she writes, 'human beings are suspects by definition, and this suspicion
cannot be diverted by exemplary behaviour, for the human capacity to think is
also a capacity to change one's mind' (1973 [1958]: 430). It is impossible 'to
know beyond doubt another man's heart' – psychoanalysis would add that it is
no less impossible fully to know one's own. Torture then becomes a 'desperate
and eternally futile attempt' to enter completely the mind of another, 'to achieve
what cannot be achieved' (the idea of knowing another's mind is already a form of
invasion which torture elevates to a craft) (1973 [1958]: 430). It is then Schreber's
dubious privilege – as a form of childhood memory that anticipated the brutality
of totalitarianism to come – to lay bare the nerve mechanism of torture at its core
(he belongs at the tortuous, rather than ecstatic, extremity of belief). Torture is the
inverse image of mental freedom. It is the state's rejoinder to, as well as recognition of, the fact that we are all suspects. (The common official argument that it
is an exceptional measure, reluctantly embraced, is therefore as psychologically
as it is politically evasive.) Hence the mutual suspicion that pervades all social
relationships under totalitarian rule.

Taking my cue from Schreber, I am tempted to say that Arendt is describing
the deep, violent, psychic coercion of totalitarian rule. Schreber's vulnerability
to such coercion is acute – it is precisely his paranoia to live it so literally, body
and soul – but the structure of such coercion has its germ in the origins of mental life (the argument, made first by Morton Schatzman [1973], that Schreber is
remembering his childhood, takes on an added meaning here). All children, writes

Mijolla-Mellor, believe in the capacity of their parents to read their thoughts. The delirium of the paranoid repeats this belief ad infinitum. In his famous 1919 essay 'On the Origin of the "Influencing Machine" in Schizophrenia', Victor Tausk – one of Freud's most important and troubled interlocutors – writes:

> We are familiar with this infantile stage of thinking, in which a strong belief exists that others know of the child's thoughts. Until the child has been successful in its first lie, the parents are supposed to know everything, even its most secret thoughts [. . .] The striving for the right to have secrets from which the parents are excluded is one of the most powerful factors in the formation of the ego, especially in establishing and carrying out one's own will.
> (in Fliess, 1969 [1948]: 45)[5]

If there is no secrecy, there is no mind. Underneath the totalitarian aim to control, as Hitler put it, 'the freedom of the human will', lies the delusion that everything, everyone, can be fully known. When Arendt writes of total domination, what she is describing therefore is the destruction of the unconscious.

In the final pages of *The Origins of Totalitarianism*, Arendt describes the ultimate freedom as being identical with the capacity to begin, just as freedom as a political reality is identical with the space of movement between men (her definition of democracy). Over such beginnings, 'no logic, no cogent deduction can have any power because the chain presupposes, in the form of a premise, the beginning' (1973 [1958]: 473). The beginning is the supreme creative capacity of man. It is therefore each new birth that totalitarianism hates, a hatred that is wholly compatible of course with forced eugenics, because each new birth might 'raise its voice in the world', threatening a multiplicity of possible futures that are uncontrollable and unknown (1973 [1958]: 473). Once again we can turn to Kermode's (1985) 'equivocally offered futures' of Shakespearean tragedy as the antidote. Political freedom and psychic freedom are therefore inseparable. Only if the child is allowed its secrets and lies, only if language can circulate in the head and in the city space, will there ever be freedom for mankind.

Of course I am pushing Arendt further than she would probably wish to go. Arendt may be against the tyranny of logic, she may at moments come close to a psychoanalytic vision of the mind, but she is also cautious. In these final pages 'duality and equivocality and doubt' – what we might call the core of the Freudian subject – reappear as something which the citizen must be protected against (1973 [1958]: 476). But this is because they are the attributes of the bereft, lonely man in the crowd, whose uncertainty makes him vulnerable to totalitarian coercion. The lonely man is surrounded by a hostile world (Schreber would then be the loneliest man on earth), whereas the solitary man is alone but 'together with himself' since men have the capacity 'of talking with themselves' (she is citing Cicero; 1973 [1958]: 476). In solitude, I am '"by myself", together with myself, and therefore two-in-one, whereas in loneliness I am actually one, deserted by all the others' (1973 [1958]: 476). Once again Arendt is talking about the innermost life – here it is the resonances with D.W. Winnicott's capacity to be alone in the presence of the other that are striking. It is by means of thought, as I see it – myself alone with myself, alone with a thousand thoughts or none – that Arendt strives to deliver the modern subject from the crowd (the subject mass of totalitarian coercion) in order to restore his civic and psychic dignity.

'Work and the free play of the imagination', Freud writes to Swiss pastor, Oskar Pfister in 1910, 'are for me the same thing, I take no pleasure in anything else' (6 March 1910, in Freud and Pfister, 1964: 35). For Freud, such freedom requires a full reckoning with the horrors of the world which, even by the 1930s, Pfister can only with the greatest reluctance be brought to contemplate. Freedom consists in freedom from idealization and, with it, from any form of sacred belief. Pfister himself suggests that the point in ethical matters is to be 'free thinkers without being heroes' (18 February 1909, in Freud and Pfister, 1964: 18). No false gods. Freud was less immune to their powers than it might seem from his later writings on religion. In 1899 he wrote a poem to Fliess extolling him as 'the valiant son who at the behest of his father appeared at the right time,/To be his assistant and fellow worker in fathoming the divine order' (29 December 1899, in Freud, 1985: 393–4). By the time he starts his correspondence with Pfister ten years later, something has happened to place any such appeal to the divine order under erasure. Psychoanalysis will henceforth join the ranks of the disbelievers. Of *The Future of an Illusion*, he writes to Pfister somewhat mercilessly, 'I wanted to strike a blow at superstition, stupidity and goggle-eyed self-abasement' (1 April 1926, in Freud and Pfister, 1964: 102). Even in the poem, Freud had called on the 'higher powers to claim as his right, conclusion, belief and doubt' – something of an odd mix (as if one could appeal to the higher powers for the right to doubt them). But by 1909, probably because he has started to father his own movement, Freud has become acutely aware of the danger to psychoanalysis of its demanding any such allegiance, of its becoming its own form of faith. 'The value of what we write must depend,' he insists, 'on its containing nothing accepted on authority . . . I do not call for any act of faith on your part' (30 March 1909, in Freud and Pfister, 1964: 22). 'I have deliberately set myself up only as an example, but never as a model, let alone an object of veneration' (10 May 1909, in 1964: 23). More defensively, when an acquaintance of Pfister's, sympathetic to psychoanalysis, demurs from being considered a member of its 'school', Freud retorts: 'Has our "school" secret signs or rites, does it swear by my words, or worship me with incense?' (12 July 1909, in 1964: 27).

Freud's disclaimers, his rhetorical question, of course neatly sidestep the place of belief inside his own movement (a key strand of Mijolla-Mellor's book). But whether or not history will bear Freud out on this question, it is crucial to psychoanalysis, crucial to Freud, that psychoanalysis dissolves belief in the crucible of transference where – at least this is the risk and challenge – it most strongly germinates and spreads. To this extent, as if in anticipation of Arendt and indeed of his own later work on mass psychology, Freud is offering psychoanalysis as its own antidote to idealization, to the sacred perversity of the group – starting with the group of two that is the analytic pair (just one reason why it is such a mistake to argue that there is no social being on the analytic couch). To call Freud a sceptic, as indeed he might call himself, is therefore not quite right, since he immerses himself, and indeed the whole practice of psychoanalysis, so firmly inside the register of belief. We could say that psychoanalysis is one of the few places in the culture where belief is given its full weight (this is also the starting premise of Mijolla-Mellor and Kristeva).

What one finds in reading Freud's correspondence with Pfister, is that it is out of the transference, a concept slow to emerge in Freud's thought, that psychoanalysis draws its understanding of belief. Thus, Freud writes to Pfister, failure to acknowledge the power of transference in the early days of psychoanalysis meant that it remained untouchable, divine. In the early cathartic method, the transference was taken for granted, 'rather like the omnipresence of the divine being' who is assumed to be the onlooker, but is unmentioned (19 July 1910, in Freud and Pfister, 1964: 42). This meant that the negative transference – hostility to the analyst 'as it is in the case of most decent neurotics' – was overlooked (there can be no negative transference to a God whose existence, whose name, remains unspoken) (19 July 1910, in 1964: 23). If psychoanalysis fails to tolerate the unconscious hostility of the patient, it will find itself in the position of Christ who pronounces 'Thy sins are forgiven thee; arise and walk' (25 November 1928, in 1964: 125). It is a startling analogy and Freud does not let it go. 'Besides,' he writes, 'the above statement calls for analysis. If the sick man had asked: "How knowest thou that my sins are forgiven?" the answer could only have been: "I, the Son of God, forgive thee." In other words, a call for unlimited transference' (25 November 1928, in 1964: 125).

Perhaps there is no other place in Freud's writing where he so unequivocally links the issue of belief to that of transference, and of both of these to the question of freedom (nor, indeed, where he so unambiguously divorces psychoanalysis from the order of Christian forgiveness). Freud has brought the issue of belief into the consulting room. This seems to me to be a far more important intervention into the question than *The Future of an Illusion*, in which belief is no more than an illusion to be dissipated by the reason of the mind (for me Freud's most un-Freudian work). And, again, more interesting than the *Papers on Technique*, where love is the daemon of the cure. Instead what counts is how the analytic process responds to the potentially sacred powers of conviction. To preserve his mental freedom and move on, the analysand must retain his right to be suspicious even of a forgiving God.

Freud does not therefore want the world to be either forgiven or saved. Like the patient, he wants it to know itself. As the correspondence progresses, it becomes clearer and clearer that the free play of the imagination – the only thing, apart from work, that gives Freud true pleasure – is the freedom to countenance the worst of what human nature has to offer (the death instinct, he states in 1930 in another revealing moment, is not 'a requirement of my heart' but a requirement of the way things are; Freud to Pfister 7 February 1930, in Freud and Pfister, 1964: 133).

Freud's own negative transference, we could say, reaches to the gods. In this he is true to his historical moment. What he wants is for the world to take the measure of what it is – or will be, since he does not live to see the worst – capable of. This, I suggest finally, might help us take the true measure of the distance, or radical antagonism, between psychoanalysis and totalitarian belief.

Notes

1 In German in Das Unbehagen in der Kultur, Gesammelte Werke, vol. 14: 496.
2 The term 'borderline', coined in the 1938 by Adolf Stern, started to acquire more general psychoanalytic currency in the 1950s, at the time Arendt was writing the book, although she may well not have taken cognisance of it.
3 The full text is: 'I want today once again to make a prophecy: In case the international Jewish financiers within and outside Europe succeed once more in hurling the peoples into a world war, the result will be, not the Bolshevization of the world and with it a victory of Jewry, but the annihilation of the Jewish race in Europe' (Goebbels, 1948, cited in Arendt 1973 [1958]: 349).
4 Although his reading is controversial, Morton Schatzman was the first to discuss this aspect of Schreber's history in *Soul Murder: Persecution in the Family* (1973).
5 Tausk's essay was first published in German in 1919 and in English in 1933.

Chapter 16

The totalitarian unconscious

Michael Rustin

There are several questions that can be asked about 'Psychoanalysis in the Age of Totalitarianism'.[1] Two of these are about relations of cause and effect: what consequences did the rise of totalitarian regimes have for psychoanalytic thinking and the psychoanalytic movement?[2] And, what influence did psychoanalytic thinking or practice have on totalitarianism, and on the intellectual and organizational responses of liberal societies to the totalitarian phenomenon? Both of these are questions appropriately addressed by historians, and are considered in many contributions to this volume.

But there is also a third question, which is not primarily one for historiography: that of whether psychoanalytic perspectives have anything to contribute to the understanding of totalitarianism as a social and psychological phenomenon. This is distinct from the issue of whether understandings of this kind, put forward in the past, had any influence or consequences at the time of their writing. Of course these questions are interconnected, in so far as understandings do have effects on social practices. 'Totalitarianism' like other social phenomena is not merely a 'fact in itself', or indeed a memory of such facts of the past, but is itself also a 'social construction'. 'Totalitarianism' like all other categories of political science or sociology is one which organizes certain 'social facts' in a particular way and from a particular perspective. The idea of totalitarianism was plainly value-oriented, since totalitarianism as a category lies at one end of an ideological spectrum, at the other end of which lie liberalism and pluralism as opposed principles of social organization.

Categories of this kind are susceptible to reinterpretation over time, as knowledge of new 'facts' emerges to further inform them and their relation to reality, and as the presuppositions which initially framed them evolve. In this chapter I will suggest that psychoanalytic thinking may contribute to such a reinterpretation, and to the identification of certain attributes of the totalitarian phenomena previously overlooked. One generic contribution of the psychoanalytic method has been to demonstrate that what is known and remembered of the past is always in part a construction of our contemporary consciousness with its own specific disavowals. One function of psychoanalysis from the beginning has been to reveal the unconscious motivation of such constructions or distortions of memory, most commonly in analytic practice with individual analysands. I am suggesting that a psychoanalytic examination of totalitarianism makes possible a parallel clarification of collectively held understandings of the past.

The idea of totalitarianism

'Totalitarianism' became a central analytic category of political science in the 1940s and 1950s, following an earlier significant discussion of the concept (in the English language) by Franz Borkenau (1940), which was deemed from the first to capture the defining attributes of two actually existing political regimes, those of Nazism and Soviet communism. The liberal democracies of the West felt threatened by both of them, following the Bolshevik Revolution of 1917, and the Nazis' coming to power in Germany in 1933. As their struggle against fascism was succeeded by the Cold War against communism, the category of totalitarianism assigned a common meaning to the two enemies, who were in both cases contrasted with the notion of liberal democracy. Against the totalitarian evil of the domination of society by an all-powerful state was proclaimed the ideal of a state whose powers were limited by laws which protected individual liberties, and were shared with other social institutions, such as the market and the family. Against the concept of a unified ideology which organized all aspects of experience were counterposed the values of freedom and plurality of thought. For liberal critics (such as Hayek, 2001 [1944] and Popper, 1945) the defining features of totalitarianism were the very obverse of their own values. The theory of totalitarianism was deployed not only to analyse and justify resistance to the Nazi and communist systems, but also to warn against the risks inherent in milder forms of political collectivism, or socialism. Hence the title of Friedrich von Hayek's 1944 warning, *The Road to Serfdom* (which, eclipsed at first, later became a canonical text of neo-liberalism), and Karl Popper's distinction between 'piecemeal' forms of social organization and the dangerous kinds, which sought to change society in 'holistic' ways (Popper, 1945, 1957).

When political scientists analysed what they viewed as the two major totalitarian systems, their primary focus was on the institutional structures and all-pervasive ideologies by which these systems were organized. In an influential text, Friedrich and Brzezinski (1956) identified six basic features which 'constituted the character of totalitarian dictatorships':

1   An official ideology, consisting of an official body of doctrine covering all aspects of man's existence to which everyone living in that society is supposed to adhere, at least passively; this ideology is characteristically focused and projected towards a final perfect state of mankind, that is to say it contains a chiliastic claim, based upon a radical rejection of the existing society.
2   A single mass party led typically by one man, 'the dictator', and consisting of a relatively small percentage of the total population (up to 10 per cent) of men and women, a hard core of them passionately and unquestioningly dedicated

to the ideology and prepared to assist in every way in promoting its general acceptance, such a party being hierarchically, oligarchically organized, and typically either superior to, or completely intertwined with, the bureaucratic government organization.

3   A system of terroristic police control, supporting but also supervising the party for its leaders, and characteristically directed not only against demonstrable 'enemies' of the regime, but against arbitrarily selected classes of the population; the terror of the secret police systematically exploiting modern science, and more especially scientific psychology.

4   A technologically conditioned near-complete monopoly of control, in the hands of the party and its subservient cadres, of all means of effective mass communication, such as the press, radio, motion pictures.

5   A similarly technologically conditioned near-complete monopoly of control (in the same hands) of all effective means of armed combat.

6   A central control and direction of the entire economy through the bureaucratic coordination of its formerly independent corporate entities, typically including most other associations and group entities.

Friedrich and Brzezinski noted some differences between fascist, Nazi and communist systems (for example regarding the continued private ownership of property under fascism and Nazism) but nevertheless held that 'these are universally acknowledged to be the features of totalitarian dictatorships to which the writings of students of the most varied backgrounds, including totalitarian writers, bear witness' (Friedrich and Brzezinski, 1956: 9–10).

In the years since this text was published, its central thesis has been subject to significant challenge and revision (Bracher, 1991; Geyer and Fitzpatrick, 2009; Kershaw, 2000; Kershaw and Lewin, 1997). Both the Nazi and Stalinist states seem to have been characterized by their irregularity, unpredictability and irrationality, in contrast to the bureaucratic consistency that the institutional theory of totalitarianism suggests. The Soviet system changed significantly during different phases of its leadership: Lenin's New Economic Policy (NEP) set out to reinstitute market relations, and the role of a bourgeoisie, before Stalin embarked on his programme of forced collectivization of agriculture. The dominant institution in Soviet society under Stalin was not the state as such, but a particular segment of it, the secret police. Stalinism was characteristically a regime of terror, whose victims included many of the ruling echelons of the system, millions of peasants, repatriated prisoners of war and dissident ethnic minorities such as the Chechens. After Stalin's death, this apparatus (for instance, the Gulags, though not the repression of dissidents) was substantially dismantled, leaving in power a self-serving bureaucratic system in which ideology had lost its previous dynamic role. It became clear from the risings and resistance in Hungary, Czechoslovakia, Poland and East Germany from 1956 onwards that, far from exercising total ideological control over their citizens, the regimes in these societies had depended largely on Soviet military power to sustain their authority. Under Gorbachev, and his programme of *glasnost* and *perestroika*, significant reforming tendencies also made themselves felt within the Soviet Union, although these were ultimately defeated by the system's conservative establishment. This failure to reform precipitated the collapse of the entire state socialist system and its virtual capitulation to the West.

The Nazi state has likewise been revealed by historians to have been an unstable mixture of conflicting jurisdictions, engaged not in orderly methods of decision-making but in chaotic battles to interpret the Führer's intentions. The institutions of the constitutional state were secondary in power and importance to the National Socialist Party, the SS and the Gestapo.[3] The more instrumental elements of the Nazi regime – for example the military high command and the economic systems organized by Speer to support the war – always had to contend with the irrationality or 'fundamentalism' of the political leadership, for whom, for example, transporting millions of Jews across Europe to their deaths took precedence over the military and economic struggle for survival, or for whom the obligation of 'honour' to fight to the last man outweighed the saving of entire armies from capture. In spite of, or because of, its 'totalitarian' character, the Nazi regime proved to be less efficient than its liberal enemies in mobilizing resources for the prosecution of war.

As for ideology, what was striking about both the Nazi and Stalinist regimes was their impoverishment of thought. The cadres of both regimes (in Russia, once the old Bolshevik leadership had been eliminated) were notable for their intellectual crudity and antipathy to ideas. One can view the anti-intellectualism of both of these regimes as an expression of a resentment of the educated classes (which one can think of in Kleinian psychoanalytic terms as a species of envious hatred). In Stalin's Russia its target included leading intellectuals of the Communist Party itself, like Trotsky and Bukharin. Elaborations of the systematic and totalizing bodies of thought known as 'ideologies' seem to depend for their possibility on a degree of free exchange of ideas. Marxism achieved its highest development as a body of ideas and research when its intellectuals worked outside regimes claiming to be Marxist. The ideas which ostensibly legitimated Stalinist and Nazi rule were for the most part mere dogmas and rationalizations of the will of political leaderships.

The Nazi and communist regimes also possessed many distinct elements. The idea that these were essentially identical systems was itself an ideological construct. What is not sufficiently acknowledged within the theory of totalitarianism is the significance of the particular 'doctrines' or 'ideals' around which totalitarian rule was organized. The Nazi commitment was to a 'racial' utopia, in which a superior 'race' believed itself entitled to dominate, enslave or indeed exterminate all other claimants to full human recognition. Furthermore, the Nazi system, following Hitler's own beliefs, idealized violence and war. It followed from this double core of Nazi ideology that the 'stabilization' or 'normalization' of its regime was unlikely to take place. Its 'racial' (which is to say quasi-biological) legitimation gave no scope for a settlement with denigrated peoples or races, whose 'inferiority' was taken as an immutable fact. In this respect Nazism went much further than the other 'Western' imperialisms, by which it had indeed been influenced (Arendt, 1951), whose primary claims to domination were cultural and political rather than biological, although racial doctrines had a significant place in their colonial practices too. The imperialisms of the British and the French were informed by universalist beliefs to the extent that the eventual emancipation of subject-peoples was at least theoretically anticipated, and was to a limited degree prepared for under colonial rule.

The communist utopia, by contrast, was justified by a theory of universal human emancipation, in which rule by a single class – 'the dictatorship of the proletariat' – was expected to be a transitional stage, after which all social classes were supposed to disappear. It was not because of their essential (still less biological) nature, but because of their imputed social roles, that the rival classes of the aristocracy and the bourgeoisie were required to be eliminated. The historical materialist theory of development on which this model was based did capture significant differences between social formations and the transitions between them. Its flaw was less in its analytic model of social change (Marx's predictive model of the unstoppable march of capitalism has even been vindicated by the current epoch of neo-liberal triumph [Desai, 2002]) than in its utopian programme for the revolutionary capture and control of this historical process. Revolutionary Communists, once in power, found a substantial lack of 'fit' between their own model of society and society's actual complexity. The failures of communism as a political system, and the disasters to which (amid achievements) it gave rise, derive from this massive discrepancy between ideology and reality.

Also, in contrast to Nazism, the communist systems, once established in power, were not essentially committed to violence, even though several of them (Stalin's Russia, Mao's China, Pol Pot's Cambodia) enacted extremely violent episodes, leading to vast numbers of deaths, even outside the exceptional context of civil war. They attempted to maintain some legitimating links with 'universalistic' political norms (human rights, social betterment, educational advance) even though these were often dishonest and based on sophistry, rather than, as with Nazism, disavowing normative constraints from 'principle'. Some evolution and mutation of communist systems has also proved possible. Thus China now combines a flourishing capitalism with the continued political rule of the Communist Party, and movements of reform communism developed in most of the West European Communist regimes, although these ultimately failed. The contrast between the self-destructive last days of Nazism and the European communists' surrender of power with scarcely a shot fired in their own defence also says something about these regimes' differences.

The other European fascisms are different kinds of regime again, although utilizing some of the technologies characterized as totalitarian, such as rule by a dictator through a mass party, the monopolistic control of mass communications, and the promulgation of a pervasive ideology. Not all fascisms (e.g. Spain) were militarily aggressive. Most (Spain, Portugal, Italy) were conservative in their accommodation with traditional sources of power and authority (landowners, army, church) compared with the Nazis, or indeed the communists. A comparative sociology of authoritarian and totalitarian regimes reveals different configurations of power.

Finally, we need to note that the differences between the liberal democratic regimes and the systems with which they are contrasted in the theory of totalitarianism, are not as absolute as the original theory proposed. In particular, a degree of symmetry developed between the 'liberal' and the 'totalitarian' systems, in the context of their antagonism with one another. The 'democratic' societies were scarcely less willing to utilize the means of mass destruction (Hiroshima, Nagasaki, the firebombing of German and Japanese cities) than the 'totalitarian' ones, when it came to war. Both sides in the Cold War were prepared to risk the destruction of civilization, through the use of nuclear weapons, to defend their ways of life. Each was also willing to condone (at the least) the destruction of hundreds of thousands of lives in their peripheral struggles in theatres of war such as Vietnam, Angola, Mozambique, Algeria, Chechnya and Nicaragua. The United States to this day maintains far more military bases throughout the world than any other power. The model of free-market capitalism has been promulgated and enforced across the world in recent decades no less energetically than the communist system once promoted its own ideology. One might also note that the levels of surveillance by the Stasi, or secret police, in East Germany, which were once so widely condemned as emblematic of totalitarian rule, have been shown by Edward Snowden's disclosures to be similar in their pervasiveness to those employed by the American and British security services. Western governments are now struggling to find a rationale to defend practices hitherto thought to be totalitarian – or Orwellian – in character. The differences between 'pluralist' and 'totalitarian' regimes remain significant, but they are far from absolute.

Psychoanalysis and totalitarianism

I will now propose that a psychoanalytic perspective can throw fresh light on the phenomenon of totalitarianism, and can characterize it with greater precision than is provided by conventional institutional and ideological formulations. There is a prior question of how far psychoanalytic understanding can extend to social and political phenomena at all, given that its primary locus has been the consulting room, in which the psychopathologies of individuals have been its primary object of study. But Freud certainly believed that psychoanalysis had application to the wider social domain, and demonstrated this in many papers. He showed (Freud, 1921, 1930) that the phenomenon of unconscious transference, manifested in clinical practice, also had a place in explaining the relations between political leaders and followers, especially in extreme situations. To Freud's understanding of the relations of followers to leaders in situations of mass popular arousal, we can add the later psychoanalytic insight into the 'counter-transference' (Heimann, 1950), which enables us to understand how leaders might reciprocally embody and act out the unconscious fantasies of their follow-ers. Social scientists (with some major exceptions) have mostly been reluctant to take account of such 'unconscious' dimensions of political life, on the grounds that these are too speculative to be amenable to empirical study. I have argued elsewhere (Rustin, 2016) that sociologists have been moved to take account of unconscious states of mind within groups and collectivities only when the 'irra-tional' disruptions of ordered social life became impossible to overlook. The perverse and destructive structures of feeling embodied in Nazism in particular called forth this analytic response, for example in the writings of members of the Frankfurt School such as Adorno, Horkheimer and Fromm. It was perhaps the impact of totalitarianism which led to the first development of what we might call psychoanalytic sociology. It is likely that key elements of psychoanalytic thought – for example Freud's positing of a death instinct, and the Kleinian emphasis on innate destructiveness – were responses to the violently destructive states of mind which became so pervasive during the wars and revolutions of the early twentieth century. Since the Second World War there has also been a sub-stantial psychoanalytic interest in the phenomena and consequences of Nazism and its crimes (Dicks, 1973; Lifton, 1961, 1986; Mitscherlich and Mitscherlich, 1975; Pick, 2012).

The essential psychoanalytic contribution to the understanding of totalitarian-ism lies in its grasp of the irrational or unconscious 'excess'[4] which manifests itself in totalitarian rule, in addition to the institutional and ideological attributes described by political scientists such as Friedrichs and Brzezinski. Totalitarianism in its extreme forms attempts the enactments of powerful fantasies, usually involving the total elimination of hated or despised enemies. We can discrimi-nate between those moments or episodes of totalitarian mobilization or rule when unconscious fantasies take over participants' grasp of reality, and those where such fantasies are constrained by a rational orientation to the world and are less toxic in their effects. There are even more and less 'totalitarian' moments within institutionally totalitarian systems, just as we may say that the psychotic elements of an individual with psychotic tendencies may be sometimes more, sometimes less in control of his mind at a given time.[5]

The contributions of Hannah Arendt and François Furet

Perhaps surprisingly, some of the descriptions of totalitarian systems which best characterize their unconscious structures of mind have been provided by writ-ers who were themselves either antipathetic or indifferent to psychoanalysis, although there have also been memorable descriptions, such as those by Adorno (1991 [1951]) and Adorno and Horkheimer (1989 [1944]), which made explicit use of psychoanalytic ideas. The most insightful of these accounts is Hannah

Arendt's classic *The Origins of Totalitarianism*, first published in 1951. Arendt's main category for understanding Nazi and Stalinist motivation is 'ideology', and her work has not therefore been understood as psychoanalytic. However, although she traces the roots of Nazi thinking back to its origins, and draws attention to its affinities with the racial thinking of other imperialisms, what she describes as an 'ideology' is as much a dynamic, destructive and perverse psychological organization as a system of ideas as such. Despite her reported dislike of psychoanalysis, Arendt finds herself using terms such as 'fantasy', 'paranoiac' and 'perverse', in characterizing both Hitler and Stalin and their milieus. It seems that she implicitly recognized that a psychodynamic register was necessary to understand this irrational phenomenon, even though she was disinclined to make overt use of it.

The structure of fantasy which dominated the Nazi mind was constituted by a belief in the superiority of the Aryan race, and its mission to impose its domination by violence on all other peoples of the world. The elimination of the Jews, defined as subhumans and as demonic conspirators against Germany (the immediate embodiment of racial virtue, though not, in the Nazi view, synonymous with it), was the first project of this mission of purification. It seems, however, that the Nazis envisaged a more extensive programme of racial elimination, during the near limitless period ('the thousand-year Reich') which they anticipated for their rule. The unfit and mentally ill had already been selected for extermination, and were being killed in large numbers, during the twelve-year period of the Nazi regime. A habit of 'concrete thinking' characterized the Nazi mind.[6] The extermination camps were a prime example of this, in that inmates who had been defined as lacking human status were denied it in practical reality as if to prove the truth of this definition. (Or as Hannah Arendt put it, because the Jews had been equated with 'vermin' or 'bedbugs', they could be exterminated as vermin or bedbugs would be by fumigation with poison gas.) And what might appear not to correspond to reality now, could be counted on or made to do so in the future, since the total victory of the Nazis was deemed to be certain. Such an equation between desire and reality is definitive of the operations of the unconscious mind, as Freud conceived it. In ideological thinking, the concept of 'inevitability' is often used to gloss over discrepancies between beliefs and facts, since it assures believers that reality will eventually be brought into line with the fantasized image of it. Hitler's disregard for truth and consistency, his erratic decisions, his consuming hatreds, and his intolerance of reality are well known. He seems to have lived for much of the time in what we would normally think of as a state of paranoid rage, which he succeeded in persuading those around him and within his larger sphere of influence to share, to varying degrees. It seems that the majority of the German people were for many years captured by this state of mind, in so far as they came to love and admire their leader, to share his vicious hatreds, and to glory in the demonstrations of his and their superiority over other nations and peoples, which was 'proved' for a time by military victories.

The problem is to explain how this delusional structure of mind was able to function in a serviceable relation to reality at all, as it did throughout the Nazi period. Arendt (1951: 477–506) provided an explanation of this paradox in a way that illuminates both its sociological and its psychodynamic aspects. She described how the inner circle of the Nazi party was surrounded by outer circles of sympathizers and fellow travellers, whose essential function was to be the intermediary between its unstable and violent unconscious psychic core and the wider world of reality. We can think of this mediating circle as a kind of 'contact barrier' between the Nazi unconscious and the real world. This circle of sympathizers enabled the Nazi fanatics to feel that their beliefs were not after all so deranged, since they seemed to be shared by many people who in most respects continued to behave as normal citizens. The function of this 'outer circle' of sympathizers for the larger population of non-believers in Nazism was to 'naturalize' or 'normalize' Nazism as not obviously irrational, since sympathizers with Nazism were themselves recognizably in most respects sane. Non-political citizens were thus exposed to the delusional beliefs of Nazism in a relatively mild and even 'disavowable' form. The apparent normality of most of what was happening around them, and the conventionality in most respects of many Nazi sympathizers, allowed them to witness, and no doubt for very many of them even covertly enjoy, cruelties and atrocities (for example the humiliation, expropriation or 'disappearance' of Jewish neighbours) while persuading themselves that these were merely anomalous events in a world which was otherwise unexceptionable, and which in the 1930s was felt even to be improving under Nazi rule. Later on, the sufferings of war, and the hatreds evoked by it, reinforced conformity to the regime, and induced paranoid-schizoid states of mind regarding Germany and its enemies, as happens in most contexts of war.[7]

One of the principal functions of terror within this system was to exclude alternative versions of reality from consideration. Ronald Britton (1998) has argued, in the context of the early Oedipal situation and of the transference relationship in psychoanalysis, that the recognition of a 'third position' – a point of view distinct from the dyad – is a precondition for thinking about psychic reality. The role of terror under totalitarian rule is to suppress and exclude such 'third positions', and thus to leave rulers and subjects confined within their shared structures of fantasy. The free expression and exchange of ideas in society is of psychological as well as political importance, since, through allowing the emergence of many 'third positions', it is the precondition of thinking and engagement with reality. Without differences and contradictions, there can be no generative thought.

The Nazi leadership was aware of the distance between its own mentality, with its endemic commitment to violence, and the habits of mind of ordinary citizens. It took care to maintain strong boundaries between its inner circle – one might say its inner world – and the wider society it sought to control and refashion, by managing flows of information between them. The other side of the flamboyance of the propaganda by which the regime conveyed what it wanted its subjects to hear, was its habit of secrecy and its cynical disregard for the truth. Thus its policy and practice of mass physical extermination was maintained as a secret (which is not to say that many did not know of it) and the regime's indifference to its people's sufferings was hidden from them.

This idea of a division between a psychotic part of a personality, and another part which remains in contact with and is able to function in relation to reality, applies to the functioning of disturbed individuals as well as collectivities such as the Nazi system.[8] Those (in the military or in government or the economy) whose task was to make the Nazi regime function rationally in relation to its 'external reality' had the continuing problem of how to mediate between Hitler and his entourage's beliefs and desires, and the obdurate external realities. This was also a continuing problem for Hitler's military commanders and for his economic minister, Albert Speer, in attempting to conduct the war in a rational manner (i.e. one which took account of military and material facts), especially when things started to go badly. One of the advantages of the Allied nations in the Second World War was the more rational decision-making processes which they maintained, through preserving some free exchange of ideas (through press, parliaments, toleration of disagreements, etc.), although some freedoms were also constrained under the conditions of war.[9] It is to the persistent irrationality of the Nazi regime that Britain probably owed its survival in 1940 and 1941 and the Soviet Union its survival in 1942.[10]

In considering the case of Stalinism as a totalitarian system, it is useful to place the work of a French historian of both the French Revolution and of European Communism, François Furet, alongside that of Arendt's. Furet's work, like hers, is 'proto-psychoanalytic' in its insights. In *The Passing of an Illusion: The Idea of Communism in the Twentieth Century* (1995) he suggests that a psychosocial dynamic similar to that of Nazism was operative under Stalinism. (The book's opening chapter is called 'The Revolutionary Passion'.) Whereas the fantasy of purification and elimination which dominated Nazism was framed in terms of racial inferiority, the 'elimination fantasy' which dominated Stalinist Russia was that of the class struggle. It was the elements of the aristocratic and bourgeois past that needed to be ruthlessly extirpated, long after their remnants had in reality been defeated. In the incessant purges of the Communist Party and the state apparatus during the 1930s, bourgeois deviations and plots were the justifications given for accusations, murder and mass incarceration in the camps. The *kulaks* or rich peasants, who had allegedly profited from the handovers of land to the peasants in the early days of the Bolshevik Revolution, were other targets for elimination. Those accused in the Moscow Trials were said to have conspired with bourgeois enemies abroad.[11] Although in these show trials evidence was fabricated, for example through forced confessions, to bring about some apparent fit between accusations and reality, it was the imputed beliefs and thus the 'objective' intentions of the accused, not their actions, which were really on trial. Individuals could be held to be enemies of the working class because of what would have been the consequences of their beliefs should they ever become embodied in actions.

The trials were a form of theatre, in which a version of political reality, sustained by fantasy, was insisted upon at the cost of the truth, and of the lives of those who dissented from the dominant beliefs.[12] The accused in these trials were sometimes trapped within the system of beliefs, or the 'psychological organization' which contained them, which they shared with their accusers. Thus, there was no 'third position' available to them to which they could appeal. The system of accusation and elimination in fact became almost indiscriminate at this time. It could both give expression to the fantasies of paranoid leaders or groups, and be used cynically, as seems to have been the case with Stalin, to destroy rivals and to concentrate all power in his own person.

Furet had previously described a similar dynamic in his book *Interpreting the French Revolution* (1981). His explanation of the Jacobin Terror focused on the role of ideas functioning as agents within a political process which had become disengaged from conventional constraints. The power of this explanation is augmented, however, if one understands the process as the pursuit not merely of a belief, but also of a collective fantasy of elimination and purification. Furet's argument (which followed that of de Tocqueville) is that the centralization of the French state had already destroyed much of civil society. The nobility had preserved its status under the monarchy, but had lost most of its integrative social functions. In the social vacuum which ensued, the ideas of individual liberty and equality were promulgated in philosophical societies which became influential in forming public opinion, and from which revolutionary leaders emerged. In a newly atomized world, Rousseau gave prime value *both* to the individual as the prime source of moral value *and* to the idea of an imaginary harmony or collectivity, formulated as the 'general will', which must prevail over all particular wills or interests. In the political vacuum left by the fall of the monarchy and by the weakness of the new representative institutions, republican clubs, in particular the Jacobins, seized the stage between 1793 and 1795. In an atmosphere of intense political theatre and continuous public meetings, an escalation of demands took place, with factions and leaders outbidding each other in their extremism. Under pressure from the mobilized 'sections' of the Parisian poor, the slogan of 'liberty, equality and fraternity' was interpreted in increasingly radical terms. A paranoid-schizoid searching out of traitors took place, with execution by the guillotine as the ritual fate of those who were defeated. Robespierre's unique 'incorruptibility', his distinctive claim to virtue, reveals the mechanism of paranoid-schizoid splitting – a combination of idealization and denigration – by which the Terror was justified. The middle-class revolutionaries were themselves always vulnerable to accusation 'from below' for their complicity with privilege. Robespierre's austerity and 'selfless devotion' to principle seemed to exempt him from such suspicion. This paranoid dynamic was exacerbated by the war which broke out between the new Republic and its monarchical and absolutist European neighbours.[13] When the Terror was brought to an end, with the fall of Robespierre, Bonaparte transformed the 'imaginary' or 'fantasied' community of the Republic into that of the conquering and liberating

French nation. This restored a kind of monarchical stability inside France at the cost of a general war with the reactionary enemies of the Republic and its allies outside France. The social classes chosen to be rooted out and destroyed in the French and Soviet revolutions were different – in the first case it was the aristocracy, in the second the bourgeoisie also. But both revolutions, according to this view, enacted fantasies of total elimination.[14]

As has been pointed out, neither Arendt nor Furet are usually recognized as writers sympathetic to psychoanalytic perspectives. Why, then, is their work so rich in its insights into the unconscious dimensions, the dominant structures of fantasy, of the extreme historical situations they described? The explanation must surely be that the situations they described were shaped by overpowering forces of fantasy. It is because both of these writers were so attentive to the phenomenology or 'lived experience' of these revolutionary situations and the regimes that arose from them (in both cases challenging more 'structural' accounts), that these irrational elements were captured in their analyses, even though each declined to make explicit use of psychoanalytic conceptions.

Totalitarian states of mind

More can be said from a psychoanalytic point of view about totalitarian states of mind, taking account of Arendt's and Furet's historical descriptions. My argument is that a distinguishing feature of 'totalitarian', compared with other kinds of authoritarian governments, is the dynamic role of a collective unconscious fantasy in their motivation and organization. From a psychoanalytic perspective, one might contend that there is no form of life, individual or collective, which does not have its shaping world of fantasy, its distinctive kinds of 'internal object', whether these are predominantly benign or malign, persecutory or nurturing. We become most aware of such collective states of mind when they take the extreme form of hatred of one group for another, when the unconscious 'excess' of sentiment shaping social relationships becomes impossible to overlook. But even when collective states of mind are more complex, embodying a measure of acceptance and trust, social bonds still have an unconscious dimension. (Using a non-psychoanalytic language, the sociologist Pierre Bourdieu (1990) referred to such implicit and taken-for-granted assumptions about the social environment as a 'habitus'.) I contend that what characterizes totalitarian systems are shared unconscious states of mind of a particularly destructive and dynamic kind.

In terms of the psychoanalytic theory derived from the writings of Melanie Klein, totalitarian states of mind are paranoid-schizoid in their organization. That is to say they are dominated by an extreme idealization of the group with which members identify, and an extreme denigration of those who are deemed to be its enemies. In totalitarian societies, or episodes in which social formations temporarily assume this character, binary distinctions between friends and enemies, between those defined in terms of good and evil, overwhelm and displace all other differences and discriminations. Hatred and destructiveness become enacted in persecution, war and atrocities directed towards aliens and enemies. Correspondingly, love and admiration – of an excessive and unrealistic kind – are directed towards the supposed virtues of 'our' side; the supposed beauty of the Aryan physical form, or the imagined utopia of the Soviet future, are examples of such idealizations. Such extreme splitting impedes or prevents the apprehension of reality, which inevitably possesses both love and hatred, desirable and undesirable attributes.[15] Totalitarian movements, regimes, and indeed individual states of mind, are notable for their intolerance of reality, and for their disposition to attack those who bring news of it.[16]

The susceptibility of large populations to succumb to such a condition has usually been the outcome of states of extreme social disorganization and the anxieties to which they give rise.[17] This was the case after Germany's defeat in the First World War, with the humiliations imposed on it by the victors, and the collapse of its economy which followed. In Russia, prior to the advent of Stalinism, there was the military defeat of the First World War, and the disruptions of the October Revolution of 1917 and the civil war which followed. Totalitarian leaders emerge and achieve power by becoming, via introjective and projective processes, the recipients and amplifiers of anxieties and hatreds among traumatized populations. In the case of the Nazis, this was through their mastery of technologies of propaganda of both word and deed, and through their deployment of terror.[18] One purpose and consequence of terror is its silencing or elimination of points of view different from those of its perpetrators. Social institutions which represent such differences – such as political parties – are destroyed, or are remade in a regime's image. The exercise of terror has the effect of further atomizing populations subject to its power, which are deprived of many of their social attachments, and are thus made vulnerable to injunctions to identify with the new dominant ideology and its institutions.

In the Soviet Union, the most active paranoid-schizoid dynamic was located in the ruling party, once its political enemies had been defeated and its power had been consolidated. It was under Stalin that this state of mind became most florid, it seems, in a toxic process, involving the paranoid demonization of internal enemies of the regime, such as Trotskyists, and the idealization of Stalin as the great leader. The larger population seemed to function in this situation in a largely passive role, as victims, bystanders or recruits of the dominant system. There were continuities in the Soviet Union between Stalinist rule and the habits of passivity and deference nurtured under the tsars. (Stalin's rule was implicitly compared in Eisenstein's (1944/1958) film *Ivan the Terrible* to that of the tsarist court.) After the October Revolution, the repressive role of the secret police morphed seamlessly between the tsarist and the Bolshevik regimes with little interruption, although with much greater severity after Stalin's accession to power.[19] 'The Great Patriotic War' of defence of the Soviet Union against Nazi invasion evoked much greater feelings of identification and loyalty than the Communist Party was ever able to achieve in support of its Marxist-Leninist political goals.[20]

Under Nazism, adherence to the Führer and the National Socialist Party were defined as coterminous with loyalty to Germany, the Fatherland. An economic resurgence during the 1930s, and early success in the Nazi regime's wars of expansion, brought the regime substantial popular support. When victories turned to defeat, and Germany suffered devastating destruction and invasion, loyalty to the regime, which was now identified with the cause of national survival, remained largely intact. The most distinctive project of the Nazis, namely the extermination of the Jews, was meanwhile maintained as a half-secret, its motivating sentiment and general intention being clear enough, while much of the operation of its machinery of mass destruction was kept from public view.

Conclusion

What then follows from this argument about the significant place of unconscious states of mind in shaping totalitarian mobilizations and regimes? First, such a psychoanalytic model helps us to demarcate 'totalitarian' from merely authoritarian forms of rule. Arendt herself made such discriminations. She argued that the Soviet Union became a totalitarian system under Stalin, but that other options for its development could have remained had Lenin not died in 1929. Whereas Stalin set out to destroy all existing social structures (repudiating 'permanent revolution' abroad, he pursued it at home), Lenin in his last years was attempting to maintain and even restore some viable social institutions. (He had said that Russia would be the easiest place in which to gain power, and the hardest in which to keep it.) The New Economic Policy (NEP) was bringing into being a nascent bourgeoisie; the peasants had been given their land, as the material base for the formation of a new social class; many different nationalities were being recognized and even constituted; the Soviets were ostensibly empowering urban workers. Arendt's argument was that Lenin's pragmatism as a politician at the time of his illness and death had gained precedence over the ideology of class struggle. It seems unlikely that Lenin would have destroyed the entire generation of the Bolshevik party which had made the revolution, as Stalin did after his death.

Arendt further argued that the Soviet Union ceased to be totalitarian following the death of Stalin, and with the dismantling of the Gulag and the large-scale and indiscriminate apparatus of terror following Krushchev's speech to the Twentieth Congress in 1956. She argued that a one-party authoritarian state is significantly different from a totalitarian regime. In psychoanalytic terms, we can say that this is because such a state is no longer primarily animated by delusional passions and fantasies, by the perverted and destructive idealism of totalitarian movements. It seeks some accommodation with realities, even if (unfortunately) these are mainly the realities of the dysfunctional institutions it has itself created.

Thus I contend that totalitarianism is characterized by an acute imbalance between fantasy and reality in political life, and by the domination of fundamentally paranoid-schizoid states of mind. The recognition of the power of collective fantasy, and of the force of paranoid-schizoid mechanism, might also help to explain something of the destructive energy unleashed in the Jacobin, Nazi and Stalinist revolutionary (or counter-revolutionary) struggles, and why projects for the entire elimination of categorized enemies – and thus of all differences – seem to be so central to totalitarian rule.[21]

It is not being suggested that 'fantasy' should be altogether banished from political life. This is because of the damage that can result when the connection between fantasy and reality is lost. Psychoanalysis teaches us that contact with the internal world of fantasy and the imagination, and rational engagement with the constraints of reality, are both necessary for creative lives. Virtuous political change can be inspired by desires and dreams of alternative futures. These may be rooted in particular experiences of the good which have been remembered and elaborated in universalist terms. Raymond Williams (1961) memorably argued that the movement for democracy in Britain was based not only on abstract principles, but also on the lived and remembered practices of working-class men and women who had fashioned democratic institutions for themselves. When Wordsworth wrote of his journeys in France at the time of the French Revolution, he was describing a transformed social climate, in which a sense of human worth seemed to have been claimed by everyone, regardless of their social status. He later wrote in disillusionment when he encountered the consequences of the Terror, and both of these descriptions offer testimony to their readers, through the passions they evoke, of the potentialities and risks inherent in radical political change.

A rich political process may be one in which there is a self-reflexive awareness of the 'springs of action' which lie in people's primary objects of love and hate, such that actions are rooted in feelings and convictions concerning the good. But what is also necessary is a grasp of the relations between fantasy and actuality, between what the imagination, or the unconscious, proposes as objects of desire, and what our reality sense informs us exists, or is possible (Rustin, 2001). [22] One outcome of the displacement of reality by fantasies is totalitarian states of mind, with their paranoid-schizoid fantasies about the locations of good and evil. Conversely, an outcome of the suppression of imagination and fantasy by an overbearing sense of the 'real' and the 'possible' can be a politics which embodies neither life nor hope. The retention of the capacity for reflection and thought as the mediator between fantasy and reality, is essential to creative political life.

Notes

1 This chapter arose from a concluding contribution by the present author to the London Conference in 2012 already referred to in the editors' introduction above, and from a panel on 'The Totalitarian Mind' at the International Psychoanalytical Association Congress in Prague in August 2013.
2 For the impact of totalitarianism on the psychoanalytic movement see Damousi and Plotkin (2012), Etkind (1997), Miller (1998) and Rustin (1985).

3 Arendt (1951) pointed out that appointment to a superior role in the 'official' state system signified a move to the margins of the Nazi hierarchy. Normally, state institutions are characterized by their commitment to a measure of legality and consistency, thus to a rationality of means if not ends. The principle of obedience to a leader, whatever he may command, is the antithesis of rationality. Arbitrary will, and whatever fantasies may motivate it, becomes the ultimate source of authority. Stalin's method of rule seems to have been different, but only superficially, in its preservation of a façade of collective decision-making by the leadership of the Party.

4 The term 'excess' has been deployed with great effect by the Lacanian Slavoj Žižek (1990, 1993) to describe the elements of unconscious fantasy and often transgressive 'enjoyment' (*jouissance*) which motivate certain political enactments.

5 Richard Lucas (2013) valuably discusses the struggles for domination which take place between the psychotic and non-psychotic parts of the mind of psychiatric patients.

6 Psychoanalysts such as Hanna Segal (1957) differentiate between 'concrete thinking', characteristic of paranoid-schizoid states, and 'symbolic thinking', a capacity for which emerges in the 'depressive position'. The difference between the two, further elaborated by Ronald Britton (1998), is that concrete thinking involves an equation between the symbol and the object it represents. In symbolic thinking, the symbol is distinct from its object, such that it becomes possible to recognize that an object may be thought about, or symbolized, in different ways, according to different points of view.

7 Arendt's conception of these 'concentric circles' of true believers, active sympathizers, and less involved citizens, all held in different degrees within the orbit of a totalitarian mentality, throws light on the broader questions of culpability and consent. There is a need to maintain a terrorizing apparatus of repression of action and opinion in totalitarian regimes because there are very different degrees of ideological commitment to them within their populations (Arendt, 1951: 477–506).

8 'Psychotic states' are of various degrees and kinds. At one extreme, they amount to insanity, but they may also occupy only part of the mind, and be more-or-less adequately contained, depending on circumstances. Some severe acts of violence are the outcome of 'psychotic episodes' or dispositions which do not preclude periods of relatively normal functioning in their perpetrators.

9 Stalin too retreated (temporarily) from personal absolutism, and conceded some power to his generals during the war with Nazi Germany, when he came to realize that the survival of the Soviet Union depended on this.

10 However, collusive decisions by various Allied governmental agencies not to give credence, or public visibility, to reports being received about Nazi extermination programmes left the Nazi regime a freer hand than they would otherwise have had to pursue them to the end.

11 The Soviet show trials had no exact equivalent under Nazism, which saw little need even for a public façade of justice. The Führer's will, not the law (however spurious) was the regime's main source of authority. Hitler eliminated his potential SA rival, Röhm, in 1934, by the equivalent of a gangland mass execution.

12 In *Humanism and Terror*, Maurice Merleau-Ponty (1969 [1947]), at the time when he was still a Communist Party member, developed a defence of this kind of 'historicist' reasoning as a justification for political actions. There he gave credence to the idea that opposition to the regime's policies, for example of the collectivization of agriculture, might amount to 'objective' support for the regime's enemies, by which in 1938 it felt threatened. In *The Adventures of the Dialectic* (1974 [1955]), after he had left the Communist Party, he repudiated this view, noting the invariable degeneration of revolutionary movements once they had achieved power, and rejecting the idea that a revolution conducted in the name of the working class (seen as a 'universal class')

was an exception to this pattern. 'Revolutions are true as movements, and false as regimes.' He asked: 'whether there is not more of a future in a regime that does not attempt to remake history from the ground up but only to change it and whether this is not the regime one must look for, instead of once again entering the circle of revolution' (1974 [1955]: 209–10). The '"internal mechanism" which makes the revolution exalt itself and, in meaning and power, go beyond the strict framework of the average objective conditions, the given historical surroundings' seems to refer, in the terms of my argument, to an underlying structure of fantasy or desire, always tending towards omnipotence, which revolutionary governments usually seek to impose on recalcitrant realities.

13 In an article on the Terror in *A Critical Dictionary of the French Revolution* (Furet and Ozouf, 1989), Furet points out that the terror increased in its severity (the numbers killed) in Paris, Lyon, the Vendée and elsewhere after the most serious threat to the Revolution from its external enemies had been held off. Whether from the desire for revenge, or deferred anxieties arising from the fear of defeat, internal terror came to its climax in a context of relative security. But the Revolution's supporters no doubt had reason to fear the retribution that would have followed their defeat.

14 Needless to say, although I am suggesting similarities in the psychological processes operating in these different regimes, this is not to imply that they are identical. The Nazi state was distinctive for its extreme addiction to conquest, destruction, and racial elimination, which was different from the universalist aspirations embodied in different forms in both the Jacobin and Bolshevik projects.

15 A realization equated in Klein's writing with the 'depressive position'. Her concepts of the paranoid-schizoid and depressive positions are set out in Klein (1940 and 1946).

16 The extremes of perfectionism and denigration which characterize totalitarianism were described in different historical embodiments by Norman Cohn (1957), in *The Pursuit of the Millennium*. His account illuminated millennial religious movements among the 'rootless poor of Europe' between the eleventh and sixteenth centuries. Such extremes were also captured by J.L. Talmon (1952) in *The Origins of Totalitarian Democracy*, which traces what he calls Political Messianism back to eighteenth-century rationalism, with Jacobinism as its principal historical instance. Both works are warnings concerning the dangers of these absolutist and totalizing states of mind, especially as these may be embodied in contemporary revolutionary political perspectives. But while Cohn proposes a connection between seventeenth-century millennial movements and modern totalitarianism, we can note another affinity in the behaviour of the churches and states and their agencies (such as the Holy Inquisition) during the religious wars of the seventeenth century, in their campaigns to extirpate heresies.

17 C. Fred Alford (1997) gives a psychoanalytic dimension to this, in the link he proposes between evil and the experience of annihilation anxiety. This is applicable to both individual and collective forms of psychopathy.

18 Adorno's 1951 essay 'Freudian Theory and the Pattern of Fascist Propaganda' traced the subtle correspondences between the Nazi's propaganda and the states of mind which it reflected and to which it gave symbolic shape. It is one of the classic psychoanalytic analyses of a political phenomenon.

19 Victor Serge (2012 [1951]), who was part of the revolutionary circle in Moscow, and on good terms with Lenin, cited the decision to set up the Cheka as a decisive early moment in the degeneration of the revolution.

20 During the years of war with Nazi Germany, some of the repressive features of Stalinist rule were in fact abated, as a means of broadening wartime support for the regime, only to be resumed as soon as the war ended.

21 It is evident that during the Cold War, a fantasy of total elimination of the enemy, the 'ideological other', at times prevailed on both sides, through a process of 'mirroring' which is common in situations of severe conflict. Hanna Segal (1987, 1995) argued that the paranoid structures of mind that had dominated the West in this period would prove difficult to renounce. The Cold War has in some influential minds been replaced by the 'war on terror', with 'Islamic fundamentalism' conceived as the West's new enemy (Rustin, 2004).

22 After all, the last infusion of idealism and passion in the Soviet Communist system came from Gorbachev and his anti-totalitarian ideas of *perestroika* and *glasnost*. Although this project of political renewal failed, one would not mainly blame its idealism for this failure, but rather the resistance of the decaying shell of the old system to renewal, or, in psychoanalytic terms, to new thought. The Soviet system after its 50 years of repression lacked the capacity to negotiate the complex realities which the reforms had created.

Chapter 17

Post-psychoanalysis and post-totalitarianism

Ruth Leys

Before even considering how we might theorize or historicize the relationship between psychoanalysis and totalitarianism, I want to suggest that we are living today in a post-psychoanalytic and post-totalitarian age. By this I mean, first, that wherever we look we see either that psychoanalysis has been widely rejected – especially in the United States where it flourishes, if at all, only at the margins of mainstream psychiatry and psychotherapy – or that it's being retooled in biological-materialist terms that involve the marginalization or abandonment of its central insights. And second, although I think it's fair to claim that the ravages of economic inequality have nothing to do with totalitarianism but are the result of neo-liberalism and global capitalism, there is a tendency in sections of both the political left and the political right today to regard totalitarianism as the greatest threat confronting the world. If both of these developments are true, what is their significance? Put slightly differently, what has gone missing when psychoanalysis is so widely discarded and totalitarianism is (still) cast as the central challenge of our times? Briefly, I suggest that what has gone missing in an age that is post-psychoanalytic is a concern with issues of intentionality and meaning. And I propose that what has gone missing in what I am calling post-totalitarianism is a concern with issues of class and economic inequality. My question then becomes: what, if anything, links these two developments together?

Post-psychoanalysis

As regards post-psychoanalysis, it would not be difficult to show that scholars and theorists of many kinds in the human and social sciences, as well as theorists of psychology and emotion, are bent on throwing off what they view as the straitjacket of psychoanalysis. Their reactions are motivated in part by the idea that the body in its lived materiality has been occluded or neglected by Freudian approaches to subjectivity. The result has been a widespread post-psychoanalytic embrace of biology and the neurosciences. This development is obvious in many domains, especially in the recent 'turn to affect'. For example, in the field of literary criticism and theory, the late Eve Kosofsky Sedgwick, a pioneer of postmodernist and queer theory, has been especially influential in her decision to discard psychoanalysis in her later work, and to emphasize instead the value of a biological approach to the affects for understanding the role of embodiment in (queer) identity formation and change. Borrowing from the (to my mind theoretically and empirically mistaken) ideas of the American psychologist Silvan S. Tomkins (1911–91), she proposed that the affects are to be understood in non-intentionalist, materialist terms as a set of universal, discrete, quasi-reflex 'affect programmes' or 'basic emotions' located subcortically in the brain and defined by signature bodily responses, especially by characteristic facial expressions. For Freud, emotions are intentional states: they are directed toward objects and depend on our desires and beliefs about the world. But according to Sedgwick, who follows Tomkins in this regard, emotions are bodily states that can be triggered by what might be called their objects – but it turns out that the objects are nothing but stimuli or tripwires for built-in, reflex-like corporeal responses (Sedgwick, 2003). Tomkins' Darwinian-inspired ideas have been embraced by Sedgwick's followers and many others, while the related non-intentionalist theory of the emotions proposed by Tomkins' follower and successor, the psychologist Paul Ekman, dominates mainstream affective neuroscience, as in the writings of the influential emotion theorist Antonio Damasio. Likewise recent affect theorists in political science and related fields, such as Brian Massumi and William E. Connolly, who claim to be influenced by the writings of Gilles Deleuze and other philosophers, are committed to the same non-intentionalism when they assert that affect is independent of cognition, signification and meaning, and when they draw on the same or similar problematic neuroscientific views to support their opinions.

It is of course possible to deny that affects are rightly understood in anti-intentionalist, materialist terms. It could be argued (in fact, I have made the argument elsewhere) that the affects are embodied, intentional states in which the question of the meaning to the organism or subject of the objects in its world is a central issue and concern (Leys, 2007, 2010a, 2010b, 2012a). Nor am I alone in thinking that the anti-intentionalist view of the affects is erroneous. But for a host of reasons the idea of non-intentionality has a powerful grip on contemporary culture and thought and is not easily dislodged.

Moreover, many psychoanalysts have also recently begun arguing the need to redefine Freudian ideas in terms amenable to the neurosciences. This has led to, among other consequences, the uncritical acceptance of non-intentionalist theories of emotion of the kind found in the work of Ekman and Damasio. The result has been a repudiation of the role of intention and belief in emotion in terms that are alien to Freud's own meaning-centred approach to affect. To take just one example, the neuro-psychoanalyst Mark Solms writes that 'emotion is the aspect of consciousness that is left if you remove all externally derived contents' – a statement I can't imagine Freud making (or indeed Wittgenstein), and one that is striking for its hostility to the idea that emotions are intentional states that are directed at objects (Solms and Turnbull, 2002: 106).

For quite a few years now many theorists have also been committed to a non-intentionalist approach to trauma. They have turned away from the Freudian emphasis on *Nachträglichkeit* ('deferred action'), or the retroactive conferral of meaning in trauma, in favour of a post-psychoanalytic emphasis on the traumatic collapse of all meaning and representation. The deconstructive account of trauma put forward by literary critic Cathy Caruth is exemplary in this regard (Caruth, 1996). At the heart of Caruth's approach to trauma is a 'performative' theory of language based on the work of the Belgian-born literary critic and theorist of deconstruction Paul de Man, according to which a 'death-like' break or resistance to meaning inheres in language itself. For Caruth, an analogous 'death-like break' lies at the heart of trauma: the victim of trauma who cannot symbolize or represent the traumatic event or scene nevertheless obsessively 'performs' or re-experiences it in the form of flashbacks, nightmares, and related neurobiological symptoms. Although aspects of Caruth's theory are linked to Freud's discussions of examples of traumatic repetition seen in shell-shocked soldiers in the First World War and in clinical settings, her account of trauma has been fortified by appeals to the findings of neurobiologists who, viewing trauma in literalist-causal terms, reinterpret the traumatic dream as a veridical memory of the traumatic event, a memory that is said to be 'engraved' in the brain with uncanny accuracy.

Although to my mind Caruth's ideas are mistaken (see Leys, 2000, ch. 8), they continue to attract attention and support. In fact, it is worth emphasizing that the new affect theorists are simply offering a reworking of the basic themes of trauma theory as put forward by Caruth. Both share the same commitment to anti-intentionalism, according to which affect and trauma are held to be characterized by the absence of intentionality or meaning; both share the same commitment to materialism, with the result that affect and trauma are literalized or corporealized in the body; and both share the same commitment to neuroscientific interpretations of affect and trauma (Leys, 2012b). They also share a commitment to the importance of (a certain notion of) ontology, a topic on which I have more to say below.

A striking manifestation of these trends can be found in the work of the French philosopher Catherine Malabou who, in a recent book, *The New Wounded: From Neurosis to Brain Damage*, first published in 2007, combines affect and trauma theory to suggest that we are living in an age in which a wide range of people can be defined as 'wounded' and hence as post-traumatic subjects (Malabou, 2012a). Malabou includes in one single category the effects of traumas resulting from actual head wounds or cerebral lesions, traumas due to natural catastrophes, and traumas resulting from political violence or social conflict, in order to propose that none of those traumas can be interpreted in psychoanalytic terms. Instead, inspired by the work of Damasio and others, as well as by the literature on the war neuroses, she proposes that trauma must be understood in corporeal-materialist terms as the consequence of damage to the (so-called) 'emotional brain'. She therefore paints a portrait of the 'new wounded' as persons who, through the impact of a cerebral accident of some kind, are so altered, so absolutely cut off from their previous identities, so emptied of memory, interiority and subjectivity, and so indifferent to others and to the world, as to be altogether deprived of feeling of any kind. Alzheimer patients, schizophrenics, autistics, epileptics, survivors of the concentration camps, patients with war neuroses or post-traumatic stress disorder, and the victims of natural and political disasters – all emerge in her account as emblematic of the zero-degree of subjectivity that supposedly characterizes the global form of life in the twenty-first century. So expansive is Malabou's account of the new wounded that she claims, with considerable hyperbole, that the post-traumatic condition is one that 'reigns everywhere today' (Malabou, 2012a: 17).

Malabou denies that she has created a false amalgam by fusing together such apparently disparate conditions. She claims rather that the phenomenon of the amalgam is precisely what needs to be discussed today: the heterogeneous mixture, as she sees it, of nature and politics at work in all types of violence, this mixture where 'politics is annulled as such so that it assumes the face of nature and where nature disappears beneath the mask of politics' (Malabou, 2012a: 156). According to her, what unites the new wounded as a group is that, no matter their different clinical forms, they all suffer from the same aetiology and the same emotional abnormalities. For Malabou, trauma produces a cerebral pathology that is identical in all cases and contexts, a pathology that she asserts resists any interpretation or assignment of meaning. She introduces the concept of 'cerebrality' to capture her sense of what she calls the 'causal value' of the damage done by traumatic events to the emotional brain, regardless of whether those events are accompanied by definable cerebral impairments (Malabou 2012a: 2). She writes: 'The "new wounded" . . . are not merely people with brain lesions. Cerebrality designates a regime of eventality that recognizes the psychic weight of accidents stripped of any signification' (Malabou, 2012a: 10). Trauma thus reveals the 'ability of the subject to survive the senselessness of its own accidents' (Malabou, 2012a: 5). In Malabou's approach, political and social conflicts become as anonymous and meaningless as natural catastrophes and the victims of trauma are emptied of all interiority and subjectivity. In her words:

> The distinction between organic traumas and political traumas becomes blurred precisely because of the type of event that gives rise to them – a brutal event, without signification, that tends to efface its intentionality in order to appear as a blow inflicted on any possible hermeneutics in general.
>
> (Malabou, 2012a: 214)

Malabou's definition of trauma as a pure 'accident' – as a completely unanticipated, ungraspable, unmediated external event that bears no relation to the past and destroys meaning – is not new. Rather, her proposal needs to be seen for what it is – as a reworking, that is, as yet another expression of the recent, I am tempted to say standard, postmodernist and post-Holocaust emphasis on the unspeakable and unrepresentable in trauma. Indeed, as I have indicated, the same emphasis on trauma, defined as an accident that unsettles semantic expectations and meanings, is basic to the work of Caruth, whose work in this regard Malabou cites favourably (Malabou, 2012a: 201). But Malabou takes these by now familiar ideas a step further. Her argument is not just that trauma is an experience that has no significance for the victim. She suggests that even the perpetrator's deliberate acts of violence lack meaning and intention. According to her, traumatic events are incidents that tend to 'mask their intentionality', with the consequence that, as she puts it, 'politics itself is defined by the renunciation of any hope of endowing violence with a political sense' (Malabou, 2012a: 155). Traumatic events thus appear 'either as perfectly unmotivated accidents or as the necessary blindness of natural laws' (Malabou, 2012a: 11). In both cases, the intentional orientation of the event is 'disguised' (Malabou, 2012a: 11). As she puts it:

> The meaning of armed conflicts . . . is masked behind the impersonal and signatureless character of their attacks. Between a car bomb and an accidental detonation of a gas tank there is both an enormous difference and no difference. The sinister lesson of terrorism lies in its refusal to formulate a lesson. Responsibility for attacks is claimed less and less. The situation in Iraq, for example, remains illegible. Who perpetrates terrorist attacks today, and why? The dissimulation of the reason for the event is the new form of the event. The increasingly radical effacement of the distinction between accident and crime, between disastrous incidents and war, the multiform presence of the absence of any responsible instances or author, makes the natural catastrophe of contemporary politics into a daily occurrence.
>
> (Malabou, 2012a: 155)

Malabou thus treats terrorist acts as unmotivated by any political reasons the terrorists themselves might give for them (Malabou, 2012: 155) and places the emphasis instead on the terrorists' emotional emptiness – as if terrorists are merely helpless carriers of an impersonal, destructive-neuronal death drive. But it is one thing to say that certain acts of terrorism are illegible to those of us who do not know who the terrorists are, do not know their culture, and do not understand their motives; it is another thing to suggest, as Malabou does, that the refusal of terrorists to publicly take responsibility for their acts is not a political strategy for which they have their reasons but points rather to the absence of any reasons, intentions, or meanings. The obliteration of the distinction between perpetrators and victims – already seen in the work of both Caruth and Giorgio Agamben – could hardly be taken further. In short, Malabou treats terrorists not as intentional agents but as new forms of identity – the identity of those whose cold indifference marks them as members of the class of the 'new wounded'. For Malabou, what matters is not the terrorists' intentions and beliefs but simply *who they are*. What is novel is that rather than proposing that terrorists have an identity different from that of their victims, she now asks us to imagine that they have exactly the same identity – the identity of the new wounded.

A further point in this connection: by substituting an interest in personal identity for an interest in issues of meaning and intention, Malabou's work conforms to the general turn to a certain notion of ontology that marks the post-psychoanalytic. By stressing the fundamental importance of affect and subjectivity – or their complete disappearance under the traumatic conditions that produce the class of the 'new wounded' – Malabou replaces questions about ideology and what people believe and think with questions about sheer 'being' or what people are, since what matters to her are not beliefs and intentions but simply the identity of subjects as the 'new wounded'. The title of another of Malabou's recent books, *Ontology of the Accident*, signals her commitment to the idea that the post-traumatic subject is the new form of 'being' in the twenty-first century (Malabou, 2012b).

The trouble with this 'ontological' (but in fact merely identitarian) turn, however, is that it forecloses the possibility of disagreement and dispute. In particular, replacing an emphasis on *what we believe* with an emphasis on *who we are* changes the entire basis on which we can have arguments and debates. Indeed, it closes down the possibility of dispute altogether. For how can there be a debate over the meaning of terrorism if all that matters is who the terrorists are, not the beliefs they hold? As the literary critic and theorist Walter Benn Michaels has argued in connection with Michael Hardt's and Antonio Negri's similar replacement of political beliefs and ideas with the 'biopolitical', defined by them as 'struggles over the forms of life':

> [S]truggles over the form of life are 'ontological' rather than ideological; they have nothing to do with the question of what is believed and everything to do with the question of what is. For Hardt and Negri, of course, Empire is what is, and in their efforts to imagine 'resistance' to it, they are as skeptical of political alternatives to it as . . . George W. Bush. Just as the point of the war on terrorism is to insist that there is no alternative ethico-legal order (you either follow the law or break it), the point of Empire is that it, too, is 'total' and that resistance to it can only take the form of negation – 'the will to be against'. So if political conflict may be imagined as a conflict between two competing commitments as to what's right, biopolitical conflict appears as conflict between what is and what isn't, or (in its more forward-looking mode) between what is and what will be.
>
> (Michaels, 2004: 173)

Michaels goes on to cite Hardt and Negri as stating: 'Those who are against . . . must also continually attempt to construct a new body and a new life'. Just so, by emphasizing bodies over ideas, and who we are over meaning, Malabou offers a vision of the twenty-first century as a world inhabited by millions of empty or vacant post-traumatic subjects, the new wounded, rather than by persons with different and hence competing political ideas and beliefs.

Post-totalitarianism

To turn now to the topic of post-totalitarianism, I suggest that a similar concern with difference and identity as opposed to a concern with disagreement over beliefs characterizes recent developments in political theory. Here the question becomes: what does it mean to insist, as Giorgio Agamben, Judith Butler and others on the left have done, that the West has normalized the state of exception that characterized the Nazi totalitarian state, with the result, so it is claimed, that the West has normalized totalitarianism itself? And what does it mean if the conservative, or neo-liberal, opponents of Agamben and Butler likewise treat totalitarianism as the most important threat confronting the world? These are precisely the questions raised by Michaels when he observes that for Agamben the threat of the Nazi camps remains central today. Indeed, arguing that the state of emergency declared in the United States after 9/11 has ceased to be the 'exception' and instead has become the 'rule', such that the normalization of the state of exception 'leads inevitably to the establishment of a totalitarian regime', Agamben identifies the Guantánamo Bay detention camp with Auschwitz (Michaels, 2011b). In other words, for Agamben the greatest threat confronting the world is totalitarianism itself. Michaels notes in this regard that people with theoretical positions very different from his and with very different politics characteristically share Agamben's fear of the return of the camps as well. In fact, as he argues, the threat of a new Hitler looms as large in some of the writings of the right as it does in those of the left, the only difference being that for the right it was Saddam Hussein who after 9/11 posed the biggest threat, whereas for the left it was Bush himself. (Today for the right it is probably Obama.)

But Michaels rightly suggests in this regard that the relevant question for both left and right ought to be, not whether Saddam Hussein or Bush is more like Hitler, nor about where the totalitarian threat is coming from. The relevant question ought to be: what does it mean for both the left and the right that totalitarianism is indeed the threat? The short answer to that question is that by treating totalitarianism – specifically the Nazi form of totalitarianism as exemplified by the concentration camps – as the most fundamental threat to modernity, both the left and the right can ignore the very real contemporary problem of economic poverty resulting from global capitalism or neo-liberalism. And just as in the case of post-psychoanalysis, so here too, theorists on the left and the right refuse the 'inequality of differing ideologies (i.e. the different beliefs about what is true)' (Michaels, 2011a: 311), in favour of a pluralist emphasis on the importance of differences in identity. Indeed, as Michaels shows, the status of the poor emerges in the work of theorists of pluralism and diversity such as William E. Connolly as precisely a new form of cultural identity, one that deserves 'respect' or 'recognition' rather than amelioration through income redistribution. In short, the case can be made that by treating poverty as a form of economic identity, pluralists such as Connolly do the work of neo-liberalism rather than critiquing it (Michaels, 2011a, 2011b).

We can approach the same topic from the perspective of affect theory by noting that the commitment to diversity and difference of identity is accompanied in the work of Connolly and many other commentators by a related commitment to the view that ideology and belief have been overrated in political life. Thus Connolly denies that people have what he calls 'abstract beliefs' and insists instead that our beliefs are embodied in our daily practices and routines, conceived as aspects of our identity to the extent that it is bodies, and not beliefs, that drive personal and political behaviour. Hence the importance attached by Connolly and others to affect, defined in non-intentionalist terms as involving corporeal changes occurring below the level of consciousness. Hence also his turn to the work of neuroscientists, such as Damasio, LeDoux and others, to confirm his views about the non-cognitive nature of affect. The result is a commitment to notions of self-transformation by everyday 'techniques' of the self or 'tactics' of the body – e.g. listening to music, exercise, taking Prozac, mental concentration, meditation, and so on – that are said to alter or remap body-brain connections and thereby change our identities. Stressing bodies over beliefs, affect over reason, Connolly claims that what is crucial is not our ideas and intentions but the non-cognitive affective processes that produce them, with the result that political change becomes a matter not of persuading others of the truth of our ideas but the 'ontological' challenge of producing new bodies, new 'becomings', and new lives (Connolly, 2002; see also Leys, 2011a; Connolly, 2011; and Leys, 2011b).

Slavoj Žižek's response to Malabou's book is an interesting commentary on these several trends. On the one hand, Žižek rejects the non-Freudian, more specifically the non-Lacanian, terms in which Malabou describes the new wounded, accusing her of naïveté in her discussion of psychoanalysis. According to Malabou, interpretations of trauma based on the existence of previous psychical conflicts, or the history of the patient, are disqualified. This means that she rejects the Freudian idea that trauma has 'always already' occurred because of a prior, more originary trauma – say, the trauma of infantile psychosexuality. Instead, she argues that her newly coined concept of cerebrality:

> allows for the possibility of a disastrous event that plays no role in an affective conflict supposed to precede it. Accordingly, it determines the survival of the psyche in terms of a perfectly and definitively aleatory effraction . . . These patients, each in his or her own way, challenge us to think pure, senseless danger as an unexpected event – incompatible with being fantasized . . . Cerebrality is thus the causality of a neutral and destructive accident – without reason.
>
> (Malabou, 2012a: 8–9)

Not surprisingly, as a staunch follower of Lacan, Žižek refuses the deflationary account of subjectivity implied by Malabou's move to the post-psychoanalytic. He insists rather that traumatic events always occur on the basis of a 'more profound and originary trauma, understood as the Real or as the "transcendental" trauma' (cited Malabou, 2012b: 226). As he observes:

When Malabou insists that the subject who emerges after a traumatic wound is not a transformation of the old one, but literally a new one, she is well aware that the identity of this new subject does not arise out of a *tabula rasa*: many traces of the old subject's life-narrative survive, but they are totally restructured, torn out of their previous horizon of meaning and inscribed in a new context.

> (Žižek, 2008–9: 23–4)

On the other hand, Žižek endorses Malabou's 'ontological' approach to trauma. He accepts the idea that what is at stake in trauma is the production of a new 'form' of life, the form that he calls 'post-traumatic' or 'autistic' and Malabou calls 'the new wounded'. 'Malabou is right to emphasize the philosophical dimension of the new autistic subject', he acknowledges:

In it, we are dealing with the zero-level of subjectivity, with the formal conversion of the pure externality of meaningless real (its brutal destructive intrusion) into the pure internality of the 'autistic' subject detached from external reality, disengaged, reduced to the persisting core deprived of its substance . . . If one wants to get an idea of the elementary, zero-level, form of subjectivity, one has to look at autistic monsters.

> (Žižek, 2008–9: 26–7)

Žižek adds an economic dimension to his discussion by including the abstract violence of global capitalism among the forces that produce today's 'autistic monsters'. Indeed, he appears to want to resist the tendency of Malabou's ideas to naturalize capitalism by depriving social conflicts of the 'dialectics of political struggle proper' (Žižek, 2008–9: 13), that is, by treating global capitalism as if it were an anonymous, natural force like any other, thereby collapsing the distinction between nature and culture (or the political). Nevertheless, Žižek risks obfuscating the role of economic exploitation in producing inequality precisely because he is committed to the same 'ontological' assumptions that govern Malabous's analysis. Thus Žižek treats the post-traumatic, autistic subject as one of the figures of the proletariat of the 'commons', in the sense of Hardt and Negri (Žižek, 2008–9: 28–9), in effect turning an economic class into an identity – as if being poor were not a matter of being located in a structure or system defined by inequality but simply a matter of being a *specific kind of subject*. As Žižek observes:

Overdoing it a bit, perhaps, one is tempted to say that this subject deprived of its libidinal satisfactions is the 'libidinal proletariat'. When Malabou develops her key notion of 'destructive plasticity', of the subject who continues to live after its psychic death . . . she touches the key point . . . In other words, when we are dealing with a victim of Alzheimer's, it is not merely that his awareness is severely constrained, that the scope of the Self is diminished – we are literally no longer dealing with the same Self. After the trauma, ANOTHER subject emerges, we are talking to a stranger.

(Žižek, 2008–9: 23)

Even more problematically, Žižek follows Malabou in equating the proletariat, defined as post-traumatic subjects or 'autistic monsters', with victims of the Nazi camps, thereby suggesting – in terms not unlike that of Agamben and others – that the post-traumatic subject must be viewed as in some sense a victim of totalitarianism. Early in her book, via a reference to Bruno Bettelheim's well-known comparison between the 'Muselman' and the victim of autism, Malabou links today's 'new wounded' with the 'Muselmans' or 'Muslims' of the extermination camps – those doomed, abject 'non-men who march and labour in silence, the divine spark dead within them, already too empty to really suffer', as Primo Levi described them (Malabou, 2012a: xvii–xviii; Levi, 1993: 90). Žižek picks up on Malabou's suggestion, asking:

If the twentieth century was the Freudian century, the century of the libido, so that even the worst nightmares were read as (sado-masochistic) vicissitudes of the libido, will the twenty-first century be the century of such post-traumatic disengaged subjects whose first emblematic figure, that of the Muslim in concentration camps, is not [*sic*, now?] multiplying in the guise of refugees, terror victims, survivors of natural catastrophes, of family violence?

(Žižek, 2008–9: 12; for other references to the 'Muslims' see also 21 and 28)

But why does Žižek link the fate of today's poor with the Nazi genocide? Why does he think the status of the proletariat in our time has anything to do with the fate of the Jews under Nazi totalitarianism? Does he really mean us to think that the rising income inequalities between rich and poor today are best understood as involving the transformation of the poor into 'autistic monsters' who have been deprived of 'engaged existence and reduced to indifferent vegetating' (Žižek, 2008–9: 21)? Does he truly believe that the situation of the poor is best understood in quasi-medical or pathological terms as one in which, as a result of the forces of capitalism, they have been transformed into persons who, like the Muslim victims of the Nazis, lack emotion, affect, memory, and even the capacity for anything but the merest kind of instrumental agency (Žižek, 2008–9: 21)? In most of the world poverty today has nothing to do with totalitarianism. On the contrary, the problem of the poor is the problem of a growing economic inequality resulting from the operations of global capitalism. This is a problem (again, as Michaels has argued) whose solution demands beliefs and commitments, themselves liable to provoke disagreements, not ontological analyses that render our political and economic beliefs irrelevant. (For an interesting argument that, in spite of his commitment to a non-reductive materialism, Žižek emphasizes 'experience' at the expense of meaningful expression and hence eliminates belief altogether, see Bartulis, 2012.)

In other words, just as the transformation of Freud's thought into neuro-psychoanalysis distracts from issues of intentionality, so worries about the alleged continual threat of totalitarianism distract from issues of economic class. Which suggests that what ensures that concerns about intentionality and about economic class go missing in post-psychoanalysis and post-totalitarianism is their shared 'ontological' commitment to the primacy of identity at the expense of issues of meaning.

Conclusion

Some final remarks. I regard Malabou's detailed critique of psychoanalysis as the strongest feature of *The New Wounded*. Nevertheless, I question the limitations of her analysis. She regards Freud's inability to separate the death drive from the pleasure principle in his discussion of traumatic repetition as a serious failing on his part. She argues instead that the death drive is unmixed with libido and hence is a force without relation to any other. She thus defines the traumatic event as that which comes to the passive subject as a strictly external act of violence, uncontaminated with libido or desire and hence as lying beyond the pleasure principle. But in arguing this position, Malabou not only fails to provide any serious discussion of the social bond, she actually suppresses issues of identification with the other that are so central to Freud's analysis of group psychology and indeed to his analysis of the neuroses.

As I have tried to show in *Trauma: A Genealogy*, from the moment of its invention in the late nineteenth century the concept of trauma has been fundamentally unstable, balancing uneasily, or rather veering uncontrollably, between two theories or paradigms. The first or 'mimetic theory' holds that in the moment of trauma the subject is immersed in the scene of violence in a mode of hypnotic or 'mimetic' identification, with the result that, like a post-hypnotic person, the victim cannot afterwards recall the original trauma but is fated to act it out or imitate it in various ways. The idea is that the traumatic-mimetic experience shatters the victim's cognitive and perceptual capacities so that the experience never becomes part of the ordinary memory system. The second or 'antimimetic' theory also tends to make imitation or identification basic to the traumatic experience, but it interprets imitation differently. In this model, even as she may imitatively yield to the scene of violence the victim remains essentially aloof from the event, in the sense that she remains a spectator of the traumatic scene, which she can therefore see and represent to herself and others. The antimimetic theory is compatible with, and often gives way to, the idea that trauma is a purely external event that befalls a fully constituted subject; whatever the damage to the latter's psychic autonomy and integrity, there is in principle no problem of eventually remembering or otherwise recovering the event, though this may involve a long and arduous therapeutic process. And in contrast to the mimetic theory's assumption of an identification with the aggressor, the antimimetic theory depicts violence simply as an assault from without.

As I also attempted to demonstrate, from the turn of the nineteenth century to the present there has been a continual oscillation between these two paradigms; indeed, the interpenetration of one by the other or alternatively the collapse of one into the other has been recurrent and unstoppable. The antimimetic model in particular lends itself to positivist interpretations of trauma, epitomized by the several neurobiological theories widely accepted today. Especially common are antimimetic theories which shift the focus of research from the notion of trauma as a psychic phenomenon troubling the mind to the idea that trauma essentially concerns the body by modelling trauma on an animal's response to inescapable shock and proposing that the traumatic event is encoded in the brain in a different way from ordinary memory. The goal of such research is to identify the neurohormonal mechanisms thought to be at the basis of such traumatic memories.

Malabou's analysis of the new wounded needs to be situated in this lineage. Hers is an antimimetic approach to trauma in which, as I have put it, the passionate identifications said to inhere in the mimetic incorporation of violence are transformed into claims about identity, and the negativity and ambivalence that according to Freud necessarily inhere in identification are violently expelled into the external world, from where they return to the fully constituted, autonomous subject in the form of an absolute exteriority. The result is a rigid dichotomy between the internal and the external such that violence is imagined as coming to the subject entirely from the outside (Leys, 2000: 37–9). It is not surprising in this regard that Malabou cites favourably the work of contemporary psychiatric theorists, such as Bessel van der Kolk and Judith Herman, who likewise treat violence as a strictly exogenous event that comes to the passive but autonomous subject purely from the outside and who ignore the role of identification in the traumatic response.

The value of the view that violence is external to the subject is that it serves to forestall the possibility of scapegoating victims of trauma by denying that they participate in or collude with the scene of abjection or humiliation. But – as I also argued in my book – it is a view of the location of violence that also has its costs. For one thing, it:

> makes unthinkable, or renders incoherent, the mimetic-suggestive dimension of the traumatic experience, a dimension that . . . calls into question any simple determination of the subject from within or without and that is present in the tendency to suggestibility that is still recognized as symptomatic of patients suffering from trauma.
>
> (Leys, 2000: 38)

It is only by ignoring the issue of mimesis-identification that Malabou can describe the victims of the war neuroses as so cut off from the world as to be deprived of all emotion, even though the literature on the war neuroses is replete with descriptions of the victim's painful emotional responses – including survivor guilt, shame, extreme fright, overwhelming anxiety, murderous hate, profound despair, and remorse – suggesting that such patients don't suffer from the absolute affec-tive 'anaesthesia' or indifference to the world that Malabou attributes to them. By proposing a stark opposition between the subject and the world, I believe Malabou misreads the literature on the war neuroses on these points, a literature on which she otherwise leans heavily.

Just as problematic is the fact that the rigid dichotomy she proposes between the external and the internal inevitably reinforces a concept of the subject of trauma as a completely passive and helpless victim. Indeed, as Malabou herself admits at the end of her book, insisting on the brutal character of the catastrophic accident and on the external dimension of violence 'could suggest that the victim counts for nothing in what comes to pass' (Malabou, 2012a: 214) – a worry about the complete loss of agency in the new wounded that she is unable to resolve. In short, I am arguing that Malabou antimimetically shifts attention from a notion of trauma as a psychic phenomenon to one that portrays trauma victims as devoid of all subjectivity and agency – an extreme claim, to say the least. Malabou's commitment to the primacy of identity is compatible with her claim that the new wounded figure the death of the subject in its lack of all emotion and mental con-tent. It is central to her claims to originality that she has distinguished for the first time the very form of the new identity of our violent times – the identity of the affectless post-traumatic subject.

From this perspective, Theodor Adorno's much earlier discussion, in 'Freudian Theory and the Pattern of Fascist Propaganda' (1991 [1951]), of the relevance of Freud's 'doctrine of identification' to totalitarian propaganda offers a striking contrast to, or commentary on, Malabou's treatment of Freud. On the basis of his understanding of Freud's ideas about mass psychology, specifically the role of identification–suggestion in group behaviour, Adorno warns against the loss of psychic interiority and autonomy that occurs when individuals, sub-stituting an idealized image for their own paternal ego ideal, identify with the Leader or Führer. By imitating the leader, Adorno suggests, individuals become the manipulable–suggestible crowd of mass movements. A detailed discussion of Adorno's understanding of Freud's views on identification and crowd men-tality lies outside the scope of this chapter (but for perceptive analyses of these topics see especially Borch-Jacobsen, 1988, 1992). Yet it is worth emphasizing that Adorno viewed with alarm the very loss of subjectivity under conditions of totalitarianism that Malabou seeks to establish. He saw in Freud's analysis of group psychology and fascist society the emerging obsolescence of the inten-tional subject and anticipated with a sense of foreboding and dismay the appear-ance under fascism of a global norm of post-individuality that Malabou and even Žižek seem to embrace.

Bibliography

Abram, J. (1996) *The Language of Winnicott: A Dictionary of Winnicott's Use of Words*. London: Karnac.

Adorno, T. (1967) *Prisms*. Cambridge, MA: MIT Press.

Adorno, T. (1978) *Minima Moralia*. London: Verso.

Adorno, T. (1990 [1966]) *Negative Dialectics*. London: Routledge.

Adorno, T. (1991 [1951]) 'Freudian Theory and the Pattern of Fascist Propaganda'. *The Culture Industry: Selected Essays on Mass Culture*. London: Routledge. 114–35.

Adorno, T. (1998 [1953]) 'Television as Ideology'. *Critical Models: Interventions and Catchwords*. New York: Columbia University Press.

Adorno, T. (2006) *Letters to His Parents 1939–1951*. Cambridge: Polity Press.

Adorno, T., Frenkel-Brunswik, E., Levinson, D.J. and Sanford, R.N. (1950) *The Authoritarian Personality*. New York: Harper & Brothers.

Adorno, T. and Horkheimer, M. (1989 [1944]) *Dialectic of Enlightenment*. London: Verso.

Aichhorn, A. (1935 [1925]) *Wayward Youth*. New York: The Viking Press.

Ainsworth, L.H. and Ainsworth, M.D. (1962a). 'Acculturation in East Africa (I): Political Awareness and Attitudes toward Authority'. *Journal of Social Psychology* 57: 391–9.

Ainsworth, L.H. and Ainsworth, M.D. (1962b) 'Acculturation in East Africa (II): Frustration and Aggression'. *Journal of Social Psychology* 57: 401–7.

Albarelli Jr, H.P. (2009) *A Terrible Mistake: The Murder of Frank Olson and the CIA's Secret Cold War Experiments*. Walterville, OR: Trine Day.

Alexander, S. (1995) 'A Note on British Psychoanalysis'. *History Workshop Journal* 45: 135–43.

Alexander, S. (2009) 'London Childhoods'. In Radstone, S. and Schwarz, B., eds. *Mapping Memories*. n.p.: Fordham Press.

Alexander, S. (2011) '"Primary Maternal Preoccupation"': Winnicott and Social Democracy in Mid-Twentieth-Century Britain'. In Alexander, S. and Taylor, B., eds. *History and Psyche, Culture, Psychoanalysis and the Past*. New York and London: Palgrave Macmillan: 149–72.

Alexander, T. (1972, October) 'The Social Engineers Retreat Under Fire'. *Fortune* 86: 132–48.

Alford, C.F. (1997) *What Evil Means to Us*. Ithaca, NY: Cornell University Press.

Alpers, B.L. (2003) *Dictators, Democracy, and American Public Culture: Envisioning the Totalitarian Enemy, 1920s–1950s*. Chapel Hill, NC: University of North Carolina Press.

Anderson, W., Jenson, D. and Keller, R.C., eds. (2012) *Unconscious Dominions: Psychoanalysis, Colonial Trauma, and Global Sovereignties*. Durham, NC: Duke University Press.

Anon. (n.d.) http://ezitis.myzen.co.uk/paddingtongreen.html.
Anon. (1933, August–September) 'Die Rolle des Juden in der Medizin'. *Deutsche Volksgesundheit aus Blut und Boden*: 15.
Anon. (1937) 'Review of Richard Müller-Freienfels, *The Evolution of Modern Psychology* (1935, New Haven: Yale University Press).' *Psychoanalytic Review* 1937, 24b: 207–8.
Anon. (1941) 'Notes and News'. *Psychoanalytic Review* 28: 555–6.
Anon. (1944) 'List of Members of the International Psycho-Analytical Association'. *Bulletin of the International Psycho-Analytical Association* 25: 196.
Anon. (1948) *International Congress on Mental Health*: 4 vols. London: H.K. Lewis.
Anon. (1949). 'Events in the Psychoanalytic World'. *Bulletin of the American Psychoanalytic Association* 5D: 1–9.
Anon. (1950) 'List of Members of the International Psycho-Analytical Association'. *Bulletin of the International Psycho-Analytical Association* 31: 302–17.
Anon. (1951) 'New Members'. *Bulletin of the American Psychoanalytic Association* 7: 47.
Anon. (1953) 'Soviet Brain-Washing'. *Princeton Alumni Weekly* 53, 23: 8.
Anon. (1959) 'News and Proceedings of Affiliate Societies and Institutes'. *Bulletin of the American Psychoanalytic Association* 15: 373.
Anon. (1968, 18 November). 'Was für Zeiten'. *Der Spiegel* 47: 46–7.
Anon. (1971a, 26 June). 'Gefährliches Gerede'. *Der Spiegel* 27: 108–9.
Anon. (1971b, 9 August) 'Der Wille zur Macht lebt'. *Der Spiegel* 33: 90–1.
Anon. (1972, 5 June) 'Was brutalisiert den Menschen?' *Der Spiegel* 24: 124–8.
Anon. (1973, 22 October) 'Ausmerzung ethisch minderwertiger'. *Der Spiegel* 43: 22.
Antic, A. (2014) 'Therapeutic Fascism: Re-Educating Communists in Nazi-Occupied Serbia, 1942–1944'. *History of Psychiatry*. 25, 1: 35–56.
Applebaum, A. (2003) *Gulag: A History of the Soviet Camps*. New York: Doubleday.
Ardrey, R. (1966) *The Territorial Imperative*. New York: Atheneum.
Ardrey, R. (1970) *The Social Contract*. New York: Atheneum.
Arendt, H. (1951) *The Origins of Totalitarianism*. New York: Schocken Books.
Arendt, H. (1972) 'Lying In Politics'. *Crises of the Republic*. New York: Harcourt Brace Jovanovich.
Arendt, H. (1973 [1958]) *The Origins of Totalitarianism*. New York and London: Harcourt Brace Jovanovich.
Arendt, H. (1983) 'On Humanity in Dark Times: Thoughts about Lessing', trans. C. Winston and R. Winston. *Men in Dark Times*. New York: Harcourt Brace Jovanovich.
Arendt, H. (1994 [1963]) *Eichmann in Jerusalem: A Report on the Banality of Evil*. Harmondsworth: Penguin.
Arendt, H. (1998 [1958]) *The Human Condition*. Chicago: Chicago University Press.
Arendt, H. (2003) 'Truth in Politics'. In Baehr, P., ed. *The Portable Hannah Arendt*, Harmondsworth: Penguin.
Arendt, H. (2003 [1964]) 'Personal Responsibility under Dictatorship'. In Kohn, J., ed. *Responsibility and Judgment*. New York: Schocken Books.
Arendt, H. (2003 [1971]) 'Thinking and Moral Considerations'. In Kohn, J., ed. *Responsibility and Judgment*. New York: Schocken Books: 159–89.
Augustine. (1961) *Confessions*. Harmondsworth, Middlesex: Penguin Classics.
Azima, H. (1955) 'Prolonged Sleep Treatment in Mental Disorders (Some New Psychopharmacological Considerations)'. *Journal of Mental Sciences* 101: 593–603.
Azima, H. (1961) 'Anaclitic Therapy: Outline of Therapeutic Techniques Based upon the Concept of Regression'. In Canadian Psychiatry Association and McGill University, eds. *Proceedings: The Third World Congress of Psychiatry*, vol. II, *Montreal, Canada*,

4–10 June 1961. Montreal and Toronto: McGill University Press/University of Toronto Press: 1070–4.

Bacu, D. (1971) *The Anti-Humans: Student Re-Education in Romanian Prisons*. Englewood, CO: Soldiers of the Cross.

Bailey, V. (1987) *Delinquency and Citizenship: Reclaiming the Young Offender, 1914–1948*. Oxford: Oxford University Press.

Bailkin, Jordanna (2012) *The Afterlife of Empire*. Berkeley: University of California Press.

Bailly, L. (2009) *Lacan*. London: Oneworld.

Bakovic, T. (1998) 'Psiholoski aspekti golootocke torture I sadistickog mucenja' [Psychological aspects of the torture and sadistic torments at Goli Otok]. *Goli Otok (1949–1956): Radovi sa okruglog stola, Podgorica 27. juna 1995*. Podgorica: CANU.

Balandier, Georges (1950) Review of Mannoni, O. (1950) *La psychologie de la colonisation: Cahiers internationaux de sociologie* 9: 183–6.

Banac, I. (1988) *With Stalin against Tito: Cominformist Splits in Yugoslav Communism*. Ithaca, NY: Cornell University Press.

Banner, L.W. (2003) *Intertwined Lives: Margaret Mead, Ruth Benedict, and Their Circle*. New York: Alfred A. Knopf.

Barham, P. (2004) *Forgotten Lunatics of the Great War*. London and New Haven: Yale.

Bartlett, D. and F. (1971, Summer) 'Social Implications of Biological Determinism.' *Science and Society* 35: 209–19.

Bartulis, Jason (2012–13) 'The (Super)Naturalistic Turn in Contemporary Theory'. nonsite.org, no. 8.

Bauman, Z. (1989) *Modernity and the Holocaust*. Ithaca, NY: Cornell University Press.

Bell, D. (1962 [1958]) 'Ten Theories in Search of Reality: The Prediction of Soviet Behavior'. *The End of Ideology: On the Exhaustion of Political Ideas in the Fifties*, rev. edn: 326–7. New York: The Free Press.

Bell, D. (2007) *The First Total War: Napoleon's War and the Birth of Modern Warfare*. London: Bloomsbury.

Benedict, R. (1942) *Race and Racism*. London: George Routledge & Sons.

Benedict, R. (1946) *The Chrysanthemum and the Sword: Patterns of Japanese Culture*. Boston: Houghton Mifflin.

Benjamin, J. (2002) 'Terror and Guilt: Beyond Them and Us'. *Psychoanalytic Dialogues* 12: 473–84.

Benjamin, J. (2007) 'The End of Internalization: Adorno's Social Psychology'. In Jarvis S., ed. *Theodor W. Adorno: Critical Evaluations in Cultural Theory*, vol. 2. London: Routledge.

Berlin, I. (1969) 'Two Concepts of Liberty'. *Four Essays on Liberty*. Oxford: Oxford University Press.

Bernays, B. (1940) *Speak Up for Democracy*. New York: Viking Press.

Bertoldi, A. (1998) 'Oedipus in (South) Africa? Psychoanalysis and the Politics of Difference'. *American Imago*, 55, 1: 101–34.

Bettelheim, B. (1943) 'Individual and Mass Behaviour in Extreme Situations'. *The Journal of Abnormal and Social Psychology*, vol. 38, 4: 417–52.

Bexton, W.H., Heron, W. and Scott, T.H. (1954) 'Effects of Decreased Variation in the Sensory Environment'. *Canadian Journal of Psychology* 8, 2: 70–6.

Bhabha, Homi K. (1994) *The Location of Culture*. London: Routledge.

Bidermann, A. (1963) *March to Calumny: The Story of American POWs in the Korean War*. New York: Macmillan.

Biko, S. (1978) *I Write What I Like*. London: Bowerdean.

Birnbach, M. (1962) *Neo-Freudian Social Philosophy*. Stanford, CA: Stanford University Press.

Bloch, M. (1997) 'La psychanalyse au secours du colonialisme: A propos d'un ouvrage d'Octave Mannoni'. *Terrain* 28: 103–18.

Bock, G. and Thane, P., eds. (1991) *Maternity and Gender Policies: Women and the Rise of the European Welfare States 1880s–1950s*. Abingdon and New York: Routledge.

Bohleber, W (2009) 'Alexander Mitscherlich, die Psyche und die Entwicklung der Psychoanalyse in Deutschland nach 1945'. *Psyche* 63: 99–128.

Borch-Jacobsen, M. (1988) *The Freudian Subject*, trans. Catherine Porter. Stanford, CA: Stanford University Press.

Borch-Jacobsen, M. (1992) *The Emotional Tie: Psychoanalysis, Mimesis, and Affect*. Stanford, CA: Stanford University Press.

Borkenau, F. (1940) *The Totalitarian Enemy*. London: Faber and Faber.

Borkovic, M. (1966) 'Zavod za prinudno vaspitanje omladine u Smederevskoj Palanci' [Institute for compulsory education of youth in Smedervska Palanka], *Istorijski Glasnik*. 1: 97–116.

Boudry, Robert (1950) Review of Mannoni, O. (1950) *La psychologie de la colonisation*. *Europe* 28: 117–18.

Bourdieu, P. (1990) *The Logic of Practice*. Cambridge: Polity Press.

Bourke, J. (1999) *An Intimate History of Killing: Face to Face Killing in Twentieth-Century Warfare*. London: Granta Books.

Bracher, K. (1991) *The German Dictatorship: Origins, Structure and Effects of National Socialism*. London: Penguin.

Brick, H. (2006) *Transcending Capitalism: Visions of a New Society in Modern American Thought*. Ithaca, NY: Cornell University Press.

Brickman, C. (2003) *Aboriginal Populations in the Mind*. New York: Columbia University Press.

Brickner, R.M. (1943) *Is Germany Incurable?* Philadelphia, PA: J.B. Lippincott.

Britton, R. (1998) *Belief and Imagination*. London: Routledge and Institute of Psychoanalysis.

Brockmann, S. (2003) 'Inner Emigration: The Term and Its Origins in Post-War Debates'. In Donahue, N.H. and Kirchner, D., eds. *Flights of Fantasy: New Perspectives on Inner Emigration in German Literature 1933–1945*. Oxford: Berghahn Books: 11–26.

Bronner, S. and Kellner, D., eds. (1989) *Critical Theory and Society: A Reader*. London: Routledge.

Brooke, S. (1996) 'Reassessing a Labour Revisionist'. *Twentieth Century British History* 7, 1: 27–52.

Burleigh, M. (2006) *Sacred Causes: Religion and Politics from the European Dictators to Al Qaeda*. London: HarperCollins.

Burton, D.E. (2000) '"Sitting at the Feet of Gurus": The Life and Ethnography of Claire Holt'. PhD dissertation, New York University.

Caffrey, M.M. (1989) *Ruth Benedict: Stranger in This Land*. Austin, TX: University of Texas Press.

Caine, B. (2005) *Bombay to Bloomsbury: A Biography of the Strachey Family*. Oxford: Oxford University Press.

Calder, A. (1992 [1969]) *The People's War, Britain 1939–1945*. London: Pimlico.

Calder, R. (1948) 'Sanity Fair'. *New Statesman*, 21 Aug.: 148.

Caldwell, L., ed. (2007) *Winnicott and the Psychoanalytic Tradition*. London: Karnac.

Cameron, D.E. (1956) 'Psychic Driving'. *American Journal of Psychiatry* 112, 7: 502–9.

Cameron, D.E. (1959) 'The Effects of the Repetition of Verbal Signals Upon the Reorganization of the Schizophrenic Patient Subsequent to Intensive Physical Treatments': 291–5. *IInd International Congress for Psychiatry, Zurich (Switzerland), September 1st to 7th 1957. Congress Report*, vol. III. Zurich: Orell Füssli Arts Graphiques: 291–5.

Cameron, D.E., Levy, L., Ban, T. and Rubenstein, L. (1964) 'Automation of Psychotherapy'. *Comprehensive Psychiatry* 5, 1: 1–14.

Carroll, D., Hubert, W.H. de B., Rees, J.R. and Woodcock, O.H. (1937) 'Symposium on "The Unwilling Patient"'. *British Journal of Medical Psychology* 17: 54–77.

Caruth, C. (1996) *Unclaimed Experience: Trauma, Narrative, and History*. Baltimore, MD: Johns Hopkins University Press.

Casey, S. (2005) 'The Campaign to Sell a Harsh Peace for Germany to the American Public, 1944–1948'. *History* 90: 62–92.

Cavin, S.E. (2006) 'War Propaganda: From World War II Radio to Internet Terrorism and Video War Games'. Paper presented at the annual meeting of the American Sociological Association, Montreal Convention Center, Montreal, Quebec, Canada, 11 August, 2003 URL: http://citation.allacademic.com/meta/p_mla_apa_research_citation/0/9/4/9/1/pages94916/p94916-1.php (accessed 13 September 2014).

Cenic, V. (1994) *Kanjec filjma* [The end of the film]. Vranje: Knjizevna zajednica 'Borisav Stankovic'.

Cesarani, D. and Sundquist, E., eds. (2012) *After the Holocaust: Challenging the Myth of Silence*. London: Routledge.

Chamayou, G. (2015) *A Theory of the Drone*. New York: The New Press.

Chase, A. (2003) *Harvard and the Unabomber: The Education of an American Terrorist*. New York: W.W. Norton.

Churchill, W., n.d. www.winstonchurchill.org/learn/speeches (accessed October 2014).

Cieply, D. (2006) *Liberalism in the Shadow of Totalitarianism*. Cambridge, MA: Harvard University Press.

Clarke, Simon (2003) *Social Theory, Psychoanalysis and Racism*. Houndmills, Basingstoke: Palgrave Macmillan.

Cocks, G. (1985) *Psychotherapy in the Third Reich*. Oxford: Oxford University.

Cohen-Cole, J. (2014) *The Open Mind: Cold War Politics and the Sciences of Human Nature*. Chicago: University of Chicago Press.

Cohn, N. (1957) *The Pursuit of the Millennium*. London: Secker & Warburg.

Collini, S. (2000 [1991]) *Public Moralists: Political Thought and Intellectual Life in Britain 1850–1930*. Oxford: Clarendon Press.

Combrichon, A., ed. (1999) *Psychanalyse et décolonisation: Hommage à Octave Mannoni*. Paris: L'Harmattan.

Connolly, William E. (2002) *Neuropolitics: Thinking, Culture, Speed*. Minneapolis and London: University of Minnesota Press.

Connolly, William E. (2011) 'The Complexity of Intention'. *Critical Inquiry* 37, 4 (2011 Summer): 791–8.

Corsi, M. (2015) *El Libro de Mariel*. Buenos Aires: Argenta Sarlep.

Couve, C. (1986) 'Psychology and Politics in Manganyi's Work: A Materialist Critique'. *Psychology in Society* 5: 90–130.

Covington, C., Williams, P., Arundale, J. and Knox, J., eds. (2002) *Terrorism and War: Unconscious Dynamics of Political Violence*. London and New York: Karnac.

Cullather, Nick (2010) *The Hungry World: America's Cold War Battle against Poverty in Asia*. Cambridge, MA: Harvard University Press.

Curthoys, N. (2010) 'A Diasporic Reading of *Nathan the Wise*'. *Comparative Literature Studies* 47, 1: 70–95.

Damousi, J. and Plotkin, M.B., eds. (2012) *Psychoanalysis and Politics: Histories of Psychoanalysis under Conditions of Restricted Political Freedom*. Oxford: Oxford University Press.

Danto, E.A. (2005) *Freud's Free Clinics, Psychoanaysis and Social Justice, 1918–1938*. New York: Columbia University Press.

Daunton, M. (1996) 'Payment and Participation: Welfare and State-Formation in Britain 1900–1951'. *Past and Present* 150: 169–216.

David-Fox, M. (2012) *Showcasing the Great Experiment: Cultural Diplomacy and Western Visitors to the Soviet Union, 1921–1941*. New York: Oxford University Press.

Davids, F. (2011) *Internal Racism*. Houndmills, Basingstoke: Palgrave Macmillan.

Davin, A. (1978) 'Imperialism and Motherhood'. *History Workshop Journal* 1: 9–66.

Dedijer, V. (1969) *Izgubljena bitka J. V. Staljina* [The battle Stalin lost]. Belgrade: Prosveta.

Denker, R. (1966) *Aufklärung über Aggression: Kant, Darwin, Freud, Lorenz*. Stuttgart and Berlin: W. Kohlhammer.

De Ridder, J.C. (1961) *The Personality of the Urban African in South Africa*. London: Routledge and Keegan Paul.

Derrida, J. (2002) 'History of the Lie: Prolegomena'. *Without Alibi*, ed. and trans. P. Kamuf. Stanford, CA: Stanford University Press.

Desai, M. (2002) *Marx's Revenge: The Resurgence of Capitalism and the Death of Statist Socialism*. London: Verso.

Devereux, G. (1953) 'Cultural Factors in Psychoanalytic Therapy'. *Journal of the American Psychoanalytic Association* 1: 629–55.

Dicks, H.V. (1950) 'Personality Traits and National Socialist Ideology: A War-Time Study of German Prisoners of War'. *Human Relations* 3: 111–54.

Dicks, H.V. (1951) 'German Personality Traits and National Socialist Ideology'. In D. Lerner, ed. *Propaganda in War and Crisis*. New York: Ayer Co.: 100–61.

Dicks, H.V. (1973) *Licensed Mass Murder: A Socio-Psychological Study of some SS Killers*. New York: Basic Books.

Dower, J.W. (1986) *War without Mercy: Race and Power in the Pacific War*. New York: Pantheon.

Dower, J.W. (1999) *Embracing Defeat: Japan in the Aftermath of World War II*. New York: W.W. Norton.

Drucker, P. (1939) *The End of Economic Man: A Study of the New Totalitarianism*. London: William Heinemann.

Dubcovsky, S., Garcia Reinoso, G., Marotta, J., Paz, Lea de, Paz, J., Schutt, F. (1971) 'Realidad y Violencia en el proceso psicoanalitico'. In Langer, M. ed. *Cuestionamos*. Buenos Aires: Busqueda.

Dubow, S. (1996) Introduction: Part I. In Sachs, W. (1996 [1937]). *Black Hamlet: The Mind of an African Negro Revealed by Psychoanalysis*. Johannesburg: Wits University Press.

Duggan, C. (2012) *Fascist Voices: An Intimate History of Mussolini's Italy*. Oxford: Oxford University Press.

Duniec, E. and Raz, M. (2011) 'Vitamins for the Soul: John Bowlby's Thesis of Maternal Deprivation, Biomedical Metaphors, and the Deficiency Model of Disease'. *History of Psychiatry* 22: 93–107.

Eissler, K., ed. (1949) *Searchlights on Delinquency: New Psychoanalytic Studies Dedicated to Professor August Aichhorn*. New York: International Universities Press.

Ekbladh, D. (2010) *The Great American Mission: Modernization and the Construction of an American World Order*. Princeton, NJ: Princeton University Press.

Elias, N. (1994 [1939]) 'State Formation and Civilization'. *The Civilizing Process*. Oxford: Blackwell.

Embree, J.F. (1945) 'Applied Anthropology and Its Relationship to Anthropology'. *American Anthropologist* n.s. 47: 635–7.

Engerman, D.C. (2003) *Modernization from the Other Shore: American Intellectuals and the Romance of Russian Development*. Cambridge, MA: Harvard University Press.

Engerman, D.C. (2009) *Know Your Enemy: The Rise and Fall of America's Soviet Experts*. Oxford: Oxford University Press.

Erikson, E.H. (1942) 'Hitler's Imagery and German Youth'. *Psychiatry* 5: 475–93.

Erikson, E.H. (1974) *Identity Youth and Crisis*. London: Faber and Faber.

Etkind, A. (1997) *Eros of the Impossible: The History of Psychoanalysis in Russia*. Boulder, CO: Westview Press.

Fairbairn, W.R.D. (1935) 'The Sociological Significance of Communism Considered in the Light of Psychoanalysis'. *British Journal of Medical Psychology* 15: 218–29. Reprinted in *Psychoanalytic Studies of the Personality*. London: Tavistock Publications Limited: 233–46.

Fanon, F. (1986 [1952]) *Black Skin, White Masks*. London: Pluto.

Fanon, F. (1990 [1961]) *The Wretched of the Earth*. London: Penguin.

Farley, L. (2013) 'Squiggle Evidence: The Child, the Canvas, and the "Negative Labour" of Writing History' (2011). In Abram, J. ed. *Donald Winnicott Today*. London and New York: Routledge: 418–52.

Federn, P. (1940) 'Psychoanalysis as a Therapy of Society'. *American Imago* 1, 4: 125–41.

Fees, C. (n.d.) 'A Fearless Frankness', http://www.thetcj.org/child-care-history-policy/a-fearless-frankness (accessed 10 November 2011).

Feldman, M. (2009) *Doubt, Conviction and the Analytic Process: Selected Papers of Michael Feldman*. London: Routledge.

Fenichel, O. (1946) 'Elements of a Psychoanalytic Theory of Anti-Semitism'. In Simmel, D., ed. *Anti-Semitism: A Social Disease*. NY: International Universities Press: 11–32.

ffytche, M. (2013) 'Freud and the Neocons: The Narrative of a Political Encounter from 1949–2000'. *Psychoanalysis and History*, 15, 1: 5–44.

Figlio, K. (2006) 'The Absolute State of Mind in Society and the Individual'. *Psychoanalysis, Culture and Society* 11: 119–43.

Finkelstein, N. (2000) *The Holocaust Industry: Reflections on the Exploitation of Jewish Suffering*. London: Verso.

Fliess, R., ed. (1969 [1948]) *The Psychoanalytic Reader*. New York: International Universities Press.

Flügel, J.C. (1962) *Man, Morals and Society: A Psychoanalytical Study*. Harmondsworth, Middlesex: Penguin.

Foster, D. (1991) 'Introduction'. In Foster, D. and Louw-Potgieter, J., eds. *Social Psychology in South Africa*. Johannesburg: Lexicon Publishers: 3–23.

Freimüller, T. (2007) *Alexander Mitscherlich: Gesellschaftsdiagnosen und Psychoanalyse nach Hitler*. Göttingen: Vandenhoeck & Ruprecht.

Freud, A. (1967) *The Ego and the Mechanisms of Defense* (first published 1936, rev. edn 1966). New York: International Universities Press.

Freud, A. (1998 [1949]) 'Notes on Aggression'. In Ekins, R. and Freeman, R., eds. *Selected Writings*. Harmondsworth: Penguin.

Freud, A. (1998 [1967]) 'About Losing and Being Lost'. In Ekins, R. and Freeman, R., eds. *Selected Writings*. Harmondsworth: Penguin.

Freud, A., with Sander, J. (1985) *The Analysis of Defense: The Ego and the Mechanisms of Defense Revisited*. New York: International Universities Press.

Freud, A. (1949) 'Report on the Sixteenth International Psycho-Analytical Congress'. *Bulletin of the International Psycho-Analytical Association* 30: 178–208.

Freud, E.L. (1984 [1968]) 'Freud to Zweig, 31 May 1936'. *Sigmund Freud/Arnold Zweig Briefwechsel*. Frankfurt am Main: Fischer.

Freud, S. (1900) *The Interpretation of Dreams*. In *The Standard Edition of the Complete Psychological Works of Sigmund Freud [SE]*, volume IV: *The Interpretation of Dreams (First Part)*. Translated from the German under the General Editorship of James Strachey in collaboration with Anna Freud, assisted by Alix Strachey and Alan Tyson. London: Hogarth.

Freud, S. (1911) 'Formulations on the Two Principles of Mental Functioning'. *SE* vol. XII: 2–226.

Freud, S. (1913) *Totem and Taboo*. *SE* vol. XIII: vii–162.

Freud, S. (1915) 'Zeitgemässes über Krieg und Tod'. *Gesammelte Werke:* Bd. X: 324–55.

Freud, S. (1916) 'Some Character-Types Met with in Psycho-Analytic Work'. *SE* vol. XIV: 309–33.

Freud, S. (1917) 'Mourning and Melancholia'. *SE* vol. XIV: 237–58.

Freud, S. (1918) 'Letter from Freud to Ferenczi, 17 November 1918'. In Falzeder, E. and Brabant, E., eds. *The Correspondence of Sigmund Freud and Sándor Ferenczi*, vol. 2, *1914–1919*.

Freud, S. (1919) 'Lines of Advance in Psycho-Analytic Therapy'. *SE* vol. XVII: 157–68.

Freud, S. (1920) *Jenseits des Lustprinzips. Gesammelte Werke:* Bd. XIII: 3–69.

Freud, S. (1921) *Group Psychology and the Analysis of the Ego. SE* vol. XVIII: 65–144.

Freud, S. (1923) *The Ego and the Id. SE* vol. XIX: 1–66.

Freud, S. (1924a) 'The Dissolution of the Oedipus Complex'. *SE* vol. XIX: 171–80.

Freud, S. (1924b) 'Das ökonomische Problem des Masochismus'. *Gesammelte Werke:* Bd. XIII: 371–83.

Freud, S. (1926) *The Question of Lay Analysis. SE* vol. XX: 177–258.

Freud, S. (1927) *The Future of an Illusion. SE* vol. XXI: 1–56.

Freud, S. (1928) 'Dostoevsky and Parricide'. *SE* vol. XXI:173–94.

Freud, S. (1930) *Civilization and Its Discontents. SE* vol. XXI: 57–146.

Freud, S. (1930) *Das Unbehagen in der Kultur. Gesammelte Werke*: Bd. XIV: 421–506.

Freud, S. (1931) 'The Expert Opinion in the Halsmann Case'. *SE* vol. XXI: 251–3.

Freud, S. (1933) *New Introductory Lectures On Psycho-Analysis. SE* vol. XXII: 1–182.

Freud, S. (1939) *Moses and Monotheism. SE* vol. XXIII: 1–138.

Freud, S. (1985) *The Complete Letters of Sigmund Freud to Wilhelm Fliess 1887–1904*, trans. and ed. J. Moussaieff Masson. Cambridge, MA: Harvard University Press.

Freud, S. and Breuer, J. (1895) *Studies on Hysteria. SE* vol. II: 21–47.

Freud, S. and Einstein, A. (1933) 'Why War?' *SE* vol. XXII: 197–216.

Freud, S. and Pfister, O. (1964) *Psycho-Analysis and Faith*, ed. H. Meng and E.L. Freud. New York: Basic Books.

Friedlander, K. (1943) 'Delinquency Research'. *The New Era*, June.

Friedlander, K. (1960 [1947]) *The Psycho-Analytic Approach to Juvenile Delinquency: Theory, Case Studies, Treatment*. New York: International Universities Press.

Friedman, L.J. (1999) *Identity's Architect: A Biography of Erik H. Erikson*. London: Free Association Books.

Friedrich, C.J. (1933) 'The Development of Executive Power in Germany'. *American Political Science Review* 27: 185–203.

Friedrich, C.J. (1937) *Constitutional Government and Politics: Nature and Development*. New York: Harper & Brothers.

Friedrich, C.J. (1954) 'The Unique Character of Totalitarian Society'. In Friedrich, C.J., ed. *Totalitarianism: Proceedings of a Conference Held at the American Academy of Arts and Sciences, March 1953*. Cambridge, MA: Harvard University Press.

Friedrich, C.J. and Brzezinski, Z.K. (1956) *Totalitarian Dictatorship and Autocracy*. Cambridge, MA: Harvard University Press.

Fromm, E. (1973) *The Anatomy of Human Destructiveness*. New York: Holt, Rinehart.

Fromm, E. (1991 [1934]) 'The Theory of Mother Right and Its Relevance for Social Psychology'. *The Crisis of Psychoanalysis: Essays on Freud, Marx and Social Psychology*. New York: Henry Holt.

Fromm, E. (1994 [1941]) *Escape from Freedom*. New York: H. Holt: 111–39, 207–10.

Fromm, E., Horkheimer, M., Mayer, H., Marcuse, H. (1936) *Studien über Autorität und Familie*. Paris: Félix Alcan.

Frosh, S. (2005) *Hate and the Jewish Science: Anti-Semitism, Nazism and Psychoanalysis*. Houndmills, Basingstoke: Palgrave Macmillan.

Frosh, S. (2011) 'Psychoanalysis, Anti-Semitism and the Miser'. *New Formations* 72: 94–106.

Furet, F. (1981) *Interpreting the French Revolution*. Cambridge: Cambridge University Press.

Furet, F. (1995) *The Passing of an Illusion: The Idea of Communism in the Twentieth Century*. Chicago: University of Chicago Press.

Furet, F. and M. Ozouf, eds. (1989) *A Critical Dictionary of the French Revolution*. Cambridge, MA: Harvard University Press.

Garland, D. (1988) 'British Criminology before 1935'. *British Journal of Criminology* 28: 1–17.

Garland, D. (2001) *The Culture of Control: Crime and Social Order in Contemporary Society*. Chicago: University of Chicago Press.

Gay, P. (1998) *Freud: A Life for Our Time*. New York: Norton.

George, A.L. (1988) 'Nathan, My Teacher'. *Remembering Nathan Leites: An Appreciation*. Santa Monica, CA: RAND Corporation.

Gerhardt, U. (1966) 'A Hidden Agenda of Recovery: The Psychiatric Conceptualization of Re-Education for Germany in the United States During World War II'. *German History* 14: 297–324.

Geyer, M. and S. Fitzpatrick, eds. (2009) *Beyond Totalitarianism: Stalinism and Nazism Compared*. Cambridge: Cambridge University Press.

Gherovici, P. (2003) *The Puerto Rican Syndrome*. New York: Other Press.

Gibianskii, L. (1997) 'The Soviet–Yugoslav Split and the Cominform'. In Naimark, N. and Gibianskii, L., eds. *The Establishment of Communist Regimes in Eastern Europe, 1944–1949*, Boulder, CO: Westview Press.

Gitre, E.J.K. (2010) 'The Great Escape: World War II, Neo-Freudianism, and the Origins of US Psychocultural Analysis'. *Journal of the History of the Behavioral Sciences* 46: 17–18.

Glaser, H. (1967) *Eros in der Politik*. Köln: Verlag Wissenschaft und Politik.

Gleason, A. (1995) *Totalitarianism: The Inner History of the Cold War*. New York: Oxford University Press.

Glover, E. (1941) 'Notes on the Psychological Effects of War Conditions on the Civilian Population'. *International Journal of Psychoanalysis*. 22: 132–46.

Glover, E. (1942) 'Notes on the Psychological Effects of War Conditions on the Civilian Population'. *International Journal of Psychoanalysis*. 23: 17–37.

Glover, E. (1946) *War, Sadism and Pacifism: Further Essays on Group Psychology and War*. London: George Allen and Unwin.

Glover, E. (1950) *Minutes of Evidence: Memorandum Submitted on behalf of the ISTD by Dr. Edward Glover, Royal Committee on Capital Punishment*. London: HMSO.

Glover, E. (1960a) 'Recent Advances in the Psycho-Analytical Study of Delinquency'. *The Roots of Crime*. New York: International Universities Press: 292–310.

Glover, E. (1960b) 'Team Research?' *The Roots of Crime*. New York: International Universities Press.

Glover, E. (1960c [1949]) 'Outline of the Investigation and Treatment of Delinquency in Great Britain, 1912–1948'. *The Roots of Crime*. New York: International Universities Press.

Gobodo-Madikizela, P. (2008) 'Radical Forgiveness: Transforming Traumatic Memory Beyond Hannah Arendt'. In du Bois, F. and du Bois-Pedain, A. eds. *Justice and Reconciliation in Post-Apartheid South Africa*. Cambridge: Cambridge University Press: 37–61.

Goebbels, J. (1948) *The Goebbels Diaries (1942–1943)*, ed. L. Lochner, New York: Doubleday.

Goldberger, L. (1970) 'In the Absence of Stimuli' (book review). *Science* 168 (3932): 709–11.

Goldberger, L. and Holt, R.R. (1961) *A Comparison of Isolation Effects and Their Personality Correlates in Two Divergent Samples*. ASD Technical Report 61-417, Aeronautical Systems Division, Wright-Patterson Air Force Base, Ohio, August.

Goldensohn, L. (2006) *The Nuremberg Interviews*, ed. R. Gellately. London: Pimlico.

Green, A. (2013 [1975]) 'Potential Space in Psychoanalysis'. In Abram, J., ed. *Donald Winnicott Today*. London and New York: Routledge: 183–204.

Greene, G. (2002 [1934]) *It's a Battlefield*. London: Vintage.

Grosskurth, P. (1986) *Melanie Klein, Her World and Her Work*. London: Maresfield Library.

Hacker, F. (1971) *Aggression: Die Brutalisierung der modernen Welt*. Vienna: Molden.

Harper, D. (2007) 'The Complicity of Psychology in the Security State'. In R. Roberts, ed. *Just War: Psychology and Terrorism*. Ross-on-Wye: PCCP Books: 15–45.

Harris, J. (1992) 'Political Thought and the Welfare State 1970–1940: An Intellectual Framework for British Social Policy'. *Past and Present* 135: 116–41.

Harrison, B. (1977) 'Interview'. *Red Rag: a Journal of Marxist Feminism*.

Harrison, T. (2000) *Bion, Rickman, Foulkes, and the Northfield Experiments: Advancing on a Different Front*. London: Jessica Kingsley Publishers.

Hayek, F. (2001 [1944]) *The Road to Serfdom*. London: Routledge.

Hayes, G. (1997) Review of Sachs, W. (1996) *Black Hamlet* (with new introductions by Saul Dubow and Jacqueline Rose). *Free Associations*, 7(2): 304–17.

Hayes, G. (2008) 'A History of Psychoanalysis in South Africa'. In van C. Ommen and D. Painter, eds. *Interiors: A history of Psychology in South Africa*. Pretoria: UNISA Press.

Hayes, G. (2011) '(Re-)introducing Chabani Manganyi'. *Psychology in Society* 41: 1–6.

Heimann, P. (1950) 'On Counter-Transference.' *International Journal of Psychoanalysis* 31(1–2). (Reprinted in Heimann, P., *About Children and Children-No-Longer: Collected Papers 1942–80*, ed. M. Tonnesman. London: Tavistock/Routledge, 1986.)

Heimann, P (1969) 'Entwicklungssprünge und das Auftreten der Grausamkeit'. In Mitscherlich A., ed. *Bis hierher und nicht weiter: Ist die menschliche Aggression unbefriedbar?* Munich: Piper, 104–18.

Hendrick, H. (1990) *Images of Youth: Age, Class and the Male Youth Problem 1880–1920*. Oxford: Oxford University Press.

Hendrick, H. (2003) *Child Welfare: Historical Dimensions, Contemporary Debates*. Bristol: Polity Press.

Hennessy, P. (1993) *Never Again, Britain 1945–1951*. London: Vintage.

Herman, E. (1995) *The Romance of American Psychology: Political Culture in the Age of Experts*. Berkeley, CA: University of California Press.

Heron, W., Doane, B.K. and Scott, T.H. (1956) 'Visual Disturbances after Prolonged Perceptual Isolation'. *Canadian Journal of Psychology* 10, 1: 13–18.

Herzog, D. (2005) *Sex after Fascism: Memory and Morality in Twentieth-Century Germany*. Princeton: Princeton University Press.

Hinshelwood, R.D. (1991) 'Unconscious Phantasy'. *A Dictionary of Kleinian Thought*. London: Free Association Books: 32–46.

Hitler, A. (1988) *Mein Kampf*. Mumbai: Jaico.

Hixson, W.L. (1997) *Parting the Curtain: Propaganda, Culture, and the Cold War, 1945–1961*. Basingstoke: Macmillan.

Hobman, J.B. ed. (1945) *David Eder, Memoirs of a Modern Pioneer*. London: Victor Gollancz.

Hobsbawm, E.J. (1994) *Age of Extremes: The Short Twentieth Century, 1914–1991*. London: Michael Joseph.

Hoffman, L.E. (1982) 'Psychoanalytic Interpretations of Adolf Hitler and Nazism, 1933–1945: A Prelude to Psychohistory'. *Psychohistory Review* 11: 68–87.

Hoffman, L.E. (1993–4) 'Erikson on Hitler: The Origins of "Hitler's Imagery and German You"'. *Psychohistory Review* 22: 69–86.

Hofstadter, R. (1964) *The Paranoid Style in American Politics, and Other Essays*. New York: Knopf.

Hollander, N.C. (1998) 'Exile: Paradoxes of Loss and Creativity'. *British Journal of Psychotherapy* 15: 201–15.

Holmes, J. (1993) *John Bowlby and Attachment Theory*. London: Routledge.

Hook, D. (2012) *A Critical Psychology of the Postcolonial: The Mind of Apartheid*. London and New York: Routledge.

Horkheimer, M. (1941) 'The End of Reason'. In *Studies in Philosophy and Social Science* 9, 3: 366–88.

Horkheimer, M. (1949) 'Authoritarianism and the Family Today'. In Anshen, R., ed. *The Family: Its Function and Destiny*. New York: Harper.

Horkheimer, M. (1982 [1940]) 'The Authoritarian State'. In Arato, A. and Gebhardt, E., eds. *The Essential Frankfurt School Reader*. New York: Continuum: 95–117.

Horkheimer, M. (1989 [1939]) 'The Jews and Europe'. In S. Bronner, and Kellner, D., eds. *Critical Theory and Society: A Reader*. London: Routledge: 77–94.

Horkheimer, M. (1996) *Gesammelte Schriften, Band 17: Briefwechsel 194–1948*. Frankfurt am Main: S. Fischer.

Horkheimer, M. (2002 [1936]) 'Authority and the Family'. In *Critical Theory: Selected Essays*. New York: Continuum.

Horkheimer, M. (2004 [1947]) *Eclipse of Reason*. London: Continuum.

Horkheimer, M. (2007) *A Life in Letters: Selected Correspondence*. Lincoln, NE: University of Nebraska Press.

Horkheimer, M. and Flowerman, S. (1950) 'Foreword to *Studies in Prejudice*'. http://www.ajcarchives.org/AJC_DATA/Files/AP1.pdf.

Horn, K. (1974a) 'Die humanwissenschaftliche Relevanz der Ethologie im Lichte einer sozialwissenschaftlich verstandenen Psychoanalyse'. In Roth, G., ed. *Kritik der Verhaltensforschung: Konrad Lorenz und seine Schule*. Munich: C. H. Beck: 190–221.

Horn, K. (1974b) 'Gesellschaftliche Produktion von Gewalt: Vorschläge zu ihrer politpsychologischen Untersuchung'. In Rammstedt, O. *Gewaltverhältnisse und die Ohnmacht der Kritik*. Frankfurt am Main: Suhrkamp: 59–106.

Horney, K. (2000 [1939]) *New Ways in Psychoanalysis*. New York: W.W. Norton.

Houghton, Bernard (1921) *The Psychology of Empire*. Madras: S. Ganesan.

Howarth, D. (2000) 'The Difficult Emergence of a Democratic Imaginary: Black Consciousness and Non-Racial Democracy in South Africa'. In Howarth, D. Norval, A. and Stavrakakis, Y., eds. *Discourse Theory and Political Analysis: Identities, Hegemonies and Social Change*. Manchester: Manchester University Press: 168–92.

Hoyer, T. (2008) *Im Getümmel der Welt: Alexander Mitscherlich*. Göttingen: Vandenhoeck & Ruprecht.

Hoyland, John S. (1937) *That Inferiority Feeling*. London: Allen & Unwin.

Hull, Matthew (2010) 'Democratic Technologies of Speech: From WWII America to Postcolonial Delhi'. *Linguistic Anthropology* 20, 2: 257–82.

Hull, Matthew (2011) 'Communities of Place, Not Kind: American Technologies of Neighborhood in Postcolonial Delhi'. *Comparative Studies in Society and History* 53, 4: 757–90.

Hunger, H. (1943) 'Jüdische Psychoanalyse und deutsche Seelsorge'. In Grundmann, W., ed. *Germanentum, Judentum und Christentum*, vol. 2. Leipzig: G. Wigand, 307–53.

Huxley, Elspeth (1956) 'To Rule in Hell'. *Time and Tide* (21 July): 879–80.

Hyslop, J. (2007) 'Rock and Roll Marxists?' In McGregor, L. and Nuttall, S., eds. *At Risk: Writing On and Over the Edge of South Africa*. Johannesburg: Wits University Press.

Ierunca, V. (1990) *Fenomenul Pitesti* [The Pitesti phenomenon]. Bucharest: Humanitas.

Immerwahr, D. (2015) *Thinking Small: The United States and the Lure of Community Development*. Cambridge, MA: Harvard University Press.

Isaac, J.C. (2003) 'Critics of Totalitarianism'. In Ball, T. and Bellamy, R., eds. *The Cambridge History of Twentieth-Century Political Thought*. Cambridge: Cambridge University Press: 181–201.

Jahoda, G. (1961) *White Man: A Study of the Attitudes of Africans to Europeans in Ghana before Independence*. London: Oxford University Press.

Jakovina, T. (2003) *Americki komunisticki saveznik: Hrvati, Titova Jugoslavija i SAD 1945–1955* [The American Communist Ally: Croats, Tito's Yugoslavia and the USA 1945–1955]. Zagreb: Srednja Europa.

Jay, M. (1973) *The Dialectical Imagination: A History of the Frankfurt School and the Institute of Social Research, 1923–1950*. Boston, MA: Little, Brown.

Jeanson, F. (1950) Review of Mannoni, O. *La psychologie de la colonisation. Les Temps modernes* (1 July): 161–65.

Jobs, R. (2007) *Riding the New Wave: Youth and the Rejuvenation of France after the Second World War*. Stanford, CA: Stanford University Press.

Jones, E. (1945 [1910]) 'Psychology and War Conditions'. *Psychoanalytic Quarterly*. 14:1–27.

Judt, T. (2008) *Reappraisals: Reflections on the Forgotten Twentieth Century*. New York: Penguin.

Jung, C. (1970 [1934]) 'The State of Psychotherapy Today'. In Jung, C.G. *Collected Works*. London: Routledge, vol. 10: 157–73.

Kalafatic, E. (1990) 'Pismo Predsedniku SFR Jugoslavije i Saveza Komunista Jugoslavije Josipu Brozu Titu' [Letter to the President of the SFR Yugoslavia and the Association of Communists of Yugoslavia Josip Broz Tito]. In Mihailovic, D. *Goli Otok*. Belgrade: NIP Politika.

Karolinska Institutet (1973) Press release. Available at: http://www.nobelprize.org/nobel_prizes/medicine/laureates/1973/press.html.

Karpf, A. (2015) 'Constructing and address "The Ordinary and Devoted Mother"'. *History Workshop Journal* 78: 82–106.

Kasper, A. (1965) 'The Narcissistic Self in a Masochistic Character'. *International Journal of Psychoanalysis* 46: 474–86.

Kauders, A. (2014) *Der Freud-Komplex: Eine Geschichte der Psychoanalyse in Deutschland*. Berlin: Berlin Verlag.

Keller, Richard C. (2007) *Colonial Madness: Psychiatry in French North Africa*. Chicago: University of Chicago Press.

Kennan, G.F. (1954) 'Totalitarianism in the Modern World'. In Friedrich, C.J., ed. *Totalitarianism: Proceedings of a Conference Held at the American Academy of Arts and Sciences, March 1953*. Cambridge, MA: Harvard University Press.

Kermode, F. (1966) *The Sense of an Ending: Studies in the Theory of Fiction*. Oxford: Oxford University Press.

Kermode, F. (1985) *Forms of Attention: Botticelli and Hamlet*. Chicago: University of Chicago Press.

Kermode, F. (2004) 'Clutching at Insanity'. *London Review of Books*, 26, 5: 12–13.

Kerr, Madeline (1952) *Personality and Conflict in Jamaica*. Liverpool: Liverpool University Press.

Kershaw, I. (2000) *The Nazi Dictatorship: Problems and Perspectives of Interpretation*, 4th edn. London: Bloomsbury Academic.

Kershaw, I. (2004) 'Hitler and the Uniqueness of Nazism'. *Journal of Contemporary History* 39, 2: 239–254.

Kershaw, I. and Lewin, M., eds. (1997) *Stalinism and Marxism: Dictatorships in Comparison*. Cambridge: Cambridge University Press.

Keynes, J.M. (1919) *The Economic Consequences of the Peace*. London: n.p.

Khanna, Ranjana (2003) *Dark Continents: Psychoanalysis and Colonialism*. Durham, NC: Duke University Press.

King, P. and Steiner, R., eds. (1991) *The Freud–Klein Controversies*. London: Tavistock-Routledge.

Klajn, V. (1958) 'Problem rehabilitacije: rehabilitacija neuroticara' [The problem of rehabilitation: rehabilitation of neurotics]. *Vojno-Sanitetski Pregled*. 7: 7–8.

Klajn, P. (1989) *Razvoj psihoanalize u Srbiji* [Development of psychoanalysis in Serbia]. Subotica: Pedagoska akademija.

Klein, M. (1932) *The Psycho-Analysis of Children*. Revised 1975 ed. London: Hogarth Press.

Klein, M. (1934) 'On Criminality'. *British Journal of Medical Psychology* 14: 312–15.

Klein, M. (1975 [1940]) 'Mourning and its Relation to Manic-Depressive States'. *Love, Guilt and Reparation and Other Works 1921–1945 (The Writings of Melanie Klein*, vol. 1). London: Hogarth Press.

Klein, M. (1975 [1946]) 'Notes on Some Schizoid Mechanisms'. *Envy and Gratitude and Other Works 1946–63 (The Writings of Melanie Klein*, vol. 3). London: Hogarth.

Koestler, A. (1940) *Darkness at Noon*. London: Jonathan Cape.

Kosier, B. (1991) *Bezboznici* [The godless] 2. Sarajevo: Svjetlost.

Kosofsky Sedgwick, E. (2003) *Touching Feeling: Affect, Pedagogy, Performativity* (Durham, NC: Duke University Press).

Kostic, P. (2012) *Psiholoska anatomija Golog Otoka* [Psychological anatomy of Goli Otok]. Belgrade: Nezavisna izdanja Slobodana Masica.

Kovel, J. (1995) 'On Racism and Psychoanalysis'. In Elliott, A. and Frosh, S., eds. *Psychoanalysis in Contexts*. London: Routledge.

Kracauer, S. (2004 [1947]) *From Caligari to Hitler: A Psychological History of the German Film*. Princeton, NJ: Princeton University Press.

Krieger, H. (1969, 14 November) 'Der Mensch – von Natur aus destruktiv?' *Die Zeit* 46: 32–3.

Kris, E. and Speier, H. (1944) *German Radio Propaganda: Report on Home Broadcasts During the War*. London: Oxford University Press.

Kristeva, J. (2007) *Cet incroyable besoin de croire*. Paris: Bayard.

Krovoza, A. (2001) 'Zum Verhältnis von Psychogenese und Soziogenese im Gewaltdiskurs'. *Psyche* 55: 906–33.

Kubie, L.S. and Margolin, S. (1945) 'The Therapeutic Role of Drugs in the Process of Repression, Dissociation and Synthesis'. *American Journal of Psychiatry* 7, 3: 147–51.

Kuklick, B. (2006) *Blind Oracles: Intellectuals and War from Kennan to Kissinger*. Princeton, NJ: Princeton University Press.

Kullaa, R. (2012) *Non-Alignment and Its Origins in Cold War Europe: Yugoslavia, Finland and the Soviet Challenge*. London: I.B. Tauris.

Kutcher, G. (2006) 'Cancer Clinical Trials and the Transfer of Medical Knowledge: Metrology, Contestation and Local Practice'. In Timmermans, C. and Anderson, J., eds. *Devices and Designs: Medical Innovations in Historical Perspective*. Houndmills: Palgrave.

Kutcher, G. (2009) *Contested Medicine: Cancer Research and the Military*. Chicago: University of Chicago Press.

Kynaston, D. (2007) *Austerity Britain 1945–51*. 2008 edn. London, Berlin, New York: Bloomsbury.

Lacan, J. (1988) 'Discourse Analysis and Ego Analysis'. *The Seminar of Jacques Lacan: Book I*, edited by J.-A. Miller, trans. J. Forrester. Cambridge: Cambridge University Press.

Lacan, J. (2002 [1966]) 'The Freudian Thing'. *Écrits*, trans. B. Fink. New York: W.W. Norton.

Lacan, J. (2006) *Book XVII: The Other Side of Psychoanalysis*, ed. Miller, J.A. New York: Norton.

Lane, C. (2002) 'Psychoanalysis and Colonialism Redux: Why Mannoni's "Prospero Complex" Still Haunts Us'. *Journal of Modern Literature* 25, 3–4: 127–50.

Langer, M. (1989) *From Vienna to Managua: Journey of a Psychoanalyst*. London: Free Association Books.

Langer, W. and Gifford, S. (1978) 'An American Analyst in Vienna During the Anschluss, 1936–1938'. *Journal of the History of the Behavioral Sciences* 14, 1: 37–54.

Laplanche, J. and Pontalis, J.-B. (1988) *The Language of Psychoanalysis*. London: Karnac.

Latham, M. (2000) *Modernization as Ideology: American Social Science and 'Nation Building' in the Kennedy Era*. Chapel Hill: University of North Carolina Press.

Latham, M. (2011) *The Right Kind of Revolution: Modernization, Development, and US Foreign Policy from the Cold War to the Present*. Ithaca, NY: Cornell University Press.

Leites, N. (1951) *The Operational Code of the Politburo*. New York: McGraw-Hill.

Lepenies, W. and Nolte, H. (1971) *Kritik der Anthropologie*. Munich: Carl Hanser.

Levi, P. (1993). *Survival in Auschwitz: The Nazi Assault on Humanity*. New York: Collier Books.

Lewis, J. (1980) *The Politics of Motherhood: Child and Maternal Welfare in England 1900–1939*. Montreal: Croom Helm.

Lewis, J. (1988) 'Anxieties about the Family and the Relationships between Parents, Children and the State in Twentieth-Century England'. In Richards, M. and Light, P., eds. *Children of Social Worlds*. London: Polity Press.

Leys, R. (2002) *Trauma: A Genealogy*. Princeton, NJ: Princeton University Press.

Leys, R. (2007) *From Guilt to Shame: Auschwitz and After*. Princeton, NJ: Princeton University Press.

Leys, R. (2010a) 'How Did Fear Become a Scientific Object and What Kind of Object Is It?' *Representations* 110: 66–104.

Leys, R. (2011a) 'The Turn to Affect: A Critique'. *Critical Inquiry* 37, 3: 434–72.

Leys, R. (2011b) 'Affect and Intention: A Reply to William E. Connolly'. *Critical Inquiry* 37, 4: 799–805.

Leys, R. (2012a) '"Both of Us Disgusted in *My* Insula": Mirror Neuron Theory and Emotional Empathy'. nonsite.org. no. 5.

Leys, R. (2012b) 'Trauma and the Turn to Affect'. In Mengel, E. and Borzaga, M., eds. *Trauma, Memory, and Narrative in the Contemporary South African Novel: Essays*. Amsterdam: Editions Rodopi: 3–28.

Leys, R. and Goldman, M. (2010) 'Navigating the Genealogies of Trauma, Guilt, and Affect: An Interview with Ruth Leys'. *University of Toronto Quarterly* 79, 2: 656–79.

Lifton, R.J. (1961) *Thought Reform and the Psychology of Totalism: A Study of 'Brainwashing' in China*. New York: Norton.

Lifton, R.J. (1986) *The Nazi Doctors: Medical Killing and the Psychology of Genocide*. New York: Basic Books.

Lilly, J.C. (1997 [1988]) *The Scientist: A Metaphysical Autobiography*. Oakland, CA: Ronin Publishers.

Linstrum, E. (2016) *Ruling Minds: Psychology in the British Empire*. Cambridge, MA: Harvard University Press.

Lorenz, K. (1949) *Er redete mit dem Vieh, den Vögeln und den Fischen*. Vienna: G. Borotha-Schoeler.

Lorenz, K. (1950) *So kam der Mensch auf den Hund*. Vienna: G. Borotha-Schoeler.

Lorenz, K. (1963) *Das sogenannte Böse: Zur Naturgeschichte der Aggression*. Vienna: G. Borotha-Schoeler.

Lorenz, K. (1970, 2 January) 'Von Wölfen und Menschen: Die Feindschaft zwischen den Generationen und ihre Ursachen'. *Christ und Welt*: 12.

Lorenz, K. (1973) 'Konrad Lorenz: Biographical'. Available at: http://www.nobelprize.org/nobel_prizes/medicine/laureates/1973/lorenz-bio.html.

Lorenz, K. (1988) 'Gespräch anlässlich seines 85. Geburtstags'. *Natur* 11.

Lowell, R. (1963) 'Pigeons'. *Imitations*. London: Faber & Faber.

Lowenthal, L. (1987) 'Towards a Psychology of Authoritarianism'. *False Prophets: Studies on Authoritarianism. Communication in Society*, vol 3. New Brunswick, New Jersey: Transaction.

Lowenthal, L. (1989) 'Sigmund Freud'. *Critical Theory and Frankfurt Theorists: Lectures – Correspondence – Conversations. Communication in Society*, vol 4. New Brunswick, NJ: Transaction.

Lucas, R. (2013) *The Psychotic Wavelength: A Psychoanalytic Perspective for Psychiatry.* London: Routledge/Institute of Psychoanalysis.

Lucas, S. (1999) *Freedom's War: The US Crusade Against the Soviet Union, 1945–56.* Manchester: Manchester University Press.

Lunbeck, E (2014) *The Americanization of Narcissism.* Cambridge, MA: Harvard University Press.

Macey, D. (1999) 'The Recall of the Real: Frantz Fanon and Psychoanalysis'. *Constellations* 6, 1: 97–107.

Macey, D. (2000) *Frantz Fanon: A Life.* London: Granta.

Macrone, I.D. (1937) *Race Attitudes in South Africa: Historical, Experimental and Psychological Studies.* Johannesburg: Wits University Press.

Makari, G. (2008) *Revolution in Mind.* New York: Harper-Perennial.

Malabou, C. (2012a) *The New Wounded: From Neurosis to Brain Damage,* trans. Steven Miller. New York: Fordham University Press.

Malabou, C. (2012b) *Ontology of the Accident: An Essay on Destructive Plasticity,* trans. Carolyn Shread. Cambridge: Polity Press.

Malabou, C. (2012c) 'Post-Trauma: Toward a New Definition?' *Telemorphosis: Theory in the Era of Climate Change,* ed. Tom Cohen, vol. 1. Ann Arbor, MI: Open Humanities Press: 226–38.

Malitz, S. (1987) *P.I. from the Cat Bird Seat: A Highly Personalized Retrospective.* New York: New York State Psychiatric Institute.

Mandler, P. (2013) *Return from the Natives: How Margaret Mead Won the Second World War and Lost the Cold War.* New Haven, CT: Yale University Press.

Manganyi, N.C. (1973) *Being-Black-in-the-World.* Johannesburg: Ravan Press.

Manganyi, N.C. (1977) *Mashangu's Reverie and Other Essays.* Johannesburg: Ravan Press.

Manganyi, N.C. (1981) *Looking Through the Keyhole: Dissenting Essays on the Black Experience.* Johannesburg: Ravan Press.

Manganyi, N.C. (1985) 'Making Strange: Race, Science and Ethnopsychiatric Discourse'. In Barker, F., ed. *Europe and its Others: Proceedings of the Essex Conference on the Sociology of Literature,* July 1984. Colchester: University of Essex.

Manganyi, N.C. (2011) 'The Violent Reverie: The Unconscious in Literature and Society'. *Psychology in Society* 41: 7–19.

Mangcu, X. (2012) *Biko: A Biography.* Cape Town: Tafelberg.

Mannoni, O. (1990) *Prospero and Caliban: The Psychology of Colonization,* trans. Pamela Powesland. Ann Arbor, MI: University of Michigan Press.

Manson, W.C. (1988) *The Psychodynamics of Culture: Abram Kardiner and Neo-Freudian Anthropology.* Westport, CT: Greenwood Press.

Marcus, L. (2012) 'European Witness: Analysands Abroad in the 1920s and 1930s'. In Alexander, S. and Taylor, B. eds. *History and Psyche: Culture, Psychoanalysis and the Past.* London: Palgrave: 105–28.

Marcuse, H. (1972 [1955]) *Eros and Civilization*. London: Sphere.

Marcuse, H., Mitscherlich, A. and Senghaas, D. (1968) *Aggression und Anpassung in der Industriegesellschaft*. Frankfurt am Main: Suhrkamp.

Marks, J. (1988 [1979]) *The Search for the 'Manchurian Candidate': The CIA and Mind Control – The Secret History of the Behavioral Sciences*. New York: W.W. Norton.

Martin, J.P. (1988) 'The Development of Criminology in Britain 1948–1960'. *British Journal of Criminology* Spring: 38–9.

Mason, P. (1954) *An Essay on Racial Tension*. London: Royal Institute of International Affairs.

Mason, P. (1957) 'Review of Mannoni, O. *Prospero and Caliban: The Psychology of Colonization*', trans. Pamela Powesland. *Journal of African Administration* 9: 100–1.

Masson, J. (1992) *Final Analysis: The Making and Unmaking of a Psychoanalyst*. London: Fontana.

Mausfeld, R. (2009) 'Weiße Folter'. *Blätter für deutsche und internationale Politik* 54, 10: 90–100.

Mayhew, B. (2006) 'Between Love and Aggression: The Politics of John Bowlby'. *History of the Human Sciences* 19, 4: 19–35.

Mazower, M. (1999) *Dark Continent: Europe's Twentieth Century*. London: Penguin.

Mazower, M. (2008) *Hitler's Empire: Nazi Rule in Occupied Europe*. London: Penguin.

McClintock, A. (1995) *Imperial Leather: Race, Gender and Sexuality in the Colonial Contest*. London and New York: Routledge.

McCoy, A.M. (2006) *A Question of Torture: CIA Interrogation, From the Cold War to the War on Terror*. New York: Henry Holt.

McCoy A.M. (2012) *Torture and Impunity: The US Doctrine of Coercive Interrogation*. Madison, WI: University of Wisconsin Press.

McCulloch, J. (1995) *Colonial Psychiatry and 'the African Mind'*. Cambridge: Cambridge University Press.

McLaughlin, N.G. (1998) 'Why Do Schools of Thought Fail? Neo-Freudianism as a Case Study in the Sociology of Knowledge'. *Journal of the History of the Behavioral Sciences* 34: 113–34.

Meisel, P. and Kendrick, W.K., eds. (1986). *Bloomsbury/Freud: The Letters of James and Alix Strachey*. London: Chatto and Windus.

Menninger, W.C. (1945) 'Psychiatric Objectives in the Army'. *American Journal of Psychiatry* 102, 1: 102–7.

Merisca, C. (1997) *Tragedia Pitesti* [The tragedy of Pitesti]. Iasi: The European Institute.

Merleau-Ponty, M. (1969 [1947]) *Humanism and Terror*. Boston, MA: Beacon Press.

Merleau-Ponty, M. (1974 [1955]) *The Adventures of the Dialectic*. London: Heinemann.

Micale, M.S. and P. Lerner (2001) *Traumatic Pasts: History, Psychiatry and Trauma in the Modern Age*. Cambridge: Cambridge University Press.

Michaels, W.B. (2004) *The Shape of the Signifier: 1967 to the End of History*. Princeton and Oxford: Princeton University Press.

Michaels, W.B. (2011a) 'The Beauty of a Social Problem (e.g. Unemployment)'. *Twentieth Century Literature* 57, 3 and 57, 4: 309–27.

Michaels, W.B. (2011b) 'Homo Sacher-Moser: Agamben's American Dream'. In Fluck, W., Motyl, K., Pease, D. and Raetzscl, C., eds. *States of Emergency – States of Crisis: Yearbook of Research in English and American Literature* 27: 25–36.

Mihailovic, D. (1990) *Goli Otok*. Belgrade: NIP Politika.

Mijolla-Mellor, S. de (2004) *Le Besoin de croire: metapsychologie du fait religieux*. Paris: Dunod.

Milam, E. (2010) *Looking for a Few Good Males: Female Choice in Evolutionary Biology*. Baltimore, MD: Johns Hopkins University Press.

Mill, J.S. (1910) 'On Liberty', ch. 3. *Utilitarianism, Liberty, Representative Government*. London: Dent.

Miller, M. (1998) *Freud and the Bolsheviks: Psychoanalysis in Imperial Russia and the Soviet Union*. New Haven, CT: Yale University Press.

Millet, J. (1963) 'The Influence of Psychiatry on Psychoanalysis in the USA'. 2 February 1963, Unpublished Manuscript. Oskar Diethelm Library, Weill Cornell Medical College, New York, Millet Papers, Box 3, Folder 3.3: 9.

Mills, D. (2006) 'Life on the Hill: Students and the Social Life of Makerere'. *Africa* 76, 2: 247–66.

Mitchell, Juliet (1974) *Psychoanalysis and Feminism*. New York: Pantheon.

Mitscherlich, A. (1956) 'Aggression und Anpassung'. *Psyche*. 10: 177–93.

Mitscherlich, A. (1958) 'Aggression und Anpassung' (II). *Psyche*. 12: 523–37.

Mitscherlich, A. (1964) 'Psychoanalyse heute'. *Gesammelte Schriften:* VIII. Frankfurt am Main: Suhrkamp: 171–93.

Mitscherlich, A. (1969a) 'Aggression ist eine Grundmacht des Lebens'. *Der Spiegel* 13 October 42: 206–12.

Mitscherlich, A., ed. (1969b) *Bis hierher und nicht weiter: Ist die menschliche Aggression unbefriedbar?* Munich: Piper.

Mitscherlich, A. (1969c) *Die Idee des Friedens und die menschliche Aggressivität*. Frankfurt am Main: Suhrkamp.

Mitscherlich, A. (1970) 'Freuds Sexualtheorie und die notwendige Aufklärung der Erwachsenen'. *Versuch, die Welt besser zu bestehen*. Frankfurt am Main: Suhrkamp: 141–56.

Mitscherlich, A. (1974a) 'Toleranz: Überprüfung eines Begriffs'. *Toleranz: Überprüfung eines Begriffs*. Frankfurt am Main: Suhrkamp: 7–34.

Mitscherlich, A. (1974b) 'Zwei Arten der Grausamkeit'. *Toleranz: Überprüfung eines Begriffs*. Frankfurt am Main: Suhrkamp: 168–89.

Mitscherlich, A. and Mitscherlich, M. (1967) *Die Unfähigkeit zu trauern: Grundlagen kollektiven Verhaltens*. Munich: Piper.

Mitscherlich, A. and Mitscherlich, M. (1975) *The Inability to Mourn: Principles of Collective Behavior*. New York: Grove Press.

Money-Kyrle, R. (2014 [1961]) *Man's Picture of His World: A Psychoanalytic Study*. London: Karnac.

Money-Kyrle, R. (1978) *The Collected Papers of Roger Money-Kyrle*. Perthshire: Clunie Press.

Moore, J. (1955) 'Beneficial Brain-Washing'. *Weekend Magazine* 5, 40: 6–8.

Moore, M.H. (2010) *Know Your Enemy: The American Debate on Nazism, 1933–1945*. Cambridge: Cambridge University Press.

Morris, D. (1967) *The Naked Ape*. New York: McGraw-Hill.

Müller, K. (2013) 'Im Auftrag der Firma'. PhD thesis, Free University Berlin, Germany.

Müller-Doohm, S. (2005) *Adorno: A Biography*. Cambridge: Polity.

Murray, H.A. (1943) *Analysis of the Personality of Adolph Hitler with Predictions of His Future Behavior and Suggestions for Dealing with Him Now and After Germany's*

Surrender. OSS Confidential, October 1943, available at: http://www.lawschool. cornell.edu/library/WhatWeHave/SpecialCollections/Donovan/Hitler/Download.cfm (accessed 10 May 2014).

Mzamane, M.V., Maaba, B. and Biko, N. (2006) 'The Black Consciousness Movement'. In Ngubane, B. ed. *The Road to Democracy in South Africa,* vol. 2, *1970–1980.* Pretoria: South African Democracy Education Trust & UNISA Press.

Nengwekhulu, R. (1981) 'The Meaning of Black Consciousness in the Struggle for Liberation in South Africa'. In Denis, L. and Daniel, C.J., eds. *Political Economy of Africa: Selected Readings.* Essex: Longman Group Limited: 198–204.

Nietzsche, F. (1992) 'The Four Great Errors'. *Twilight of the Idols,* trans. D. Large. Oxford: Oxford University Press: 19–98.

Opie, I. and P., eds. (1951) *The Oxford Dictionary of Nursery Rhymes.* Oxford: Oxford University Press.

Panic, R. (1997) *Titovi Havaji* [Tito's Hawaii]. Belgrade: Nezavisna izdanja Slobodana Masica.

Parker, I. (2004) 'Psychoanalysis and Critical Psychology'. In Hook, D., ed., with Mkhize, N., Kiguwa, P. and Collins, A. (section eds.) and Burman, E. and Parker, I. (consulting eds.) *Critical Psychology.* Cape Town: UCT Press: 138–61.

Parsons, T. (1970 [1952]) 'The Superego and the Theory of Social Systems'. *Social Structure and Personality.* London: The Free Press.

Paskauskas, R.A., ed. (1995) *The Complete Correspondence of Sigmund Freud and Ernest Jones, 1908-1939.* Cambridge, MA: Harvard University Press.

Pedersen, S. (1993) *Family, Dependence, and the Origins of the Welfare State: Britain and France, 1914–1945.* Cambridge: Cambridge University Press.

Peglau, A. (2013) *Unpolitische Wissenschaft? Wilhelm Reich und die Psychoanalyse im Nationalsozialismus.* Gießen: Psychosozial-Verlag.

Perucica, K. (1990) *Kako su nas prevaspitavali* [How they re-educated us]. Belgrade: Dereta.

Peters, O., ed. (2014) *Degenerate Art: The Attack on Modern Art in Nazi Germany.* Exhibition at the Neue Gallerie, New York. Munich: Prestel.

Phillips, A. (1988) *Winnicott.* London: Fontana Modern Masters.

Pick, D. (2012) *The Pursuit of the Nazi Mind: Hitler, Hess, and the Analysts.* Oxford: Oxford University Press.

Plack, A. (1967) *Die Gesellschaft und das Böse: Eine Kritik der herrschenden Moral.* Munich: List.

Plack, A. (1973) Aggressivität als Frage an die Wissenschaften. In Plack, A., ed. *Der Mythos vom Aggressionstrieb.* Munich: List, 9–39.

Plotkin, M.B. (2013) 'On Psychoanalysis and its History: Some Reflections'. In Segal, N. and Kivland, S., eds. *Vissicitudes: Histories and Destinies of Psychoanalysis.* London: Institute of Germanic and Romance Studies, School of Advanced Study, University of London.

Poiger, U.G. (2000) *Jazz, Rock, and Rebels: Cold War Politics and American Culture in a Divided Germany.* Berkeley: University of California Press.

Pols, H. (2011) 'The Totem Vanishes, the Hordes Revolt: A Psychoanalytic Interpretation of the Indonesian Struggle for Independence'. In Anderson, W. Jenson, D. and Keller, R. C. eds. *Unconscious Dominions: Psychoanalysis, Colonial Trauma, and Global Sovereignties.* Durham, NC: Duke University Press.

Pols, H. and Oak, S. (2007) 'War and Military Mental Health: The US Psychiatric Response in the 20th Century'. *American Journal of Public Health* 97, 12: 2132–42.

Pommier, G. (2001) *Erotic Anger: A User's Manual.* Minneapolis: University of Minnesota Press.

Popovic, M. (1989) *Udri bandu* [Hit the bandits]. Belgrade: Filip Visnjic.

Popper, K. (1945) *The Open Society and Its Enemies,* 2 vols. London: Routledge and Kegan Paul.

Popper, K.R. (1957) *The Poverty of Historicism.* London: Routledge and Kegan Paul.

Proceedings (1948). *Proceedings of the International Congress on Mental Health,* 4 vols. London.

Radonjic, B. (1995) *Poruseni ideali* [Destroyed ideals]. Belgrade: Interpress.

Raitt, S. (2000) *May Sinclair, a Modern Victorian.* Oxford: Clarendon Press.

Rapaport, D. (1958) 'The Theory of Ego Autonomy: A Generalization'. *Bulletin of the Menninger Clinic* 22, 1: 13–35.

Rauch, H.-G. (1973) 'Der sogenannte Gute'. *Die Zeit* 14 December 51: 21.

Raynor, E. (1990) *The Independent Mind in British Psychoanalysis.* London: Free Association Books.

Reeves, M.P. (1979 [1913]) *Round About a Pound a Week.* London: Virago reprint.

Reik, T. (1975 [1948]) 'Who Am I?' *Listening with the Third Ear.* New York: Farrar, Straus and Giroux.

Richards, A.D. (1985) 'Interviews with Dr Charles Fisher'. *New York Psychoanalytic Institute and Society Oral History Project* Part IV. Available at: http://international psychoanalysis.net/wp-content/uploads/2007/08/fisher-int-scan-part-3-barbara.pdf (accessed 22 February 2012).

Riesman, D. (1950) *The Lonely Crowd: A Study of the Changing American Character.* New Haven, CT: Yale University Press.

Riesman, D. with Glazer, N. (1961) '*The Lonely Crowd*: A Reconsideration in 1960.' In Lipset, S.M. and Lowenthal, L., eds. *Culture and Social Character: The Work of David Riesman Reviewed.* New York: The Free Press.

Riley, D. (1983) *War in the Nursery: Theories of the Child and Mother.* London: Virago.

Ritchie, J.F. (1968) *The African as Suckling and as Adult.* Manchester: Rhodes-Livingstone Institute.

Roazen, P. (2000) *Oedipus in Britain: Edward Glover and the Struggle over Klein.* New York: Other Press.

Robin, R. (2001) *The Making of the Cold War Enemy: Culture and Politics in the Military-Intellectual Complex.* Princeton, NJ: Princeton University Press.

Rodman, F. (1999 [1987]) *The Spontaneous Gesture: Selected Letters of D.W. Winnicott.* London: Karnac.

Rodman, F. (2003) *Winnicott, Life and Work.* Cambridge MA: Da Capo Press.

Rose, J. (1993) 'War in the Nursery'. *Why War? Psychoanalysis, Politics and the Return to Melanie Klein.* Oxford: Blackwell: 191–230.

Rose, J. (1996) 'Introduction: Part II.' In Sachs, W. (1996 [1937]). *Black Hamlet: The Mind of an African Negro Revealed by Psychoanalysis.* Johannesburg: Wits University Press.

Roseman, M. (2001) *The Past in Hiding.* Harmondsworth: Penguin.

Rosenfeld, H. (1971) 'A Clinical Approach to the Psychoanalytic Theory of the Life and Death Instincts: An Investigation Into the Aggressive Aspects of Narcissism'. *International Journal of Psychoanalysis,* 52:169–78.

Ross, E. (2007) *Slum Travelers, Ladies and London Poverty 1860–1920.* London and Los Angeles: University of California Press.

Rosten, L. (1951) 'How the Politburo Thinks'. *Look* 13 March: 31–5.

Rothschild, Emma (1994) 'Psychological Modernity in Historical Perspective'. *Rethinking the Development Experience: Essays Provoked by the Work of Albert O. Hirschman.* Washington, DC: Brookings Institution.

Roustang, F. (1982) *Dire Mastery: Discipleship from Freud to Lacan.* Baltimore, MD: Johns Hopkins University Press.

Rowbotham, S. (2010) *Dreamers of a New Day: Women Who Invented the Twentieth Century.* London: Verso.

Rustin, M.J. (1985) 'The Social Organisation of Secrets: Towards a Sociology of Psychoanalysis'. *International Review of Psychoanalysis* 12, 22: 143–59.

Rustin, M.J. (1991) *The Good Society and the Inner World.* London: Verso.

Rustin, M.J. (2001) 'The Roots of Reason'. *Reason and Unreason: Psychoanalysis, Science, Politics.* London: Continuum: 113–34.

Rustin, M.J. (2004) 'Why Are We More Afraid than Ever? The Politics of Anxiety After Nine-Eleven' in Lemma, A. and Levy, S., eds. *The Perversion of Loss.* London: Whurr.

Rustin, M.J. (2016) 'What Happened to Psychoanalytic Sociology?'. In Elliott, A. and Prager, J., eds. *Routledge Handbook on Psychoanalysis in the Social Sciences and Humanities.* London: Routledge.

Rutschky, M. (2006) 'Von Prof. Freud zu Dr. Caligari'. *Cicero* January 132.

Sachs, W. (1934) *Psychoanalysis: Its Meaning and Practical Applications.* London: Cassell & Co.

Sachs, W. (1943) 'Racism: A Study in Psychology'. *The Democrat* 4 November: 5.

Sachs, W. (1944) 'Racism: The Solution'. *The Democrat* 20 January: 15–16.

Sachs, W. (1947) *Black Anger.* Boston: Little, Brown.

Sachs, W. (1996[1937]) *Black Hamlet: The Mind of an African Negro Revealed by Psychoanalysis.* Baltimore, MD: Johns Hopkins University Press.

Said, E. (1993) *Freud and the Non-European*, Response by Jacqueline Rose, introduced by Christopher Bollas. London: Verso.

Sampson, Anthony (1956) 'White Settlers on the Couch'. *Times Literary Supplement* 27 July: 452.

Sartre, J.-P. (1990 [1961]) 'Preface'. In Fanon, F., *The Wretched of the Earth.* London: Penguin: 7-26.

Saville, E. and Rumney, D. (1992) *Let Justice be Done: A History of the ISTD – A Study of Crime and Delinquency from 1931 to 1992.* London: ISTD.

Schatzman, M. (1973) *Soul Murder: Persecution in the Family.* New York: New American Library.

Scheflin, A.W. and Opton, E.M., Jr (1978) *The Mind Manipulators.* New York: Paddington Press.

Schlein, S., ed. (1987) *Erik H. Erikson: A Way of Looking at Things – Selected Papers from 1930 to 1980.* New York: W.W. Norton.

Schmideberg, M. (1948) *Children in Need.* London: Allen & Unwin.

Schmideberg, M. (1953–4) 'Is the Criminal Amoral?' *British Journal of Delinquency* 4: 272–81.

Schreber, D.P. (1988) *Memoirs of My Nervous Illness*, trans. and ed. by I. Macalpine and R.A. Hunter, new introduction by S. Weber. Cambridge, MA: Harvard University Press.

Schubert, G. (1973) 'Biopolitical Behavior: The Nature of the Political Animal'. *Polity* Winter 6: 240–75.

Schwarz, H. (1950–1) 'Dorothy: The Psycho-Analysis of a Case of Stealing'. *British Journal of Delinquency* 1: 29–47.

Schwartz, T.A. (1991) *America's Germany: John J. McCloy and the Federal Republic of Germany*. Cambridge MA: Harvard University Press.

Segal, H. (1957) 'Notes on Symbol Formation'. *International Journal of Psychoanalysis* 38: 391–7.

Segal, H. (1987) 'Silence is the Real Crime'. *International Review of Psychoanalysis* 14, 3: 3–11.

Segal, H. (1995) 'From Hiroshima to the Gulf War and After: A Psychoanalytic Perspective'. In Elliott, A. and Frosh, S., eds. *Psychoanalysis in Contexts*. London: Routledge.

Segel, H. (2012) *The Walls behind the Curtain: East European Prison Literature, 1945–1990*. Pittsburgh: University of Pittsburgh Press.

Selg, H., ed. (1971) *Zur Aggression verdammt?* Stuttgart: Kohlhammer.

Senate Select Committee on Intelligence, eds. (2014) *The Senate Intelligence Committee Report on Torture: Committee Study of the Central Intelligence Agency's Detention and Interrogation Program*. Foreword by Senate Select Committee on Intelligence Chairman Dianne Feinstein, Findings and Conclusions, Executive Summary. Declassification Revisions 3 December, 2014. URL: https://web.archive.org/web/20141209165504/ http://www.intelligence.senate.gov/study2014/sscistudy1.pdf (accessed 25 February 2016).

Sereny, G. (1995) *Albert Speer: His Battle with the Truth*. London: Picador.

Serge, V. (2012 [1951]) *Memoirs of a Revolutionary*, new edn. New York: New York Review of Books.

Shabecoff, P. (1965) 'Germans Shunt Psychoanalysis To a Minor Role, Scholar Says: Professor Deplores Neglect of Practice in Region Where It Took Root'. *New York Times*: 22 February 23.

Shapira, M. (2013) *The War Inside: Psychoanalysis, Total War, and the Making of the Democratic Self in Post-War Britain*. Cambridge: Cambridge University Press.

Simic, D. and Trifunovic, B. (1990) *Zenski logor na Golom Otoku: Ispovesti kaznenica i islednice* [Women's prison camp at Goli Otok: testimonies of inmates and the investigator]. Belgrade: ABC Produkt.

Simmel, E. (1946) 'Anti-Semitism and Mass Psychopathology'. In Simmel, E.. ed. *Anti-Semitism: A Social Disease*. New York: International Universities Press.

Sitze, A. (2007) 'Treating Life Literally'. *Law Critique* 18: 55–89.

Sitze, A. (2013) *The Impossible Machine: A Genealogy of South Africa's Truth and Reconciliation Commission*. Ann Arbor, MI: University of Michigan Press.

Slater, E. (1944) 'Psychological Aspects of Family Life'. In Horder, L., ed. *Rebuilding Family Life in the Post-War World: An Enquiry with Recommendations*. London: Odhams Press: 92–106.

Smith, D. (1994) 'Juvenile Delinquency in the British Zone of Germany, 1945–51'. *German History* 12: 39–63.

Solms, M. (2010) 'The Establishment of an Accredited Psychoanalytic Training Institute in South Africa'. *Psycho-Analytic Psychotherapy in South Africa*. Downloaded from http://www.readperiodicals.com/201001/2113454891.html#ixzz36gIfP 7JR (accessed 2 July 2014).

Solms, M. and Turnbull, O. (2002) *The Brain and the Inner World: An Introduction to the Neuroscience of Subjective Experience*. New York: Other Press.

Solomon, P.H. (1980) 'Soviet Penal Policy, 1917–1934: A Reinterpretation'. *Slavic Review* 39, 2: 195–217.

Solovey, M. and Cravens, H., eds. (2012) *Cold War Social Science: Knowledge Production, Liberal Democracy, and Human Nature*. New York: Palgrave Macmillan.

Spitzer, H.M. (1944) 'Considerations on Psychological Warfare Directed Against Japan'. 9 Dec. 1944: National Archives (US), RG208/378/443, Foreign Morale Analysis Division, 1944–5.

Spitzer, H.M. (1947) 'Psychoanalytic Approaches to the Japanese Character'. *Psychoanalysis and the Social Sciences* 1: 131–56.

Stanescu, M. (2010) *The Re-Education Trials in Communist Romania, 1952–1960*. Boulder, CO: East European Monographs.

Steedman, C. (1995) *Strange Dislocations: Childhood and the Idea of Human Interiority 1780–1930*. London and Cambridge, MA: Harvard University Press.

Steiner, J. (1993) *Psychic Retreats: Pathological Organizations in Psychotic, Neurotic and Borderline Patients*. London: Routledge.

Steiner, R. (1985) 'Some Thoughts about Tradition and Change Arising from an Examination of the British Psychoanalytical Society's Controversial Discusssions (1943–1944)'. *International Review of Psychoanalysis* 12: 27–71.

Stewart-Steinberg, S. (2011) *Impious Fidelity: Anna Freud, Psychoanalysis, Politics*. Ithaca, NY: Cornell University Press.

Stirk, P. (1992) *Max Horkheimer: A New Interpretation*. Hemel Hempstead: Harvester Wheatsheaf.

Stoetzel, J. (1955) *Without the Chrysanthemum and the Sword: A Study of the Attitudes of Youth in Post-War Japan*. London: William Heinemann.

Stojanovic, M. (1991) *Goli Otok: Anatomija zlocina*. [Goli Otok: anatomy of a crime]. Belgrade: Strucna knjiga.

Stonebridge, L. (1998) 'Anxiety at a Time of Crisis'. *History Workshop Journal* Spring 45: 171–82.

Strachey, J. (1934) 'The Nature of the Therapeutic Action of Psycho-Analysis'. *International Journal of Psychoanalysis*, 15: 127–59.

Swanson, M. (1977) 'The Sanitation Syndrome: Bubonic Plague and Urban Native Policy in the Cape Colony 1900–1909'. *Journal of African History* 18, 3: 387–410.

Swartz, S. (2006) 'A Long Walk to Citizenship: Morality, Justice and Faith in the Aftermath of Apartheid'. *Journal of Moral Education*, 35, 4: 551–70.

Swartz, S. (2007) 'Reading Psychoanalysis in the Diaspora: South African Psychoanalytic Psychotherapists' Struggles with Voice'. *Psycho-Analytic Psychotherapy in South Africa* 15, 2: 1–18.

Talmon, J.L. (1952) *The Origins of Totalitarian Democracy*. London: Secker & Warburg.

Taschwer, K. (2013) 'Konrad Lorenz' bester Freund'. *derStandard.at*. 5 November. Available at: http://derstandard.at/1381370977060/Konrad-Lorenz-bester-Freund.

Terada, R. (2004) 'Thinking for Oneself: Realism and Defiance in Arendt'. *English Literary History* 71, 4: 839–65.

Thane, P. (1991) 'Visions of Gender in the Making of the British Welfare State; the Case of Women in the British Labour Party and Social Policy 1906–1945'. In Bock, G. and Thane, P., eds. *Maternity and Gender Policies: Women and the Rise of the European Welfare States, 1880s–1950s*. London and New York: Routledge: 93–118.

Theweleit, K. (1978) *Male Fantasies*, vol. 2. Minneapolis: University of Minnesota Press.

Theweleit, K. (1987 [1977]) *Male Fantasies*, vol. 1. Cambridge: Polity.

Thimm, K (2001) Ruf nach dem Rassepfleger. *Spiegel* 8 October 41: 209.

Thomson, M. (2006) *Psychological Subjects: Identity, Culture, and Health in Twentieth-Century Britain*. Oxford: Oxford University Press.

Thomson, M. (2013) *Lost Freedom: The Landscape of the Child and the British Post-War Settlement*. Oxford: Oxford University Press.

Thornton, A.P. (1965) 'Jekyll and Hyde in the Colonies'. *International Journal* 20, 2: 221–9.

Tidd, C.W. (1960) 'Symposium on 'Psycho-Analysis and Ethology' I. Introduction. *International Journal of Psychoanalysis*, 41: 308–12.

Todd, S. (2014) *The People: The Rise and Fall of the Working Class 1910–2010*. London: John Murray.

Tolokontseva, D. (2012) 'Use of Correctional and Labour Measures on the Inmates of the Solovetsky Camp in the 1920s and 1930s'. *Arctic Review on Law and Politics* 2: 186–99.

Tooze, A. (2006) *The Wages of Destruction: The Making and Breaking of the Nazi Economy*. London: Penguin.

Torres, N. (2013) 'The Psycho-Social Field Dynamics: Kurt Lewin and Bion'. In *Bion's Sources: The Making of His Paradigms*. Torres, N. and Hinshelwood, R. D., eds. Hove: Routledge.

Torriani, R. (2005) *Nazis into Germans: Re-Education and Democratisation in the British and French Occupation Zones, 1945–1949*. PhD dissertation, University of Cambridge.

Urwin, C. and Sharland, E. (1992) 'From Bodies to Minds in Childcare Literature: Advice to Parents in Interwar Britain'. In Cooter, R., ed. *In the Name of the Child: Health and Welfare in England, 1880–1940*. London: Routledge: 174–99.

van der Horst, F.C.P. (2011) *John Bowlby from Psychoanalysis to Ethology: Unravelling the Roots of Attachment Theory*. Chichester: Wiley-Blackwell.

Vaughan, M. (1991) *Curing Their Ills: Colonial Power and African Illness*. Palo Alto, CA: Stanford University Press.

Vicedo, M. (2013) *The Nature and Nurture of Love: From Imprinting to Attachment in Cold War America*. Chicago: University of Chicago Press.

Videla, J.R. (1980) Speech at the 'Camara de Comercio' La Prensa 30 October 1980. In Caraballo, L., Chartier, N., Garulli, L. (2011) *La Dictadura: Testimonios y Documentos 1976–1983*. Buenos Aires: Eudeba.

Wachsmann, N. (2004) *Hitler's Prisons*. New Haven, CT: Yale University Press.

Warne, A. (2013) 'Psychoanalyzing Iran: Kennedy's Iran Task Force and the Modernization of Orientalism, 1961–3.' *International History Review* 35, no. 2: 396–422.

Watkins, F. (1940) 'The Problem of Constitutional Dictatorship'. In Friedrich, C. and Mason, E., eds. *Public Policy*. Cambridge, MA: Harvard University Press: 324–79.

Watson, P. (1978) *War on the Mind: The Military Uses and Abuses of Psychology*. New York: Basic Books.

Webb, B. (1926) 'Appendix B'. In *My Apprenticeship*. London, New York, Toronto, Bombay, Calcutta, Madras: Longmans, Green, and Co.

Weidman, N. (2011) 'Popularizing the Ancestry of Man: Robert Ardrey and the Killer Instinct'. *Isis* 102: 269–99.

West, D.J. (1988) 'Psychological Contribution to Criminology'. *British Journal of Criminology* Spring: 77–91.

Westad, O.A. (2005) *The Global Cold War: Third World Interventions and the Making of Our Times*. Cambridge: Cambridge University Press.

Wheatland, T. (2009) *The Frankfurt School in Exile*. Minneapolis: University of Minnesota.

White, J. (2008) *London in the Twentieth Century*. London: Vintage.

Wiggershaus, R. (1994) *The Frankfurt School: Its History, Theories, and Political Significance*. Cambridge, MA: MIT Press.

Wiggershaus, R. (1995 [1986]) *The Frankfurt School*. Cambridge: Polity.

Williams, R. (1961) *The Long Revolution*. London: Chatto & Windus.

Winnicott, C. (1989) 'D.W.W.: A Reflection'. In Winnicott, C., Shepherd, R. and Davis, M., eds. *Psychoanalytic Explorations*. London: Karnac: 1–18.

Winnicott, D.W. (1931) *Clinical Notes on the Disorders of Childhood*. London: William Heinemann.

Winnicott, D.W. (1950) 'Some Thoughts on the Meaning of the Word "Democracy"'. *Home is Where we Start From: Essays by a Psychoanalyst*. London: Penguin Books: 239–59.

Winnicott, D.W. (1958) *Collected Papers: Through Paediatrics to Psychoanalysis*. London: Tavistock Publications.

Winnicott, D.W. (1958 [1936]) 'Appetite and Emotional Disorder'. *Collected Papers: Through Paediatrics to Psychoanalysis*. London: Tavistock Publications: 33–51.

Winnicott, D.W. (1958 [1947]) 'Hate in the Countertransference'. *Collected Papers: From Paediatrics to Psychoanalysis*. London: Tavistock Publications: 194–203.

Winnicott, D.W. (1958 [1949]) 'Mind and its Relation to the Psyche-Soma'. *Collected Papers: From Paediatrics to Psychoanalysis*. London: Tavistock Publications: 243–54.

Winnicott, D.W. (1958 [1948]) 'Paediatrics and Psychiatry'. *Collected Papers: Through Paediatrics to Psychiatry*. London: Tavistock Publications: 157–73.

Winnicott, D W. (1958) 'Primary Maternal Preoccupation (1956)'. *Collected Papers: Through Paediatrics to Psychoanalysis*. London: Tavistock Publications: 300–5.

Winnicott, D.W. (1958 [1945]) 'Primitive Emotional Development'. *Collected Papers: Through Paediatrics to Psychoanalysis*. London: Tavistock Publications: 145–56.

Winnicott, D.W. (1958 [1935]) 'The Manic Defence'. In *Collected Papers: Through Paediatrics to Psychoanalysis*. London: Tavistock Publications: 129–44.

Winnicott, D.W. (1958) 'The Antisocial Tendency'. *Collected Papers: Through Paediatrics to Psycho-Analysis*. New York: Basic Books.

Winnicott, D.W. (1964) *The Child, the Family and the Outside World*. London: Penguin.

Winnicott, D.W. (1965 [1935]) 'The Capacity to be Alone'. *Maturational Processes and the Facilitating Environment*. London: The Hogarth Press: 29–36.

Winnicott, D.W. (1969) 'James Strachey 1887–1967'. *International Journal of Psycho-Analysis*: 129–31.

Winnicott, D.W. (1984 [1962]). 'A Personal View of the Kleinian Contribution'. *The Maturational Processes and the Facilitating Environment*. London: Maresfield Library, The Winnicott Trust: 171–8.

Winnicott, D.W. (1986 [1940]) 'Discussion of War Aims'. *Home Is Where We Start From: Essays by a Psychoanalyst*. London: Penguin: 210–20.

Winnicott, D.W. (1986 [1964]) 'This Feminism'. *Home Is Where We Start From: Essays by a Psychoanalyst*. London: Penguin Books: 183–94.

Winnicott, D.W. (1986 [1965]) 'The Price of Disregarding Psychoanalytic Research'. *Home Is Where We Start From: Essays by a Psychoanalyst*. London: Penguin: 172–82.

Winnicott, D.W. (1986 [1968]) 'Adolescent Immaturity'. *Home Is Where We Start From: Essays by a Psychoanalyst*. London: Penguin: 150–66.

Winnicott, D.W. (1986 [1969]) 'Freedom'. *Home Is Where We Start From: Essays by a Psychoanalyst*. London: Penguin Books: 228–38.

Winnicott, D.W. (1986 [1969]) 'The Pill and the Moon'. *Home Is Where We Start From: Essays by a Psychoanalyst*. London: Penguin: 195–209.

Winnicott, D.W. (1988) *Human Nature*. London: Free Association Books.

Winnicott, D.W. (1989) 'Part Four: On other Forms of Treatment'. In Winnicott, C., Shepherd, R. and Davis, M., eds. *Psychoanalytic Explorations*. London: Karnac: 515–54.

Winnicott, D.W. (1989 [1959]) 'Melanie Klein: On her Concept of Envy'. In Winnicott, C., Shepherd, R. and Davis, M., eds. *Psychoanalytic Explorations*. London: Karnac: 443–6.

Winnicott, D.W. (1989 [1965]) 'Growth and Development in Immaturity'. *The Family and Individual Development*. London: Routledge Classics: 29–41.

Winnicott, D.W. (1989 [1967]) 'D.W.W. on D.W.W.'. In Winnicott, C., Shepherd, R. and Davis, M., eds. *Psychoanalytic Explorations*. London: Karnac: 569–82.

Winnicott, D.W. (1990 [1963]) 'Communicating and Not Communicating Leading to a Study of Certain Opposites'. In Khan, M.M.R., ed. *The Maturational Processes and the Facilitating Environment: Studies in the Theory of Emotional Development*. London: Karnac: 179–92.

Winnicott, D.W. (1991 [1977]) *The Piggle: An Account of the Psychoanalytic Treatment of a Little Girl*. London: Penguin.

Winnicott, D.W. (1996a) 'Notes on the Time Factor in Treatment'. In Shepherd, R., Johns, J. and Taylor Robinson, H., eds. *Thinking About Children*. London: Karnac: 231–4.

Winnicott, D.W. (1996b) 'Towards an Objective Study of Human Nature'. In Shepherd, R., Johns, J. and Taylor Robinson, H., eds.. *Thinking About Children*. London: Da Capo Press, Perseus Books: 3–12.

Winnicott, D.W. (1998 [1936]) 'The Teacher, the Parent and the Doctor'. In Shepherd R., Johns, J. and Taylor Robinson, H., eds. *Thinking About Children*. London: Perseus Books: 77–96.

Winnicott, D.W. (2006 [1965]) 'Advising Parents' (1957). *The Family and Individual Development*. London: Routledge 2006: 165–75.

Winnicott, D.W. (2012 [1984]) 'Evacuation of Small Children' (1939). In Winnicott, C., Shepherd, R. and Davis, M., eds. *Deprivation and Delinquency*. London: Routledge: 11–12.

Winnicott, D.W. (2012 [1984]) 'Review of The Cambridge Evacuation Survey' (1941). In Winnicott, C., Shepherd, R. and Davis, M., eds. *Deprivation and Delinquency*. London: Routledge: 19–21.

Winnicott, D.W. (2012 [1984]) 'The Deprived Mother' (1939). In Winnicott, C., Shepherd, R. and Davis, M., eds. *Deprivation and Delinquency*. London: Routledge: 27–33.

Winnicott, D.W. (2012 [1984]) 'Home Again' (1945). In Winnicott, C., Shepherd, R. and Davis, M., eds. *Deprivation and Delinquency*. London: Routledge: 44–8.

Winnicott, D.W. (2012 [1984]) 'Children's Hostels in War and Peace' (1984). In Winnicott, C., Shepherd, R. and Davis, M., eds. *Deprivation and Delinquency*. London: Routledge: 65–8.

Winnicott, D.W. (2012 [1984]) 'The Antisocial Tendency' (1956). In Winnicott, C., Shepherd, R. and Davis, M., eds. *Deprivation and Delinquency*. London: Routledge: 103–12.

Winnicott, D.W. (2012 [1984]) 'The Foundation of Mental Health' (1951). In Winnicott, C., Shepherd, R. and Davis, M., eds. *Deprivation and Delinquency*. London: Routledge: 145–7.

Winnicott, D.W. (2012 [1984]) 'The Deprived Child and How He Can Be Compensated For Loss of Family Life' (1950). In Winnicott, C., Shepherd, R. and Davis, M., eds. *Deprivation and Delinquency*. London: Routledge: 148–61.

Winnicott, D.W. (2012 [1984]) 'Residential Care as Therapy' (1970). In Winnicott, C., Shepherd, R. and Davis, M., eds. *Deprivation and Delinquency*. (London: Routledge: 190–6.

Winnicott, D.W. and Britton, C. (2012 [1984]) 'Residential Management as Treatment for Difficult Children' (1947). In Winnicott, C., Shepherd, R. and Davis, M., eds. *Deprivation and Delinquency*. London: Routledge: 49–64.

Wolpe, H. (1989) 'South Africa: The Case for Sanctions'. *Issue: A Journal of Opinion* 18(1): 17–21.

World Federation for Mental Health, The (1950). *UNESCO International Social Science Bulletin* 2: 71–5.

Yerushalmi, Y.H. (1991) *Freud's Moses: Judaism Terminable and Interminable*. New Haven, CT: Yale University Press.

Young-Bruehl, E. (1982) *Hannah Arendt: For Love of the World*. New Haven, CT: Yale University Press.

Young-Bruehl, E. (1988) *Anna Freud: A Biography*. New Haven, CT: Yale University Press.

Zaretsky, E. (2004) *Secrets of the Soul: A Social and Cultural History of Psychoanalysis*. New York: Knopf.

Žižek, S. (1989) *The Sublime Object of Ideology*. London: Verso.

Žižek, S. (1990) 'Eastern European Republics of Gilead'. *New Left Review* 1, 183: 50–62.

Žižek, S. (1993) *Tarrying with the Negative: Kant, Hegel and the Critique of Ideology*. Durham, NC: Duke University Press.

Žižek, S. (1994) *The Metastases of Enjoyment*. London: Verso.

Žižek, S. (1997) *The Plague of Fantasies*. London: Verso.

Žižek, S. (2008–9) 'Descartes and the Post-Traumatic Subject'. *Filozofski vestnik* 29, 2: 9–29.

Index

Abraham, Karl 56
Abrams, Allan 161
Adler, Alfred 182–3
Adorno, Theodor W. 16, 33–5, 37–8, 55–9,
    61–8, 100, 110, 136, 227, 237, 251
affect theory 246, 251
Agamben, Giorgio 243, 245, 248
aggression 87–101, 103; as drive 89, 94,
    96; as learned behaviour 94; Lorenz
    on 88–9, 91, 93, 95–6, 99–101;
    Mitscherlich on 87, 90–2, 95, 97–100
Ainsworth, Mary 188
Alexander, Franz 149
Alford, C. Fred 237
Allan Memorial Institute 156–7
Amendola, Giovanni 21–3
American Psychiatric Association 148
American Psychoanalytic Association,
    Committee on Morale 149–50, 160
anaclitic therapy 157
anti-fascism 75, 85, 92, 127
anti-Semitism 11, 29–41, 58, 134;
    Holocaust 29–41, 92; as madness
    36; as mass psychosis 39; psychic
    interpretation 36–7; responsibility for
    34–5; and socially induced misery 38;
    see also Nazism
anxiety xviii–xix, 8, 47, 67, 75, 77, 81, 83,
    88, 118–21, 135, 140, 153, 157, 200,
    250; of conscience 51; social 52
apartheid 193–204; Black Consciousness
    Movement 198–9; Black Hamlet (Sachs)
    195–8; infantilization of Africans 202;
    'The Violent Reverie' (Manganyi)
    198–202

Ardrey, Robert 88
Arendt, Hannah xvi–xvii, 5–6, 13, 18,
    43–8, 52, 93, 128, 193–4, 207–20,
    227–32, 234, 236
Argentina: 'disappeared' xvi–xviii;
    National Reorganization Process xvii;
    psychoanalysis in xx, 134, 139
atavism 30–2
authoritarian personality 38, 58, 61–2, 67,
    69, 100, 110
authoritarianism 7, 32, 58–62
autonomy 64–5, 69, 155, 157, 191, 249,
    251
Azima, Hassan 156–8, 162

Bakovic, Todor 169–71
Balandier, Georges 191
Bauman, Zygmunt 31, 40
Bell, Daniel 111
Benedict, Ruth 104–5, 107, 109
Benjamin, Jessica 57, 64, 69
Berlin, Isaiah 21
Bernal, J.D. 141
Bernays, Edward 6
Bettelheim, Bruno 140, 248
Bevan, Aneurin 128–9
Beveridge Report 85, 128
Beveridge, William 117, 128
Bion, Wilfred 9, 190
Blauer, Harold 156
Bloomsbury Group 141
Bolshevism 4, 11, 136
Borkenau, Franz 222
Boudry, Robert 191
Bourdieu, Pierre 232

Bowlby, John 73–4, 124, 127, 188, 191
Bradfish, Otto 44, 47
brainwashing 5, 7–8, 16, 92, 148, 155–8,
    176
Brickner, Richard 105–6, 108, 151;
    conferences organized by 105–6, 112
British Psychoanalytical Society (BPAS)
    116, 118–19
Britton, Clare 124–6
Britton, Ronald 229, 236
Burns, Alan 187
Burt, Cyril 75
Bustamante, Alexander 188
Butler, Judith 245

Cameron, Donald Ewen 156–7
Carothers, J.C. 184
Carroll, Denis 74, 85
Carstairs, Morris 188
Caruth, Cathy 241
Cattell, James P. 156
Cenic, Vera 172
Cesarani, David 30
Chadwick, Mary 119
Chavafambira, John 195–8
Chicago Psychoanalytic Institute 149
children 14, 200; child guidance 73–86;
    'disappeared' xvi–xvii; father-child
    relationship 58, 60–1, 66–9; loss of
    parental attachment 63–4; mother-child
    relationship 65, 88, 157, 188–9; mother-
    child separation 124–5; psychoanalysis
    50–2, 87–8, 116–23; secrets and lies
    216–17; superego 56, 208; wartime
    evacuees 124–7; see also Oedipus
    complex
Children Act 1948 125
Chile xvii
Churchill, Winston 114, 129
cinema 6, 8
civilization 29–31, 37, 39–40, 60–1, 83,
    103, 114, 226; failed 34
'clamour of need' 120–3
clinical encounters 15–17
Cocks, Geoffrey 13
coercion 191, 213–14, 216–17
Cold War 3–4, 6–7, 13, 16, 21, 29,
    95, 110–11, 115, 140, 182, 222,

226, 238; brainwashing 7–8, 155–9;
    de-psychologizing of national
    difference 107–9; re-education of
    political prisoners 163–77; swaddling
    controversy 109–10
Collini, Stefan 116
Comfort, Alex 190
communism/communists xx, 5, 7–8,
    10–11, 20–1, 23, 29, 104, 107, 109,
    111, 133, 136–8, 142, 222, 224–5; mind
    control 7–8, 155–8; re-education
    163–77; see also Cold War; Soviet
    Union
community development 190
concrete thinking 228, 236
Connolly, William E. 240, 245–6
counter-transference 120, 123, 227
counterintelligence, use of psychoanalysis
    in 147–62; brainwashing 5, 7–8, 16,
    92, 148, 155–8, 176; Cold War 154–9;
    OSS Truth Drug Committee 152–4, 158;
    Second World War 148–52
criminology 73–86; ISTD 73–8;
    psychoanalytic understanding 78–84
cruelty 98–9, 213–14
cultural nomadism 32–4
cultural relativism 102–13
'culture of law, order and reason' 30–1

Damasio, Antonio 240, 246
Damousi, Joy 13
Darwinism 141
de Man, Paul 241
De Ridder, J.C. 202–3
death-drive 98–9, 227
decolonization 181–92; community
    development 190; dependency 183, 188,
    190; as mother-child separation 188–9;
    'traumatic weaning' 183, 189
dehumanization 18, 47, 200
Delay, Jean 142
Deleuze, Gilles 240
delirium 210, 212, 217
democracy 49, 73–7, 81, 83–4, 105,
    115–18, 127–8, 137, 217
denial xviii, 10, 18, 23, 29–30, 35, 49–50,
    53, 114, 208
denigration 231–2, 237

Denker, Rolf 93
dependency 183, 186, 188, 190, 200
Derrida, Jacques 54
Devereux, George 151
Dicks, Henry 102–3, 108
'disappeared' of Argentina xvi–xviii
Dollard, John 94
Donovan, Colonel William 148, 150
Drucker, Peter 6
Du Bois, Cora 112

Eastern Europe, re-education of political
    prisoners 163–77
Eder, David 74
education 32, 55, 78, 82; see also
    re-education
ego psychology 36, 90, 140–1, 155
Eibl-Eibesfeldt, Irenäus 93
Eichmann, Adolf 47, 99
Eissler, Kurt xx
Ekman, Paul 240
Elias, Norbert 55
elite groups 209–10
elite psychology 111
empathy 91, 122
Engerman, David 110
Erikson, Erik 7, 57, 103, 105, 148
Etkind, Alexander 13

'failed civilization' 34
Fairbairn, W.R.D. 11
families 11, 59–60, 66–7, 73, 75, 78;
    break-up 75, 82; extended 189;
    matriarchal 187; patriarchal 13,
    16, 59–61, 66–8, 174, 182;
    psychoanalysis 119; societal role 125,
    127; undermining of 60–1; see also
    children; father-child relationship;
    mother-child relationship
family values xvii
Fanon, Frantz 140, 181–4, 195, 200–1
Farley, Lisa 130
fascism/fascist 4–5, 7, 10–11, 21–3, 35,
    41, 56–62, 67, 69, 97, 133, 136, 138,
    140, 142, 159, 182, 222, 225–6; anti-
    fascism 75, 85, 92, 127; Islamo-fascism
    137; postfascism 92–5; see also anti-
    Semitism; Nazism

fathers 59–60, 66–9, 188; authority of
    59–61, 123; lack of 66; Little Hans 50;
    murdered 31, 55, 64; 'primal' 55–6,
    58, 64; role of 133; superego 56, 59;
    unconscious impact 58; weakness 187–8;
    see also Oedipus complex; patriarchy
father figures 123, 182–4, 191
father-child relationship 58, 60–1, 66–9
Faulkner, William 46–7
Federn, Paul 9
feminism 41, 119, 123, 127–8, 136
Fenichel, Otto 10, 38
Finkelstein, Norman 29
First World War 46–7, 53, 87, 115, 119,
    136, 141, 214, 233; shellshock 147
Flowerman, Samuel 29–41
Flugel, J.C. 57
Foucault, Michel 16
Foulkes, S.H. 9
Frank, Anne 47
Frankfurt School 36, 55–70, 181–2; see
    also Adorno; Fromm; Horkheimer;
    Marcuse
Franklin, Marjorie 74, 124
freedom i, 3, 6, 33, 65, 94, 102, 109, 115,
    117, 128, 213, 222, 230; personal 18;
    political 13; of speech 136–7; of thought
    xvi, 7, 17, 45, 216–19
Freilichkeit 140
French Revolution 231–2, 235
French, Thomas 106
Freud, Anna xvi, 12–13, 48–52, 73, 87,
    118, 130, 138
Freud, Sigmund 3–4, 8–9, 11–12, 17, 31,
    34, 49, 55–6, 64, 74, 87, 89, 93, 95,
    116, 120, 130, 134, 137, 140, 147, 165,
    208, 226–7; correspondence with Oskar
    Pfister 218–20; death-drive 98–9, 227;
    Little Hans 50; superego 55–70
Friedlander, Kate 73, 77, 82–3
Friedrich, Carl J. 20, 24
Fromm, Erich 10, 16, 57, 59, 93, 96, 103,
    105–6, 110, 227
Furet, François 230–2, 237

Gentile, Giovanni 23
Germany/German 7, 21, 114; crime
    and punishment 76, 85; imagined

communities 5; inner emigration 42–54; national character 102–6; Nazi *see* Nazism; pathologization of 110; post-war 10, 76, 87–101, 108, 111; psychoanalysis in 10–11, 63, 159–60; social change 58
Gestalt psychology 135
Glaser, Hermann 93–4, 100
Glazer, Nathan 67
Gleason, Abbott 21
Glover, Edward 56–7, 73–4, 77–9, 85, 118
Goebbels, Joseph 6
Goebbels, Magda 213
Goering, Hermann 208–9
Goldberger, Leo 158
Goldensohn, Leon 208–9
Goli Otok prison camp (Yugoslavia) 163–77; *istraga* 172, 174; psychotherapeutic techniques 169–76; *raskritikovanje* (self-criticism) 174
'good enough' concept 115, 117, 126–9
Gorbachev, Mikhail 223–4, 238
Gorer, Geoffrey 105, 109
Göring, Hermann 97
Great War *see* First World War
Grotjahn, Michael 149
group psychology 9, 64
group think 7–8
guerrilla groups xvii
Gutteridge, William 187

Hacker, Friedrich 93, 95
Halliday, James 190
hallucinogens 158
Hamletism 195–8
Hardt, Michael 244
Harper, David 160
Hartmann, Heinz 87
Hayek, Friedrich 21–2, 222
Hebb, Donald 157–8
Heidegger, Martin 45
Heimann, Paula 93, 97
Hellman, Ellen 195
Herman, Judith 250
Himmler, Heinrich 211
Hitler, Adolf 5–6, 12, 23, 87, 105, 114, 207–11, 217, 224, 228; *Mein Kampf*

207, 213; psychobiographical studies 148; *see also* Nazism
Hobsbawn, Eric 135
Hoch, Paul 156
Hofstadter, Richard 8
Holocaust 29–41, 92; *see also* anti-Semitism; Nazism
Holt, Clare 112
hope 117–18
Horkheimer, Max 29–41, 50, 57–9, 61, 63, 65–7, 69, 100, 103, 227
Horn, Klaus 93, 95
Horney, Karen 10, 57, 103, 106, 167
Houghton, Bernard 185
Hoyland, John 185
Huxley, Elspeth 184
Hyslop, Jon 193

idealization xviii, 67, 102, 218, 231–3
ideology 224, 228–9
imperialism 14, 20, 22, 105, 107, 185, 194, 225; *see also* decolonization
impoverishment of thought 224
incest 196; *see also* Oedipus complex
innate destructiveness 227, 232–3
inner emigration 42–54; Anna Freud 49–52; Hannah Arendt 43–8
Institute of Race Relations 186
Institute for the Scientific Treatment of Delinquency (ISTD) 73–4; establishment and early work 74–8
irrationality 30–2, 36, 39–40, 96, 223–4, 230
Isaacs, Susan 119
Islamo-facism 137
ISTD *see* Institute for the Scientific Treatment of Delinquency

Jahoda, Gustav 186
Jakobson, Edith xx
Jaspers, Karl 45, 50
Jennings, Ivor 187
Jews: anti-Semitism *see* anti-Semitism; cultural nomadism 32–4; dehumanisation of 228; foreignness of 38; victim status 37–8; and women as outsiders 34
Jones, Arthur Creech 190

Jones, Ernest 9–10, 74, 118–19, 138, 149–50, 159
Judt, Tony 20
Jung, Carl 33
Jünger, Ernst 21, 23
juvenile delinquency 73–86; ISTD 73–8; as maladjusted citizenship 76; psychoanalytic understanding 78–84

Kalafatic, Emilijan Milan 168
Kardiner, Abram 103–4
Karnac, Henry 130
Karpf, Anne 117
Kennan, George F. 22, 111
Kermode, Frank 211–13, 217
Kerr, Madeline 187–8
Keynes, John Maynard 116–17
Kinsey, Alfred 95
Kis, Danilo 173
Klajn, Vladislav 166–7, 170, 177
Klein, Melanie xxi, 9, 12, 17, 55–6, 73, 83, 87, 117–20, 126, 130, 142, 232, 237; innate destructiveness 227, 232–3; see also paranoid-schizoid position
Koestler, Arthur 5
Kohut, Heinz 99
Kracauer, Siegfried 70
Krieger, Hans 93
Kris, Ernst 9, 87, 161
Kristeva, Julia 210
Kristol, Irving 66–7
KUBARK mind-control program 155, 159
Kubie, Lawrence 106, 152–3
Kubrick, Stanley 8

Lacan, Jacques 10, 12, 49, 51, 90, 140, 142, 182, 200–1, 208, 216
Laing, R.D. 16
Langer, Marie xx, 139
Langer, Walter 148, 150–2, 160
Lasswell, Harold 6
Leites, Nathan 111
Lenin, Vladimir 223
Lepenies, Wolf 93
Lessing, Gotthold Ephraim 42, 44–5, 53–4
Lévy-Bruhl, Lucien 183
Levy, David 149, 161
Lewin, Kurt 190

liberalism/liberal 3–4, 6, 8, 20–2, 24, 64, 66–7, 90–1, 95, 110, 115–17, 128, 136–40, 163, 166, 193–4, 221–2, 224–6; neo-liberalism 222, 225, 239, 245
libido 87, 89, 94, 98, 103
Lifton, Robert Jay 7, 168
Linton, Ralph 104
Lorenz, Konrad 88–9, 91, 93, 95–6, 99–101
Low, Barbara 74, 77, 119
Lowell, Robert 46
Lowenthal, Leo 59
Lucas, Richard 236

MacArthur, Douglas 109
McCoy, Alfred 158
MacCrone, I.D. 193–4
Macey, David 191, 194
Malabou, Catherine 241–4, 246–9, 251
Malitz, Sidney 156
Manganyi, Chabani 194–5, 203; 'The Violent Reverie' 198–202
Mann, Thomas 43–4
Mannoni, Octave 181–5, 187–8, 191
Maoism 5
Marcuse, Herbert 57–9, 63, 91, 93–5, 103, 136
Margolin, Sydney 153, 157
Marxism 10, 39, 65, 224; see also communism/communists
Mason, Philip 185–6
mass murder 30, 96, 100; see also Holocaust
mass psychology 30, 218
Masson, Jeffrey 133–4
Massumi, Brian 240
Masters, William 95
matriarchy 187
Mead, Margaret 104–7, 109
Medico-Psychological Clinic 119
Mekeel, Scudder 104
Menninger, Karl 135
Menninger, William 147
Merleau-Ponty, Maurice 236–7
metapsychology 201, 214; see also psychology
Michaels, Walter Benn 244–5
Mihailovic, Dragoslav 168, 175
Mijolla-Mellor, Sophie de 214–19

militarism 11, 116
Mill, John Stuart 116
Miller, Emanuel 74
Miller, Martin 13
Millet, John 147, 161
mimetic theory of trauma 249–50
mind control 7–8, 155–8; *see also*
    brainwashing
mind-altering drugs 148, 152–6
Misovic, Dragisa 167
Mitchell, Juliet 140
Mitchell, Philip 184
Mitscherlich, Alexander 87, 90–2, 95,
    97–100, 142
Mitscherlich, Margarete 87, 98
MKULTRA mind-control program 155,
    158–9
Money-Kyrle, Roger xvii–xviii, 10, 16, 128
morality: promotion of 98; true 52–3
Morgenthau Plan 112
Morris, Desmond 88
mothers: dependence on 118, 127;
    domineering 188; emotional importance
    of 117; 'generous mothering' 189; good
    enough 117, 127, 129; intuition 123;
    respect for 122; 'traumatic weaning'
    183, 189; working 127, 191; *see also*
    matriarchy; Oedipus complex
mother-child relationship 65, 70, 83, 88,
    122–3, 127, 157, 188–9
mother-child separation 124–6, 188–9
mourning 63–9
Murray, Henry 151
Murray, Jessie 119
Mussolini, Benito 4, 6, 23, 128
mutative interpretation 120

Nachträglichkeit (deferred action) 241
Nahiri, Eva 173
Nazism xviii, xx, 4–5, 7, 21, 44, 47, 61,
    63, 65, 75–6, 85, 92, 114, 128, 147,
    207–20, 222, 224–5, 228–9, 234, 245;
    elite superiority 209–10; Holocaust
    29–41, 92; ideology 224, 228–9; Nazi
    mentality 148–52, 209–10, 229–30;
    neo-Freudian viewpoint 102–13; post-
    Nazi Germany 87–101; prophecy as
    justification 211–12; sado-masochistic
    patterns 102–3; *see also* anti-Semitism

Negri, Antonio 244
neo-Freudian movement 102–13
neo-liberalism 222, 225, 239, 245; *see also*
    liberalism/liberal
New York Psychoanalytic Society 149
Nietzsche, Friedrich 212
Nkrumah, Kwame 186
Nolte, Helmut 93

Oedipus complex 55–6, 59, 62, 68, 74,
    196, 229
Office of Strategic Services (OSS) 148;
    Truth Drug Committee 152–4, 158
Orwell, George 17
Overholser, Winfried 152

pacifism 114–15
Pailthorpe, Grace 74
Panic, Rade 171–5
paranoid-schizoid position 35,
    232–3
parental attachment, loss of 63–4
Parsons, Talcott 55, 106
patriarchy 13, 16, 59–60, 66–7, 174, 182;
    dismantling of 61, 68
Peglau, Andreas 159
Penrose, Lionel 141
perfectionism 237
Perham, Margery 187
Perry, Ethel 81–2
Perucica, Kosta 173–4
Pfister, Oskar 218–20
Pick, Daniel 36
Plack, Arno 93–4
Plotkin, Mariano 13
Podhoretz, Norman 66–7
politicization of psychoanalysis xx,
    87, 198, 202–3; re-education of
    political prisoners 163–77; use in
    counterintelligence 147–62
Pollock, Friedrich 59
Popovic, Marija Zelic 172–3
Popovic, Milovan 165, 170
Popovic, Veselin 177
Popper, Karl 21, 222
post-Nazi Germany 87–101
post-psychoanalysis 239–44
post-totalitarianism 245–51
postfascism 92–5

prejudice: anti-Semitism *see* anti-
Semitism; cultural nomadism 32–4;
purity and projection 34–40
projection 34–40
psychic driving 156–7
psychic regression *see* regression therapy
psychoanalysis xix–xx, 8–11;
Argentina xx, 134, 139; children 50–2,
87–8, 116–23; in counterintelligence
147–62; definition of 11–12; families
119; Germany 10–11, 63, 159–60;
as 'Jewish science' 11; politicization
of xx, 87, 147–77, 198, 202–3;
post-psychoanalysis 239–44; and
totalitarianism 226–32
psychological torture 148; mind control
147–62; re-education 4, 163–77, 708
'psychological totalitarianism' 35
psychology 5–8, 11, 13, 36, 58–9,
75, 239; of authoritarianism 29; of
dependency 183, 186, 188, 190, 200;
of disengagement 190–1; of economic
development 189; ego psychology 36,
90, 140–1, 155; elite 111; Gestalt 135;
group psychology 9, 64; and mass
democracy 6; mass psychology 30,
218; obsolescence of 62–3; political
leadership 55; of power i; social 32;
women 152
psychopathy 85, 108
psychosis xix, 35, 39, 236
purity 34–40
Pyke, Geoffrey 141

racial inferiority 224–5, 228
racism 30, 35, 52
Rapaport, David 155
rational behaviour xvii–xviii
Rauch, Hans-Georg 93
Rawls, John 51
re-education 4, 7–8; brainwashing 5, 7–8,
16, 92, 148, 155–8, 176; Goli Otok
prison camp 163–77; political prisoners
163–77; psychotherapeutic techniques
169–76; wartime origins 164–7
reality xvii, 44–5; denial of xviii, 50;
engagement with xvi; realness of 46, 49;
true morality 52–3; unwillingness to
contemplate 48

regression therapy 14, 126, 154–5, 157
Reich, Wilhelm 10, 94, 98, 140, 159
Reik, Theodor 208
religion 3, 23, 31, 37, 56, 107, 116, 141,
218
religious hatred 30–1; *see also* anti-Semitism
Richards, Arnold D. 147
Riesman, David 110
Riley, Denise 130
Ritchie, J.F. 183
Riviere, Joan 119–20, 126
Rose, Jacqueline 54
Rosenfeld, Herbert 17
Roudinesco, Elisabeth 140–1
Roustang, François 139

Sachs, Wulf 183, 185, 193–8, 203; *Black
Hamlet* 195–8
sadism 57, 100, 102–3
Sampson, Anthony 184
Sandler, Joseph 51, 53
Sanford, R. Nevitt 61
Sartre, Jean-Paul 142, 195
Schatzman, Morton 216–17, 220
Schmideberg, Melitta 73–4, 83–4, 86, 119
Schmitt, Carl 21, 23
Schreber, Daniel Paul 214–17
Schwarz, Hedwig 79–81, 85
Searl, Nina 119
Second World War 3, 29, 55, 124–7,
230; evacuation 124–5; Japanese
involvement 107–9; psychoanalysis in
counterintelligence 147–62; *see also*
Nazism
Sedgwick, Eve Kosofsky 239–40
Segal, Hanna 238
Selg, Herbert 93
sensory deprivation 157–8
Sereny, Gitta 213
Serge, Victor 237
Shapira, Michal 129
Sharpe, Ella 119
Simmel, Ernst 38–9, 150–1
Sitze, Adam 194
Snowden, Edward 226
social anxiety 52
social democratic vision 114–30
social psychology 32
Soddy, Kenneth 189

South Africa, apartheid 193–204
Soviet Union 23, 109–10; Communism 5,
    136, 222, 224–5; *glasnost/perestroika*
    224, 238; New Economic Policy 223,
    234; show trials 5, 236; Stalinism 5, 75,
    223, 230–4
Speer, Albert 213, 224, 230
Speier, Hans 9
Spitzer, Herman 103
splitting xxii, 39, 231, 233
Stalinism 5, 75, 223, 230–4
Steiner, John 17
Stevens, Wallace 211–12
Stewart-Steinberg, Suzanne 49–51, 54
Strachey, Alix 119, 187
Strachey, James 119–20, 129
Strecker, Edward 152
Studies in Prejudice 29–41
Sugar, Nikola 177
Sullivan, Harry Stack 103
superego 55–70, 102; authority and
    totalitarianism 58–62; children 56;
    mourning the fathers 63–9
swaddling controversy 109–10
Swanson, Maynard 195

Talmon, Jacob 6, 237
Tausk, Victor 217
Temple, Nicholas 16–17
Terada, Rei 45, 47
terrorism xvii, 18, 93, 204, 243–4
therapeutic violence 163–77; Goli Otok
    prison camp 164–9
Theweleit, Klaus 35, 97
'third position' of psychoreality 229, 231
thought: freedom of xvi, 7, 17, 45, 216–19;
    impoverishment of 224
Thouless, Robert 187
Tinbergen, Nikolaas 100
Titmuss, Richard 116
Tomkins, Silvan S. 240
Tooze, Adam 22
torture xviii, 7, 99, 157, 216; as mind
    control 216; promotion of morality 98;
    psychological *see* psychological torture;
    sadism 57, 100, 102–3; white 158
total behaviour 114
total state 21, 24
totalism 7

totalitarian spirit 22, 24
totalitarian states of mind 232–4
totalitarian unconscious 221–38
totalitarianism xvi, 4–5, 7–8, 20–5, 133–43;
    apartheid 193–204; characteristics of
    222–3; clinical encounters 15–17; and
    cultural relativism 102–13; idea of 22,
    222–6; novelty 20–1; present crises
    17–19; and psychoanalysis 226–7;
    psychological 35; spiritual domination
    213–14; superego 58–62; theory 24; *see
    also* Nazism
trauma 241–4, 246–9, 250–1; mimetic
    theory 249–50
'traumatic weaning' 183, 189
truth drugs 148, 152–4
Turner, Julia 119

USA, psychoanalysis and
    counterintelligence 147–62; 1940–45
    148–52; Cold War 154–9; OSS Truth
    Drug Committee 152–4, 158

van der Kolk, Bessel 250
violence 250–1; *see also* torture
Vispo, Raúl 156
von Frisch, Karl 100

Wakefield, Edward 184
war neuroses 147, 241–2, 250–1
Warnes, Hector 156
welfare discipline 75
Whitehorn, John 152
Williams, Cicely 183
Williams, Raymond 235
Wills, David 124
Winnicott, Alice 119, 126
Winnicott, Donald 12, 14, 73, 114–30,
    139, 218; 'clamour of need' 120–3;
    Clinical Notes 121–2; 'War Aims'
    114–18; war work 124–7
Winter, David 189
women: exclusion of 34; matriarchy
    187; mother-child relationship 65,
    70, 88, 157, 188–9; mother-child
    separation 124–5, 188–9; psychology
    of 152

xenophobia 52

Young-Breuhl, Elisabeth 42–3, 49–50, 213
Yugoslavia: Goli Otok prison camp 163–77;
    Institute for Compulsory Re-education of
    Communist Youth 164–5; re-education
    of political prisoners 163–77

Zaretsky, Eli 13, 16
Zelic, Marija 163–4
Žižek, Slavoj 32–3, 38–41, 236,
    246–9
Zweig, Arnold 154

eBooks
from Taylor & Francis

Helping you to choose the right eBooks for your Library

Add to your library's digital collection today with Taylor & Francis eBooks. We have over 50,000 eBooks in the Humanities, Social Sciences, Behavioural Sciences, Built Environment and Law, from leading imprints, including Routledge, Focal Press and Psychology Press.

Choose from a range of subject packages or create your own!

Benefits for you

- Free MARC records
- COUNTER-compliant usage statistics
- Flexible purchase and pricing options
- All titles DRM-free.

Benefits for your user

- Off-site, anytime access via Athens or referring URL
- Print or copy pages or chapters
- Full content search
- Bookmark, highlight and annotate text
- Access to thousands of pages of quality research at the click of a button.

Free Trials Available

We offer free trials to qualifying academic, corporate and government customers.

eCollections

Choose from over 30 subject eCollections, including:

Archaeology	Language Learning
Architecture	Law
Asian Studies	Literature
Business & Management	Media & Communication
Classical Studies	Middle East Studies
Construction	Music
Creative & Media Arts	Philosophy
Criminology & Criminal Justice	Planning
Economics	Politics
Education	Psychology & Mental Health
Energy	Religion
Engineering	Security
English Language & Linguistics	Social Work
Environment & Sustainability	Sociology
Geography	Sport
Health Studies	Theatre & Performance
History	Tourism, Hospitality & Events

For more information, pricing enquiries or to order a free trial, please contact your local sales team: www.tandfebooks.com/page/sales

www.tandfebooks.com